African American
Performance and
Theater History

African American Performance and Theater History

A CRITICAL READER

Edited by

Harry J. Elam, Jr.

David Krasner

OXFORD
UNIVERSITY PRESS

2001

OXFORD

UNIVERSITY PRESS

Oxford   New York

Athens   Auckland   Bangkok   Bogotá   Buenos Aires   Calcutta
Cape Town   Chennai   Dar es Salaam   Delhi   Florence   Hong Kong   Istanbul
Karachi   Kuala Lumpur   Madrid   Melbourne   Mexico City   Mumbai
Nairobi   Paris   São Paulo   Shanghai   Singapore   Taipei   Tokyo   Toronto   Warsaw

and associated companies in
Berlin   Ibadan

Published by Oxford University Press, Inc.
198 Madison Avenue, New York, New York 10016

Oxford is a registered trademark of Oxford University Press.

Library of Congress Cataloging-in-Publication Data

African American performance and theater history: a critical reader /
edited by Harry J. Elam, Jr. and David Krasner.
p.   cm.
Includes bibliographical references and index.
ISBN 0–19–512724–2; ISBN 0–19–512725–0 (pbk.)
1. Afro-American theater.   2. American drama—Afro-American authors—History
and criticism.   I. Elam, Harry Justin.   II. Krasner, David, 1952–
PN2270.A35A46   2000
792'.089'96073—dc21   00–022463

9 8 7 6 5 4 3 2 1

Printed in the United States of America
on acid-free paper

Acknowledgments

Many people have contributed to making this book possible. We would like to begin by thanking our first editor, T. Susie Chang, for all her work and support of this manuscript. We also thank her successor, Elissa Morris, for seeing this book through to fruition. We are grateful to all the contributors for their commitment, hard work, and insightful chapters.

Lisa Thompson and Nicole Hickman, two Ph.D. candidates in the Modern Thought and Literature Program at Stanford, worked diligently to compile the bibliography on African American theater and performance. Hickman also helped with the editing and proofreading processes. We appreciate the efforts of Ron Davies, the administrator in the Department of Drama at Stanford, for preparing the manuscript for publication and of Susan Sebbard, Assistant Director of the Humanities Center at Stanford, for her careful proofreading of the volume.

Harry Elam acknowledges the support of Janelle Reinelt, Professor of Drama at the University of California, Davis, and his life partner, Leonade Jones, for their readings and honest critiques of his contributions to this anthology. David Krasner acknowledges the support and hard work of the Theater Studies' assistant at Yale, Jan Foery, and his most significant other, Lynda Intihar. This book was published with the assistance of the Frederick W. Hilles Publication Fund of Yale University.

We owe an enormous debt to those who went before us, and we are grateful that they have constructed a ground on which we now walk. Our study is a continuation of a tradition built on the works of historians, scholars, and critics, such as William Branch, Winona Fletcher, Paul Carter Harrison, Samuel Hay, Errol Hill, James Weldon Johnson, Lofton Mitchell, Thomas Pawley, and Bernard Peterson. We dedicate these chapters to these scholars, in particular, Professor Errol Hill—brilliant historian, editor, and researcher. If our efforts come close to reaching the standards he has set, we will have accomplished our goals.

Stanford, California   HJE jr
New Haven, Connecticut   DK
September 2000

Contents

Contributors

TELIA U. ANDERSON teaches English and African studies at New York City Technical College. She graduated cum laude from Yale in 1991 and earned an M.A. in theater studies from Brown in 1997. She won the New Scholar's Prize, given by the International Federation for Theatre Research, in 1996 for an earlier version of her chapter, "Calling on the Spirit."

ANNEMARIE BEAN is an assistant professor of Theater at Williams College, Williamstown, Massachusetts. She was managing editor of the *Drama Review* for three years; is the coeditor, with James V. Hatch and Brooks McNamara, of *Inside the Minstrel Mask: Readings in Nineteenth-Century Black-face Minstrelsy* (1996); winner of the 1997 Errol Hill Award, given by the American Society for Theatre Research for outstanding scholarship in African American theater studies; and she is editor of *A Sourcebook of African-American Performance* (1999). Her current project is a study of gender impersonation by white and African American nineteenth-century minstrels.

KIMBERLY D. DIXON is completing her dissertation on contemporary African American women playwrights in Northwestern University's interdisciplinary Ph.D. program in Theater and Drama. She is a graduate of Yale University and UCLA, with degrees in theater, African American studies, and psychology. She has published on Suzan-Lori Parks in *American Drama*. In addition, Dixon is an emerging playwright and screenwriter.

HARRY J. ELAM, JR., is Christensen Professor for the Humanities, director of graduate studies in Drama, and chair of the Committee on Black Performing Arts at Stanford University. He is author of *Taking It to the Streets: The Social Protest Theater of Luis Valdez and Amiri Baraka* (1997) and coeditor, with Robert Alexander, of *Colored Contradictions: An Anthology of Contemporary African American Plays* (1996). He is finishing a book entitled *(W)Righting History: The Past as Present in the Drama of August Wilson*. He has published articles in *Theatre Journal, Text and Performance Quarterly*, and *American Drama*, as well as contributed to several critical anthologies.

HENRY LOUIS GATES, JR., is the chair of the Afro-American Studies Department and director of the W. E. B. Du Bois Institute for Afro-American Studies at Harvard University. He is a prolific writer and scholar, who has authored and coauthored several books, edited or coedited many more, and written numerous articles for such magazines as the *New Yorker, Time,* and the *New Republic*. His many books include *Figures in Black: Works, Signs, and the "Racial" Self* (1987), *The Signifying Monkey: A Theory of Afro-American Literary Criticism* (1988), *Loose Canons: Notes on the Culture Wars* (1992), *Colored People: A Memoir* (1994), *The Future of the Race* (1996), and *Thirteen Ways of Looking at a Black Man* (1997).

JAMES V. HATCH is professor emeritus of English and Theater at City College of the City University of New York. His publications include a biography, *Sorrow Is the Only Faithful One: The Life of Owen Dodson*, which won the Bernard Hewitt Award for best theater history book published in 1993. He is co-founder, with his wife, Camille Billops, of the Hatch-Billops Collection and Archive in African American cultural history.

DAVID KRASNER is director of undergraduate Theater Studies at Yale University, where he teaches theater history and literature, dramatic criticism, acting, and directing. His book *Resistance, Parody, and Double Consciousness in African American Theatre, 1895–1910* (1997) received the 1998 Errol Hill Award from the American Society for Theatre Research. He is the editor of *Method Acting Reconsidered: Theory, Practice, Future* (2000) and is currently working on his next book, *Black Performance and the Harlem Renaissance: African American Theater and Drama, 1910–1930*.

DIANA R. PAULIN is an assistant professor in American Studies and English at Yale University. Her articles on representations of cross-racial liaisons have been published in *Cultural Critique, Theatre Journal*, and the *Journal of Dramatic Theory and Criticism*.

JAY PLUM is Program Manager for the Center for the Study of Media & Society at the Gay & Lesbian Alliance Against Defamation (GLAAD). He received his Ph.D. in Theatre from the Graduate School and University Center of the City University of New York. His articles have appeared in *African American Review, Modern Drama, Text and Presentation*, and *Theatre Survey*.

TINA REDD is an assistant professor of Theory and Criticism at the University of Washington. She has published on Negro units and the Federal Theater Project in *The Journal of American Drama and Theatre*.

SANDRA L. RICHARDS is chair of African-American Studies and professor of Theater at Northwestern University. She is author of *Ancient Songs Set Ablaze: The Theater of Femi Osofisan* (1996) and a widely recognized authority on African American and African Drama.

JOSEPH R. ROACH is the Charles C. and Dorothea S. Dilley Professor of Theater at Yale University. He is author of *The Players' Passion: Studies in the Science of*

Acting (1985 reprinted 1993), which won the Bernard Hewitt Award in 1986, and *Cities of the Dead: Circum-Atlantic Performance* (1996), which won the James Russell Lowell Award in 1997. He has directed more than forty plays and operas.

MIKE SELL is an assistant professor of English at Indiana University of Pennsylvania. He has published essays on a variety of topics, including Vsevelod Meyerhold, Samuel Beckett, film violence, performance art, Arthur Miller, and the relationship of the avant-garde to transformative economic systems. He is currently writing a book devoted to case studies in the relationship of avant-garde performance, the counterculture, and Cold War capitalism.

SANDRA G. SHANNON is professor of African American literature and criticism in the Department of English at Howard University. She has published extensively on August Wilson. Her book *The Dramatic Vision of August Wilson* (1995) traces Wilson's evolution from his boyhood interest in black literature to his phenomenal success as a Pulitzer Prize–winning playwright. Other works include an essay in *African American Review*'s Winter 1998 issue, a chapter and annotated bibliography in *May All Your Fences Have Gates: Essays on the Drama of August Wilson* (1994), and chapters in *August Wilson: A Casebook* (1994) and *Memory and Cultural Politics: New Approaches to American Ethnic Literature* (1996).

CHRISTINA E. SHARPE is an assistant professor in the Department of English at Tufts University; she teaches courses in multiethnic American literature and women's studies. She has published work on race and cyberspace and on Cherrié Moraga.

WILLIAM SONNEGA is associate professor of Communication and Theater at St. Olaf College; he teaches theater, media, and cultural studies. He is the author of a variety of articles on race and performance, including "Re[pre]senting Jews in Postwar German Theatre" (*Theatre History Studies*, 1994) and "Morphing Border: The Remanence of MTV" (*The Drama Review*, Spring 1995). He is currently writing a book on liberalism and live performance.

MARGARET B. WILKERSON is Director of Media, Arts and Culture at the Ford Foundation. Formerly the director of the Center for Theater Arts, chair of the Department of African American Studies and professor in the Department of African American Studies at the University of California, Berkeley, she is the editor of *9 Plays by Black Women* (1986). She is currently completing a literary biography on playwright Lorraine Hansberry. Wilkerson was the recipient of the 1996 Career Achievement Award for

Outstanding Educator from the Association of Theater in Higher Education and of the Black Theater Network's Winona Fletcher Award for outstanding scholarship (1994).

JUDITH WILLIAMS received her Ph.D. from the Department of Drama at Stanford University.

African American
Performance and
Theater History

The Device of Race

An Introduction

HARRY J. ELAM, JR.

As our title, *African American Performance and Theater History: A Critical Reader*, suggests, this anthology explores the intersections of race, theater, and performance in America. The interactions among them are always dynamic and multidirectional. Accordingly, the social and historical contexts of production can critically affect theatrical performances of blackness and their meanings. At the same time, theatrical representations and performances have profoundly impacted African American cultural, social, and political struggles. This book argues that analyzing African American theater and performance traditions offers insight into how race has operated and continues to operate in American society. Significantly, this examination of African American theater and performance history reflects not only on the historical evolution and cultural development of racial representations but also on the continuity and continuum of performance theories and theatrical practices over time. Dramatic tropes, aesthetic and cultural images, artistic agendas, and political paradigms are repeated and revised as the past is continually made present, and the present is constituted in the African American past.

The desire to implement a critical strategy that recognizes the continued presence of the past in African American theater and performance has led us to construct this anthology differently from traditional studies of theater history. Ordinarily, investigations of theater history and performance unfold chronologically, beginning with articles on the earliest eras and concluding with contemporary considerations. Such structures, however, do not allow for analyses of the intersection of issues and themes, for theoretical continuities across and through time. Consequently, we have employed a more genealogical strategy and organized the essays contained in this volume into four parts, which are representative of the ways black theater, drama, and performance, past and present, interact and enact continuous social, cultural, and political dialogues. Part I covers Social Protest and the Politics of Representation; part II discusses Cultural Traditions, Cultural Memory, and Performance; part III looks at the Intersections of Race and Gender; and part IV focuses on African American Performativity and the Performance of Race. By structuring the chapters along these lines, we are able to observe particular performance practices at specific historic moments and also examine how African American theatrical moments and movements talk to, comment on, build upon each other.

Each part contains at least one chapter that focuses on a particular playwright or analyzes a specific text, one that examines a theatrical group or movement, and one that considers a particular historical moment and its import. Each of the four areas reflects significant and resilient issues within African American theatrical practice. And yet, at the same time, we acknowledge that this book's categories draw a map that could have been arranged differently; issues of black drama and performance overlap and interact in numerous ways, and the complexity of African American theater, drama, and performance defies rigid boundaries. Consequently, articles in this volume talk to each other across the parts as well as within them. This book is a cross-disciplinary study that explores new terrain revealed by recently developed methodologies, while offering fresh insights into familiar topics. It juxtaposes the work of established historians and critics with those of emerging scholars. The diversity of research, viewpoints, and ideologies in this work will, we hope, contribute to a growing interest in black theater and performance. The underlying purpose of this volume, then, is to position African American theater and performance scholarship as pivotal in the discussion of African American history and culture.

Our anthology of African American theater and performance proceeds from the assertion that, at its inception, the American "race question" is inherently theatrical. From the arrival of the first African slaves on American soil, the discourse on race, the definitions and meanings of blackness, have been intricately linked to issues of theater and performance. Definitions of race, like the processes of theater, fundamentally depend on the relationship between the seen and unseen, between the visibly marked and unmarked, between the "real" and the illusionary. In the past, Western science, philosophy, and literature repeatedly associated black skin and the "negroid" race with intellectual inferiority and cultural primitivism. The visible differences among peoples signified that "real," unquestionable, biologically based racial differences existed.[1] More recently, racial theorists, such as Michael Omi and Howard Winant, have defined race as a construct that is historically, socially, and culturally determined.[2] Such constructivist analyses have eroded the perception that there are essential or ontological bases for race. Yet the visual markings of race continue to have real meanings and effects.

The play *Les Blancs* (1969), by Lorraine Hansberry,[3] offers one of the clearest and most powerful discourses on the constructed reality and situational meanings of race. Throughout the play, an African intellectual character, Tshembe Matoseh, and a white American liberal, Charlie Morris, engage in a series of polemical debates on race. During one such encounter, the following discussion unfolds:

TSHEMBE: Race—racism—is a device. No more. No less. It explains nothing at all.

CHARLIE: Now what in the hell is that supposed to mean?

TSHEMBE: I said racism is a device that, of itself, explains nothing. It is simply a means. An invention to justify the rule of some men over others. . . . I am simply saying that a device is a device, but that it also has consequences; once invented it takes on a life, a reality of its own. So, in one century, men invoke the device of religion to cloak their conquests. In another, race. Now in both cases you and I may recognize the fraudulence of the device, but the fact remains that a man who has a sword run through him because he is a Moslem or a Christian—or who is shot in Zatembe or Mississippi because he is black— is suffering the utter reality of the device. And it is pointless to pretend that it doesn't exist—merely because it is a lie!⁴

In this passage from *Les Blancs*, Hansberry theorizes that the meanings of race are conditional, that the illusion of race becomes reality through its application. Despite its being written more than thirty years ago, this passage has a particular contemporary relevance. It locates the current debates over the definitions of race in decidedly and purposefully theatrical terms: "Race is a device." The contemporary import of this passage speaks not only to Hansberry's prescience but also to the unique nature of theatrical representation and, thus, to the significance of this critical anthology.

Theater is built upon devices. In the theatrical environment, the signification of objects results from their specific usage in the moment. In *Les Blancs*, for example, Hansberry uses the device of a black woman dancer to represent "Mother Africa" and to incite Tshembe's call to revolutionary consciousness. Relying on the audience's suspension of disbelief and the magic of theater, the dancer exists solely in Tshembe's mind. Although she appears on stage with both Tshembe and Charlie, Charlie cannot see her; she is visible only to Tshembe and to the audience. Thus, the device of the woman dancer directs the dramatic action, while it foregrounds the unique theatrical negotiation of illusion and reality. Every theatrical performance depends on performers' and spectators' collaborative consciousness of the devices in operation and their meanings. This consciousness is coconstructed in a new way with each performance.

The inherent "constructedness" of performance and the malleability of the devices of the theater serve to reinforce the theory that blackness, specifically, and race, in general, are hybrid, fluid concepts whose meanings depend upon the social, cultural, and historical conditions of their use.⁵ Consequently, African American theater and performance have been and remain powerful sites for the creation, application, and even the subversion of notions of blackness and of concepts of African American identity. Reflecting on the transformative potential of Heater in his important 1968 manifesto, "The Black Arts Movement," critic Larry Neal calls theater, "potentially the most social of arts" and "an integral part of the socialization process."[6] Neal and other artist/activists of the Black Arts Movement championed the theater as a potent space for the articulation of black social and cultural agency and self-determination. Most significantly, their conceptions of blackness and their cultural plan for revolutionary action were rooted in the urgencies of that particular historic moment.

Our anthology affirms that the meanings and the constructions of race generally and blackness particularly are contextual and historically specific. At the same time, it reveals that contemporary African American theater and performance practices are inherently connected to the performance theories, rhetoric, and representations of the past. This is not to suggest that contemporary African American representations and theories of representation have not moved away from prior essentialized or monolithic visions of blackness. And yet, we must assert that representing and performing blackness remain politically and culturally charged. Racism and its impact on African American life and culture have not disappeared. Race remains a device with very real meanings. As a consequence, the black figure on the American stage is always and already fraught with political, cultural, and social significance.

Social Protest and the Politics of Representation

Black theater practitioners have been continually concerned with the viability of black theater as a means of social protest. Consequently, the desire to control "the politics of representation," as Stuart Hall terms it,[7] has played a significant role in the history of African American theater and performance. The politics of representation concern not only understanding the power inherent in the visible representation of African Americans but also recognizing the mechanisms of production, which dictate the dissemination of these images. Accordingly, African American theater critics and artists, from W. E. B. Du Bois to Amiri Baraka to August Wilson, have asserted that black theater practitioners must not only have authority over the representational apparatus but must use the theater as a means of protest and revolt in order to change black lives and fight oppressive conditions.

In his well-known 1926 manifesto for a black theater, Du Bois states that "a real Negro theatre" must be "About us, By us, For us, and Near us."[8] To Du Bois, theatrical representation is critical to the perpetuation of an African American cultural politics of transformation and emancipation. Notably, Du Bois's call for a segregated black theater resonates in both Amiri Baraka's 1965 radical proclamation, "The Revolutionary Theatre," and August Wilson's more contemporary speech to the Theatre Communications Group's 1996 national convention, "The Ground on Which I Stand." Baraka (then, as LeRoi Jones) proclaims that the revolutionary theater is "a political theatre, a weapon to help the slaughter of these dimwitted fatbellied white guys who somehow believe that the rest of the world is here for them to slobber on."[9] Aligning himself with the African American history of struggle and survival, as well as the black tradition of a functional art of protest, Wilson states:

> I stand myself and my art squarely on the self-defining ground of the slave quarters, and find the ground to be hallowed and made fertile by the blood and bones of the men and women who can be described as warriors on the cultural battlefield that affirmed their self-worth.[10]

The strategies of Wilson, like those of Baraka and Du Bois, reify the continuous intersections of culture, power, identity, and representation.[11]

The chapters in the first part of this anthology, Social Protest and the Politics of Representation, consider such intersections of politics and performance. They confront ways in which African American theater and performance have operated as social weapons and tools of protest. The four chapters in part I discuss the actual, real-life consequences and effects that result from the theatrical representation of African Americans. The opening essay examines the most popular play ever produced on the American stage, *Uncle Tom's Cabin*. Harriet Beecher Stowe's novel *Uncle Tom's Cabin* (1851–52) spawned at least two major stage adaptations as well as a variety of off-shoots and parodies. As the author Judith Williams observes, *Uncle Tom's Cabin* perhaps seems a strange place to begin a discussion of black theater and performance history. And yet the original novel, written by Harriet Beecher Stowe, and the subsequent stage adaptations, Williams maintains, have had a profound effect on African American culture, as well as on subsequent representation of blackness. In "Uncle Tom's Women," Williams notes how the performances of *Uncle Tom's Cabin* contributed to the creation of three transcendent black female archetypes: the mammy, the tragic mulatto, and the Topsy figure, the black "pickaninny," who was not born but "just growed." Significantly, when white actresses played these black figures on stage in the nineteenth century, Williams argues, it both stereotyped and silenced real black women. She analyzes how this silence served to fuel white desire and to suppress black subjectivity. The representations of these stereotypes were not, however, totalizing; they also contained in performance the potential for subversion.

Margaret B. Wilkerson, in "Political Radicalism and Artistic Innovation in the Works of Lorraine Hansberry," focuses on one of the most prescient and perceptive playwrights of the modern American stage. Eschewing the identification of Hansberry as a conciliatory integrationist found in 1960s and 1970s Black Arts criticism, Wilkerson establishes Hansberry as an advocate of radical change. She documents the political significance of the playwright's personal history and underscores the importance of Africa and African liberation efforts in Hansberry's dramaturgy. This rereading of Hansberry identifies ways in which race, gender, and politics dynamically interact in her work.

The Black Arts Movement of the 1960s and early 1970s still stands out in African American theater history as the most significant collective effort of black social protest theater. The movement advocated not only social change but cultural transformation through the institutionalization of a particularly black aesthetic. Contemporary critics have attacked the essentialism and misogyny of the movement. Within this volume, in fact, Henry Louis Gates, Jr., questions whether the movement did function as effective protest. Here in this section, Mike Sell's chapter, "The Black Arts Movement: Performance, Neo-Orality, and the Destruction of the 'White Thing,' " reevaluates the movement and sounds a cautionary note against previous critiques. Sell points out that critics need to factor in the politics of their positionality as they are implicated in the very institutions against which the Black Arts Movement struggled. The Black Arts Movement, Sell maintains, formulated an alternative structure of history, community, and aesthetic, the impact of which continues to be felt.

The Black Arts Movement spoke specifically and exclusively to black audiences; it "preached to the converted." What happens when white audiences attend African American protest theater? How does the performance work with a clientele whose expectations, socialization, and rationale for attendance may be decidedly different from the particular African American audience for whom the social protest performance was intended? William Sonnega, in "Beyond a Liberal Audience," addresses these questions by examining two contemporary performances in Minneapolis, Minnesota: a black production of *Death of a Salesman* by Arthur Miller and *Sally's Rape* by African American performance artist Robbie McCauley. Sonnega starts from the assumption that white audiences attending these productions can be constructed as "liberal." Sonnega then critiques notions of white liberalism and notes how white liberal attendance can reinforce rather than subvert ideas of white privilege and normative whiteness. Using reactionary racial critics, such as Dinesh D'Souza and Shelby Steele, in innovative ways, Sonnega considers whether these productions operated as sites for effective cross-cultural communication, for interracial dialogue and healing, or for the development of new coalitions and new ideological communities. In order for such effects to occur, Sonnega argues, white liberalism must be continually interrogated, and practices need to be constructed that expose rather than reinvent racism. He challenges and critiques how artists and activists have employed the device of race to influence attitudes and to incite social change.

The chapters in this part reflect on the potential cultural and political power of representing and performing blackness. Juxtaposed to each other, these four authors provide perspectives on the salient interplay between black politics and the politics of black representation. They further the discourse on the social efficacy of theatrical representation and comment on the ability of black theater to affect thought, behavior, and even social action.

Cultural Traditions, Cultural Memory, and Performance

The chapters in the second part of this anthology engage in an interactive dialogue on the power of cultural memory and how it is constructed through performance. In their introduction to *Memory & Cultural Politics*, Amritjit Singh, Joseph Skerrett, Jr., and Robert Hogan discuss the African American "struggle to remember." They maintain:

> African Americans, brought hither in chains from their homes across the Atlantic, have struggled to remember a past from which they were cut off by the Middle Passage and slavery. As with Native Americans, this feat of memory could not have been undertaken without conflict with the dominant national narrative, which denied any value to the African American past and its cultural products.[12]

Notably, for African Americans physically separated from their African past, the "struggle to remember" has continually involved performance and other forms of African American cultural expression because of their ability to shape perceptions and even rewrite history. African American theatrical works across historical periods such as May Miller's *Harriet Tubman* (1935), William Branch's *In Splendid Error* (1953), and Suzan-Lori Parks's *Imperceptible Mutabilities in the Third Kingdom* (1989) all reimagine the past. In addition, African American performance practices, from the slave ring shout to contemporary Hip Hop contain vestiges of earlier African cultural traditions. Consequently, performance can constitute, contain, and create "cultural memory." By cultural memory, we mean those collective memories that are culturally constructed over time and whose meanings are historically and culturally determined. Cultural memories of slavery and past racial oppression continue to play a critical role in the formation of African American cultural politics and in the shaping of African American identities.

Significantly, three of the chapters in this second part explore examples of African American performance practices in venues outside of the conventional theater; they thus expand our discussion of performance. Together, these chapters assert that such "performances of everyday life" have been critical to black cultural expression, struggle, and survival. Richard Schechner, in *Between Theater and Anthropology*, defines performance as "restored behavior" or "twice-behaved behavior."[13] Following this argument, if performance is restored behavior, then it is inherently connected to social and cultural interactions. Augmenting Schechner's definition, Elin Diamond perceives performances as cultural practices that "conservatively re-inscribe or passionately reinvent the ideas, symbols, and gestures that shape social life."[14] Inevitably, then, performances must negotiate systems of power, cultural and social mores, values, and beliefs. As we will see, the performances and sites of performance examined in these chapters engage not only with social and cultural codes but also with cultural memory.

Joseph Roach, in his essay "Deep Skin," calls for a critical approach to African American performance traditions that recognizes their living memory, that incorporates and validates African methodologies of remembrance, and that imagines and examines "environments of memory." Roach develops the innovative theoretical concept of "deep skin," a "melanoma of the imagination," which stereotypes the behaviors and attitudes of one people toward another. Deep skin, he theorizes, plays a critical role in the interpretation and veneration of African American cultural traditions. Roach's exploration of Congo Square in New Orleans, Louisiana, the site of slave performances from 1790 through 1851, as well as jazz funeral processions in more recent times, locates the square not only as a repository of performances but as an environment of memory that itself continues to perform.

Telia U. Anderson, in "Calling on the Spirit," considers the black church as a site of performance and an environment of memory. Anderson examines the history of African American women calling on the spirit within the black Baptist church service. She theorizes that this practice constitutes a radical Africanist performance strategy and a space of gendered resistance. When black women respond to the service in this way, they challenge the doctrinal authority of the male preacher, engage in a form of "guerrilla sermon," and transform the meanings present in the service of worship. Anderson's work not only recognizes the subversive power present in black women's calling on the spirit but also expands our definitions of performance.

A critical element within the dramaturgical project of August Wilson is the celebration of the collective cultural memory of Africa in African American experiences. Wilson believes that African Americans must rediscover this Africanness in order to survive in contemporary America. In response to Wilson's now-famous speech to the Theatre Communication Group in January 1996, Henry Louis Gates, Jr., in "The Chitlin Circuit," takes issue not with Wilson's cultural aesthetics but with his polemics. The first part of Gates's chapter revisits the questions of representation and social efficacy addressed in part I of this anthology. Gates challenges Wilson's call for and conception of an "authentically" black theater and Wilson's celebration of the Black Arts Movement. While Sell effectively argues that the Black Arts Movement had a broad impact on grassroots, community-based theaters and future playwrights and practices, Gates maintains that the impact of the movement was more limited. More significantly, Gates turns to a black theater practice that has been underexamined and even denigrated within black theater scholarship. And yet the so-called Chitlin Circuit is a tradition of a decidedly black theater that is for, by, and about black people. The black touring companies that comprise the Chitlin Circuit reflect the cultural memory and traditions of the TOBA (Theatre Owners Booking Association, often euphemistically referred to as "tough on black asses") of the Harlem Renaissance. Using stock characters and broad acting techniques and encouraging frequent and active audience participation, the Chitlin Circuit productions operate within a system of black working-class aesthetic values. The performances occur in a distinctly black, "racially sequestered," environment of memory. As a result, they require a system of evaluation sensitive to their particular practices.

Sandra G. Shannon, in "Audience and Africanisms in August Wilson's Dramaturgy," examines how Wilson incorporates African symbolism and practices into his work. Shannon interrogates the insensitivity of Wilson's audiences and critics to his Africanist agenda. Using the work of Pierre Nora, she theorizes that Wilson's dramas function as *lieux de memoire*, sites of memory, and that his dramatic cycle is an act of personal and collective memory, "a 400-year autobiography." Not unlike Roach, Shannon challenges critics to recognize different modes of analysis and to eschew Western standards of criticism, which fail to appreciate African aesthetic practices. A different cultural and aesthetic sensibility, she posits, is at operation in Wilson's plays.

Part II, then, presents new perspectives on the intersections of black cultural traditions and performance criticism. African American cultural retentions, conventions, and collective memories not only continue to inform and shape African American cultural production but must affect our critical interpretations and analyses of African American performance practices as well.

Intersections of Race and Gender

Another critical concern that African American theater and performance criticism must address which will expand our perspective and inform our understandings of performances both past and present, is gender. Recent scholarship inside as well as outside of the theater establishes gender as a fundamental condition of experience as well as a critical category of analysis. More than just the opposition of and differences between masculinity and femininity, gender operates as a "system of beliefs, of ideology and behaviors mapped across the bodies of males and females."[15] Gender is not a product of biology but of social, cultural, and historical forces. When critical analyses of gender enter into the theoretical discourse on blackness, they help disrupt and challenge homogenized definitions and essentialized concepts of African American identity. The constructed nature and devices of the theater can foreground the fluidity of gender. Theatrical representations of gender can compel audiences and critics to reconsider the fixity and naturalness of gender categories. Examining the complex intersections of gender, sexuality, and race within African American theater and performance practices compounds the meanings of race and racial representation.

The third part of this anthology, Intersections of Race and Gender, makes use of contemporary critical articulations of gender to elucidate African American play texts and performances past and present. Annemarie Bean, in "Black Minstrelsy and Double Inversion," examines the interactions of race and gender on the minstrel stage. Bean addresses how both black and white minstrel players performed color and gender. They performed "color" rather than race, she notes, as both black and white minstrels appeared literally blackened on stage. The performances of African American minstrels, how-ever, manipulated and inverted the rules of performance and the derogatory stereotypes established by white minstrelsy. Bean uncovers and explores new critical territory in the history of blackface performance, as she interrogates the very particular experience of African American women who portrayed men on stage. She terms these performances a "double inversion" because they inverted conventional white minstrel representations of both men and women. While the subject of minstrelsy has been the site of much recent scholarly analysis,[16] these cross-gendered double inversions have rarely been documented or discussed. These performances blurred the lines and chal-lenged the distinctions between masculinity and femininity. Bean's work explores how both race and gender were constructed on and through these cross-gendered performances.

Continuing the discussion of black female performers' struggle against racial and gendered stereotypes, David Krasner, in "Black *Salome*," examines the plight of black female choreographers fighting for recognition at the inception of modern dance. He focuses on the work of Aida Overton Walker and her performance of Salome in 1908 and 1912. Krasner documents the racist origins of modern Western cultural conceptions of "the primitive" and black cultural inferiority and their impact upon the representations and expectations of black women. According to Krasner, the notion of black primitivism along with the legacies of slavery directly contributed to the exoticization of the black woman and a belief in her hypersexuality. The black female response to her own sexualized representation was to maintain a "puritan" respectability and propriety. Thus, Krasner explains, the partic-ular historical and cultural contexts of the times not only played a significant role in determining how Walker performed Salome but in how we must understand and interpret this performance's meanings.

Kimberly Dixon, in "Uh Tiny Land Mass Just Outside of My Vocabulary," considers how what she terms "creative nomadism" works as a strategy to counter the constraints and restraints of gender and race placed upon African American playwrights. Dixon defines creative nomadism as a "liberating hybridity" that allows the playwright to negotiate between worlds from a fluid and constantly changing vantage point. She cites Obie Award–winning playwright Suzan-Lori Parks as a key practitioner. The creative nomadism of Parks and other contemporary African American playwrights, Dixon main-tains, celebrates and illuminates the constructed, contextual nature of time and space and of race and gender.

Jay Plum, in "Attending Walt Whitman High," points out that the pol-itics of gender do not simply concern the opposition of and differences be-tween masculinity and femininity. Through this study of the group Post-modern African American Homosexuals (Pomo Afro Homos) and their performance piece *Dark Fruit,* Plum considers the meanings and definitions of contemporary black masculinity. According to Plum, the sexual politics of the Pomos' performances confront conventional and pejorative represen-tations of black homosexuality, attack black homophobia, and implicate the audience. Equally significant, Plum's criticism implicitly challenges the heterosexism of traditional black theater scholarship. Within his analysis, as in the other essays of this part, considerations of gender and sexuality complicate and disrupt conventional racial readings and representations of blackness.

The discussions of gender in these four chapters also inform our understanding of identity. As Stuart Hall notes, "Identity is constructed within not outside of representation." The question of who African Americans are is never distinct from representation but is always invented or constructed in the moment. According to Hall:

> Identities are about questions of using the resources of history, language and culture in the process of becoming rather than being: not "who we are" or "where we have come from" so much as what we might become, how we have been represented and how that bears on how we might represent ourselves.[17]

Identity, then, is not fixed but is the site of multiple contestations and fluid locations. There is not simply one African American identity but many African American identities.

African American Performativity and the Performance of Race

If identity is not fixed, and if the meanings of race are the product of social, cultural, and historic constructions, then can race be performed? Are there times in everyday life when African Americans act out or "do" blackness?[18] Adapting Richard Schechner's definition of performance as "twice-behaved behavior," at such moments one could argue that the performer repeats, reinscribes, or even reconfigures established gestures, behaviors, linguistic patterns, cultural attitudes, and social expectations associated with blackness. Accordingly, in slavery times, slaves would wear the mask of ignorance and perform the expected role of black subservience in order to avoid punishment from the slave master's lash. Historically, such performances of blackness have functioned as methods of cultural or personal survival as well as reaffirmations and renegotiations of cultural identity.

Using theories of performance and performativity, the chapters in part IV probe into the ways blackness and racial identity have been constructed in and through performance. Diana Paulin, in "Acting Out Miscegenation," theorizes that the theatrical representation of interracial desire has the potential to disrupt static definitions of race and that staged portrayals of interracial unions between black and white characters destabilize definitions of both blackness and whiteness. Adapting Judith Butler's concept of gender performativity, Paulin considers how race operates in performative terms as she analyzes *The White Slave* (1882) by Bartley Campbell. Even as this play, written by a white playwright, ends with the affirmation of racial difference, Paulin shows that the introduction of interracial desire complicates racial readings and any ontological separation of black and white.

In her analysis of the Federal Theater Project's Negro Unit in Birmingham, Alabama, "The Administration of Race," Tina Redd chronicles how certain racialized social "performances" reinforced the static borders and constructions of race on and off stage. Redd's study of the all-too-brief existence of the Birmingham Negro Unit between 1935 and 1936 reveals that white bureaucrats, in their efforts to control and to define the Negro unit, "performed whiteness" by silencing and excluding any black participation. She documents the history of a Negro unit under white hegemony and subject to a particular politics of racial segregation, which defined and delimited all representations of blackness. As cultural capital, the Birmingham Negro Unit was subject to economic and administrative practices within a racialized social field that constructed blackness as separate and unequal and denied black artistic legitimacy.

While Paulin and Redd observe the constructions of blackness by white playwrights and under the control of white producers, Harry Elam examines the power of black performers to exploit their "productive ambivalence" and transgress, transcend, and even subvert established racial categories. In "The Black Performer and the Performance of Blackness," Elam argues that the black performance artist can purposefully utilize his or her ambivalent status—as a real person, as a theatrical representation, as a sociocultural construction—to expose and perhaps even explode definitions of blackness. He analyzes the work of black performance artists in two significant works of black theater history, *The Escape; or, A Leap to Freedom* by William Wells Brown (1858), the first black play published in the United States, and *No Place To Be Somebody* by Charles Gordone, the Pulitzer Prize–winning play of 1969. In both of these works, black performers exploit the theatricality of race as well as the situational meanings and constructions of blackness.

Unlike the other works in this part or in the anthology as a whole, Christina Sharpe examines the role that performance plays in a novel, Gayl Jones's *Corregidora* (1975). Sharpe, in "The Costs of Re-Membering," argues that performance functions as a strategy of remembrance and resistance in this "blues" novel. Within the story of Corregidora, the characters enact a ritualistic remembering of their slave past, the history of African enslavement in Brazil. The blues themselves, Sharpe argues, operate within the novel as a cultural intervention and as a source of collective cultural memory. Sharpe analyzes the relationships among the sexual, gendered, and racial performances in Jones's text and the contemporary intraracial interactions of black men and black women. In this chapter and in this part of the volume, questions of visibility, the marked and unmarked in black performance, figure prominently.[19]

Discussion with Senior Scholars

Part V, a roundtable discussion on African American theater historiography, featuring some of the leading scholars in the field of African American theater and performance—James Hatch, Sandra Richards, and Margaret Wilkerson—concludes the anthology. Questioned by the editors, Elam and Krasner, these scholars assess the past and present state of African American theater and performance studies. Among many issues, this roundtable examines the relationship of black theater criticism to black theater and performance studies practice; considers the role of the scholar in perpetuating as well as analyzing black performance; analyzes the relationship between African American "legitimate" theater and what Gates calls the Chitlin Circuit;[20] and discusses some of the issues raised by the August Wilson–Robert Brustein debate in January 1997.

The roundtable discussion, conjoined with the other parts of this anthology, recasts the past with an awareness of critical and theoretical developments in the present. We show that, in theatrical moments and movements throughout American history, blackness has functioned as a complex, powerful signifier loaded with historical baggage and yet still dependent on the situational contexts of its use. This book affirms the power of theater to act as a cultural force within and as a social barometer of African American experiences. Analyzing African American performance traditions offers us insight into how blackness has been produced and even *performed* as the device of race is continually reconstructed and redefined within the theater.

NOTES

1. Nineteenth-century theories of polygenism proposed that geographical origins and biological inheritance determined racial categories. Using pseudoscientific and biased methodology, authorities on "craniometry" claimed a clear relationship between the size of human skulls and the shape of human brains and, as a consequence, racial difference. In 1858, while on tour in Odessa Russia, the great black Shakespearean actor, Ira Aldridge, consented to having his head measured by the American consul there. The consul concluded:

> The head of this eminent coloured man is very much larger than the average size for a white man which, as is generally known, is above the Negro type of head. . . . his [head], like that of Fred Douglass, is an isolated case and proves only rare possibilities or outcroppings from common stock.

Thus, Aldridge's big head was dismissed as a biological aberration. Other biological interpretations of race in the nineteenth century and even into the early twentieth century maintained that inherited gene pools determined race, that race was in the blood.

2. See Michael Omi and Howard Winant, *Racial Formation in the United States*, 2d ed. (New York: Routledge, 1994); and David Theo Goldberg, *Racist Culture* (Cambridge, Mass.: Blackwell, 1993).

3. While Hansberry wrote the play *Les Blancs*, her former husband, Robert Nemiroff, completed it for the stage in 1969. Hansberry was extremely ill with cancer at the time. See Margaret Wilkerson's discussion of the play in chap. 2 of this volume.

4. Lorraine Hansberry, *Les Blancs, Collected Last Plays of Lorraine Hansberry,* ed. Robert Nemiroff (New York: New American Library, 1983), 92.

5. See Omi and Winant, *Racial Formation in the United States*; Goldberg, *Racist Culture.*

6. Larry Neal, "The Black Arts Movement," *Drama Review* 12, no. 4 (Summer 1968): 33.

7. Stuart Hall, "New Ethnicities," in *The Post-Colonial Studies Reader*, ed. Bill Aschroft, Gareth Griffiths, and Helen Tiffin (London: Routledge, 1995), 223–228.

8. W. E. B. Du Bois, "Krigwa Little Theatre Movement," *Crisis* 32 (July 1926): 135.

9. LeRoi Jones, "The Revolutionary Theatre," in *Selected Plays and Prose of Amiri Baraka/LeRoi Jones* (New York: William Morrow, 1979), 131.

10. August Wilson, "The Ground on Which I Stand," *American Theatre* (Sept. 1996): 16.

11. Spurred on by the vociferous responses to this speech, Wilson helped to organize a National Black Theatre Summit at Dartmouth College in March 1997. More than 300 black theater scholars, theater practitioners, entrepreneurs, and community activists came together to discuss the future of black theater. Significantly, the summit led to the creation of a new national black theater organization, the African Grove Institute, named after the first documented black theater in this country, Mr. Brown's African Grove Company (1821–1823).

12. Amritjit Singh, Joseph T. Skerrett, Jr., and Robert E. Hogan, *Memory & Cultural Politics* (Boston: Northeastern University Press, 1996), 4.

13. Richard Schechner, *Between Theater and Anthropology* (Philadelphia: University of Pennsylvania Press, 1985), 35.

14. Elin Diamond, *Performance & Cultural Politics* (New York: Routledge, 1996), 2.

15. Mimi McGurl, unpublished essay, 9.

16. See W. T. Lhamon, Jr., *Raising Cain* (Cambridge, Mass.: Harvard University Press, 1998); Eric Lott, *Love and Theft* (New York: Oxford University Press, 1993); James Hatch, Annemarie Bean, and Bruce McNamara, *Inside the Minstrel Mask* (Hanover, N.H.: Wesleyan University Press, 1996); and Dale Cockrell, *Demons of Disorder* (Cambridge: Cambridge University Press, 1997).

17. Stuart Hall, "Who Needs Identity?" in *Questions of Cultural Identity*, ed. Stuart Hall and Paul du Gay (London: Sage, 1996), 4.

18. These questions are appropriated from Eve Sedgwick and Andrew Parker, "Introduction," *Performance and Performativity* (New York: Routledge, 1995), 1.

19. See Peggy Phelan, *Unmarked: The Politics of Performance* (New York: Routledge, 1993).

20. Henry Louis Gates, Jr., "The Chitlin Circuit," *New Yorker* (3 Feb. 1997): 44–55 (reprinted as chap. 7 in this vol.).

Part I

Social Protest and the Politics
of Representation

1

Uncle Tom's Women

~~~~~~

JUDITH WILLIAMS

In an anthology dedicated to African American theater history, perhaps it seems odd to consider dramatizations of *Uncle Tom's Cabin*, the abolitionist novel written in 1852 by Harriet Beecher Stowe. Neither the original text nor the multiple stage adaptations that followed were authored by African Americans, and within the theater conventions of the era, African Americans seldom appeared on the stage except in the form of "jubilee singers," a nineteenth-century hypertext that interpolated spirituals and slave songs into the performances. It was not until 1878 that a black Uncle Tom, Sam Lucas, appeared on the stage. Lucas was a well-known minstrel performer, who was as attractive for his large resources (rumors of his diamonds abound in clippings of the period) as for the novelty of a black man on the stage in a serious role. Black female performers appeared, later, in the role of Topsy but without the fanfare of Lucas; they were little more than a footnote in the long history of the "Tom Show"—a fact reflected in this chapter itself. The question remains: what does Uncle Tom have to do with African American theater history?

In teaching the university-level course African American Theater, I begin with *Uncle Tom's Cabin* because of the permanence of the images that it inspired. Although Stowe's novel is no longer as widely read as it once was, many individuals who have not read *Uncle Tom's Cabin* have a clear picture of Uncle Tom. Similarly, the stage productions had a tenacious staying power. The "Tom Show," as the eventual cavalcade of adaptations of *Uncle Tom's Cabin* were called, was the most widely produced play in the history of the United States, and despite the longevity of contemporary musicals, has yet to be surpassed. Its first adaptation appeared while the novel was still in serialization in the *New Era*, and performances continued all around the globe through World War II, although some articles erroneously note the death of this venerable form in 1930. These blackface performances schematized the stereotype of the black character and repeated it for almost a century. All African American traditions were forced to combat the incredible archetypal power of the "Tom Show," which competed with the other stage images well into the twentieth century.

"Tom Shows" incorporated the blackface, music, and spectacle of the minstrel show with the pathos and abolitionist sentiment of Stowe's novel. Although early black images appeared before those depicted by *Uncle Tom's Cabin,*[1] in this essay, I use the "Tom Show" as a site where the formation of stereotypes of black female characters can be evaluated. Stowe's self-professed objective was to appeal to whites in an arena that was dear to their hearts, and it was on the terrain of motherhood that she chose to wage her battle. However, in her depiction of black female characters, Stowe repeated the tropes of black female representation already developing in the nineteenth-century imagination, and the enormous stage caricatures that emerged were not solely the interpolations of her dramatic interpreters. Stowe employs three primary icons of the black female: the mammy, the tragic mulatto, and the Topsy figure. The mammy was a favorite of sentimental literature, and her appearance, typically fat, black, and kerchiefed, linked her to the minstrel stage. A second figure that gained currency through the nineteenth century was the tragic mulatto: the near-white, genteel heroine, depicted as a beautiful and articulate woman, whose virtue was threatened by her Negro status. Stowe added a third type of black female character: Topsy, the disrespectful child who "never was born" yet became an icon of the American imagination.

In her creation, Stowe engaged in the highly ambivalent process of stereotyping that, in Homi Bhabha's description, attempts to ascribe a "fixity" to a subject. According to Bhabha, "The stereotype is a form of knowledge that facilitates between what is already 'in place,' and something that must be anxiously repeated."[2] Stowe's characters merely repeated what had already been "fixed" by earlier racial discourse.

The nineteenth-century representation of these characters was plagued by what George Fredrickson describes as "romantic racialism" in *The Black Image in the White Mind* in which "benevolent reformers tended to see the Negro more as a symbol than as a human being with the normal range of virtues and vices."[3] Although these figures had a symbolic value, they were implicated in the stereotypes of the time. Intrinsic to the process of stereotyping is an ambivalence that includes:

> a repertoire of conflictual positions [that] constitutes the subject in colonial discourse. The taking up of any one position, within specific discursive form in a particular historical conjuncture, is thus always problematic— the site of both fixity and fantasy. . . . As a form of splitting and multiple belief, the stereotype requires for its successful signification, a continual repetitive chain of other stereotypes.[4]

In the case of *Uncle Tom's Cabin,* this trope functions in its reinscription of already-held stereotypes, its elevation of stereotype to archetype, and, finally, the continued repetition of these images on the stage, which yield a cultural penetration that is so deep that, despite the fact that *Uncle Tom's Cabin* is no longer read widely, its stereotypical figures are well fixed in the American imagination.

Although Stowe's novel was immensely popular, the proliferation of the "Tom Shows" that followed the novel increased the potency and size of its stereotypes. "Tom Shows" changed the landscape of American theater, increased its audience base, and spawned a long-lasting genre of their own. The essence of stereotype was present in Stowe's novel, yet the embodiment that occured on stage added another dimension to it. On stage, ideas achieve corporeality, and the stereotype gains a greater semblance of reality. In *Unmarked*, Peggy Phelan contends:

> Performance implicates the real through the presence of living bodies. In spectatorship there is an element of consumption: there are no left-overs, the gazing spectator must try to take everything in. Without a copy live performance plunges into visibility—in a maniacally charged present— and disappears into memory, into the realm of invisibility and unconscious where it eludes regulation and control.[5]

Unlike the permanence of pictures or words, performance can only be captured through the memories of its documenters, and studying it historically entails the mediation of those other writers. The texts of nineteenth-century plays tell one story, their production history another, which is unrecoverable in its totality. What remains are descriptions by reviewers, memoirs of the performers, programs, posters, and other artifacts from the shows; from these pieces of historical memory, one can attempt to recover the lost moment of the stage presentation.

Each production began with an adaptation of Stowe's text, and entwined within the stage adaptations is a tension between Stowe's vision and that of her adapters. Their additions as well as those of actors and producers changed the stereotypes and created a dynamic interplay of ideas and images. Of these numerous adaptations, two have been placed at the forefront of historical analysis. H. J. Conway's version was the most popular, and George Aiken's has proven the most durable and has become the standard.

The Aiken version of the play began at the Troy Museum in Troy, N.Y., and after a very successful run, the production moved to Albany and then to New York City, where it played at Purdy's National Theater. It opened in 1852 and closed on May 13, 1854, after 325 performances. The Conway adaptation was created for the Boston Museum and opened November 15, 1852. P. T. Barnum then mounted a New York production, which competed directly with the Aiken version. Conway's version is widely considered more sentimental and less didactic in tone than Aiken's. Because of their unique combination of the sentimental elements of the melodrama and the burlesque blackface comedy of the minstrel show, these stage shows proved immensely popular. In *Melodramatic Formations*, Bruce McConachie characterizes *Uncle Tom's Cabin* as a "moral reform play," a form that grew in popularity through the middle of the nineteenth century. In McConachie's discussion, it is the

Conway, not the Aiken version, that typifies this form, and it is primarily the white characters who take on the roles of moral reformers. McConachie describes the problematic representations of both black and female characters: "Because they can never be men of principle or women of honor, the African-American characters are pictured as childish buffoons, their characterization taken directly from the stereotypes of the minstrel show."[6] Conway took his inspiration from the stereotypes and assumptions of the time rather than from any more humanizing aspects of Stowe's novel. This type of portrayal is obvious even from the introduction of the characters; for example, Topsy is called "a rough but true [example] of neglected undereducated black humanity."[7] This character, a child in Stowe's text, was most often portrayed by a grown woman or a boy on stage.

The Aiken version was the first adaptation to include the Topsy character, and it set the convention for her minstrel-like depiction. Although Stowe states explicitly in the novel that Topsy is a child of eight or nine years old, on the stage the character was first played by Caroline Fox, mother to Cordelia Howard, who played Little Eva, and wife to George Howard, who portrayed St. Clare. The presence of an adult woman in this role changed the nature of the relationships among Topsy and the other characters. What may have been subtle undercurrents of sexuality within the novel were magnified by the unavoidable presence of a grown woman on the stage. Behaviors that in children are merely unseemly become vulgar when demonstrated by an adult woman. The illusion of childhood also increases the sense of potential and possibility that surrounds Topsy; in a child, "wickedness" has a more innocent connotation than in an adult woman. Wicked for adult women is most often linked to sexuality and licentiousness.

Adult women were not alone in their portrayal of Topsy. Like other black female characters, white men as well as white women enacted her. As Harry Birdoff comments in his 1947 history, *The World's Greatest Hit: "Uncle Tom's Cabin"*: "Little Evas grew to Topsies, Maries, Elizas and then Aunt Chloes. Gangling boys attempted the irrepressible Topsies, went on to Markses, then to Legrees and in old age achieved the epitome—Uncle Toms."[8] In the stage vocabulary, black characters appeared almost genderless with a movable sexuality. In the representation of black women, the stereotype elided not only any sense of history but even erased the presence of the black female body from the stage. In this erasure we see the problem of stereotype that Bhabha describes: "Like the mirror phase, 'the fullness' of the stereotype— its image as identity is always threatened by a 'lack.' "[9] On the stage, this metaphorical "lack" is doubled and reinforced by the actual lack of a black body.[10]

Topsy is simultaneously the opposite of the more virtuous black figures of Stowe's novel and the foil to the purity of Little Eva. Eva's appearance marks her as graceful yet ethereal; Topsy's countenance marks her as "goblinlike" or "heathenish." Stowe describes Eva as "always dressed in white, she seemed to move like a shadow through all sorts of places, without contracting spot or stain,"[11] whereas Topsy "was dressed in a single filthy, ragged garment, made of bagging."[12] Despite these differences, Stowe describes Eva's behavior on the boat as pure mischief. She wanders without restraint and is not responsive to the mild chastisements of her father and guardian. Stowe describes Topsy with equal inclinations toward mischief, yet whereas Eva's explorations are childlike and endearing, Topsy's games are valanced with a more insidious and threatening character.

On stage, these differences are magnified by the power of the visual image. The young girl playing Eva is opposed to the larger, more active, full-grown woman or young boy playing Topsy. They seem not to be potential playmates at all but clear opposites—any childish innocence for Topsy is drained by the blackened stage image. At the same time, there is a contrast in the coloring of the two. Eva's fair face and hair highlighted by her white clothes heightens the blackness of the cosmetic coloring of the white actor playing Topsy. Eva's goodness and kindness provide the impetus for Topsy's eventual reform and the inevitable triumph of light over dark. The Topsy character realizes the value of whiteness in antebellum southern society as she constantly espouses her desire to become white. She links whiteness with goodness. In *White*, Richard Dyer emphasizes that "to be seen is to have one's corporeality registered yet true whiteness resides in the noncorporeal."[13] Although Eva is initially embodied, she fades away and dies, only to be remanifested in a final tableau in the Aiken version as a purely spiritual being, highlighting the purity of her whiteness.

In contrast, Topsy's corporeality is ever-present. In her extremes of behavior and appearance, Topsy embodies darkness and resembles the female caricatures of the minstrel stage. On stage, these black female characters, who do not "speak" on the lives of black women, have a long history. The minstrel wench was first created by white men in black face and in drag. When not a fair-skinned, mulatto belle, the image of a black woman was usually one of lascivious nature, grotesque physical proportions, and enormous appetites. This profile once again echoes the absence of a black woman as a substantial stage presence. On the minstrel stage, the displacement and absence of the black woman occurs at a second level. The audience sees the image of a black woman but without the presence of a black female body—or even a white female body. The false image of a black woman is instead inscribed on a white male body.

In *Love and Theft*, Eric Lott argues that "misrecognition and identification" were the foundation of the myths of blackness that arose in the nineteenth century. Given the repression that abounded in nineteenth-century society, representations of blackness served as an outlet for baser instincts and an attempt to project them onto black bodies and distance them from polite society. Dyer describes white masculinity as including both light and dark elements, yet it is the triumph of the white aspects, linked to mental or spiritual pursuits, over their corporeal dark opposites that provides the strength of white manhood. The employment of the blackface embodies these baser aspects but projects them out of the white body and underlines the white's mastery of them. Embodied in these images is at once a repulsion of the black and a desire for the black. "The desire 'to be black' expressed in white people's relationship to black music and dance may well inform the fashion of tanning, but the point about tanning is that the white person never does become black."[14] A similar appropriation occurs in minstrelsy, where whites can take on the spectacular elements of a perceived blackness but just as easily shrug them off. These images, however, silence the black figure. The stereotype replaces a real presence and encodes it in silence. These immense characterizations became the standard by which any "darky" portrayal could be measured, especially in the theaters of the North, where most of the patrons had limited personal exposure to blacks with which to mediate their experience of the images that they saw. In Lott's analysis of *Uncle Tom's Cabin* he argues, however,

> Mrs. G. C. Howard's Topsy . . . was a departure from the minstrel show's typical female types, whose ridicule depended on their overripe aptitude or special ineptness for courtship and love; Topsy, by contrast, was Miss Ophelia's mischievous, unruly sidekick, a sort of female match for the rustic Jim Crow.[15]

This part of Lott's argument fails to cover the magnitude of Topsy's stage performance. Very few spectators (or reviewers) of the nineteenth century made the trip to the theater to view Miss Ophelia and her sidekick. Topsy is the stronger of the two characters, and I would posit that the opposite relationship is more compelling. Within the milieu of the "Tom Shows," Topsy had a tendency to just grow. There arose shows in which the original story of Tom was excised from the presentation, and the interactions of Topsy and Little Eva solely were emphasized. For white actresses, Topsy was the most promising role in the "Tom" circuit. Elizabeth Corbett argues in a 1930 article in *Theatre Guild* Magazine that

> twenty years ago all the celebrated actresses on our stage used to claim that they began as Topsy. Some of them undoubtedly did. If they were exceptionally good Topsies, that was their chance of leaving off Uncle Tom-ming.[16]

We are reminded here that, for the white actresses who donned the black face and bagging dress of Topsy, there was seldom shame; it often proved a way for actresses to launch their careers and gain notice in the theater circuit. The stereotypical image of Topsy became a testing ground for young actresses to prove their mettle. The black face and character of Topsy allowed the creation of a space of license or transgression for whites. This space permitted them to take on the more uninhibited attributes that the stereotype allowed for blacks and inhabit it. When whites put on the black, they reinscribed and inflated the already existing negative stereotypes of black people.

In a review of a London presentation of the play, the actor who portrayed Topsy was praised for her ability to convincingly embody the role, which was seen to be an accurate representation of blackness:

It seems almost impossible to believe that Miss Chippendale is a white young lady, but such is the fact. Her command of Nigger [*sic*] mannerisms appears to be second nature, and where she picked up that extraordinary croaking intonation in which she makes Topsy speak is one of those things which no fellow can understand. In her Mrs. Stowe's Topsy stands confessed.[17]

Another actress is similarly praised:

One of the best impersonations of the evening, was found in the irrepressible "Topsy," played with equal care and comicality by Miss Marie Bates, who sacrifices all scruples of feminine vanity on the altar of art, by making herself the perfection of Negro ugliness, adopting the most uncouth and ungraceful dress and demeanor, and tumbling head over heels with a pantomimic dexterity, which a London street boy might despairingly envy.[18]

In both of these reviews, the performances are judged by the distance from the accepted set of behaviors for white women. The space of license and the actresses' ability or willingness to occupy it fully is what provides the substantive merit of their performances. Yet the seeming reality that these reviewers find in the performances is questionable. Even more than Stowe herself, these London denizens are distanced from the day-to-day activities of motherless, fatherless slave children. The Emancipation Act abolished slavery in Great Britain and its colonies in 1833. The small population of blacks in Britain in 1878 consisted of all free people, many of whom had been emancipated for almost two generations. Race sentiments, however, were influenced by stereotype and prejudice as the debate on the inferiority of blacks was waged in Britain as well as in the United States. Thus Londoners, including the reviewers, although they did not have much firsthand knowledge of blacks, had ample material on which to base their conceptions of "Negro ugliness" or "Nigger mannerisms" in the scientific and political debates of the era. Again, the power of the stereotype asserts itself as "a form of knowledge that vacillates between what is already 'in place' and something that must be anxiously repeated."[19]

The primary arbiters of the Topsy character, Stowe, Aiken, Conway, and other adapters, as well as the actors like Cordelia Howard, were northerners who reflected northern views of slavery and slave children. For both Aiken and Conway, Topsy was a comic character. In the Conway version, Topsy is thoroughly minstrelized and, as McConachie reports, "delivers a stump speech promising to join a 'benevolence s'ciety' in the North to 'lucidate to dat s'ciety de necessity ob doin' somethin' for dere coloured brethren in bondage.' "[20] Although the stage presence of Topsy was very different from the vision that Stowe presents of Topsy in the novel, the language of the Aiken text almost replicates Stowe's words and gives insight into the nature of Topsy's character and the image that other characters (and the authors) hold of her. The St. Clares describe Topsy as a "purchase," an "article," a "heathenish, shiftless looking object," and a "thing." It is clear that Topsy's humanity in their eyes (and in the eyes of Stowe?) is in question.

Despite Topsy's dehumanization, within the representational excess of black women's portrayals on the nineteenth-century stage lies the possibility of subversion. In seeking to create a comic character who drew audiences accustomed to ludicrous black female impersonations, playwrights allowed Topsy to grow, and along with her stereotype, the revolutionary potential of Topsy became part of that representational excess. The extremity of her character, which makes it humorous, also makes it subversive. Because she was so distant from appropriate behaviors, audiences could revel in her ridiculousness. Yet, even at her most ridiculous, she is threatening. As a character, she is a black woman who behaves badly and who cannot be controlled. As a stage presence, she is a white woman covered in blackness and freed to enact behaviors well outside of the realm of a proper woman's etiquette. Echoing Peggy Phelan's argument in *Unmarked*, "Representation follows two laws: It always conveys more than it intends; and it is never totalizing."[21] Even in the most stereotypical reading of Topsy, there is a representational excess: Topsy is still a stereotype, but she grows.

Topsy was not, however, Stowe's sole black creation, and she is only one of the three characters who I will consider here. Outside of the minstrel milieu in nineteenth century theater, mulatto women were almost always portrayed by white women in metaphoric blackface. Stage adaptations of *Uncle Tom's Cabin* were some of the first plays that popularized this type of heroine. They included the story of the fair-skinned Eliza and George Harris, as well as the tragedies of Cassy and Emmeline. Of the three different types of black female characters that Stowe presents, the tragic mulatto figures were the most intelligent and the most sympathetic. Through these figures, she demonstrates the cost of slavery to the institution of motherhood. At the close of the novel, in her "Concluding Remarks," Stowe addresses:

> Mothers of America,—you who have learned by the cradles of your own children, to love and feel for all mankind,—by the sacred love you bear your child; by your joy in his beautiful spotless infancy; by the motherly pity and tenderness with which you guide his growing years; by the anxieties of education; by the prayers you breathe for his soul's eternal good; I beseech you, pity the mother who has all your affections, and not one legal right to protect, guide, or educate the child of her bosom.[22]

Although Stowe uses the term *mother* without qualification as though to indicate all slave mothers, in the novel she highlights the separation stories of only the fairer-skinned characters: Cassy, Eliza, Emmeline. For these heroines, Stowe's portrait is richer. The mulatto figure is by her nature less fixable; she holds in her body the union of the two races and the possibility of change. The tragic mulatto was tragic because, although she had the appearance of a white woman, she was tainted by her relation to her black mother. This taint also allowed her virtue to be questionable. The tragic mulatto occupied a liminal space neither white nor black with access neither to full virtue nor its lack. The ability of a white woman to play this role without cosmetic enhancement underlined the tragic notion of her fate—to look white but to be black. She appeared as a white woman, but she was without the protections that white status conferred on her: she could be raped without consequence. The fact that these women were portrayed on stage by white women further complicated the idea of an intelligent black woman. The audience was always aware that the intelligent "black" character on the stage who inspired compassion was a white woman. At the same time, the audience was aware that the "black" woman who flouted the norms of society and stepped out of her place was also a white woman. The images that the white women created reinforced the need for control of black women.

Through her near-white characters, Stowe sought to bring the tragedy of slavery close to the sympathies of her readers. But Stowe's picture of pure black mothers is not so sympathetic. Stowe presents three mulatto figures who are subject to the loss of the bonds of motherhood: Eliza, the mother who escapes with her son to prevent their separation; Emmeline, the daughter who is taken from the protection of her mother and falls prey to indecent sexual advances; and Cassy, the degraded mother whose children were sold away from her and who resorted to murder to prevent the same fate for her third child.

In addition to showing aspects of motherhood under siege, these three figures are also vulnerable as women. Each of the women is cast as a sexual object without the protection of the law that white women have. Their appearance marks them as white—they "tragically" look white—yet the unmarked presence of their blackness brands them as commodities within a sexual exchange. When Eliza's owner, George Shelby, is in debt and is forced to sell Eliza's son Harry, the slave trader offers to buy Eliza for the New Orleans market instead, but Shelby refuses. Eliza is spared this fate because of the affections of her mistress and because her mistress depends on her services. After Eliza escapes, the slave trader attempts to catch her and sell her south, but Eliza is not caught. Emmeline is separated from her mother and is sold to Simon Legree, a character portrayed by Stowe as degenerate and cruel; his intent is sexual. Cassy eventually falls into the estate of Legree and serves as his mistress. She had been the mistress of several men, some of whom treated her more honorably than others, and she bore children who she was not, as a mother, able to protect. All three of these characters suffer through the slave system's denial to black women of the rights to their own bodies or to the children they produce. Aiken includes all three characters in his adaptation. Conway, however, eliminates Emmeline and portrays only Cassy as a mother. Here, I will consider in more depth only the figure of Cassy, since it is she who most closely approximates the tragedy of the mulatto.

Although Richard Yarborough describes Cassy as a "proud, willful, mixed-blood woman who has been driven to infanticide by broken promises, sexual exploitation, and horrible suffering, Cassy resists her enslavement more fiercely and actively than any black character besides George Harris,"[23] Cassy also exemplifies the Victorian image of the fallen woman. As previously noted, Cassy had been mistress to three men—one whom she loved and two whom she despised. Cassy is powerless to prevent her violations by her various masters. Even in the case of her single "consensual" relationship, she did not have the power to prevent it. In Stowe's story, Cassy's first paramour is described as having kindness and beauty, and he tells Cassy, in her words, that "he had loved me a great while, and that he would be my friend and protector;—in short, though he didn't tell me, he had paid two thousand dollars for me, and I was his property."[24] Although this man came to Cassy kindly and asked for love, the relationship was legally little different from the one she endured with Legree. This relationship ended when the master found himself indebted to a less kind man who desired Cassy and acquired her and her children in payment of that debt. When Stowe introduces Cassy, it is after years of illicit sexual relationships, which have compromised her honor and her beauty.

Stowe places Cassy first in the cotton field where, despite seeming out of place, she completes her field work with incredible facility, seeming "to work by magic."[25] Stowe describes Cassy more exotically than either of the two earlier representations of the tragic mulatto. She says of her:

> It was a woman, tall and slenderly formed, with remarkably delicate hands and feet, and dressed in neat and respectable garments. By the appearance of her face she may have been between thirty-five and forty; and it was a face once seen, could never be forgotten,—one of those at a glance, seem to convey to us an idea of a wild painful sexual history. Her forehead was high, and her eyebrows marked with beautiful clearness. Her straight well-formed nose, her finely cut mouth, and the graceful contour of her head and neck, showed that she once must have been beautiful; but her face was deeply wrinkled with lines of pain, and of proud and bitter endurance. Her complexion was sallow and unhealthy, her cheeks thin, her features sharp, and her whole form emaciated. But her eye was the most remarkable feature,—so large, so heavily black, overshadowed by long lashes of equal darkness, and so wildly, mournfully despairing. There was fierce pride and defiance in every line of her face, in every curve of the flexible lip, in every motion of her body; but in her eye was a deep settled night of anguish,—an expression so hopeless and unchanging as to contrast fearfully with the scorn and pride expressed by her whole demeanor.[26]

In this description, Stowe specifies her age and, though identified by her appearance as a tragic mulatto figure, Cassy's age places her in the same generation as the conventional mammy figure. But Cassy's sexual usage sets her apart from the mythic mammy. Stowe places Cassy at the end of her youth, and her value as a concubine to Legree is on the decline. Were Cassy a more complacent character, and Legree less ruthless, she might have evolved from her role in sexual service to simply a service role like that of the mammy figure.

Susan Roberson contends, in "Matriarchy and the Rhetoric of Domesticity," that "Victorian writers constructed an elaborate sign system whereby, theoretically, the inner self could be known by external signs such as manners and dress"[27] and that Stowe, like other writers of her era, was proficient in the use of this system. In the above description, Cassy's wrecked beauty links her to a ravaged illicit sexual history and presents her as a clearly sexualized woman. Despite her sexualized past, Stowe depicts her sympathetically as a victim of a cruel system and implies in the description a sense of defiance and internal strength. Additionally, Legree and his slave drivers perceive Cassy as having access to magical powers. Cassy may not have magical powers, but she is able to insinuate herself into Legree's fears and superstitions and appears to have power where she does not.

On stage, Cassy loses her confrontational desire for freedom and appears more a character of desperation than defiance. In the Aiken version, Cassy first appears on the stage when she gives Tom water after his initial whipping by Legree. She seems so convincingly white that Tom mistakes her for the mistress, and she corrects him roughly: "Don't call me missis. I'm a miserable slave like yourself—a lower one than you can ever be!"[28] She then admonishes Tom to give up his battle against Legree and recounts her own record of disgrace at Legree's hands. She has neither the majesty nor the suggestion of magical powers that Stowe's Cassy manifests.

A similar conversation occurs between the two in the novel, but the language is slightly different. Tom says, "The Lord forbid, missis," and Cassy responds not to the title of "missis" but to the appeal to God. She says, "The Lord never visits these parts."[29] Cassy defies even the idea of divine intervention rather than dwell on her own plight and wretchedness as does her stage counterpart.

Stowe shows two faces for Cassy: the one she wears in public view, which is filled with a potent defiance, and a more defeated one, which she reveals to Tom when she brings him water after his brutal beating at Legree's hands. This scene alone is reproduced in the play text, removing the small power or agency that Stowe seemed to grant Cassy in the novel. In the play, Cassy seems less defiant; she is simply debased and defeated. As Yarborough concludes, Stowe's Cassy is almost as rebellious a figure as George Harris, who escapes slavery on his own, but Aiken's stage Cassy does not maintain this type of defiant energy.

Conway, in his version, introduces Cassy early in Act II. Cassy is placed in a New Orleans jail where she has spent the past three months. It is Legree who enters, not Tom. She is sleeping when he enters and he rouses her. Legree says he will take her back if she obeys. She tells him of how she dreamed about her life before her father's funeral, and she provides the exposition of her life to Legree, not to Tom. Legree is exasperated by her repetition of what he has heard many times before. In this case Legree is the evil cousin who led Cassy's beloved to gamble and leave her out of his affections. She also talks of her lost child "Eliza," who was sold by Legree. Although Aiken maintains the three tragic mulatto characters—Cassy, Eliza, and Emmeline—he merges Eliza and Emmeline into a single character so that it is Cassy and Eliza who plot against Legree, as well as Cassy and Eliza who are revealed to be mother and daughter.

Despite the sanitization of the Conway version of true abolitionist sentiment, Conway creates a stronger character for Cassy than Aiken does and like Yarborough sees the revolutionary possibility of Cassy. When she is in jail, Cassy remains defiant and she narrates to Legree a dream of vengeance in which all of Legree's murdered victims rise up against him. Although Legree responds by physically attacking her, he seems somewhat frightened by the power of her dream.

When Cassy appears in Act V, Scene 2, with the newly purchased Eliza, it is Eliza who speaks of escape and Cassy who tries to convince her that it is not possible. Cassy tells Eliza that if she refuses to submit to Legree's sexual advances, Legree will murder her as he has murdered others in the past. In the end, Cassy and Eliza formulate a plan of escape dependent on Cassy's knowledge of Legree's fears. They plan to have Eliza appear dressed as Legree's mother in a bloody gown in order to scare him away.

Cassy's insinuations are essential to the success of the plan. She prods Legree's fears about the haunted room where his mother died. Cassy tells Legree of the things that she has heard and seen in the room. When Legree checks the room, Eliza emerges dressed as they described. Later when Legree beats Tom, Cassy again suggests that his mother's ghost is at hand. Then, at the moment Legree discovers the talisman that Tom carries and picks it up, Eva's hair curls around his finger and he screams. Cassy says the hair comes from Legree's murdered mother's head, and in the window Eliza is visible in the bloody white dress. Legree has a fit and says that he is choking. He dies shortly after of fright. It is largely through Cassy's manipulations that Legree comes to this end. The rebellious energy of the novel is maintained and the representational excess of this character, although seemingly tragic, is one of power and agency.

A British version of the play by Mark Lemon and Tom Taylor maintains a defiant and willful Cassy and shows the malleability of the mulatto character. This version of the play describes a cooperation among the black female characters that is missing in both Stowe's novel and other versions of the play. Emmeline does not appear in the play; instead, it is Eliza whom Legree purchases as Cassy's replacement. Cassy tells her story not to Tom but to Eliza, as a way of warning her. She says, "For six years I have been the companion of a man—brutal, drunken, and inhumane. I have daily witnessed cruelty that you believe impossible, and now my tyrant has grown weary of me and has bought another mistress."[30] In this version, Cassy, not Eliza, warns Tom of his impending sale. When he refuses to take her advice and run away, she chastises him that his sale is not the will of heaven: "It is the laws of devils. Your mass'r would not have sold you, Eliza told me so, but must sell you, or sell all. You thank him for this."[31] At the conclusion of the play, Lemon and Taylor position the figures of Eliza, Topsy, Cassy, and George together as they all attempt an escape from Legree's plantation. In a final act of defiance, Cassy shoots and kills Legree, ensuring the safety of the party.

Despite the vehemence of Cassy's rebellion, even this version of the play elides many of the facts of Cassy's story, which Stowe presents in the novel. One fact that is not revealed in the play is that Cassy murdered her third child rather than have him sold away from her: "I took the little fellow in my arms when he was two weeks old, and kissed him and cried over him," Cassy describes, "and then I gave him laudanum, and held him close to my bosom, while he slept to death."[32] Here, Stowe's Cassy is her most threatening and subversive as she refuses to reproduce the slave children to maintain the system. She is similar to the Lemon-Taylor Cassy, who is willing to take a life in order to save her own, but she is an entirely different creature than the relatively helpless heroine who Aiken provides. Unlike the proactive Cassy of the novel, the Cassy of George Aiken's text did not take the life of her child and does not establish the destructive potential of a violated mother. Cassy as a stage character never gained the popularity or attention that either Topsy or Eliza did. Already far from a Victorian heroine in her role as a sexually compromised woman, the crime of baby killing might have made her almost a stage villain. The elision of the more horrific facts of her story grant her less agency and make her a more sympathetic and "womanly" supporting character. McConachie argues that "Stowe's conservative feminism helped to insure that many of her women did not make it to the stage."[33] Those that did were no longer as strong as they had appeared in the novel. This is due partly to the nature of the audience, which McConachie reconstructs as primarily male, working class, and unlikely to have strong abolitionist leanings. For this group, the mulatto provides a particular attraction; she is a woman who, despite her white appearance, maintains a hidden darkness—the same darkness that Dyer links with male desire. This construction of the female implies a passivity, and thus a stronger, more assertive Cassy would be less desirable to the audience.

Clearly, the translation of *Uncle Tom's Cabin* from the page to the stage is not a smooth one. Stage conventions change and undermine crucial elements of Stowe's abolitionist project. Sensationalization of triumphant acts, like Eliza's escape across the Ohio River, overshadow the more horrific elements of the story, like Emmeline's mishandling on the auction block by Legree. A defiant female character like Cassy translates from the novel as a weak or pathetic "womanly" character. Despite being called tragic mulattos, none of Stowe's fair heroines truly experiences a tragic ending. Stowe and her theatrical imitators rescue their heroines from slavery and abuse.

Like the tragic mulatto, the mammy has inspired a variety of critical material. For example, in *Plantation Mistress*, Catherine Clinton contends that the mammy myth was a creation of the white imagination.

> She existed as a counterpoint to the octoroon concubine, the light-skinned
> product of a "white man's lust" who was habitually victimized by slave

owners' sexual appetites. In addition the Mammy was integral to the white male's emasculation of slavery, since she and she alone projected an image of power wielded by blacks—a power rendered strictly benign and maternal in its influence. Further, her importance was derived from her alleged influence over whites; in her tutelary role, she was, in fact, invented as the desired collaborator within white society: idealized by the master class, a trumped-up, not a triumphant, figure in the mythologizing of slavery.[34]

Clinton implicitly echoes Toni Morrison's argument in *Playing in the Dark*. The mammy is an example of what Morrison describes as an "enabler" of whiteness; the black character serves as a darker reflection through which the white character is established. Morrison suggests four methods in which African Americans are marked as different and as integral functions in the performance of an American white identity. In the first role, the black Other is an "enabler" for whiteness, as described above. Second, Morrison suggests that white writers use the African American dialect as a marker of difference. Third, she argues, "We need studies of the technical ways in which an Africanist character is used to limn out and enforce the invention and implications of whiteness."[35] Finally, Morrison indicates an approach to the appropriation of the narrative of an African American experience in order to mediate "one's own humanity."[36] The mammy is a fiction that, in its representation, fulfills all of the criteria that Morrison proposes.

Within the myths of black femininity of the nineteenth century, only the mammy is free of the taint of sexuality. Her physical traits place her beyond the pale of sexual attraction. However, like Topsy, her representation entails an excess, and the same traits that mark her as undesirable can be read as sexualized. Although the myth marks the mammy as a woman whose body is denuded of sexuality, in literature, as in reality, this separation is impossible. In *Uncle Tom's Cabin*, Stowe described her own character, Aunt Chloe, as a woman with "a round, black, shiny face" and wrote that "her whole plump countenance beams with satisfaction and contentment from under a well-starched turban."[37] Encoded within this visual representation are the stereotypical features of the mammy. Although Stowe's project was abolitionist, her depiction of this black character repeats stereotypical tropes, which link Aunt Chloe to the mammy and allow her appropriation as a mammy figure. However, the representational excess of her portrait (and of the mammy more broadly) refutes this interpretation at the same time that it suggests it.

Stowe presents a Chloe who is surrounded by young children, black and white. In Stowe's novel, Chloe is a mother with two small children and an infant. At the same time that the infant reinforces Chloe's nurturing role, it also suggests her sexual one. A woman with an infant is one that cannot be too far from the sexual act that led to its conception. Chloe's concern for her husband, the father of her children, can certainly be read as that of a nurturer but also as that of a woman connected by a sexual relationship to her man. And, although she takes great care to accommodate the young master, George

Shelby, it is clear at the outset that Chloe's primary concern is her husband, Uncle Tom. As Stowe presents her, Aunt Chloe's mothering of her own children may be questionable, but her loyalty to her mate is not. She, when warned by Eliza of Tom's impending sale, urges Tom to run away. Stowe also presents a scene in which Aunt Chloe conspires with Mrs. Shelby in order to prolong a dinner after which the slave trader Haley plans to take possession of Eliza's son Harry. Chloe's "unusually leisurely and circumstantial manner" gives Eliza a head start away from the plantation.[38] Chloe also reappears at the end of the novel, having presented the Shelbys with the fruit of her labor as a baker in order to purchase Tom's freedom. When she learns that Tom has died, she gives the money to Mrs. Shelby: " 'Thar,' said she, gathering [the money] up, and holding it, with a trembling hand, to her mistress, 'don't never want to see nor hear on 't again. Jist as I knew 't would be,— sold, and murdered on dem ar' old plantations!' "[39] These words again reveal that, despite Chloe's pivotal role in the Shelby household, her first obligation remains her conjugal tie to Uncle Tom. Sarah Duckworth, however, criticizes Stowe's articulation of Aunt Chloe and argues that Stowe places her as a less-adequate mother than the white (or near-white) mothers in the novel:

These white women know full well their spiritual mission as shepherdesses for God, but Chloe can only identify herself in terms of the physical services she performs. She focuses always on tangibles—abstract concepts of evil and good are beyond her mental grasp. Consequently the one thing that makes Chloe's "fat sides" shake with honest pride and merriment is not a favorite child, but knowing that her baked goods are better than her "compeers."[40]

Duckworth's critique emphasizes that Chloe, unlike the white mothers, is shown as primarily a body in service, not as a fully realized subjectivity. Although Chloe may not make abstract distinctions between good and evil, she is consistent in her loyalty to her family and implicitly understands the "evil" inherent in Uncle Tom's sale. Chloe, despite any lack of abstract conception, further understands that her physical service can return Tom to his family, and by the end of the novel, she has converted the strength of her baking ability into the capital that might have bought Tom's freedom—had he survived. Duckworth's analysis certainly illustrates the deficiencies in Stowe's depiction of Chloe and of the black female characters, and it also points to Morrison's discussion of the role of black characters in literature. Chloe's lack of abstract thought highlights the social principles of her mistress; when Chloe and the mistress conspire together to delay the dinner, Chloe's ineptitude becomes the surrogate expression for Mrs. Shelby's opposition to Tom's sale. Thus, in Stowe's depiction, one sees a constant tension between the representation and its excess—the former promoting a traditional stereotypical reading of Chloe while the latter creates spaces of subversion.

These interstices, which allow a resistant reading, are truncated in Stowe's own dramatization of the novel, *The Christian Slave*. In this dramatization,

Stowe moves closer to the portrait that Duckworth describes as she emphasizes only the service aspect of Chloe's character, largely because Chloe's
statements from the novel are reproduced without the mediating effect of
Stowe's narration. Chloe appears first in her cabin, cooking, and is seldom far
from the kitchen. In both the novel and the dramatization, she cooks Tom a
special breakfast before he leaves and rails against the injustice of Tom's being
sold. She says:

> "Sich a faithful crittur as ye've been and allers sot his business 'fore yer own
> every way, and reckoned on him more than yer own wife and chil'en! Them
> as sells heart's love and heart's blood, to get out of that scrapes, and the
> Lord'll be up to 'em! Now mind, I tell ye de Lord'll be up to 'em."[41]

Here, Chloe describes Tom in the terms that usually describe the mammy;
his devotion to his master overwhelms any other ties that he may have. Yet,
implicit in her criticism of Tom are the assumptions that Tom should not
place his master before his family and that Chloe maintains the opposite set
of values.

In the Conway version, it is not loyalty but humor that characterizes Chloe.
Instead of entering the opening scene in an intimate family setting, Chloe
performs a minuet and then a dance accompanied by a banjo with another
slave for the entertainment of George Shelby in the plantation house. As
McConachie suggests, the role of black characters in this adaptation of the
play is little more than comic relief, and the contrast between the white
reformer characters and the comic black characters highlights the strengths
of the white characters. To use Morrison's language, these characters become
enablers of the white characters. When another slave suggests that Tom
might be sold, Chole responds, "Part wid my old man. No—no—Massa
won't do it nebber lib to see dat day."[42] Rather than the defiance of her masters
depicted by Stowe, Conway shows a Chloe whose faith in her masters makes
Tom's impending sale seem impossible; the space of resistance thus seems
smaller in this version.

Although less comic, George Aiken's Chloe appears only once in the
stereotypical attire of the mammy. Birdoff reports that, on opening night,
her mere entrance "set [the crowd] roaring and applauding vociferously."[43]
Here, the audience reads the visual text in the minstrel context, where pure
black women were objects of ridicule. The expectation of the audience was
humor, but it was soon sobered by the seriousness of Uncle Tom's situation:

> When Eliza tells Chloe of Tom's impending sale she says to him:
> "Well, old man, why don't you run away too? Will you wait to be toted
> down the river, where they kill niggers with hard work and starving? I'd
> a heap rather die than go there, any day! There's time for ye; be off with—
> You've got a pass to come and go anytime. Come, hustle up, and I'll get
> your things together."[44]

Chloe states plainly that her loyalty to the masters is not valued above her
life and suggests that Tom exploit his trusted position in order to escape.

Chloe's prophetic words are ignored, and Tom convinces her that, if he is loyal to his master and has faith in God, he will be fine. She expresses her faith in Tom's belief and accepts *his* decision, not the hierarchical order of the white society. In this instance, the representational excess depicts Chloe as mammy, whereas the text suggests a different role. No matter that this Chloe's physical appearance is fat, dark, and kerchiefed—she is not the docile mammy of the myth. She is complicated by her relationship to her own family, and the mere presence of that family gives her an identity outside of her white masters. She grows larger than simply a vehicle for establishing the whiteness of the other characters.

In addition to Chloe, a figure that is given the name "Mammy" appears in Stowe's novel and dramatization. Although Mammy appears in neither the Aiken nor the Conway version of the play, she is important to discuss because she functions in the roles that Morrison assigns to black characters in white literature. When the St. Clares return to their plantation, their family and their slaves greet them. Eva first hugs and kisses her mother, who complains that she is ill; Eva then hurries into the arms of Mammy. Here, we see the elements of the mammy myth come into focus. This character, like Tom, served first the parent, Marie St. Clare, and then grew to love the child, Eva. Eva, like young George Shelby, understands the value of a loyal servant even when her mother does not. Marie complains that Mammy does not show proper devotion to her:

> If Mammy felt the interest in me she ought to, she'd wake easier—of course she could. I've heard of people who had such devoted servants, but it never was *my* luck. Now Mammy has a *sort* of goodness; she's smooth and respectful, but she's selfish at heart. Now, she never will be done fidgeting and worrying about that husband of hers. You see when I was married and came to live here, of course I had to bring her with me, and her husband my father couldn't spare. He was a blacksmith, and, of course, very necessary; and I thought, and said at the time that Mammy and he better give each other up, as it wasn't likely to be convenient for them ever to live together again. I wish now I'd insisted on it, and married Mammy to somebody else; but I was foolish and indulgent, and didn't want to insist. I told Mammy at the time she mustn't ever expect to see him more than once or twice in her life again, for the air of father's place doesn't agree with my health, and I can't go there; and I advised her to take up with somebody else; but no—she wouldn't. Mammy has a kind of obstinacy about her, in spots that everybody don't see as I do.[45]

Marie laments that Mammy is not as faithful to her as the mythical mammy, to the exclusion of her own family. Marie also reiterates that Mammy cannot feel love toward her children or husband in the same way that Marie does and that her separation from them is essentially meaningless. And, like the character of Chloe, Mammy's conjugal and filial ties also serve to link her to sexuality. Furthermore, Marie repeats race sentiments that describe slaves' insensitivity to pain and normal affections. Beyond Marie's criticisms,

Mammy also falls short of the myth in her appearance. Although "dressed neatly, with high red and yellow turban on her head," Stowe describes her as a "decent mulatto woman" not as the heavy brown woman generally associated with the figure of the mammy. Mammy does, however, fit Stowe's prototype of black motherhood. Whenever Stowe presents an idealized black mother figure, she is always of mixed race, like Eliza or Cassy. Even when Stowe creates a character explicitly called "Mammy," she does not fulfill all the criteria of the mythic mammy.

In Marie St. Clare, Stowe presents a failed motherhood, and Marie's criticism of Mammy, whose devotion is clearly stronger than her own, serves to underscore that point. Mammy's function for Stowe is to illustrate the deficiencies in Marie St. Clare's character and to suggest that slavery may abuse blacks, but it also denigrates whites; this portrait underlies Morrison's theses. Stowe wishes to upset what she sees as the northern mythical view of the South: "It is supposed that domestic servitude in slave states is a kind of paradise; that house servants are invariably pets; that young mistresses are always fond of their 'mammies,' and young masters always handsome, good natured, indulgent."[46] Thus, the presentation of Mammy is a deliberate effort by Stowe to challenge the relationship between white masters and black slaves; this usage suggests the roles Morrison defines: enabler, mediator of humanity, and enforcer of the implications of whiteness. This role is underscored in Stowe's representations because in neither the novel nor *The Christian Slave* does this character speak. In the novel, Mammy does make an occasional physical appearance. In Stowe's dramatization, however, even her appearance is occluded; she is merely discussed by Marie and Ophelia. Her presence is invoked, although her voice is absent. Like Stowe herself, her characters speak for the absent black woman; Mammy's existence is tied only to her physical service to the characters' needs and to her thematic service as a vehicle for Stowe's politics.

Any discussion of the mammy figures in *Uncle Tom's Cabin* would be incomplete without a recognition of Uncle Tom himself. Tom embodies many of the qualities suggested for women by the cult of true womanhood, which idealized motherhood. Uncle Tom, as feminized hero of the novel, displays many aspects of the mammy. He responds to Chloe's accounting of his relationship to his master: "Wan' he [the master] put in my arms a baby?"[47] Like many slave nurses, Tom began care of his master when the man was born. He extends this loyalty to his master's son, and he retains a strong relationship with the young master, George Shelby. In the novel, Tom's parting from his young white charge seems more poignant than that from his actual family. The Shelbys had contrived to have young George away at another plantation. Tom asks as he leaves that Mrs. Shelby give his regards to George, and then the emotional boy runs his horse up to the parting scene. "Young Master George sprang into the wagon, threw his arms tumultuously round his neck, and was sobbing and scolding with energy."[48] Tom returns his affection and exclaims: "O! Mas'r George! This does me good! . . . I couldn't bar to go off without seein' ye!"[49] The intimacy of this relationship foreshadows the close affection that grows between Tom and Little Eva. Tom cares for his young charges like a mother and suggests the idealized qualities of the audience, which Stowe desired to address. His gender, however, at once aids in his heroic depiction and undermines it. As a man, he does not necessarily suggest the same possibility of sexual compromise that characters like Eliza, Cassy, or even Topsy and Chloe do. Despite his feminization, he is a man, who Stowe describes as at the prime of his life, and that image suggests sexual compromise of another sort, making images of the young Eva on Tom's lap evoke additional meaning. At the same time that these two tensions are in play, we return to Morrison in order to understand that, more so than any other character, Tom serves as the barometer and enabler for the humanity of the other characters. It is Tom's relationships with George Shelby and Little Eva that best illustrate their nobility, just as it is Legree's relationship with Tom that definitively elucidates his depravity.

Ideas of black women that began in the nineteenth century continue to be perpetuated through the modern era. In the case of the three images of black female characters, each was visually codified by a set of physical traits: the tragic mulatto by her fair skin, the mammy through her size and her kerchiefed head, Topsy by the wild tails protruding from her head and her rough clothing. Each set of traits reflected a set of assumptions, which evolved into stereotypes ultimately reenacted and played out on the stage and through American culture. Despite the painful and denigrating nature of the images, they are also part of the landscape of the American consciousness. At the same time that these images serve as a reminder of a painful history, they are markers of a tenacious survival.

NOTES

1. Jo A. Tanner, *Dusky Maidens* (Westport, Conn: Greenwood, 1992), 8–9. Tanner describes two early productions that included a black female character. A white woman in blackface played the servant in William Miln's *All in a Bustle* (1798), but no white woman willing to black her face could be found in Cincinnati in 1823, so in Edwin Forrest's presentation that year of the farce *The Tailor in Distress*, the author hired a black woman to perform the part.

2. Homi K. Bhabha, "The Other Question: Stereotype, Discrimination and the Discourse of Colonialism," in *The Location of Culture* (New York: Routledge, 1994), 66.

3. George Fredrickson, *The Black Image in the White Mind: The Debate on Afro-American Character and Destiny, 1817–1972* (New York: Harper & Row, 1972), 109.

4. Bhabha 77.

5. Peggy Phelan, *Unmarked: The Politics of Performance* (New York: Routledge, 1993), 148.

6. Bruce McConachie, *Melodramatic Formations: American Theatre and Society, 1820–1870* (Iowa City: University of Iowa Press, 1992), 182.

7. H. J. Conway, *Uncle Tom's Cabin*, Uncle Tom's Cabin Collection, Harry Rangoon Humanities Center, University of Texas, Austin, 1.

8. Harry Birdoff, *The World's Greatest Hit: "Uncle Tom's Cabin."* (New York: Vanni, 1947), 6. A program held in the Harvard Theatre Archive's Uncle Tom's Cabin Collection from a performance on 20 Jan. 1853 at Ordway Hall on Washington Street lists Mr. Mitchell as Topsy in the cast list.

9. Bhabha 77.

10. Within the minstrel milieu after the Civil War, the minstrel show included the growing presence on the stage of black men and, in rare instances, women. Within black minstrel companies, black men cross-dressing as black female characters never became a particularly popular convention. In the case of the "Tom Shows," although there is evidence of several black actors, beginning with the minstrel performer Sam Lucas, portraying Uncle Tom, there is little evidence that a black woman enacted Topsy on the stage. George Clinton Densmore Odell, *Annals of the New York Stage* (New York: Columbia University Press, 1927–1944), vol. 11, records instances of two black women, Abbie Hampie and Bella Martin, who were both billed as "the only colored Topsy." They both appeared in "Tom Shows" in October 1879. In an unidentifiable newspaper clipping from the Harvard Theatre Archive, "Uncle Tom's Strong Grip: A Unique Class of Actors Which the Play Has Created," the unknown author states: "There were real Negro Topsies and genuine Negro Uncle Toms" but does not provide any concrete examples of said black Topsies. C. A. Leonard points to a specific instance in his *New York Herald Tribune* (19 May 1929) article, "Negro Theater Is No New Thing; It Started Hereabouts in 1821." He writes that, in "1897, Lew Payton, who played Pa Williams in 'Harlem,' attempted an all colored version of 'Uncle Tom's Cabin' himself playing Uncle Tom." However, attempts to find more documentation of this production have been unsuccessful.

11. Harriet Beecher Stowe, *Uncle Tom's Cabin* (1852; reprint, New York: Harper & Row, 1965), 147.

12. Stowe 239.

13. Richard Dyer, *White* (New York: Routledge, 1997), 45.

14. Dyer 49.

15. Eric Lott, *Love and Theft: Blackface Minstrelsy and the American Working Class* (New York: Oxford University Press, 1993), 217–218.

16. Elizabeth Corbett, *Theatre Guild Magazine* (1930), clipping file, Uncle Tom's Cabin Collection, Harvard Theatre Archive.

17. Untitled article, *London Era*, (25 Aug. 1878), clipping file, Uncle Tom's Cabin Collection, Harvard Theatre Archive.

18. Untitled article, *London Daily Telegraph* (1 Sept. 1878), clipping file, Uncle Tom's Cabin Collection, Harvard Theatre Archive.

19. Bhabha 66.

20. McConachie 183, citing Conway 4:1.

21. Phelan 2.

22. Stowe 447.

23. Richard Yarborough, "Strategies of Black Characterization in *Uncle Tom's Cabin* and the Early Afro-American Novel," in *New Essays on "Uncle Tom's Cabin"*, ed. Eric Sundquist (Cambridge: Cambridge University Press, 1986), 55.

24. Stowe 364.

25. Stowe 355.

26. Stowe 353.

27. Susan L. Roberson, "Matriarchy and the Rhetoric of Domesticity," in *The*

Stowe Debate: Rhetorical Strategies in "Uncle Tom's Cabin," ed. Mason I. Lowance (Amherst: University of Massachusetts Press, 1994), 131.

28. George Aiken, *Uncle Tom's Cabin*, in *Representative Plays by American Dramatists*, ed. Montrose Moses (1925; reprint, New York: Benjamin Blom, 1952), 681.

29. Stowe 355.

30. Mark Lemon and Tom Taylor, *Slave Life; or, Uncle Tom's Cabin*, 24. Uncle Tom's Cabin Collection, New York Public Library, Performing Arts Library.

31. Lemon and Taylor 30.

32. Stowe 367.

33. McConachie 12.

34. Catherine Clinton, *Plantation Mistress* (New York: Pantheon, 1982), 202.

35. Toni Morrison, *Playing in the Dark: Whiteness and the Literary Imagination* (Cambridge, Mass: Harvard University Press, 1992), 52.

36. Morrison 53.

37. Stowe 31.

38. Stowe 56.

39. Stowe 440–441.

40. Sarah Smith Duckworth, "Stowe's Construction of an African Person and the Creation of White Identity for a New World Order," in Lowance 220.

41. Stowe 97. *"The Christian Slave": A Drama Founded on a Portion of "Uncle Tom's Cabin,"* dramatized by Harriet Beecher Stowe expressly for the readings of Mistress. Mary E. Webb (Boston: Philips, Sampson and Co., 1855), 19.

42. H. J. Conway, *Uncle Tom's Cabin*, Conway's Boston Museum version of text, 1876 (as combined with Aiken's text), 1:8. Harry Ransom Humanities Research Center, University of Texas, Austin. The text is not complete, and act 4 is an interpolation from the Aiken text.

43. Birdoff 69.

44. Aiken 621.

45. Stowe 166.

46. Harriet Beecher Stowe, *The Key to "Uncle Tom's Cabin"* (1854; reprint, New York: Arno, 1968), 74.

47. Stowe, *Uncle Tom's Cabin*, 97; Stowe, *The Christian Slave*, 19.

48. Stowe, *Uncle Tom's Cabin*, 102.

49. Stowe, *Uncle Tom's Cabin*, 102.

2

Political Radicalism and Artistic Innovation in the Works of Lorraine Hansberry

MARGARET B. WILKERSON

Lorraine Hansberry (figure 2.1) was a visionary playwright whose belief in humankind's potential to overcome its own excesses of avarice, oppression, and inhumanity compelled her to raise provocative questions on the American stage. Ironically, her success with *A Raisin in the Sun*, which won the 1959 New York Drama Critics Circle Award and which won acclaim from white as well as black audiences during its Broadway production, led some critics to view her work as integrationist and accommodationist. A virile, confrontational Black Arts Movement in the 1960s, which challenged its parent, the Civil Rights Movement, following Hansberry's death, seemed to eclipse her work and to label it as "old-fashioned," both in form and content. However, persistent voices continued to claim for Hansberry a more radical stance, and during the 1990s, they have been joined by some of her earlier detractors. A close examination of two of her plays, *A Raisin in the Sun* and *Les Blancs*, combined with information about her sources and facts about her life affirm a political stance more radical than previously recognized and artistic choices that challenge the boundaries of theatrical realism.

A Raisin in the Sun remains one of the most-produced plays in the United States and one of the most popular with audiences of all colors. A drama filled with humor and pathos, it depicts the conflicts in a working-class black family in Chicago over the use of a $10,000 insurance benefit paid on the death of the family's patriarch. The mother Lena, insists on placing a down payment on a house, which happens to be in a white neighborhood, countermanding her son, Walter Lee, who wants to invest in a liquor store. Both characters seem to be pursuing the American dream of upward mobility—property and money—when, in fact, Hansberry is using their aspirations as metaphors for the dream of freedom and the right to be regarded as not only a citizen but as a human being. Because the play uses the family's efforts to

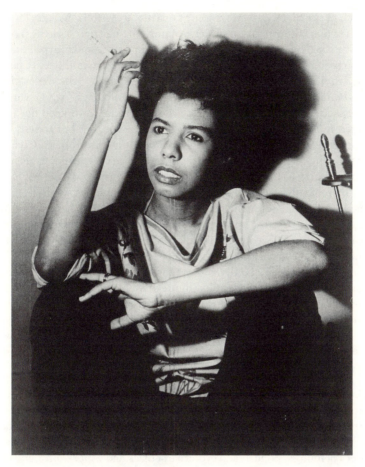

Figure 2.1   Lorraine Hansberry. Gin Briggs photo, courtesy Estate of Robert Nemiroff (Jewel Greshan Nemiroff, executrix).

move into a white neighborhood as its major metaphor, some black artists of the 1960s considered *A Raisin in the Sun* an example of a failed and degrading integrationist philosophy.

Amiri Baraka, whose work in the 1960s emerged as the sine qua non of black militant drama, epitomized this attitude as he, along with other black artists, claimed that the play represented a bygone era:

> We thought Hansberry's play was part of the "passive resistance" phase of the movement, which was over the minute Malcolm's penetrating eyes and words began to charge through the media with deadly force. We thought her play "middle class" in that its focus seemed to be on "moving into white folks' neighborhoods," when most blacks were just trying to pay their rent in ghetto shacks.[1]

Much of the Black Arts Movement's discomfort with Hansberry lay in the character and interpretation of Lena/Mama, the matriarch of the Younger family. Played by Claudia McNeil in the original stage and film productions, she was seen by audiences, particularly whites, and critics alike, as a familiar figure from the American literary and dramatic canon: the dark-skinned, white-haired, conservative mammy of the "good old days," who revered the master, sought to emulate his lifestyle, and struggled to keep her unruly children in line. Visually, McNeil fit the stereotype, but her actions belied the concept. Walter Lee's decision not to take the money from the Clybourne Park residents, who want to keep their neighborhood white, was seen often as a capitulation to his mother's will rather than as a personal triumph. Some angry men of the Black Arts Movement took umbrage at Walter Lee, who seemed ineffectual, impotent, and proven wrong by his mother, a reductionist view of their situation, demeaning the black man's struggle for manhood in a racist society. The controversy over whose story it was—Walter's or Mama's—was waged during the play's out-of-town trials in 1958 as Sidney Poitier and Claudia McNeil vied for central focus. Audiences of that time took greater comfort in the familiar figure of Mama, finding Poitier's restless and explosive Walter Lee more disturbing.

However, in 1986, Baraka, after seeing a revival of *A Raisin in the Sun*, which restored some material cut from the original production and which eventually became an "American Playhouse" television production, wrote a dramatic reassessment of the play:

> [In the 1960s,] we missed the essence of the work—that Hansberry had created a family on the cutting edge of the same class and ideological struggles as existed in the movement itself and among the people. What is most telling about our ignorance is that Hansberry's play still remains overwhelmingly popular and evocative of black and white reality, and the masses of black people dug it true.[2]

Baraka argues that this play "typifies American society in a way that reflects more accurately the real lives of the black U.S. majority than any work that ever received commercial exposure before it, and few if any since. It has the life that only classics can maintain (20)." Baraka makes this reevaluation of the play without any reference to the passages cut from the original but restored in the Roundabout Theatre production that he witnessed. When he compares the next two explosions in black drama, James Baldwin's *Blues for Mr. Charlie* and his own *Dutchman*, (the first constructs a debate of the ideas of Martin Luther King, Jr., and Malcolm X, and *Dutchman* openly advocates the use of armed resistance), he finds them both wanting because "for one thing, they are both (regardless of their 'power') too concerned with white people."[3] In contrast, Baraka notes:

> It is Lorraine Hansberry's play which, though it seems "conservative" in form and content to the radical petty bourgeoisie (as opposed to revolutionaries), is the accurate telling and stunning vision of the real struggle.

Both Clay [*Dutchman*] and Richard [*Blues . . .*] are rebellious scions of the middle class. The Younger family is part of the black majority, and the concerns I once dismissed as "middle class"—buying a house and moving into "white folks' neighborhoods"—are actually reflective of the essence of black people's striving and the will to defeat segregation, discrimination, and national oppression. There is no such thing as a "white folks' neighborhood" except to racists *and to those submitting to racism.*[4]

Baraka's concise deconstruction of the term *white folks' neighborhood* reminds us that the phrase accepts the terms of segregation and discrimination; the more radical view taken by Mama is the right to live where she can afford with no regard to claims of neighborhood "ownership." Baraka rightfully equates the Younger family with the Fannie Lou Hamers, Malcolm Xs, and Angela Davises, advocates of a radical vision of full participation in society and full acceptance as human beings for the majority, not just the elite class, of blacks. The Youngers are the incarnation of the "ghetto-variety" masses who would burst forth from "the bloody southern backroads and the burning streets of Watts and Newark onto TV screens and the *world* stage" in the years following the original production of the play.[5]

Walter Lee, a frustrated and restless chauffeur, who desires the opportunities that the "white boys" have, is a precursor to the overtly militant male characters of the 1960s. Hansberry foresaw the explosion to come as the curtailment of the black male's possibilities became unbearable. Hansberry intends Walter to be the protagonist in the play who, according to the principles of Western dramaturgy, undergoes major change and overcomes his human flaws. However, because Walter represents a despised class, which has been ridiculed on the stage, it was difficult for audiences not to impose stereotypes with which they were most familiar. Hansberry recognized that the audience brought into the theater "prior attitudes . . . from the world outside. "In the minds of many," she wrote, "Walter remains, despite the play, despite performance, what American [racial] traditions *wish* him to be: an exotic."[6]

Hansberry was very aware of the tensions between her creation and the audiences' perceptions. In fact, she also believed that her play was flawed and contained "dramaturgical incompletions":

> Fine plays tend to utilize one big fat character who runs right through the middle of the structure, by action or implication, with whom we rise or fall. A central character as such is certainly lacking from *Raisin*. I should be delighted to pretend that it was *inventiveness*, as some suggest for me, but it is, also, craft inadequacy and creative indecision. The result is that neither Walter Lee nor Mama Younger loom large enough to monumentally command the play. I consider it an enormous dramatic fault if no one else does.[7]

When she wrote the screenplay, she attempted to "correct" this flaw by providing greater context for Walter Lee's dilemma in several scenes added to the original stage script. She inserts one particularly telling scene on a Chicago street, which sets Walter's frustration against a global backdrop of freedom struggles. After learning that Mama has used a portion of the insurance money as a down payment on a house, a dejected Walter leaves the apartment. He comes upon a street orator, who is rousing a crowd of black males by comparing their economic deprivation with the rising fortunes of emerging African nations:

> Well, my brothers, it is time to ask ourselves what the black man is asking himself everywhere in this world today. . . . Everywhere on the African continent today the black man is standing up and telling the white man that there is someplace for *him* to go . . . back to that small, cold continent where he came from—Europe! . . .
>
> How long before this mood of black men everywhere else in the world touches us here? How long! How much has to happen before the black man in the United States is going to understand that God helps those who help themselves? . . .
>
> What is the difference, my friends—between the black man here and every other man in the world? It's what every one of you knows . . .
>
> We are the only people in the world who are completely disinherited! . . .
>
> We are the only people in the world who *own* nothing, who make nothing! I ask you, my friends, where are your factories . . . ?
>
> . . . Where are your textile or steel mills? Heh? Where are your mighty houses of finance? . . . *Answer me, my brothers—Where are they?*[8]

Freedom is hollow, the orator (and Hansberry) reminds us, without economic power. However, this scene along with most of her additions ended up on the cutting room floor as the producer and director adhered to the presumably safer course, a replication of the successful stage play.

To mainstream critics of the 1950s, Hansberry was a housewife who came out of nowhere to write this compelling play of the 1959 season. Many were surprised by her articulate command of social and political issues. Born into the comforts of the black upper middle class in 1930s Chicago, she hardly seemed destined to cultivate revolutionary attitudes. However, her family home was a cultural mecca where, as a child, she met black artists and leaders, such as Paul Robeson and Langston Hughes. While her father's real estate business gave the family an affluent lifestyle, she came to know the stories and struggles of working-class families through his tenants and the public schools to which he sent her. She admired and envied the independence and defiant attitudes of the latchkey children. The foundation for her political views were laid in her childhood by a combination of influences: the strong black pride taught by her father and mother; the tradition of fighting segregation and discrimination modeled by her father's legal challenge before the Supreme Court of restrictive covenants in housing; and early association with and influence by Ray Hansborough, a black Communist. Hansborough did not school her in the doctrinaire views of the Communist party but rather nurtured in her democratic ideas of freedom and social justice for all people and, especially, African Americans.

Hansberry chose to attend the University of Wisconsin at Madison, a predominantly white university known for its progressive faculty, rather than a black college (as had her parents and siblings), where the social requisites reminded her of the high school sororities and activities of the middle class that she so detested. At Wisconsin, she joined the Communist party and, later, the Labor Youth League. She served as the president of the Young Progressives Association, a campus-based national organization of college students who campaigned for Henry Wallace and the Progressive party in the 1948 election. Under her presidency, the campus chapter of the YPA produced several dramatic productions with political import.

Bored and disappointed with college, Hansberry left after her second year and moved to New York City, with her mother's permission, to pursue "an education of a different kind" in the progressive political and cultural circles of the city. There, she took a course on Africa from W. E. B. Du Bois and worked as associate editor with Paul Robeson on his newspaper, *Freedom*. Robeson devoted the pages of his newspaper to the political upheaval and exploitation of Africa; to Senator Joe McCarthy's campaign against Communists, which was engulfing many writers and artists; and to racial discrimination in the United States. This job brought Hansberry into contact with many international visitors, who came to speak with Robeson, and exposed her to news stories affecting people of African descent all over the world.

It was impossible for a person of Hansberry's consciousness to ignore the momentous social and political events of the 1950s and 1960s. This period marked the beginning of the Cold War between the U.S. and Soviet superpowers, a rising demand by blacks for civil rights at home, and a growing intransigence and rebellion by colonized peoples throughout the world. When Robeson's passport was revoked by the State Department, Hansberry traveled as his representative to an international peace conference in Uruguay and met there delegates from Central and Latin America and Korea, who were resisting the wars being fought on their soil by the U.S. government. She became an articulate spokesperson for these causes and enjoyed something of a celebrity status in progressive circles back home because of her association with Robeson and her experience in Uruguay. Her activities and associations had already earned her an FBI file, but the bureau pursued her in earnest after her trip to the peace conference and her marriage to Robert Nemiroff, known to the FBI for his earlier involvement with Communist party activities.

The general public did not know of these associations. And, although Hansberry did not hide her past, she did not broadcast it either, given the tenor of the 1950s and the red-baiting propensity of some congressmen. But she wrote for several leftist magazines, such as *New Challenge* and *New Foundations*, using her own name rather than a pseudonym like some of her contemporaries. And the FBI continued to collect her writings and to record her activities as it was aware of them.

When her play reached Broadway, the bureau was especially anxious to determine whether it was a subversive work so that the agency might anticipate and possibly counteract any influence and effect it might have. The agents who reviewed the play for her FBI file concluded that it "contains no comments of any nature about Communism but deals essentially with negro [sic] aspirations, the problems inherent in their efforts to advance themselves, and varied attempts at arriving at solutions" and that "relatively few [in the audience] appeared to dwell on the propaganda message."[9] Hansberry would have been amused by their conclusions. Perhaps because she avoided the catch phrases of the Left and couched her ideas in the folk idiom of African Americans and, perhaps, because certain scenes that give the play a sharper political edge were deleted, the revolutionary import of *A Raisin in the Sun* eluded the FBI.

Had the agents paid closer attention to the scenes with Asagai, the African intellectual who romances Beneatha, they might have responded differently to the play. *A Raisin in the Sun* offered important clues to the positions Hansberry would take in *Les Blancs*, a play that was produced posthumously and that focuses on the inevitability of violent revolution when discourse fails to produce positive action. The mere presence of Asagai as an African intellectual signals the populist thinking of Hansberry. He attends college in the United States but plans to return to make important social and political changes in his native Nigeria, which is still under British colonial rule. Asagai's speeches, as well as Beneatha's brief tutoring of her mother (just before Asagai's first visit to the Younger home) about the need to liberate the African continent from the British and the French, are also intended to educate an audience ignorant of African history and current affairs. Contact with her uncle, William Leo Hansberry, one of this country's earliest scholars of African history and the East Coast advisor and contact for Ethiopian students, had taught Hansberry that the African was much more than the primitive, savage exotic portrayed in American films and novels. Beneatha, modeled on a younger Hansberry, displays the romanticism about Africa seen in earlier writings by blacks, but she also embodies the yearning for a future informed by a sense of identity that proudly encompasses a more accurate knowledge of the African past. Changing her hair style to natural, donning tribal garb, and approximating African dance represent in humorous fashion Beneatha's attempts to embrace her heritage and are evidence of Hansberry poking some good-natured fun at herself and the romantic impulse. But Beneatha is not to be dismissed. For all her foibles and poor judgment in asserting her atheism in her mother's presence, she is a lightning rod for the family's attitudes about Africa, and she prepares the audience for the real revolutionary-in-the-making: Asagai.

Even more telling in *A Raisin in the Sun* is the advice that Asagai imparts to Beneatha regarding the uneasy progress and personal sacrifice often brought by change and revolution *and* the connection that he makes between African and African American aspirations. His story about the nature of change, which many critics found distracting and unnecessary (indeed, it was left out of the film), unites Mama's effort to improve the family's lot by buying a house with the struggle by African peoples to be free of colonial rule. At that moment, Asagai becomes the spiritual son of Mama, both inheritor and exponent of the ancestral and human impulse for freedom, and Mama's dream takes on broader implications.

Ideas only hinted at in *A Raisin in the Sun* emerge full-blown in *Les Blancs* (1972—first performed posthumously), having grown in Hansberry's consciousness for many years. Because of her contact with her uncle, William Leo Hansberry, she had been exposed to an Africa beyond the *Tarzan* stories known to most Americans. As a youth, she met young African intellectuals, who would later fight for their countries' independence. She had a lifelong habit of reading avidly everything in African studies available to her, from Basil Davidson's *Lost Cities of Africa* (1959) to Jomo Kenyatta's study of the Kikuyu, *Facing Mt. Kenya* (1965). She clipped articles from newspapers on Kenyatta and Kenya's struggle for independence during the early 1960s, the successful guerrilla war for independence waged by the Algerians, Katanga whites resisting the U.N. forces, postcolonial changes in the Congo, the extremes of wealth and poverty in Nigerian cities, the revolt of Angolans against the Portuguese, and U.N. reports on the effects of racial discrimination on economic development in Africa.

Africa of the 1960s was on the verge of revolution. Ghana had emerged in 1957 as the first independent African nation. Kenya was in a prolonged struggle for its liberation and, after decades of seeking land reform and human rights without success under an often brutal British rule, an underground movement had formed, which vowed violent revolution against the whites. The arrest of Jomo Kenyatta, who opposed violence, on charges of plotting to overthrow the British, only exacerbated the situation as violence exploded throughout the country. Hansberry, understanding this history from the perspective of African peoples, spoke at rallies, wrote articles, and sent letters to U.S. editors that criticized the characterization of Africa's independence movements as "Mao Mao" terrorism and that renamed them freedom fighters.

Africa was not that unusual a subject for African American writers. Harold Isaacs, in his study of black American writers and their African ancestry, analyzed the literary relationship of five major writers—Langston Hughes, Richard Wright, Ralph Ellison, James Baldwin, and Lorraine Hansberry—to the continent.[10] However, most looked to Africa as part of a nostalgic or romanticized past or as an escape from the brutalities of racism in the United States. Like her predecessors and contemporaries, Hansberry had fantasized about a romantic African past, having spent hours as a girl daydreaming about her origins. The late Robert Nemiroff, Hansberry's former husband and literary executor, noted in an essay on *Les Blancs* that, as she wrote in her unfinished, semiautobiographical novel, she believed:

> in her emotions she was sprung from the Southern Zulu and the Central Pygmy, the Eastern Watusi and the treacherous slave-trading Western Ashanti themselves. She was Kikuyu and Masai, ancient cousins of hers

had made the exquisite forged sculpture at Benin, while surely even more ancient relatives sat upon the throne at Abu Simbel watching over the Nile.[11]

Hansberry, who at the time of Isaacs's study had not yet written *Les Blancs*, also believed that African Americans might gain inspiration for their freedom fight from their African ancestors and that the future of the peoples and their continents are linked.

Set in an African country in the midst of rebellion and resistance against colonial rule, *Les Blancs* is an uncompromising drama that reveals the terrifying consequences of the failure of meaningful dialogue. Hansberry exposes her audience to the tragic choices that lead to armed resistance and violent revolution: exploitation and oppression perpetrated by greed and supremacist beliefs and fed by the crippling actions of patriarchal liberals and the complicity of organized religion. While the play charts the inevitability of violence when dialogue is used only to postpone, it does not shirk from nor romanticize the price of resistance—no matter how justified.

To speak or write about exploitation and oppression in Africa during the 1960s, when Hansberry began this play, was to court controversy and the wrath of many critics. However, as a student of African history and politics and as an advocate for African independence from colonial rule, she saw the tragic scenario unfolding: Western excuses for the continuation of colonial oppression, mounting pressure by the resistance, and the inevitable bloodshed that would happen if the people's will was thwarted. "Radical" may be an appropriate label for her views when cast against the prevailing ideas acted out by the governments of the West, but "humane" seems equally reasonable when one rejects notions of the inferiority of Africans. To continue the virtual enslavement of these people was unconscionable to Hansberry.

The central character of the play is Tshembe Matoseh, who has returned home for his father's funeral and finds the Africans in violent, though not yet open, rebellion against the colonists. Not unlike the Mao Mao movement in the 1960s, the people of Tshembe's tribe are waging silent, deadly warfare against the settlers, killing families in the dead of night. The Africans have come to this point only after many years of thwarted efforts to gain human and civil rights through peaceful means. Upon his arrival, Tshembe is immediately confronted with the expectation of his tribal associates to join the resistance. He, however, has grown cynical and weary of the movement and prefers to quickly dispense with his familial duties and return to his English wife and son in London. But Tshembe is swept up by his own emotions, by the revelation that his father was a leader in the resistance, and by an intensifying series of events, which propel him to the wrenching decision to join and help to lead the growing revolution.

Several characters represent the face of oppression. One of the most compelling, the Reverend Torvald Neilsen, never appears on stage, but his presence is felt as the founder of the mission where much of the play takes place. Hansberry modeled this character on Albert Schweitzer, winner of the

Nobel Peace Prize in 1952 for his work as a medical missionary in the Gabon territory of West Africa. Greatly admired for bringing "civilization" to "the dark continent" and establishing a hospital in the jungles of Lambarene, Schweitzer was also a Renaissance man—holder of doctoral degrees in theology, philosophy, and medicine; author of a number of important religious texts; and principal of Strasbourg Theological College before the age of thirty. During his lifetime, he was recognized as one of the world's foremost authorities on organ architecture, as an eminent Bach scholar, and as a celebrated interpreter of Bach's organ music.

Having studied John Gunther's *Inside Africa* and various articles on Schweitzer, Hansberry was also aware that his attitudes toward the Africans he had chosen to help was typical of the West: highly paternal. Gunther, who describes his visit to Lambarene, carefully balances Schweitzer's reverence for life and personal sacrifice (living in an African jungle) against his authoritarianism and colonialist attitudes toward Africans. In a chapter on that visit, he captures in Schweitzer's words his beliefs about the African:

> The Negro is a child, and with children nothing can be done without the use of authority. We must, therefore, so arrange the circumstances of daily life that my natural authority can find expression. With regard to the Negroes, then, I have coined the formula: "I am your brother, it is true, but your elder brother."[12]

According to Gunther, Schweitzer loved the Africans only in the abstract. "He seems to be fonder of the animals in Lambarene than the human beings."[13] Hansberry's use of Schweitzer as the source for the Reverend Neilsen allowed her to unmask the seemingly benevolent and benign face of colonialism and to reveal its despotic and cruel visage. The choice was risky, given the veneration accorded Schweitzer in many parts of the Western world.

Much of Hansberry's portrayal of the mission is based on Gunther's account. Gunther reported, "No bush hospital can be tidy, any more than can a farmyard in South Carolina. There will always be things out of place, and innocent litter on the ground. But Schweitzer's hospital was, I thought, the most unkempt place of its kind I saw in all Africa."[14] In the play, Charlie Morris, a white journalist who has just arrived at the mission in order to write an article praising Neilsen, reveres the doctor and his work. When Morris justifies the unsanitary, primitive condition of the hospital with the argument he has heard—that Africans would not come for treatment if it were different—Willy DeKoven, one of the doctors who works at the mission hospital, wryly comments: "One of the first things that the new African nations have done is to set up modern hospitals when they can. The Africans go to them so freely that they are severely overcrowded."[15]

Schweitzer's recorded attitudes support Hansberry's depiction of the paternalistic, though seemingly benign oppression. In the play, Neilsen dismisses the tribal leaders as children when they bring a petition for a new constitution that would permit Africans to sit in the legislature in proportion to their numbers. "Dear children," he smiles and says, "Go home to your huts before you make me angry. *Independence indeed!*"[16] The brutal consequences of this attitude are played out through the character of Major Rice, a cruel settler who commands the local police force and who raped Tshembe's mother. The child of that assault, Eric, has become an alienated, lonely young man seeking love through a homosexual relationship. Through Charlie Morris, the American journalist who constantly reveals his ignorance of African affairs, Hansberry captures the naivete of the supposedly well informed American. Morris does not realize at first the complicity of his country in colonialism (it is U.S. or U.S.–made bombers and weaponry that defend the forces of oppression from the resistance at the end of the play). When military troops are housed at the mission at the insistence of the overtly racist Major Rice, the benevolent, violent, and naive faces of the oppressors become one. Madame Neilsen, wife of the reverend, stands in stark contrast to these multiple expressions of oppression. Physically blind, she foresees nevertheless the impending conflagration and, as Tshembe's surrogate mother and teacher, urges him to become a warrior for his people.

Hansberry reserved some of her most piercing criticism for established religion and its complicity with the forces of repression. As a child in Chicago, Hansberry had seen photographs of the pope blessing Mussolini's troops as they set forth to attack Abyssinia. The military action was much criticized at the family dinner table and among blacks in her home town. In the play, when Tshembe discovers that Abioseh, his brother, is a novice in the Catholic church and soon to be a priest, he excoriates him and the role of the church in the colonization of Africans, calling Christianity only "another cult— which has kept the watchfires of our oppressors for three centuries!"[17] The betrayal of the church is enacted in the play through Abioseh, who turns informer and exposes Peter/Ntali, a leader of the resistance, who is then shot on the spot.

Undoubtedly, one of the most radical aspects of this play is the position that it takes on violent revolution. Some critics called it "propaganda" while others asserted that it "advocated genocide of non-blacks as a solution to the race problem."[18] It would have been quite easy to reduce the issue of revolution to a black-white issue, but Hansberry saw deeper. And she attempted and achieved something much more difficult in *Les Blancs*: to chart the agonizing journey that brings a people to the point of violent rebellion. Hansberry remembered that the turning point in the South African struggle came with the Sharpeville Massacre in 1960, an action that she protested along with many others at the United Nations. In the play, there is no joy in Tshembe when he finally takes up arms against the colonialists. He has killed his brother, who betrayed their people, and the first shots fired at the mission have taken the life of his surrogate mother, Madame Neilsen. The hyena-like howl that pours forth from Tshembe as he holds her limp body in his arms is a cry of pure agony at the tragedy of human waste that has and is about to occur. Among the innocent and guilty are black and white; both will die in this struggle. The Africans in this story have chosen armed rebellion reluctantly and slowly. Ironically, the actions of Abioseh echo the warning from

Asagai in *A Raisin in the Sun* (as well as that of Hansberry) that African "winners" in the end will not guarantee peace and freedom, but the struggle for independence and democratic freedoms for the masses is likely to continue even as petty toadies of empire take over. The ideas in *Les Blancs* are a far cry from the simplistic interpretations claimed by some of its early critics.

Artistically, Hansberry faced the challenge of depicting the visceral nature of Tshembe's choice, which goes beyond logic and rationality, while communicating the often subtle and indirect role that women play in freedom struggles. A woman whose feminism was sharpened and supported by her reading of Simone de Beauvoir's *The Second Sex* (1947, French; 1953, English), Hansberry was well aware of the cultural constraints placed on the depiction of women and sought various ways to overcome these limitations in her dramaturgy. She used a clever strategy to communicate the compelling nature of Tshembe's final choice and to incorporate the powerful, though often hidden, influence of women in political affairs, while presenting these matters to a Western audience for whom women's roles (and black women, in particular) were primarily servile.

Typically, Hansberry looked to the classics—specifically, Shakespeare—for a form grand enough to encompass the monumental questions raised in this play and to give her characters and their dilemmas heroic stature. But the classical model was built on male protagonists or individuals of great wealth or power, whose actions affected the state or the lives of many people. Hansberry's desire to use this form for the ordinary human being posed structural problems for her writing with which she would struggle throughout her life. In her early drafts, for example, she had two major characters, Candace and Tshembe, returning home to their father's funeral. The two became one male character, Tshembe, prompting some writers to question whether Hansberry censored her feminist self or was unduly influenced by her husband, Robert Nemiroff. The answer, however, may lie more with the limitations of the form than with her sensibilities.

In fact, Hansberry used a very innovative device to overcome these restrictions in *Les Blancs*: the African woman warrior. This woman, who appears as a warrior-dancer, is the only woman of African descent in the play (not counting villagers, who may be added in the background). She can be seen only by Tshembe and appears to him twice, carrying a spear and eventually thrusting it into his hand. She represents the collective history of African people and depicts through movement their slaughter and enslavement.[19] She never speaks words, but her gestures communicate volumes. She has appeared to Tshembe before; wherever he goes, he cannot escape her: the streets of London, the subways of New York. A possessed Tshembe confesses, "And whenever I cursed her or sought to throw her off . . . I ended up that same night in her arms!"[20] Her power over him is hypnotic and passionate.

When Charlie questions why Tshembe is behaving so strangely (since he cannot see the warrior-dancer), Tshembe cries out, "Who! Who! When you knew her you called her Joan of Arc! Queen Esther! La Passionara!"[21] With this last name, Hansberry references the Spanish Civil War and Dolores

Ibarruri, known as La Passionara, whose words not only galvanized the imagination of the republican resistance but who epitomized the spirit of women throughout Spain. In his book on the Spanish Civil War, Richard Kisch describes her:

> She was then a tall dark woman with large eyes set deep under heavy black eyebrows. She radiated a burning intensity which was reflected in her gift of language. . . . La Passionara, like other mass leaders who were making a name for themselves as natural soldiers . . . knew how to seize the moment of action when it came.[22]

Unlike La Passionara, Hansberry's woman warrior does not speak, but she draws on an aesthetic more common to African performance in which the gesture has equal if not greater meaning than the word. In that sense, the female figure exhibits more strength than Tshembe, the major character, in that she has power over him. It may seem like a risky strategy in a play so filled with eloquent language and rhetoric, but the dancer's "silence" actually emphasizes the emptiness of words.

Tshembe and Charlie, two men representing the East and the West, the developing and the developed country, have talked and talked and talked, sparring often, showing respect for each other at times. But just as the talks on the governmental level prove fruitless, so does the conversation between Tshembe and Charlie as the revolution overtakes them all. Words do not resolve the situation. Finally, action speaks—not in words but in violent, revolutionary events. Had Hansberry retained Candace as a major, realistic character, she would have been bound by words and the limitations of her place as a woman. Had she rebelled against her place and assumed a leadership role, her unusual position (at least in Western eyes) might have distracted ultimately from the focus of the play. When the silent dancer is pitched against the backdrop of Hansberry's command of the word, the intentionality and innovativeness of this figure becomes quite clear.

It is tempting to discuss this character primarily in the context of the limited roles of women of the 1950s and the genius of creating in a woman power that encompasses intellect, artistry, and emotion. While that argument is useful in understanding perhaps why Hansberry uses only one woman of African descent, it may obscure the real genius of this choice. In an important sense, the dancer is more than woman—she embodies the spirit of a great continent, of a people, and is both man and woman. In the play, she also embodies the spirit of Tshembe's father, who was a leader in the resistance. Visually, she exhibits the movement and voluptuousness attributed to women while, at the same time, she carries a spear and calls Tshembe to the warrior role most associated with men. The dancer-warrior, like all of Hansberry's characters in this remarkable play, is multilayered and complex. It is also worth noting that the dancer pushes the boundaries of realism but is credible within the play's context because she can be seen as an extension of Tshembe's consciousness.

Figure 2.2   Tshembe (Derrick Lee Weedon) contends with the spirit of his homeland in the form of The Dancer (Melany Bell) in the Oregon Shakespeare Festival's 1998 production of Hansberry's *Les Blancs* in the Angus Bowmer Theatre. Directed by Timothy Bond, scenic design by Richard L. Hay, costume design by Helen Qizhi Huang, lighting design by Dawn Chiang. Photo by David Cooper.

Eric, Tshembe's younger brother, represents another facet of Hansberry's radical views. Hansberry, who was a lesbian, believed that homosexuals may comprise the last oppressed minority. She condemned homophobia both in essays and letters. Eric is in a homosexual relationship with Dr. Willy DeKoven. When Tshembe angrily asks if Eric is "his playtime little white hunter," a lonely Eric responds that DeKoven listens to him, cares for him, spends time with him, while his brothers have been away. Eric is the product of Major Rice's rape of his mother, so he was unable to seek solace with his brothers' father. Alienated from the familial relationships that have brought Tshembe back, Eric is adrift—and his homosexuality alienates him even more from the others at the mission.

When armed warfare breaks out, however, Eric is the first of his brothers to join the native rebellion, and he takes a prominent role in the fight. While Eric is not the focal point of the play, his inclusion in the freedom struggle is a small footnote that reinforces Hansberry's progressive views.

The popularity and success of recent productions of *Les Blancs* in Oregon (see figure 2.2) and Baltimore, along with anniversary productions of *A Raisin in the Sun* in both university and professional theaters confirm the compelling nature of the plays and Hansberry's ideas. Several decades after her death, the human issues of freedom, equality, and independence; their relevance to ethnicity, color, gender, class, sexuality, and sexual orientation; and the artistic tools used to represent these issues in provocative and persuasive forms remain challenges for the field of theater. Hansberry believed in the social and political import of art, and she demonstrated her commitment to this principle by crossing sacrosanct boundaries and taking intellectual and artistic risks.

NOTES

1. Amiri Baraka, "A Critical Reevaluation: *A Raisin in the Sun*'s Enduring Passion," in Lorraine Hansberry, *"A Raisin in the Sun" and "The Sign in Sidney Brustein's Window"* (New York: Vintage, 1995), 19.

2. Baraka 19.

3. Baraka 19.

4. Baraka 19–20.

5. Baraka 20.

6. Lorraine Hansberry, "Willy Loman, Walter Younger, and He Who Must Live," *Village Voice* (12 Aug. 1959): 7.

7. Hansberry, "Willy Loman," 7.

8. Lorraine Hansberry, *"A Raisin in the Sun": The Unfilmed Original Screenplay* (New York: Plume, 1992), 132–134.

9. Lorraine Hansberry File, 100–44090–8 (Philadelphia: Federal Bureau of Investigation, Feb. 5, 1959), 1.

10. Harold R. Isaacs, "Five Writers and Their African Ancestors," in Part I, *Phylon* 21.3 (1960): 243–265; Part II, *Phylon* 21.4 (1960): 317–336.

11. Robert Nemiroff, "A Critical Background," in Lorraine Hansberry, *"Les Blancs": The Collected Last Plays* (New York: Vintage, 1994), 27.

12. John Gunther, *Inside Africa* (New York: Harper & Brothers, 1955), 733.

13. Gunther 714.

14. Gunther 714.

15. Hansberry, *Les Blancs*, 113.

16. Hansberry, *Les Blancs*, 115.

17. Hansberry, *Les Blancs*, 61–62.

18. Hansberry, *Les Blancs*, 133–134.
19. Hansberry, *Les Blancs*, 81.
20. Hansberry, *Les Blancs*, 80.
21. Hansberry, *Les Blancs*, 81.
22. Richard Kisch, *They Shall Not Pass* (London: Wayland, 1974), 103–104.

3

The Black Arts Movement

Performance, Neo-Orality, and the
Destruction of the "White Thing"

@G@G@G@G@G@G@G@G@G@G@G@G@G@G@G@G@G@G@G@G@G@G@G

MIKE SELL

It is worth recalling that a cofounder of the Black Panther Party for Self-Defense—Bobby Seale—was at one time an actor in a San Francisco theater troupe run by an up-and-coming playwright and director named Ed Bullins. It is worth recalling because the relationships among institutions, communities, and the peculiar ontologies and epistemologies of performance are foundational dynamics of both the Black Power and Black Arts movements. Both movements devised Black Nationalist strategies to effectively respond to the complications of race politics by the peculiar characteristics of the American political scene in the 1960s, a scene dominated by a tendentiously racist mass media, which seemed intent on transforming the social and civil turmoil of the era into a multimedia spectacle.[1] However, significant differences exist between the performance politics of the two movements. While the Panthers attempted to seduce and exploit the media (and wealthy liberals) by way of outrageous, blatant displays of hypermasculine "Blackness," the Black Arts Movement sought to evade white media, tolerant liberal wealth, and Euro-American aesthetic traditions by taking their revolutionary, Afrocentric cultural program to historically African American colleges and urban, geographically distinct, African American communities.[2] These very different negotiations of what Guy Debord calls the "society of the spectacle"[3] were linked to very different understandings of the relationship between political radicalism and artistic radicalism. While the Panthers utilized alliances with radical and liberal communities of whites in pragmatic fashion and basically avoided aesthetic questions, members of the Black Arts Movement generally viewed such alliances as profoundly hazardous to their racial separatist strategy and spent much time articulating an Afrocentric "critical metaphysics," a nonobjective, ethically oriented mode of artistic production and reception. And while the Panthers saw the benefits of art primarily as a means to an end (i.e., fundraising), Black Artists viewed art—as they viewed African Americans themselves—as both the means and the end of revolution.

Roots, Rhythm, and Critical Metaphysics

Put schematically, the Black Arts Movement sought "to link, in a highly conscious manner, art and politics in order to assist in the liberation of Black people."[4] This was how Larry Neal explained the movement and its critical aesthetic methods to readers of *Ebony* magazine back in the long, hot summer of 1969. The fact that *Ebony* had devoted an entire issue to black art stands as something of an anomaly: both a high-water mark of the movement's efforts to popularize its cultural program at the grassroots level and a rare liaison with capitalist (better said, black capitalist) media. Such revolutionary writings and reports in an ostensibly liberal, popular, publication such as *Ebony* speak eloquently to the ways in which a theory and practice of cultural empowerment cultivated by a small, elite coalition of college-educated, radical, African American intellectuals struck a sympathetic chord with a relatively large segment of African American society. As Neal made clear in his *Ebony* essay, Black Art was nothing if it did not strive for "intimacy with the people."[5] Black Art was a dynamism of representation and revolution, of vanguardist experiment and the "souls of Black folk."[6]

The efforts to dynamically interweave organizational development, political activism, and racially exclusive cultural production by this revolutionary separatist movement were justified by a philosophical project that aimed to create a critical metaphysics that would help redefine and revive the ontological, epistemological, and metaphysical bases of African American society, particularly as they related to the relationship between the Black artist and his (and it was a generally male and occasionally proprietary "his") people. The primary targets of this critical metaphysics were the *art object* and the *literary text*, both viewed as linchpins of a Western power rooted in colonial domination of cultural production. The commodity-oriented tendencies of colonized cultural production were particularly galling to black intellectuals; thus, a primary target of the Black Arts Movement was not simply "consciousness" but the production and circulation of *things*. The "white thing" often cited by Black Arts critics and artists was quite literally that—a menagerie of commodities.[7] But it was also a cultural *ethos*, which justified alienation in terms of the financial profit to be gained by the buying and selling of people-as-things. As surely as commodities were destroyed during the uprisings in Watts and Detroit, this ethos was destroyed by the theoretical and dramatic works of the movement. Neal and his colleagues from the Muntu reading/performance group of North Philadelphia—a pivotal cell in the production of a critical metaphysics at the service of a grassroots Black Nationalist program—argued that objects and texts were not valuable in and of themselves but merely as material components of a much broader cultural, political, and economic renaissance. They were art "merely incidentally," since real value was to be found in the performances, artists, and communities that surrounded the object and text.[8]

The paradox of their attack on text and object is that, while Black theorists, poets, playwrights, and performers generated an avant-garde culture of unprecedented acuity and popularity, the very success of their project has in many ways guaranteed their invisibility within a fundamentally textual literary and theater history. If, as Henry Louis Gates, Jr., has recently argued, the Black Arts Movement was the shortest and least successful African American literary renaissance,[9] then I would assert that that is because the movement attempted to displace the notions of value, permanence, and significance, which ratify much of the academic establishment's sense of literariness, historicity, and success. As James Stewart, also of Muntu, argued:

> In our movement toward the future, "ineptitude" and "unfitness" will be an aspect of what we do. These are the words of the established order—the middle-class value judgments. We must turn these values in on themselves. Turn them inside out and make ineptitude and unfitness desirable, even mandatory. We must even, ultimately, be estranged from the dominant culture. This estrangement must be nurtured in order to generate and energize our black artists. This means that he cannot be "successful" in any sense that has meaning in white critical evaluations. Nor can his work ever be called "good" in any context or meaning that could make sense to that traditional critique.[10]

Stewart's essay strikes a significant note of caution against how scholars represent the Black Arts Movement. We are implicated in many of the institutions and attitudes against which it struggled. The movement's exploitation of performance and theater (1) explicitly attacked the materialism of American culture, including its celebration of texts, especially novels, as the epitome of cultural sophistication; (2) enabled a recreation and revision of pretextual, orally based West African aesthetic and ethical systems ruptured during the Middle Passage; and (3) complemented the tactical and strategic needs of organizational efforts by radical intellectuals in urban ghettos and (4) valorized a number of already existing African American cultural forms such as music, oral performance modes, food, clothing and so on. As a result, the movement fits uneasily in the canons of Euro-American culture and the relatively stable institutions of literary criticism and pedagogy.

If the artists and audiences of the Black Arts Movement discovered the soul of Black liberation in the deconstruction and partial rejection of the art object and the literary text, they also discovered that such "soul" is acutely vulnerable to economic and institutional backlash. Attempting to outmaneuver the institutional and technological power of the white thing, Black artists formulated a theory of culture and communication that, in some sense, guaranteed forgetting when their communities were disrupted in the early '70s and '80s. Musician and critic Tam Fiofori captured this paradox in a profile of Sun Ra in 1967: "Memory, like sentiment or emotion, can be replaced, diverted, or it can simply fade away."[11] While the movement founded its critique upon performance in order to meet the complex demands of a revolutionary cultural nationalist movement in the context of mass-mediated (or "spectacular") capitalism, its demise was due to demands placed upon it, which performance practices could only inadequately address, namely, the demands of institutional permanence, mass communication, and real estate.

The origins of the Black Arts Movement are instructional in this regard, for they reveal the way it is shaped by this complex dynamic of organization, performance, and cultural production. Such origins are most effectively traced to a number of small, distinctively local communities of poets and intellectuals, which gathered in Philadelphia, New York, and Oakland in the middle years of the 1960s. These groups pursued a diverse range of projects, including research into African and African American folk, popular, and high cultures; readings of the most significant political, cultural, and aesthetic theories of their day (articulating what we would now call "cultural studies" almost a decade ahead of the ground-breaking work of the Birmingham School); concrete experimentation with poetic form; self-criticism; and consciousness raising. Their sympathies, in contrast to most of the older African American middle class, were not with Martin Luther King, Jr., or the Negro church establishment from and for which he spoke. *Liberator* magazine, one of the key forums for Black Arts Movement theory, was stridently anti-King. Their sympathies fell to Patrice Lumumba, Fidel Castro, Ernesto "Che" Guevara, and (always and essentially) Malcolm X.

The more significant of these reading circles include the Umbra Poets Workshop, a group of young artists that met weekly on New York's Lower East Side from 1962 to 1965, published a short-lived poetry journal, and gave readings just around the block from the famed Five Spot jazz club.[12] The Bay Area saw a tenuously unified legal study, theater, and activist collective gather under the banner of Black House. And, in North Philadelphia, there gathered what I believe was the intellectual community most responsible for granting the Black Arts Movement lasting significance in African American theater and performance history: the Muntu reading group, a study circle of jazz musicians, poets, and critics that included Neal, Stewart, and Charles Fuller.[13] That these groups were communal gatherings should not be overlooked by the historian; indeed, in the case of the Muntu group, relationships had lasted since childhood.[14] These groups (and there were others in Detroit, New Orleans, Chicago, Los Angeles, and many African American colleges) functioned as crucial support networks, valuable sources of criticism, and, most important (according to Tom Dent, a member of Umbra and later cofounder of Blkartsouth), as performative contexts that afforded a "level of communication with kindred spirits that wasn't phony or superficial."[15]

While these small performance communities supplied potent theoretical fuel for the articulation of a "Black Aesthetic," the ignition point of the *institutional* movement is best sited at the founding of the Black Arts Repertory Theater/School (BART/S) on 30 April 1965. BART/S was organized by the increasingly ex-Beat poet LeRoi Jones with the financial aid of the Harlem Youth Project (HARYOU-ACT, upon whose board African American actor and activist Roger Furman served); the practical aid of former Umbra members Rolland Snellings (a.k.a. Askia M. Touré), Albert Haynes, and William and Charles Patterson; and the ideological aid of the editorial board of *Liberator* magazine, which included the elder statesman Harold Cruse and the prodigious young critic and folklorist Larry Neal. The fundraising brochure for BART/S tells us that "as its name indicates, [the BART/S] will be a repertory theater in Harlem, as well as a school. As a school it will set up and continue to provide instruction, both practical and theoretical, in all new areas of the dramatic arts."[16]

For purposes of generating financial support, Jones held his ideological cards fairly close to his chest; in reality, the "dramatic arts" that his school was exploring went far beyond the practice and theory of the putatively "phony" Anglo-Jewish dominated mainstream theater. As Neal described the opening of BART/S, "The idea behind . . . this event . . . is to open a dialogue between the artist and his people, rather than between the artist and the dominant white society which is responsible for his alienation in the first place."[17] As it became clear near the end of the movement's "heroic phase" (1965–1972),[18] this dialogue was tacitly revolutionary, a volatile, often contradictory dynamism of space, race, and representation.

Jones and his colleagues were attempting to create an American version of the decolonization movements that had swept through Africa, Central America, and Southeast Asia during the '50s and '60s, movements whose practical, conceptual, and decidedly performative force Jones first recognized during his visit to Cuba in 1960. Indeed, such an embodiment was necessarily a performative one, for around the time Jones was assembling staff and capital for BART/S, he was writing his seminal essay "The Revolutionary Theatre," an essay proclaiming that the theater:

> must *expose!* Show up the insides of these humans, look into Black skulls. White men will cower before this theatre because it hates them. Because they themselves have been trained to hate. . . . Even as Artaud designed *The Conquest of Mexico*, so we must design *The Conquest of White Eye*, and show the missionaries and wiggly Liberals dying under blasts of concrete. For sound effects, wild screams of joy, from all the peoples of the world.[19]

Combining a revolutionary and racially separatist nationalism with a politicized, fundamentally Artaudian theory of performance allowed Jones, who would soon change his name to Amiri Baraka, to articulate a critical metaphysics that blended avant-garde experiment, postcolonial politics, and African and African American cultural traditions. His hypothetical drama, *The Conquest of White Eye*, perfectly embodied this volatile convergence. Riffing off the "first spectacle of the Theatre of Cruelty,"[20] acidly punning on "whitey" and "white eye," Jones's conceptual drama interwove the shock of agit-prop, the antivisual bias of Artaud, and the populism of street festival. Nevertheless, we should be aware of the contradictions that plague his eclectic form of revolutionary performance. As explosive as it is, it fails to account for the racist tendencies of the European avant-garde, which supplied some of Jones's fundamental ideas about the nature and function of political theater. Thus, while Baraka's essay energized the Black Arts, it also modeled a profoundly contradictory relationship to the tradition of avant-gardism.

"Real Estatic" and the Limits of Performance

For the authorities, the metaphysical niceties of BART/S were not nearly as distressing as its shockingly frank (and decidedly theatrical) approach to the "race problem." Whether BART/S really embodied Jones's theoretical principles or managed to escape the contradictions inherent in the idea of a "Black avant-garde" is moot. Of greater significance is the fact that angry, honest art was being brought to working-class African Americans via street-corner productions of plays such as *Dutchman*, poetry readings, and impromptu performances by cutting-edge jazzmen such as Albert Ayler, Sun Ra, Ornette Coleman, and John Coltrane. Not surprisingly, BART/S lost its funding within the year as a federal investigation into alleged "mismanagement" of antipoverty funds was initiated, purportedly by liberal whites and African Americans (a constant target of Jones's invective) out to "discredit and destroy all the militant and progressive forces in Harlem."[21] The demise of the institution was also catalyzed by the intense infighting cultivated by William Patterson. As Jone described it many years later, "Even while we did our heroic work of bringing the art, the newest strongest boldest hippest most avant of the swift dark shit to the streets, you could look up at that building and swear it was in flames."[22] These flames were certainly fanned by Jones's very public "kill-Charlie" performances for the New York media establishment. Essentially "cruel," the hyperbolically violent rhetoric of his movement-era poetry and his public appearances continues to obscure the more nuanced, if no less revolutionary, theoretical work he and his colleagues pursued behind the scenes of the racist society of the spectacle and beyond the gaze of white media.

The death of BART/S was not the last time that the best lessons of Black Art would be found in the failure and disappearance of exemplary institutions. As Jones put it, "What was real survived the flame."[23] In fact, such failure dovetailed with the political, economic, and cultural implications of a Black Aesthetic intent on transformation rather than conservation, on spirit rather than object. One immediate and well-known result of this founding/disappearance was the rejuvenation of the Oakland, California, collective Black Arts/West, now called Black House. Black House served briefly as both the headquarters for the nascent Panther party and as a center for community performances of community-created theater, poetry, and music. It hosted a potent convergence of Black politics and performance. Among its founders were Eldridge Cleaver (who later engineered the expulsion of the Black Artists), Duncan Barber, Jr., Hillery X Broadus, Carl Boissiere, Ed Bullins (who would be named Minister of Culture for the Panthers after his play *In the Wine Time* met with critical success in New York), and Marvin X. The astonishing promise of Black House was short-lived, however, as Cleaver-instigated clashes over the desirability of an alliance with white radicals and, perhaps more significantly, over the validity of radical aesthetics caused a violent rift between the Black Artists and the more pragmatic Panthers.

The death of Black House—along with Bullins's dissatisfaction with the Bay Area's theater scene—resulted in yet another significant institutional event, for in 1967 Bullins was invited by Robert Macbeth to come to Harlem for a tenure as playwright-in-residence of the New Lafayette Players. With the Players (lacking a theater at the time of his arrival in Harlem and only six years away from death by economic asphyxiation), Bullins cemented his fame as a playwright, editor, and theorist, assembling the famed *The Drama Review* special issue on Black theater, running the highly influential journal *Black Theatre*, and writing some of his most important plays to date.

However, the impact of BART/S went well beyond these often-invoked institutions. The impact was felt not merely in California and New York but in those performance arenas that rarely make it into academic theater histories: community colleges, amateur groups, and regional professional theaters away from the major urban and cultural centers of the U.S. The pumping black heart of BART/S found sympathetic rhythms throughout the country, resulting in a vast number of short-lived (and some long-lived) cooperative community theaters, such as Black Arts/West of Seattle, Studio Watts Workshop of Los Angeles, the Dashiki Project Theatre of New Orleans, the Bed-Sty Street Academy Workshop in Brooklyn, Black House of Philadelphia, Concept East of Detroit (site of a memorable production of Baraka's *Slave Ship*), and the Yard Theatre of Kingston, Jamaica. Most of these theaters were run on little more than enthusiasm and spare parts, and their place in our collective memory is vague. In a sense, this historical invisibility was intended; the desire to escape a certain philosophical, aesthetic, historiographical, and critical tradition was at the heart of the movement's greatest conceptual and practical triumph.

Larry Neal, for one, continually advised the Black community to "swim on." Like the African American archetype Shine, the Black community needed to find its own "thing" ("Said the Captain: 'Shine, Shine, save poor me. I'll give you more money than a nigger ever see.' Said Shine to the Captain: 'Money is good on land and on sea, but the money on land is the money for me.' And Shine swam on."[24]). Again, the issue and the dilemma were autonomy: of institutions, of aesthetics, and of metaphysics. As Harold Cruse carefully demonstrated in his opus, *The Crisis of the Negro Intellectual*,[25] unless the Black liberation movement was accompanied by "an ideological and organizational approach to . . . the administration, the organization, the functioning, and the social purpose of the entire American apparatus of cultural communication," that movement was bound to fail.[26] Cruse's comments identify a crucial oversight of the Black Arts Movement, for it was the lack of property ownership that helped doom the movement. As Wahneema

Lubiano has pointed out, lacking a real "nation" in some sense forced Black radicals into the "cultural solution."[27] Lacking real estate, an ideologically unified model of community, and a sure foothold in the middle-class African American community, the most advanced segments of the Black Arts Movement chose the transient, situational, performative forms of avant-garde poetry and theater to forward their goals. Lacking real territory, they pursued an essentially idealist philosophy; however, this idealism was grounded in the concrete, temporary spaces of public performance.

Theater/Culture/Revolution

What constituted "cultural revolution" for these artists and activists? And what is the relationship of theater to the racially separatist revolution they sought? The answer is to be found in the theater cooperatives modeled after BART/S. The Black Arts Movement was, after all, a performance movement as much as anything else, a movement that deemed the novel, "a passive form . . . not conducive to the kind of social engagement that Black America requires at this time."[28] Poetry, too, was to be transformed by revolutionary signification and tactical necessity. That is to say, it was to be *performed*, the text utilized as a kind of score. Like many, Neal viewed soul musician James Brown as a model performer, at once popular, conscious, and infectiously activist:

> The poet must become a performer, the way James Brown is a performer— loud, gaudy, racy. He must take his work where his people are. . . .
>
> He must learn to embellish the context in which the work is executed; and where possible, link the work to all usable aspects of the music. For the context of the work is as important as the work itself. Poets must learn to sing.[29]

For Charles Fuller (Muntu member, Neal's close friend, and eventual winner of the Pulitzer Prize for *A Soldier's Play* [1981]), autonomy could only be attained by way of a complete and mutual transformation of community and artist. As he writes, "Each change must of necessity produce a change in the Black writer who addresses his community."[30]

While the concepts and practices of the movement would be refined and resited in order to adequately comprehend the political, economic, and cultural differences among African American communities, the basic urge behind its manifestations remained the same: to formulate a theory and practice of Afro-centric autonomy. This necessitated an emphatically theatrical approach to the interrelated questions of criticism and power. The critic could no longer be disengaged from the community. The ivory tower was also a white thing. Criticism is a power granted by the people to the critic, whether in direct form (as in the gathering of people in the presence of a figure of critical authority) or in indirect (as in the funding of critics through state and private institutions supported by corporate philanthropy and use fees).

This is one reason why, in "The Revolutionary Theatre," Jones explicitly invokes Wittgenstein in order to ground his assertion that "ethics and aesthetics are one."[31] To Jones—an underestimated contributor to our growing understanding of the roles that culture and performance play in domination and liberation—aesthetics and oppression were inseparable. Utilizing a Wittgensteinean logic the larger implications of which might have shocked Wittgenstein, Jones asserts that escape from oppression demands the destruction of an entire aesthetic tradition: the massive edifice known as "Western philosophy." In the revolutionary theater described by Jones, race politics, critical metaphysics, and theatricality are coaxed into a realm where action, not merely contemplation, is the litmus of artistic success. As he stated:

> The liberal white man's objection to the theatre of the revolution (if he is "hip" enough) will be on aesthetic grounds [among these, it should be noted, are issues of "success" and "longevity"]. . . . Americans will hate the Revolutionary Theatre because it will be out to destroy them and whatever they believe is real.[32]

If Jones's theater showed victims and reminded its viewers that "they [the viewers] are the brothers of victims, and that they themselves are victims if they are blood brothers,"[33] it was also the place where steely resolution and a profoundly critical aesthetics took root. As Baraka concluded, "Not history, not memory, not sad sentimental groping for a warmth in our despair" will create the revolutionary culture.[34]

If not history, memory, nor sentimental groping, then why theater, which seems to specialize in exactly those things? It is the great paradox of the Black Arts Movement that it embraced as a tool precisely that which it most radically and thoroughly criticized: the imposed theatricality of African American life. Forced to perform in both figurative and literal senses, African Americans have always been (if inconsistently and never wholly) under the white gaze and by the white clock. Even its revolutionaries kowtowed ultimately to television—witness the spectacular actions of the Panthers.

The choice of performance was mostly the result of economics, but it was also a component of the anti-commodity project. Black artists were generally distressed by the bourgeois theater's encrypted historicism, its particular use of memory and writing, its tendency to resolve social issues in individualistic terms, and (in the era after World War II) its marginalization by television.[35] But they were energized and empowered by the theater's capacity to shape time and space in contextually potent situations. However, put at risk by this thorough going critique of Western aesthetics and space-time concepts were certainty and permanence; for the theater challenges the collective capacity to define and delimit the real and the illusory, the essential and the transient. Along with the destructive capacity of the theater so acidly identified by Baraka came a more difficult search for the performative and institutional grounds upon which a distinctly black body and community could be cultivated without mortgaging that body and community to Western materialism and the contradictions of black vanguardism.

Grounding the Black Aesthetic

The blooming of an anti-Western, antimaterialist, "anti-objective" criticism in the 1960s among Black artists is inseparable from the blooming of Black theaters across the country at the time and the effort to theoretically and practically create a "new orality," a "Black Talk," to recall Ben Sidran's important phrase.[36] Attempting to evade the materialism, rationalism, and medium-centered bias of white high and vanguard culture, theoretically attuned artists such as Neal, Fuller, and James Stewart sought forms that explicitly rejected the object as such and the objectivity that separated the viewer from the viewed. The theater was a linchpin in the popular elaboration of this critique. Thus, consideration of the Black Arts Movement's critical concepts and practices (and perhaps of the Black Power Movement as well) should delve into the philosophical and practical complexities of performance.[37] And, as this project was launched in urban contexts characterized by a high degree of absentee ownership, the consideration of performance must delve into the dilemmas of property ownership. The link between Black Art and theater/performance can be discovered in such dilemmas. The fundamental struggle of experimental theater groups is not merely to create new forms—they must also pay the rent. It is within this potentially crippling dynamic of property relations, subjectivity, and aesthetics that the nonobjective critique found a time and a space, a moment of highest quality. In a theater under lease, with props and furnishings on loan (if existing at all), stage design and acting theory were creatures of profound economic crisis, devised to survive the collapse of fragile, threatened institutions.

It is therefore not by accident that the Black Arts Movement founded its politics on the valorization and exploitation of performative modes of culture; for theater and performance can answer specific sociopolitical needs, particularly to a community that is economically depressed and politically advanced. This was why Harold Cruse considered theater to be central to the question of the Black revolution.[38] While Black cultural expression had been more or less forced to settle on performative forms as an expressive solution to cultural, political, economic, and historical suffocation, such necessity enabled powerful forms of resistance, including the effervescent, efflorescent resistance of the temporary locale—of juke joint jams, theaters, church events, street corner doo-wop, and barricades, which suggest the mobile infinity of tactics described by Michel de Certeau in his discussion of pedestrians and post-Authorial readers.[39] As Cruse reminded his younger comrades, the struggle for African America's future was fought on the simultaneous fronts of economy, politics, and culture. That fight, Cruse demanded, had to begin in the theaters of the inner city, those in Harlem first and foremost.

Likewise, performance afforded a common conceptual ground for the three-headed struggle of antimaterialism, cultural retrieval, and urban organization. For Larry Neal, whose untimely death in the early '80s cruelly denied the Black Aesthetic its full flowering within contemporary criticism, the preeminence of theater and performance in the Black Arts and Black Power movements was a matter of paying attention to one's history. Discussing the work of Baraka, Neal insisted that theater "is inextricably linked to the Afro-American political dynamic. And such a link is perfectly consistent with Black America's contemporary demands. For theatre is potentially the most social of all of the arts. It is an integral part of the socializing process."[40] It is the theater that best exhibits the totality, Neal believed, the *temporality*, of "Black men in transition."[41]

There is an important distinction to be drawn between the notions of theater/performance and its efficacy vis-à-vis the project of Black Nationalism developed by Cruse and Neal in the movement-era essays I have cited. Whereas Cruse advocates the theater for practical reasons (i.e., that it, more than any other art form, completely encompasses the cultural, political, geographical, and economic needs of black liberation), Neal seems to be indicating that the theater *as process*, as a way of being and a way of knowing, is directly tied to black acculturation, self-criticism, and liberation despite the existence of concrete institutions. Theater, for Neal, is literally in the skin; Blackness is drama. The theater is "a bridge between [the community] and the spirit, a bridge between you and your soul in the progression of a spiritual lineage."[42] So while Cruse focuses on organizational concerns, such as property ownership and institutional development (the practical failure of which doomed Black Art as a revolutionary movement), Neal focuses on the special demands of Pan-African, revolutionary subjectivity, a subjectivity that transcends the specific issues that Cruse identifies—and that has survived the short-lived institutions of the movement.[43]

The distinction is an important one for us to maintain, particularly if the more radical implications of Black Art are to be understood; for that the Black Arts as *theory* survived the death of the Black Arts as *movement*. When the Nixon administration slashed corporate funding of experimental arts and the economic crisis of 1973 laid low hundreds of community theaters across the United States, the practical links forged between art and politics were fatally sundered—but the theory survived in those educated by the Black Arts Movement, proving that the people's poetry is found in the people, not in the texts. Even so, Hoover and Nixon's Counter-Intelligence Program (COINTELPRO) was devastating both practically and theoretically. In addition to careers and lives, the practical links among text, institution, and performance were critically wounded by white backlash. The Black Arts as *theater* transformed abstract aesthetic into movement, concept into politics. But once those theaters and the momentary communities that they represented were destroyed, the Black Arts Movement crossed a horizon beyond which European traditions of politics, aesthetics, historiography—and property—could not clearly see.

The Black Aesthetic as Nonobjective

In the late '60s, Maulana Ron Karenga demanded that Black Art "remind us of our distaste for the enemy, our love for each other, and our commitment to the revolutionary struggle that will be fought with the rhythmic reality of a permanent revolution."[44] Such a rhythmic reality ill accords with the traditions and trends of European aesthetics. Reflecting this iconoclastic, jazz-inflected spirit, former Muntu member James Stewart, in "The Development of the Black Revolutionary Artist" (the lead essay in Neal and Baraka's indispensable *Black Fire* anthology), reminds us, "The revolutionary understands change."[45] Like Baraka in *Blues People*, Stewart saw the "death of the artifact" in the Middle Passage as a conceptual and practical avenue into cultural revolution. A revolutionary art, he concludes, must be like the legendary temples of mud "that vanish in the rainy seasons and are erected elsewhere."[46] "Likewise," he tells us:

> most of the great Japanese artists of the eighteenth and nineteenth centuries did their exquisite drawings on rice paper with Black ink and spit. These were then reproduced by master engravers on fragile newssheets that were distributed to the people for next to nothing. These sheets were often used for wrapping fish. They were a people's newssheet. Very much like the sheets circulated in our bars today.[47]

"Revolution is fluidity," Stewart argues. Borrowing eclectically from Asian mystical traditions, African American blues riffs, the African American Baptist church, new jazz, and Voudoun, Stewart demonstrates that the revolutionary artist is part of a proud line of "misfits estranged from the white cultural present."[48] The Black artist, therefore, could not expect to be "successful," for in the context of cultural revolution, " 'ineptitude' and 'unfitness' will be an aspect of what we do."[49]

Fuller saw this spirit as energized by a "release from object," the title of one of his essays on aesthetic theory. Thinking of the relationship between the thing and the labor to make the thing, he asks "if the sacrifice [of materials in the construction of the art object] was greater than the need, or simply a manifestation of that need—a tool, a service—something to demonstrate how much was needed and which, once fulfilling the need, was abandoned."[50] The ability to answer this question was, for Fuller, the fundamental criterion of revolutionary culture:

> If we can swallow that Black writing in this country did not begin as *object*, we can understand its present need to reflect the revolution its people are engaged in, and see a fluidity.[51]

When the theme is Blackness, the perceptual habits that underwrite our collective and individual capacity to make sense of the world—that is, the criteria of aesthetics and philosophy—are put at risk. Nowhere is that risk made more apparent than in Ed Bullins's experimental play ("to be given before predominantly white audiences"), *The Theme Is Blackness*. The script runs complete as follows:

> SPEAKER: The theme of our drama tonight will be Blackness. Within Blackness One may discover all the self-illuminating universes in creation. And now BLACKNESS—
> (*Lights go out for twenty minutes. Lights up.*)
> Will Blackness step out and take a curtain call?
> BLACKNESS[52]

It is easy to imagine the sense of confusion and discomfort this antithetical thesis drama tried to inspire in its predominantly white audience when it was first staged in 1967 at various sites in and around San Francisco. There is a contradiction here that must be carefully noted. Though *Theme* easily fits into the anti-objective trend of the Black Arts Movement, its utilization of shock, audience discomfort, and the aggressive failure of assumptions traces roots to the long tradition of Western avant-garde provocation, which goes back to the European Symbolists, Futurists, and Dadaists.[53] Cultural exclusivism breaks down the moment a Black nationalist consciously or unconsciously quotes Marinetti.

This very traditional vanguard desire to *épater le bourgeoisie* aside, *The Theme Is Blackness* renders a more complicated, more fathoming judgment on the interconnection of theater and racism than was ever accomplished by the European avant-gardes. Read in the context of the antispectacular, antiobjective theory articulated by Neal, Stewart, Fuller, and Baraka, *The Theme Is Blackness* can be interpreted as targeting the long history of philosophical inertia, technological expansion, and colonialism, which had given Bullins and his community their riddled present. And while its totalizing urge (for nothing is more totalizing than nothingness) may push aside more concrete historical and cultural concerns (unlike Sonia Sanchez's *Malcolm/Man Don't Live Here No Mo*, which will receive attention below), its attack on the tendentiously abstracting, spectacular racism of the Enlightenment is effective indeed. Blackness in Bullins's one act is a metaphysic all its own. We shouldn't forget that one possible outcome of *Theme* is the formation of a group of conscious individuals fully prepared to produce their own cultural event in the absence of the expected one. Performed before politically committed Blacks, the results might be memorable. Muntu is flexibility in rhythm with social transformation and historical reclamation.

The addition of free jazz and sound effects by the Chebo Evans Third World Three Black Trio in conjunction with the Black Arts/West company during the play's run underlines the central and most problematic fact of Bullins's theatrical-political gesture: its refusal to *show* and *specify*, and therefore, to enmesh itself in the running intra-theatrical battle of realism, naturalism, symbolism, minimalism, what-have-you-ism (not to mention its refusal to communicate any specific political message). The theatrical gesture allows for shock, discomfort, and/or flexible, communal, "soulful" response—Bullins views the latter as tacitly nationalist. As Bullins makes clear in his essay

"The So-Called Western Avant-Garde Drama," the European tradition of theatrical protest was a dead end, and it had to move beyond its basic assumptions concerning text and performance space: "It would seem that in America there is no way to break away from the historical (in the Western sense) definitions of drama, though never-ending revolutions occur in theatre which are usually inappropriately named 'avant-garde.' "[54] While this view of theater was by no means original, the provocative suggestion that the Euro-American theater tradition (including its avant-garde) is racist in its most fundamental assumptions, techniques, and material certainly was. For Bullins, the history of avant-garde theater mirrored the endless victimizing round of a history dominated by Europeans and their "ways of seeing." By refusing to show "Blackness" to its "predominantly white audience"—or, from another perspective, overwhelming the show with the shown—Bullins implies that even the seemingly innocent act of watching theater is embedded in a tangled skein of oppression, ignorance, and political compromise. For Bullins, Blackness simply exceeds the essentially theatrical frame of the white thing.

When the lights go down and Blackness comes up in *The Theme Is Blackness*, the conceptual and perceptual apparatus of white racism is hobbled. The "eye of whiteness" is cast adrift, scattered on the scatological seas of a peculiarly black history: *The Conquest of White Eye/Whitey*. Blackness swamps the viewer and her small community, the audience. Unable to claim distance from the stage, no longer able to exert its powers of judgment over the spectacle of the Other, the eye of whiteness (an eye possessed not only by whites) is situated in a context of fathoming ambiguity. Perhaps more significant, Bullins's ambivalently avant-garde gesture (which recalls John Cage no less than the Greensboro sit-in) returns the viewer to his body. As we all know, even the most cramped theater seats can be forgotten in the face of effective performance. The discomfort of the situation in *Theme* is the result of the play's failure to alleviate the body through distracting or engaging dramatic action.

Most significant to my eyes—as inappropriate as those particular tools might be in this context—is Bullins's refusal to give his audience a sense of dramatic progression. That is, Bullins's play refuses to structure and thematize *time* or to make meaningful the *object*. Because the piece lacks the traditional cues of drama (visual and verbal transformations in setting, character, and thesis), it lacks the "temporal shape" of traditional plays. As a result, judgment (of character or moral action, for example) cannot cast its glance over the scene: it cannot see at all. In the darkness, character does not develop, crisis and consequence do not find dialectical resolution. Drama, as it is traditionally known, fails to take hold; time does not concretize. The theater, which always takes time, is pressed to its conceptual and formal limits by Bullins's one act. The bourgeois drama, the drama of judgment, the drama of history, meets its end. The essentially linear parade of significant individuals weathering significant events—a parade we associate with both bourgeois historical narrative and bourgeois drama—is interrupted. Performativity, in the original production, was surrendered entirely to the audience;

in the later, musical version, this performativity was augmented by free jazz. Having taken away its sight and its sense of temporal progression, Bullins utilizes theater to call the end of (white) history.[55] When this call was sounded before a politically astute, mostly Black audience (as it was at Black Arts/West), this act of visual and temporal terrorism was given an improvisational and decidedly less anarchic shape.

But even though it strikes against the *conceptual* foundations of European culture, Bullins's play is nonetheless characterized by an *ahistorical* and *apolitical* approach to the question of Black liberation (not the first nor last time this would be the case). Certainly, *The Theme Is Blackness* is a concrete, critical, theatrical gesture against racism. But it fails, at least prior to the addition of music and effects, to synthesize the freedoms of the moment with the demands of history and culture. The deep ground, the "Black (w)hole," to cite Baker,[56] of this critique is given a more concrete, more historically minded spin in Amiri Baraka's *Slave Ship*, productions of which by the Chelsea Theatre at the Brooklyn Academy of Music and by Ron Milner's Concept East in Detroit during the late '60s inspired a generation of Black artists. Like Bullins's *The Theme Is Blackness*, *Slave Ship* simultaneously confronts, exploits, and explodes the relations of visibility, race, and theatricality. But, unlike Bullins, Baraka explicitly contextualizes the "shapelessness" of Blackness in the brutality of slavery and the Middle Passage. Unlike *The Theme Is Blackness*, which utilizes the nonobjective in a more totalizing, abstract, or free-jazz manner, Baraka's play situates the nonobjective within a determinant context. Nonobjectivity is linked in *Slave Ship* both to West African culture and to a suffering that, like the Holocaust, challenges the very possibility of memory and representation.

In the Chelsea Theatre's production of *Slave Ship*, the eye of whiteness was literally cast into the hold of racism's epitomous metaphor, the slave ship, and struggled like the captured Africans in the play, to find a place to stand, a place to breathe, a place from which to make sense of the sensory assault.[57] Assaulted by smells, assaulted by the violent sonic funk of director Gilbert Moses' and Archie Shepp's free jazz score,[58] the audience's ability to judge was incapacitated. The body and the community were thrown into a Blackness not unlike that exploited by Bullins in *Theme*.

But this disabling is not portrayed as wholly negative nor as wholly a consequence of the Middle Passage. The use of strobe lights and extended periods of darkness suggest a more positive theatrical-philosophical program similar to the jazz-inflected production of *The Theme Is Blackness* at Black Arts/West. What Baraka allows us to see and hear in the flashing lights of *Slave Ship* is a shuffling Uncle Tom, a liberal Preacher (symbol of faith in historical progress and future justice) panicked by clamoring drums, seduced and nauseated by the rich stench of the event, trapped in the strobes and stage lights of a spectacle that threatens the very act of spectating. Embodied in this stage image are the volatile ambiguities of the Black revolution as an economic, political, and cultural structure. Somewhere among the precolonial, oral-based cultures of West Africa referenced in the performance, the unimaginable sufferings of the Middle Passage evoked by the performance, and the linear historical imagination of liberal Christianity deconstructed by the performance is found the Artaudian cruelty of *Slave Ship*, the cruelty of a Black nation being born, the cruelty of a cultural revolution explicitly designed to dissolve the boundaries between ethics and aesthetics. *Slave Ship* not only represents the act of cultural revolution, it is itself a concrete example of the Black Arts Movement's nonobjective aesthetic and its complex, often confusing relationship to history, economy, and activism.

Slave Ship is therefore not a social protest play. It does not seek to adjust or reform existing institutions nor is its primary address directed toward the oppressor. Likewise, it does not seek to appeal to the moral standards of the oppressor nor to those of the oppressed. Quite the opposite, in fact: the play revels in emotional excess, virtuosic jazz, intricately intertwined vocal performances, and sudden, shocking vulgarity. *Slave Ship* is a counterspectacle that attempts to create representational strategies to fundamentally challenge the conceptual, aesthetic, and ethical boundaries of Euro-American political drama. It does not supplicate. It deconstructs, satirizes, and destroys. The use of music, audience participation, and an offstage act of violence against an invisible White Voice that echoes throughout the hold of the ship reflects, in Harry Elam's phrase, "the Black masses symbolically expung[ing] the visible and invisible hegemony of the dominant culture."[59] The white thing is never even allowed on stage.

The power of representation that Elam rightly considers one of the central critical concerns of *Slave Ship* is not only a target of proposed revolutionary action but also a contested terrain. The antinarrival bias of Baraka's play not only reveals to its audiences that the present condition of the African American community is little different from that of slavery but also works to create an alternative sense or structure of historicity, community, and aesthetics. If the bourgeois tradition of protest drama, with its generally rigid narrative telos and its carefully timed deployment of ethical and progressivist assumptions, possesses any relevance in the context of *Slave Ship*, it is only in the sense of that which restrains the possibility for radical transformation. Such assumptions represent a pale, fragile bulwark against, in Gwendolyn Brooks's heady phrase, "the noise and whip of the whirlwind."[60]

The rarely discussed plays of Sonia Sanchez utilize similarly deconstructive dramaturgical strategies to demonstrate the power available to a "whirlwind commonwealth." In particular, plays such as *Sister Son/Ji* (1969) and *Malcolm/Man Don't Live Here No Mo* (1972) sever the links among individualism, heroism, and the monumentality of history. Perhaps more important, they work to undermine such white things as the untainted hero, the resolved crisis, and phallocentrism (things not always adequately undermined by Sanchez's male colleagues). Predicting the choreopoems of Ntozake Shange, these plays utilize monologue and movement to highlight personality without celebrating individuality. They are explicitly designed to cultivate memory and inspire activism. They are, with the addition of *The Bronx Is Next* (1968), among the most acutely self-critical, resolutely revolutionary plays of the Black Arts era, articulating a rigorously feminist attitude that one rarely encounters among the plays and critical works of the movement. They accomplish what other self-critical revolutionary dramas such as Richard Wesley's *Black Terror*, the four plays by Edgar White collected in *Underground* (1970), Oliver Pitcher's *The One* (1971), and Bullins's *We Righteous Bombers* (1968) fail to accomplish: they deconstruct and question without in any way diffusing the commitment to action. And, like *The Theme Is Blackness* and *Slave Ship*, her plays challenge the relationship between the "seen" and the "scene."

Malcolm/Man is a notable children's play in a movement that valued highly such plays. And, like all effective children's literature, it manages to be profound without sacrificing simplicity. The piece is essentially a dance-drama that takes place, as all of Sanchez's plays do, in a never-ending "Now" that reflects an urge much like that of *Theme* and *Slave Ship*: to render time more malleable. A chorus of "3 sistuhs," a "brotha (bout 14 or 15)," and a "sistuh (bout 12, 13, or 14)" retell the life of Malcolm X. The tale is told by the sistuh and brotha, who take on a variety of roles, the girl as various female characters ("wite/amurica," "malcolm's future wife"), the boy as various incarnations of X. The telling of the life is counterpoised to the chorus, which takes the play into its narrative movements by singing:

> we be's hero/worshippers . . . we be's death/worshippers . . . we be's leader/worshippers . . . BUT: we should be blk/people worshippers . . . AND: some of us are leaderless toooooday . . . our homes are empty cuz . . . MALCOLM/MAN DON'T LIVE HERE NO MO.[61]

As in her other plays, Sanchez complements a major theme (X as exemplum) with one or more minor themes (here, the loss of individuality caused by worship of others and the lack of political and familial leaders). This complementary dyad of major and minor themes is itself triangulated within a "feminine focus," to recall Ruby Cohn and Enoch Brater.[62] X's life is counterpoised in the text by the strong presence of the sistuh and in performance by the female chorus members. And, as in her other plays, Sanchez does not conclude but, rather, she articulates a question. If *The Bronx Is Next* locates its central question in the lies and violence directed toward women marginalized by the revolution (single mothers, prostitutes, elderly women), the centering question of *Malcolm/Man* is the origin of X: "Malcolm, Malcolm, where did u come from."[63] This question of origins is presented by Sanchez as inseparable from a community of growing young women: the rotating, fluid X is composed of five dancers, four of them female.

Thus, this search for the origins of X's revolt—an emblematic source of the Black Arts Movement—is not presented in hagiographic terms, is not viewed as the rise of a heroic masculine individual, is not portrayed as a crisis resolved by the traditional forms of dramatic denouement: tragic death or comic marriage. Quite the contrary, the primary purpose behind Sanchez's use of dance and music in *Malcolm/Man* is to place the heroic example of X within reach of the black child and her memory, to transform the historic figure of X into a kind of iconic "revolutionary spirit," and to quite literally frame that life within the transient, beautiful motions of dancing children. The transformation of X into an accessible figure was accomplished by utilizing a child actor to portray the man. The transformation into performative spirit of the heroic individual constructed by X and Alex Haley in the *Autobiography* (1964) was enabled by having the five performers periodically return to the slowly rotating X formation with which the performance began, momentarily obliterating the individual and foregrounding the icon-as-dance. By transforming the potentially intimidating example of a revolutionary hero into a role that can be performed by any child and that has to be performed in careful cooperation with other actors, Sanchez avoids the potentially antidemocratic tendencies of hero worship. By utilizing dance and iconography, she foregrounds the importance of community cooperation and collective beauty. X in *Malcolm/Man* is not as much a hero to be worshiped as an ethos to be embraced in the spirit of the drum. This spirit is rather more gentle than that which informs Bullins's *Theme* or Baraka's *Slave Ship*, but it is no less impatient with the conceptual limitations and narrative habits of Western metaphysics.

Historicizing the Black Arts Movement

For the majority of the Black Arts Movement's constituency, there was no middle ground between oppression and freedom, white and Black, text and performance. And though contemporary criticism will find such binary formulations problematic, we should not allow our own critical biases to stand in the way of our understandings of the basic intentions of the Black Arts. Though there were more than a few Black artists who challenged such broad distinctions (Bullins and Neal among them), none finally abandoned them, despite the contradictory implications of the binary. One was either with the revolution or against, and the revolution, as Gil Scott-Heron compelled us to understand, would not be televised.[64] Spectatorship was the trap, performance the key. The critical dilemma of history—that it is available, as Jameson puts it, only in textual form[65]—is particularly troublesome vis-à-vis the Black Arts Movement. The refusal of object, text, and spectatorship in some sense guaranteed the Black Arts Movement's lack of presence in the history and criticism of American literature.[66] On the other hand, it places the movement well within the orbit of an avant-garde embedded in racist colonialism.

If the movement was indeed short and unsuccessful (putting aside for the moment artists such as Sanchez, Bullins, Nikki Giovanni, bell hooks, and OyamO, who continue to produce excellent work, and those fundamentally influenced by it, such as Toni Cade Bambara, Ntozake Shange, Alice Walker, August Wilson, and Toni Morrison), it left behind a daunting legacy of poems, plays, music, theory, and polemic, not to mention the legacy of its most impressive achievement: the conceptualization and attempted implementation of a Black Aesthetic. If the movement was indeed short and unsuccessful (and the bloody work of Nixon and Hoover's COINTELPRO should not be discounted when we consider the essentially aesthetic questions of duration and success), it sounds signal lessons to those who wish to challenge the dominance of the white thing. What was left behind are objects and desiccated memories, scripts for revolutionary performances yet to come. The texts that remain tease criticism like museum fetishes, exactly the kinds of ritual objects divorced from ritual context that Stewart and Fuller found both deeply distasteful and profoundly reactionary. For without soul, without the embodied sense of self-transformation that the movement sought to implement, the movement itself becomes an object, a scholarly fetish. This is a logic that cannot be escaped; it calls to question the ethical validity of all scholarly work on the movement, including this essay, written by a white scholar at a mostly white college.

For better and worse, the soul of the Black Arts Movement is bound to the ontological and epistemological dilemmas of performance both in a tendentiously racist "society of spectacle," that makes any revolutionary gesture contradictory, and in an academic tradition of literary-critical and literary-theoretical work, which tends to have difficulty contending with the momentary, local dynamics of performance. Because it attempted to blur the boundaries between the artist and the masses, between nations, between the present, the past, and the future, and because it attempted to eradicate Western notions of time and space, the Black Arts Movement itself seemed to want to end like one of Bullins's plays: in a BLACKNESS that permanently confounds concept and narrative. Like the audience plunged into darkness, the scholar of the Black Arts Movement should be sensitive to the fact that the texts and objects she studies possess permeable boundaries, express past conditions, and contain the possibility of performative moments that challenge the very notion of textuality and objectivity. Rigorous historicization and contextualization of these texts is not merely a scholarly and pedagogical option; it is fundamental to understanding. There are voices in these plays and poems that are never explicitly indicated, title characters never named. Like the fetish divorced from ritual—a continual concern of Black Arts critics—the texts of the Black Arts Movement are ruins. Their subtext is a community destroyed by economic backlash, provoked infighting, and a vanguard sensibility incapable of escaping the tradition of the avant-garde itself.

NOTES

I wish to express respect and gratitude to Yvonne "Baubie" Paschal for her patience and inspiration. My understanding of the Black Arts Movement—and black literature in general—is deeply indebted to our conversations and collaborations.

1. The "society of spectacle" is a term coined by Guy Debord to characterize a stage in capitalism in which the logic of commodity production dominates all aspects

of life. Such domination is enabled by the various mass media that developed during and after the rise of totalitarian states in the 1920s and 1930s, media that have become ends in themselves. See Debord, *Society of the Spectacle* (Detroit: Black and Red, 1970).

2. Unlike the rest of the essays in this collection, mine will capitalize the term "Black." Among radical African Americans in the 1960s, "Black" was a proper name that indicated both an ethnic and a political identity; the specificity of the term demands its capitalization. "Black" differentiated what it named—whether art, person, or politics—from "Negro" (a now antiquated term read by radicals to mean "liberal" or "assimilationist") and specified it in terms of the general category "African American" (a term rarely used at the time). Thus, every "Black" artist was an "African American," but none were "Negroes." Or to use the term in both its contemporary and older senses, every "Black" artist was black, but not every black artist was "Black."

3. One should note that Debord's notion of "spectacle" was formulated partly in response to the violent uprisings in African American communities, which occurred throughout the middle and late '60s. See Debord, "The Decline and Fall of the Spectacle-Commodity Economy," in *Situationist International Anthology*, ed. and trans. Ken Knabb (Berkeley, Calif.: Bureau of Public Secrets, 1989), 103–180. Debord argues that the uprisings were explicit responses to and attacks on commodity culture.

4. Larry Neal, "Any Day Now: Black Art and Black Liberation," *Ebony* 24 (1969): 54.

5. Ibid., 55.

6. This dynamism is aptly described by Stephen Henderson as an "interior dynamism," which found empowering roots in the inner life of blacks. In "The Form of Things Unknown," Henderson identifies what he calls a "Soul Field," which bound the activities of artistic production and artistic reception in a "complex galaxy of personal, social, institutional, historical, religious, and mythical meanings that affect everything we say or do as Black people sharing a common heritage." See Stephen Henderson, *Understanding the New Black Poetry: Black Speech and Black Music as Poetic References* (New York: William Morrow, 1973), 41. Houston Baker cites Henderson's essay as a key note in the definition of "an entirely new object of literary-critical and literary-theoretical investigation." See *Blues, Ideology, and Afro-American Literature: A Vernacular Theory* (Chicago: University of Chicago, 1984), 74. Baker nonetheless criticizes Henderson for his "impressionistic chauvinism": "For it is, finally, *only* the Black imagination that can experience Blackness, in poetry, or in life. As a result, the creative and critical framework suggested by Henderson resembles, at times, a closed circle" (81).

I would argue that the "romanticism" of Henderson and the various other voices of cultural nationalism in the Black Arts Movement is mitigated when the critic considers the central place of theater and performance in it. Rather than relying on a pre-existing cultural identity, Black Arts performance hopes, rather, to establish a cultural identity by constructing what Leslie C. Sanders has called "the Black territory," created in the particular space-time matrix of a particular performance with a particular audience. See *The Development of Black Theater in America: From Shadows to Selves* (Baton Rouge: Louisiana State University Press, 1988), 102. Rather than nostalgically resurrecting a preexisting culture, Black Arts performance hopes to invent, in Tejumola Olaniyan's words, "a Black dramatic voice self-consciously embedded in a cultural matrix." See *Scars of Conquest/Masks of Resistance: The Invention of Cultural Identities in African, African-American, and Caribbean Drama* (New York:

Oxford University Press, 1995), 4. Blackness, rather than being essential, is made "retroactively actual," a phrase I riff off Richard Schechner's notion that:

> the project coming into existence through the process of rehearsal . . . determines the past: what will be kept from earlier rehearsals or from the "source materials." . . . rehearsals make it necessary to think of the future in such a way as to create a past.

See *Between Theater and Anthropology* (Philadelphia: University of Pennsylvania Press 1985), 39.

7. Larry Neal utilizes this term twice in his article "The Black Arts Movement," clearly indicating that "thingness" is not simply a concern about objects and commodities but about "white ideas and white ways of looking at the world." See "The Black Arts Movement," *Drama Review* 12, no. 4 (1968): 30.

8. Larry Neal, "And Shine Swam On," in *Black Fire: An Anthology of Afro-American Writing*, ed. LeRoi Jones and Larry Neal (New York: William Morrow, 1968), 649.

9. Henry Louis Gates, Jr. "Black Creativity: On the Cutting Edge," *Time* (10 Oct. 1994): 75.

10. James T. Stewart, "The Development of the Black Revolutionary Artist," in Jones and Neal 6.

11. Tam Fiofori, "The Illusion of Sun Ra," *Liberator* 7, no. 12 (1967): 13.

12. See Michael Oren, "The Umbra Poets' Workshop, 1962–1965: Some Socio-Literary Puzzles," in *Belief vs. Theory in Black American Literary Criticism*, ed. Joe Weixlmann and Chester J. Fontenot (Greenwood, Pa.: Penkevill, 1986).

13. For discussion of Neal and Fuller's theater, see Nilgun Anadolu-Okur, *Contemporary African American Theater: Afrocentricity in the Works of Larry Neal, Amiri Baraka, and Charles Fuller* (New York: Garland, 1997).

14. For discussion of the Muntu group, see James Spady, *Larry Neal: Liberated Black Philly Poet with a Blues Streak of Mellow Wisdom* (Philadelphia: PC International, 1989).

15. Quoted in Oren 193.

16. LeRoi Jones, "The Black Arts Repertory Theater School," *Liberator* 5, no. 4 (1965): 21.

17. Larry Neal, "The Cultural Front," *Liberator* 5, no. 6 (1965): 27.

18. I follow Kalamu Ya Salaam's periodization in this regard. In 1965, BART/S was founded, the first truly "Black" cultural institution. In 1976, John Johnson decided to stop publication of *Black World*, a key Black Arts Movement publication. See *The Magic of Juju: An Appreciation of the Black Arts Movement (BAM)* (Chicago: Third World Press, forthcoming).

19. LeRoi Jones, "The Revolutionary Theatre," *Liberator* 5, no. 7 (1965): 5.

20. The reference is to Artaud's term for *The Conquest of Mexico*. See *The Theater and Its Double* (New York: Grove, 1958), 128. Jones's riff resituates Artaud in the context of colonialism and the subjective demands of decolonization, an aspect of Artaud's work largely ignored in our time. An excellent and thorough discussion of Jones's appropriation of Artaudian dramaturgical/philosophical concepts can be found in Sanders 126–131. See also Mance Williams, ed., *Black Theatre in the 1960s and 1970s* (Westport, Conn.: Greenwood, 1985), 20–24.

21. Daniel H. Watts, "Cong. Powell-HARYOU-ACT," *Liberator* 5, no. 11 (1965): 3.

22. Amiri Baraka, *The Autobiography of LeRoi Jones* (Chicago: Lawrence Hill, 1997), 458.

23. Ibid., 459.

24. Neal, "And Shine Swam On," 637.

25. Harold Cruse, *The Crisis of the Negro Intellectual* (New York: Morrow, 1967). Cruse played a vital role in the Black Arts Movement by instilling a thoroughgoing sense of historicism into his younger colleagues, particularly around the historically vexed issue of the Black intellectual. The premiere party for the book took place at the New Lafayette Theatre (ironically, only three days before it was burned down by hard-core nationalists and forced to move).

26. Ibid., 14.

27. Wahneema Lubiano, "Black Nationalism and Black Common Sense: Policing Ourselves and Others," in *The House that Race Built: Black Americans, US Terrain*, ed. Wahneema Lubiano (New York: Pantheon, 1997). Lubiano's criticism does not take adequate account of the "nonobjective" aesthetics of the movement. Other considerations of the land issue include the letter from Rolland Snellings/Askia Touré to Larry Neal, 2 June 1967 (Larry Neal Papers, New York Public Library), in which Snellings argues for renewed attention to the South and a carefully planned deployment of Black Arts leaders to all parts of the country. As he puts it, "Our 'nationalism' only extends to Harlem, Philly, or Detroit for the most part. We are really *regionalists* using the rhetoric of nationalists" (8). For further discussion of the "southern shift" of the movement after 1970, see "Southern College Poets," in Henderson, 185ff.; Addison Gayle, Jr., "The Black Aesthetic Ten Years Later," *Black World* (Sept. 1974): 20–29; and Larry Neal, review of *The Sound of Soul* by Phyllis Garland, *Negro Digest* (Jan. 1970): 43–47.

28. Larry Neal, "The Black Writer's Role," *Liberator* 6, no. 6 (1966): 8.

29. Neal, "And Shine Swam On," 655.

30. Charles Fuller, "Black Writing is Socio-Creative Art," *Liberator* 7, no. 4 (1967): 10.

31. Jones, "The Revolutionary Theatre," 5.

32. Ibid.

33. Ibid., 6.

34. Ibid.

35. Georg Lukács criticized the bourgeois theater of his time in exactly such terms:

> The new drama . . . is bourgeois and historicist; we add now that it is a drama of individualism. And in fact these three formulas express a single point of demarcation; they merely view the parting of ways from distinct vantage-points.

As a result, the drama "increasingly becomes an affair of the spirit [and] increasingly misses the vital centre of personality." See "The Sociology of Modern Drama," trans. Lee Baxandall, in *The Theory of the Modern Stage*, ed. Eric Bentley (New York: Penguin, 1986), 430.

36. Ben Sidran, *Black Talk* (New York: Da Capo, 1981). In this sense, the cultural nationalism of the Black Arts Movement stands as a more positive project, not merely as a reaction against a general lack of nation status as described by Lubiano. The emphasis on culture, in fact, serves as a strategic foil to the lack of property. Of course, lacking long-term institutional development, such a strategy must ultimately prove ill-conceived.

37. However, the distinction between the two movements is important to maintain. The Black Power Movement, emblematized by the Black Panthers, was at heart

a pragmatic, working-class movement, much more willing to entertain the role of non-Blacks as allies in the struggle.

Black House was fatally wounded by this irresolvable difference (a difference, as Cruse demonstrates in *Crisis*, that has claimed more than a few left-wing African American organizations). As described in *TDR*'s special issue on black theater, a long-term goal of Black House involved a confrontation among the theater audience, black revolutionaries, and the Bay Area police force, a confrontation that failed to occur because the organizers had been unable "to establish operational relations with Black revolutionaries in the Oakland area," meaning specifically the Panthers. See *Drama Review* 12, no. 4 (1968), 84. In reality, the Panthers (led by Cleaver) were working toward the exclusion of both the artists and the cultural nationalists from their ranks. The failure of Black House—heartbreaking after the enormously successful Black Communications Project—supplied an all-too-clear answer to the question, What would happen if a revolution happened and nobody came? The tactical mistake aside, the plan was inspired—and, if it had succeeded, would have supplied a model to other theaters hoping to ignite a truly revolutionary theater.

38. Cruse 68. For Cruse, the theater best enabled the development of historically grounded cultural institutions. Most important, such theaters would be owned and operated by Blacks for Blacks.

39. Michel de Certeau, *The Practice of Everyday Life*, trans. Steven Rendall (Berkeley: University of California Press, 1984).

40. Neal, "The Black Arts Movement," 33–34.

41. Ibid., 34.

42. Neal, "And Shine Swam On," 649.

43. I am not implying that Neal had no concern with institutional development, which would be a patent absurdity. Quite the contrary, he and Cruse saw eye to eye on that issue. The comparison between Cruse and Neal's visions of the theater is limited to the specific point concerning the tension between institutional and critical visions of theatricality.

44. Maulana Ron Karenga, "Black Cultural Nationalism," in *The Black Aesthetic*, ed. Addison Gayle, Jr. (Garden City, N.Y.: Doubleday, 1971), 38.

45. James T. Stewart, "The Development of the Black Revolutionary Artist," in Jones and Neal 5.

46. Ibid., 3–4.

47. Ibid., 4.

48. Ibid., 6.

49. Ibid.

50. Charles H. Fuller, "Black Writing: Release from Object," *Liberator* 7, no. 9 (1967): 20.

51. Ibid.

52. Ed Bullins, *"The Theme Is Blackness,"* in *The Theme Is Blackness: "The Corner" and Other Plays* (New York: Morrow, 1973). For further discussion of Bullins's life and work, see Samuel Hay, *Ed Bullins: A Literary Biography* (Detroit: Wayne State University Press, 1997).

53. To understand the contradictions inherent in the notion of a Black avant-garde, it is worth recalling that the birth of modern experimental theater was formulated in terms that do not fit well with the demands of Black liberation. One might recall, first of all, the metaphoric top-loading of "darkness" by the Symbolists, particularly Maurice Maeterlinck, whose *The Intruder* explicitly links the horizons of bourgeois culture (death, the extrafamilial, the timeless) with darkness. See *The*

Intruder, in *Doubles, Demons, and Dreamers: An International Collection of Symbolist Drama*, ed. Daniel Gerould (New York: Performing Arts Journal, 1985). In Italy, the Futurists consistently linked the temporal rupture of avant-garde performance with a racialized subject. See Filippo Tommaso Marinetti, "The Foundation and Manifesto of Futurism," in *Art in Theory 1900–1990: An Anthology of Changing Ideas*, ed. Charles Harrison and Paul Wood (Cambridge, Mass.: Blackwell, 1992), 145–48, with its references to Marinetti's childhood Sudanese nurse, as an example of the cultural "ground" upon and against which the Futurist project was founded. We should also recall the self-styled "primitivism" ("Negro rhythm," as Hugo Ball had it [quoted in Roselee Goldberg, *Performance Art: From Futurism to the Present*, rev. ed. (New York: H. N. Abrams, 1988), 38]) of the Zurich Dadaists when considering the ramifications of Bullins's critique of avant-garde theater in the West. Richard Schechner noted the divergence of Blacks Arts Movement theater from the experimental trends of white countercultural theater in his introduction to the volume of *TDR* devoted to Black Theater (edited by Bullins). He writes:

> As I read over the material for this issue it became clear to me that the aesthetics most commonly discussed in *TDR*—happenings, environmental theatre, new kinds of criticism, regional theatre, actor training—are most lively in the context of a certain segment of white American society. Most of these movements are irrelevant to Black theatre. And some of them are viewed as "decadent," others as "oppressive."

See "White on Black," *Drama Review* 12, no. 4 (Summer 1968): 25–27.

54. Ed Bullins, "The So-Called Western Avant-Garde Drama," *Liberator* 7, no. 12 (1967): 16.

55. For other discussions of historicism and its limitations, see Hayden White, *Metahistory: The Historical Imagination in Nineteenth-Century Europe* (Baltimore: Johns Hopkins University, 1973), and *The Content of the Form: Narrative Discourse and Historical Representation* (Baltimore: Johns Hopkins University, 1987). See also Dominick LaCapra, *Rethinking Intellectual History: Texts, Contexts, Language* (Ithaca, N.Y.: Cornell University, 1983). For an overview of White and LaCapra's work and critical responses to both, see Lloyd S. Kramer, "Literature, Criticism, and Historical Imagination: The Literary Challenge of Hayden White and Dominick LaCapra," in *The New Cultural History*, ed. Lynn Hunt (Berkeley: University of California, 1989).

56. Baker 5.

57. Eugene Lee's set design for the production utilized the principles of environmental/Artaudian theater: it surrounded the audience with a set that suggested the interior of an Atlantic slaver.

58. For discussion of the role of music in several productions of *Slave Ship*, see Harry Elam, Jr., "Social Urgency, Audience Participation, and the Performance of *Slave Ship* by Amiri Baraka," in *Crucibles of Crisis: Performing Social Change*, ed. Janelle Reinelt (Ann Arbor: University of Michigan, 1996). See also Kimberly Benston, "Vision and Form in *Slave Ship*," in *Imamu Amiri Baraka (LeRoi Jones): A Collection of Essays*, ed. Kimberly Benston (Englewood Cliffs, N.J.: Prentice-Hall, 1978). Benston characterizes *Slave Ship*'s music (composed by Archie Shepp) as reflecting "the entire historical and mythical process of Afro-American being" (174).

59. Elam 22.

60.
> Salve salvage in the spin.
> Endorse the splendor splashes;

stylize the flawed utility;
prop a malign or failing light—
but know the whirlwind is our commonwealth.

. . . .

It is a lonesome, yes. For we are the last of the loud.
Nevertheless, live.
　　Conduct your blooming in the noise and
　whip of the whirlwind.

　　Gwendolyn Brooks, "The Sermon on the Warp-
　　　land," *Blacks* (Chicago: Third World Press,
　　　　　　　　　　　　　1989), 454–456.

61. Sanchez 24.

62. Enoch Brater, ed., *Feminine Focus: The New Women Playwrights* (New York: Oxford University Press, 1989).

63. Sanchez 24.

64. Gil Scott-Heron, "The Revolution Will Not Be Televised," *The Revolution Will Not Be Televised* (New York: BMG Music, 1988).

65. Fredric Jameson, *The Political Unconscious: Narrative as a Socially Symbolic Act* (Ithaca, N.Y.: Cornell University, 1981), 35.

66. This situation is not helped by the fact that, as of the writing of this essay, many of the central texts of the movement are no longer in print (including almost all of Bullins's work). The political economy of publishing, so often criticized by black artists, continues to restrain consideration of the movement's political, economic, and cultural project. This aside, one of the signal ironies of Gates's critical stance against the Black Arts Movement is that the first Black Studies program in the country—San Francisco State University—was created by Black Student Union president Jimmy Garrett (who cut his teeth as a playwright in Black Arts/West) and Nathan Hare. Garrett wrote the highly influential play *And We Own the Night* (1968) (its title borrowed from Baraka's "State/meant," *The Le Roi Jones/Amiri Baraka Reader*, ed. William J. Harris [New York: Thunder's Mouth Press, 1991] 169–170), one of the pieces that toured with the Communications Project.

4

Beyond a Liberal Audience

WILLIAM SONNEGA

> In 1960 it was thought by a lot of black people and a lot of white
> liberals that if the two cultures met and white Americans
> embraced our [black] culture, if they got to know our music and to
> know our dance, then somehow we could come to a better
> understanding. But that was not the case. You could be KKK and
> still watch Bill Cosby on Thursday nights.
>
> Spike Lee[1]

For the past few years, I have been thinking and writing about the conundrum Lee describes, and I have come to believe that his observations about the failure of the performing arts to progressively transform race relations in the United States are, for the most part, accurate. While many white Americans are, of course, still trying to come to a better understanding of black culture by embracing its various artistic forms, such embraces, however well-intentioned, often appear to maintain the hierarchies of white privilege rather than contest the social and economic inequities on which they are based. The wholesale commodification of black urban gangsta rap by white suburban teens comes to mind as but one of many cross-cultural appropriations, which do not substantively redress the exclusionary politics that divide the daily lives of so many blacks and whites. In this respect, I have been interested in how the epistemological question that Lee raises regarding the limits of cross-cultural knowing is enacted in the embrace of contemporary black theater by white audiences. Specifically, I have been looking at African American theatrical productions in Minneapolis and St. Paul, Minnesota, and their relation to the predominantly white, socially and politically liberal cultural landscape in which they are embedded.

Generally, my understanding of the term *liberal* in this context is derived from a credo put forward by David Spitz and based upon John Stuart Mill's perspective on toleration in *On Liberty*; namely, that liberal attitudes are founded upon the premise that acknowledgment of one's limitations implies acceptance of the limitations of others, which leads to open discussion for discovering truth and remedying social ills.[2] A white liberal audience, in this sense, is one that will attend black theater, as black theater becomes a forum in and around which such discussion may take place, a site where liberal whites, by virtue of their presence, publicly acknowledge their limitations—or Otherness—in the belief that such disclosure constitutes an important contribution to a progressive multiracial politics. Implicit for such an audience is the notion that white or mainstream theater is normative while black theater is "race theater," a classification empowered, in part, by the privilege that liberal whites associate with not being black. Yet, in the same spirit, a liberal white audience may not see the blacks in black theater at all as Other but as sites representative of cross-cultural commonality. Such attitudes may be even more liberal, in fact, than those founded on a carefully constructed Otherness, in that they presume that toleration is something liberals naturally possess rather than seek to acquire.

In Minnesota, a white liberal audience is in these problematic terms one that will attend the African American theatrical productions of St. Paul's Penumbra Theatre. As an October 1997 audience profile compiled by Penumbra attests, the theater's patrons are generally affluent, well-educated, and white: nearly half (43 percent) reported annual household incomes of $50,000 or more; one third (33 percent) reported having achieved a postgraduate degree while 58 percent reported having achieved some college or a bachelor's degree. Seventy-eight percent of the audience was white.[3] While these demographics are not common to all theater audiences, they provide a paradigm for considering the extent to which white attendance at black theater constitutes progressive social behavior. The purpose of this essay is not to conveniently target this behavior as hypocritical but rather to consider how "muddy" the relationship of liberal advocacy and social action actually is.[4] Given that the American theater at present devotes a significant portion of its resources to marking—and marketing—itself as liberal, particularly where issues of race are concerned, my critique thus emphasizes challenges facing black theater and a racial transformation of the American mise-en-scène.

A Liberal Audience

In a theater on the floor below me, there is a rehearsal underway for a production of Imamu Amiri Baraka's *Dutchman*, a play that stages a mythic confrontation between a black man and a white woman on a New York City subway train. Before the rehearsal began, the play's director, an African American female student, expressed to me her deepest concerns about the work, namely that, on our small, private, predominantly white liberal arts college campus in the Midwest, the play will likely be attended only by those for whom Baraka's penetrating discourse on sublimated black rage and its misrepresentation by whites is a commonly read text, a given circumstance of race relations in late 1990s America. In this spirit, the director confessed her fears of preaching to the choir, of seeking to convert an audience that, if not already converted, covets a culturally redeeming experience of conversion with all the ritualized faith of the devout taking communion. She wondered about how the audience would respond to Clay's claim that the blues of Bessie Smith are categorically misunderstood by Lula and by whites in general. Would this provoke them, or encourage them to reward the moment with yet one more perfunctorily politically correct (PC) nod of approval? Would Clay's prophecy to Lula—and all whites—that blacks will one day murder whites if black culture continues to be colonized by "the great intellectual legacy of the white man" challenge the audience to reconsider the politics of assimilation, or reinforce the contention that such colonizations no longer exist—particularly on liberal arts college campuses?[5] Ultimately, in an institutional environment organized by rhetorical rather than actual constructions of diversity, in which the nuanced, complicated subject positions of personal experience are often strategically masked to prevent rather than promote intercultural dialogue, what effect could *Dutchman* have on the audience other than to reproduce a dominant cultural hegemony?

Such questions, central to critical pedagogy and postcolonial and antiracist theory, are increasingly integral to contemporary theater criticism and practice. They resonated, for example, in the subtext of "On Cultural Power: The August Wilson/Robert Brustein Discussion," particularly when Wilson stated, "The Lila Wallace–Reader's Digest Fund did a tremendous disservice to blacks by giving money to white organizations to encourage diversity rather than directly to black theatres." The agenda, at that moment, addressed precisely the ideological imperatives of white liberal cultural programming. By marginalizing black theater within and through subsidies to white theaters, Wilson commented, whites are encouraged to construe intercultural performance not as a contestation of the normative patterns that maintain social, political, and economic inequities but as simply fulfilling part of a liberal agenda for social change. "Mainstream theatres should do [black] plays because they want to," he remarked, "not because they have the funding for it."[6]

Such criticism of liberalism is no longer solely an artistic or academic project. In the 1996 presidential election, for example, the term *liberal* itself was regarded by both Republican and historically liberal Democratic strategists as too fraught with derogatory connotations to productively characterize *any* candidate's platform. In such contexts, the term was often applied generically to describe the allegedly unethical, immoral, and inhumane biases of the mass media, thereby implicating the media of film, television, and radio rather than failed liberal policies in the decline of literacy and the rise of crime, among other social ills. In campaign rhetoric, *liberal* often became a four-letter word, the "*l* word," making its utterance a political taboo. This was especially true in Minnesota, where Democratic senator Paul Wellstone was tagged "embarrassingly liberal" by his opponent and, later, "The Most Liberal Man in America" by Republican campaign strategists.[7]

Satirical sketches of white liberals, once associated with Rush Limbaugh's monologues, now appear throughout mass media. In a sketch on a 19 January 1995 episode of "Saturday Night Live," for example, four male office workers, three white and one black, discussed their plans for the forthcoming holiday, Martin Luther King, Jr., Day. As the three white men spoke enthusiastically of spending the day watching basketball on television, drinking beer, and gambling in Atlantic City, their black colleague offered each of them free tickets to a marathon reading of Dr. King's speeches. Fumbling, the white men declined the tickets, then bestowed on their black colleague a series of gifts, including a laptop computer, a wallet with several hundred dollars in it, and, finally, another laptop, by way of compensating him for their apparent lack of sensitivity. Relieved, though rid of their possessions, the white men then slunk sheepishly from the office as a black woman entered and asked the black man, "How'd you do?" implying that she, too, had literally capitalized on the guilt of white liberals.

The sketch is a summary par excellence of the kind of liberalism that may shape the perceptions of many white spectators of contemporary black theater in America. In assuming the audience is conversant with the traditional liberal tenet of toleration and with how liberalism in the United States has, since the late 1960s, been driven by social policies devised more to display virtue than to solve social problems, the sketch satirizes the manner in which liberal whites have sought to atone for the victimization of minorities. As Shelby Steele observes, compassion has been reduced to a series of expedient devices—group preferences, quotas, set-asides, redistricting, race and gender norming—that proclaim the good will of their creators while doing little to end the discrimination that minorities face. What it has effected, Steele argues, is a strategy of "compensatory deference" in which liberal whites, rather than working to dismantle the infrastructures of institutional racism, simply show deference to minorities in compensating them for their suffering—a maneuver that makes "deference synonymous with social virtue."[8] Once deference is socially virtuous in itself, the three white men in the sketch are virtuous by definition, despite their resistance to spending a *token* moment listening to the speeches of Martin Luther King, Jr. (As Bismarck once remarked, "When you say that you agree to a thing in principle, you have not the slightest intention of carrying it out in practice."[9]) In concluding with the black characters' manipulation of white liberal privilege, the sketch points to the inefficacy of compensatory deference and race-based tokenism as strategies for social reform.

While these are wholly uncomplicated and overdetermined stereotypes, they nonetheless signal the emergence of a broad-based critique of liberal ideology in American culture. What does this critique portend with respect to the constitution and disposition of theater audiences, especially toward productions that are, by funding and design, committed to the inculcation of a greater degree of tolerance and understanding among people of diverse racial and ethnic backgrounds? As Eugene Nesmith reported in *American Theatre*, "The 1995–96 season schedules for the nearly 350 constituent companies of Theatre Communications Group renders up a list of at least 50 major productions dealing with African American subject matter."[10] While Henry Louis Gates, Jr., regards this as heralding a black "cultural glasnost," others, like Lou Bellamy, founder and artistic director of Penumbra Theatre in St. Paul, question how such productions alter the stakes for black artists and their works. "I tend to view the major institutions' forays into this arena as colonialist," he writes:

> Quite often they are guided by those who, because of their privileged position, occupy and extend their control over my art. They tend to place value on facets of my existence without understanding that existence in totality. When institutions become arbiter and interpreter, they even skew my perception of myself. They, by virtue of their privilege, foster the idea that those whom they choose to admit are more accomplished or more talented because those artists chose to accept their "color-blind" invitation. . . . I now have to fight to keep Penumbra from becoming a "farm team" where well-funded artistic directors come to do "one-stop shopping" for new ideas, talent and craft. And where managing and marketing directors seek replacements for their dwindling and blue-haired white subscribers.[11]

While there are, of course, few artistic directors in America at present with funds enough to do this kind of shopping, Bellamy nonetheless emphasizes how black plays and performers are frequently perceived as attractive commodities by mainstream white theaters, which have made a commitment to diversifying their repertoires. Between Gates and Bellamy sits the contemporary American theater audience, a group composed largely of white liberals, who often bring to their role the unquestioned assumption that, given the persistence of racism in society, there is no alternative to institutionalizing race as the basis of employment, law, education, and, of course, theatrical representation. In this context, how does the critique of liberalism explicate the relation of black theater and white audiences?

Liberal Conundra

Criticism of white liberal ideology unfolds in response to a complex matrix of issues. Among them, the history of civil rights and contemporary ethical debates about race, education, and the marketplace emerge as prominent sites of inquiry. On the one hand, historiographic investigations seek to account for the contributions of white liberals to the Civil Rights Movement, with emphasis on the crucial but often blurred distinction between rhetorical advocacy and political action. In her study of the Southern Conference Movement, for example, Linda Reed writes that the attempt by white southern liberals to create a more egalitarian society, in an era in which the majority of white southerners refused to consider racial equality, deserves a prominent place in American history "because it illustrates the weaknesses of organizations [that] refuse to take direct action in situations that call for revolutionary means." The Civil Rights Movement, she comments, showed that basic reform requires "unseemly acts by masses of people—boycotts, demonstrations, jailings—which [white liberal organizations] had neither the numbers nor courage to undertake."[12]

Similarly, John Kneebone writes of how white southern journalists, in the wake of the Supreme Court's 17 May 1954 declaration that racial segregation in public schools is unconstitutional, sought to console their readers with claims that segregation would survive for years, that "calm deliberation" would therefore better serve the South than "angry reaction." Desegregation would come to the South because the region must obey the law, but the change could take place gradually, without conflict. In tracing the evolution of this discourse through a series of editorials that appeared from 1954 to 1958, Kneebone demonstrates how white southern journalists employed the rhetoric of cultural relativism to suppress contradictions inherent in their "moderate" stance. As journalist Virginius Dabney wrote, his argument implied nothing "of bigotry or prejudice, and nothing having to do with supposed racial superiority or inferiority." Rather, blacks and whites alike should desire "to preserve the ethnic and cultural heritage of one's own race, and not to have it diluted or destroyed through commingling with a race that has a sharply contrasting background." Kneebone finds that, through compromises such as this, white southern journalists kept alive a liberal spirit of toleration, yet, as Dabney's editorials show, maintained a racist social infrastructure as well. He concludes that the significance of this strategy was, finally, that it ensured that white liberals would always control the cultural agenda and rate of change in race relations.[13]

On the other hand, criticism of liberal ideology addresses how the contemporary attack on racism is often reduced to policy measures aimed at eliminating racist institutional barriers or providing compensatory programs designed to increase the cultural capital and skills of African Americans in education and the marketplace. Its premise, as Henry Giroux points out, is that liberal discourse in its various forms

> rarely engages how white authority is inscribed and implicated in the creation and reproduction of a society in which the voices of the center appear either invisible or unimplicated in the historical and social construction of racism as an integral part of their own collective identity.

Though the theoretical scope is broad and oversimplified here, Giroux formulates a strategy that resists the contention that racism is solely *explicit*. That it is also *implicit* becomes the basis for an argument that dominant educational approaches to race and ethnicity, organized by the discourse of multiculturalism, generally fail to conceptualize race and ethnicity as part of a wider discourse of power and powerlessness. "Questions of representation and inclusion suppress any attempts to call into question the norm of whiteness as an ethnic category that secures its dominance by appearing to be invisible," he notes. The invisibility of white culture, fashioned in the gaze of liberal ideology, becomes for Giroux its defining and most powerful aspect, constituting white privilege even as it allegedly contests the practices that construct it.[14]

Pondering similar concerns, Dinesh D'Souza writes that "liberalism, which began as an ideology of equal rights, has degenerated into the paternalism of rigged results." What is rigged are liberal policies designed to erase differences in academic achievement, economic performance, and crime rates between blacks and other groups. By routinely abridging standards for blacks, such policies make it more likely that blacks will fail at tasks for which they are inadequately prepared. While white liberals do not want blacks to fail, D'Souza observes that many seem to behave as though, in every competition that is not fixed, they expect them to do so. Like Kneebone, he references his critique to the liberal embrace of relativism as a basis for proclaiming the equality of all cultures while rejecting the classic racist assertion of white civilizational superiority. Yet D'Souza rethinks relativism as that which also makes it impossible for liberals to confront the issue of black cultural pathology. To do so is seen as "blaming the victim," while the desire to avoid a genetic explanation forces liberals to blame group differences on racism.[15] What this form of liberalism evinces is thus not the easily targeted hypocrisy that Kneebone locates in white liberal journalists but a more epistemologically complex register of experience, one that ultimately prevents liberals from supporting policies that uphold any standard of responsibility.

As Shannon Jackson emphasizes, to push beyond a "knee-jerked condemnation of the PC-inauthenticity of . . . those who do not 'walk' their 'talk' " is to acknowledge how muddy the relationship of rhetorical advocacy and social action actually is. She writes:

> Talking and walking, like all variations on the theory/practice dichotomy, denote different registers of experience; they function imprecisely because these registers can be so different and because that difference illuminates conundra about intention, about consequence, and about what it is to be knowledgeable about one's actions.[16]

For D'Souza, such conundra are further exacerbated by the steady erosion, since the 1960s, of liberal confidence in the ability of color-blind rules to give blacks a fair chance to compete on their merits. Their faith in the efficacy of policy shaken, white liberals are now left mainly to produce alibis for black failure, abandoning activism for a litany of ritualistic apologies. D'Souza cites a few of them: the "root causes" of poverty, the "bitter hoax" of the American Dream, the mysterious disappearance of "meaningful" work, the prospect of a "resurgence" of "hate," the danger of "imposing one's morality," the need to avoid "code words," and how we should all "understand the rage."[17] For D'Souza, this rhetoric takes on a comic aspect, and he questions whether it is even believed by its advocates. In pointing out how self-deception thus becomes one of liberalism's primary modes, he claims that "many liberals may cease to believe in their own ingenious excuses and become like lawyers who suspect, finally, that their client may be guilty."[18]

While there may be little evidence to support D'Souza's thesis, rendering it debatable at best, it nonetheless converges with other critiques evoking general frustration with the liberal status quo and the intellectual and moral bankruptcy of relativism as its ideological basis. The points at which these critiques differ suggest the possibility of cultural theory that allows for a more nuanced liberal subject position, one that does not necessarily perpetuate both the white guilt and white self-righteousness that constitute its condition. Generally, by drawing into focus the invisibility of whiteness as a normative ethnic category, such criticism resists uncomplicated stereotypes of dominant members of society and counters the attempts of white liberals to secure a disingenuous position outside their own antiracist critiques. In this sense, the work of Reed and Kneebone questions implicitly the viability of doing revolutionary cultural work in mainstream theaters, while that of Giroux and D'Souza suggests how problematically the good intentions of white liberal theatergoers are translated as a coherent multiracial politics. From a Millian perspective, I have characterized the white patron of black theater as liberal, as one who desires entry into a progressive dialogue with black theater and culture, as one who comes to the theater and says, "Here I acknowledge my Otherness, and in so doing imply that I accept you—community, theater, play, and performer—as the Other. Can we talk?" Yet, as these critiques of liberalism foreground, to what extent do these talks take place? On what basis does the experience of theatergoing retain—in Minneapolis/St. Paul, for example—a socially transformative power?

Diversity Work

In the Twin Cities theater community, there have emerged in the 1990s two primary approaches to representing race and ethnicity. To some extent, these were articulated in the Wilson-Brustein discussion and are perhaps reflective generally of a binary tension in thinking and performing about race in the American theater just now. The approaches were clearly exemplified by two productions: a 1991 staging of *Death of a Salesman*, directed by Sheldon Epps, at the Guthrie Theatre in Minneapolis (see figure 4.1), in which black actors appeared in the central roles of Willy, Linda, Biff, Happy, and Uncle Ben Loman; and a 1995 staging of *Sally's Rape*, written and performed by African-American performance artist Robbie McCauley, at Penumbra Theatre in St. Paul.[19] Both productions were immensely popular with audiences and generated considerable coverage and controversy in local media. Critical reactions to the Guthrie's black *Salesman* focused on the ethical implications of promoting diversity by color-blind casting a well-known play by a prominent white author. Specific questions addressed the extent to which Willy Loman

Figure 4.1   *Death of a Salesman* by Arthur Miller, Guthrie Theatre, Minneapolis, Minnesota, 1991. Willy Loman played by Mel Winkler; Howard played by Barton Tinall. Photo by Michael Daniel.

is, as Miller has repeatedly insisted, a modern Everyman whose fall evokes universal aspects of suffering, or a figure grounded deeply in the particular ideology and cultural landscape of white middle-class America. If he is the latter, as Bellamy and Wilson have argued, then the misrepresentation of the Lomans as a black family only serves to further distort a white liberal perception of the actualities of black male, female, and cultural identities. Reactions to *Sally's Rape*, on the other hand, centered on the content and dynamics of postshow dialogues, which were moderated by McCauley. In the dialogues, white spectators were encouraged to publicly perform—for one another— their real, imagined, or desired affiliations with both the represented and actual histories of the rape of an African American slave woman, which occurred more than one hundred years ago. What emerged frequently was a series of uncomfortable confrontations—or silences—between liberal whites, who sought to maintain that their cultural sensitivity was, in fact, greater than others. Examples of each production illustrate the liberal conundra about intention, consequence, and consciousness that Jackson and others have criticized.

A Black Everyman

In keeping with Miller's minimalist concerns, Sheldon Epps's *Salesman* was set on the Guthrie's large unadorned thrust with only a single platform indicating the boys' bedroom upstage and a towering row of apartments, decaying and apparently vacant, at its rear. While there was nothing extraordinary about the structural elements of the mise-en-scène, they were nonetheless drawn into a sharp critical and cultural focus via the use of color. The floor of the stage was painted red, green, and gold, resembling a multicolored Jamaican or West African tapestry or a vast piece of Ghanaian *kente* cloth, the "cloth of kings." These colors were then picked up and highlighted by identically colored projections emanating from the apartment windows, so that the entire setting signified generally "Africanness" or, more specifically, "African Americanness." The Lomans were seen to have built their house, quite literally, upon the cultural foundations of African ancestors. It should be noted that, in the summer of 1991, when this production was staged it was not uncommon to encounter *kente* cloth on the streets of Minneapolis attached to jackets, hats, purses, and other items. Earlier that year, the Dayton-Hudson Corporation, one of the Guthrie's principal benefactors, had introduced into its chain of upscale department stores a line of goods imported from West Africa, which included small sections of *kente* cloth, at $40 each. Ironically, it is possible that some Guthrie spectators may have thus first recognized the representation of *kente* cloth on stage not as a sign of the Lomans' African heritage but simply as one of many new products they had discovered recently at the mall.

A variety of aspects of Miller's play were similarly linked to other racially constituted texts with which the Guthrie audience was likely to be familiar. To begin with, the representation of the Lomans as a black family pointed to the marginalization of blacks in American society as well as within Minnesota and the Guthrie itself. Surrounded by upper-middle-class white spectators, the Lomans were isolated in the theater much the way the lower-middle-class Jeffersons had been isolated on television in the 1980s following their move to Manhattan's affluent and predominantly white Upper East Side. While this particular positioning strongly emphasized both class and race differences between the Lomans and the audience—something a traditionally cast production of *Salesman* at the Guthrie would of course not do—it did not, in this context, contest these differences as detrimental to the status quo. African Americans, after all, comprise only 3.6 percent of the Twin Cities' population, making it common that many white residents could go for some time without immediate contact with blacks.[20] Thus, Epps's Lomans mirrored and made oddly familiar the racial imbalance explicit in Minnesota cultural life. Familiarity with such an imbalance does not always engender a commitment to its rectification, however, and it may be that, for many Guthrie spectators, the theatrical simulation of a black family in their midst simply reinforced their sense of exteriority to actual blacks and their experiences.

Epps's revisioning likewise extended to Uncle Ben, whose tales of success in the diamond mines of the African Gold Coast were radically reinterpreted as a result. "I was going to find father in Alaska," he tells Willy, but then adds that he "had a very faulty view of geography . . . [and] after a few days . . . ended up in Africa." Delivered by an African American actor, these lines consistently drew one of the largest laughs in the production. In addition to the joke about Ben's misguided travels, they signaled a search for racial ancestry not explicitly stated in the text. Followed by Ben's claim that he had discovered their father as "a man with a big beard . . . sitting around a fire . . . [playing] some kind of high music . . . [on] a flute," the audience once again laughed at how casting had cleverly rehistoricized both the absent Loman father and Uncle Ben as patriarchal figures in a kind of "Roots" miniseries saga. On the one hand, the fine sense of postmodern irony at play in the scene signaled that other "alternative" pleasures were likely to be produced as the result of intertextual layering. On the other hand, it legitimized the processes by which white spectators drew upon stereotypical associations of African Americans to produce those pleasures. Thus the production ironically appeared to promote a fresh reading of *Salesman* while reproducing yet one more stale pastiche of rearticulated racism.

The color-blind casting did not generate solely hip laughter, however. The reenactment of Biff's failure to pass high school math and earn a football scholarship to the University of Virginia, for example, became poignantly realigned with the narratives of many young black men whose academic and athletic aspirations go, as a matter of survival, hand in hand. Here again, the audience was asked to appreciate how deftly casting had sutured the Lomans to an African American cultural context, while at the same time it reinforced a particularly narrow perception of black male identity and its allegedly innate athleticism. Happy's proposed solution to his brother's hard-luck story inflated this perception further. "We form two basketball teams, see?" he tells Biff. "We play each other. It's a million dollars' worth of publicity. Two brothers, see? The Loman Brothers. Displays in the Royal Palms—all the hotels. And banners over the basketball court: 'Loman Brothers.' Baby, we could sell sporting goods!" As a pipe dream conjured by a young black man, it is likely that Happy's plan resonated for the liberal white audience with a degree of irony greater than that indicated by the text. In other words, if the production of meaning in the scene is contingent on the audience knowing what Happy does not—namely, that the Loman brothers were not born to succeed in business—to what extent did the color-blind casting also emphasize that the Loman brothers were not born to succeed in business *because they are black*? While there is not, of course, an easy answer to this, D'Souza's comments about the "rigged paternalism" of liberalism come to mind. The possibility—however modest and fleeting—that color-blind casting empowered the liberal white audience with the ability to eviscerate the Lomans by referring them to stereotypes of blacks prevalent in the dominant culture nonetheless problematizes such theater as an emblematic site for "doing" diversity work. Racial stereotypes that resonate around rather than within a performance, that are referred to rather than represented, that are not explicitly satirized or subjected to a self-reflexive critique position an audience on a compelling, potentially transformative, yet dangerous, edge. At stake is the extent to which the audience apprehends the presence of the stereotypes and, if so, questions critically their function in the performance and everyday life.

For example, when Willy comes to see his boss, Howard, about taking him off the road, the negotiation of power in the scene was unmistakably drawn along racial lines. Howard, in this context, provided a recognizable frame through which Willy and his struggles could be regarded at a safe and, perhaps, all-too-familiar distance; that is, the white boss informs the black employee that his work is substandard and then fires him. The Lomans' neighbors, Charley and his son, Bernard, provided similar frames through which Willy's identity could be formulated almost exclusively as a function of race. When Bernard prepares to return to Washington, Willy confronts him and asks, "Why didn't [Biff] ever catch on?" Bernard then briefly retraces for Willy the chronology of Biff's demise, concluding with the observation that something devastating apparently happened to Biff while visiting his father in Boston. In a traditionally cast *Salesman*, the negotiation of power in this scene is potentially intense. Bernard, the studious boy next door, who was never, according to Willy, "well liked," has become a gifted young attorney preparing to argue a case before the Supreme Court. His return painfully signifies for Willy all that Biff and Happy have not become and all that he has not become for them. When Bernard asks Willy, "What happened in Boston?" the stage is thus set for the revelation of how Biff lost his faith in his father, and ultimately in himself, after discovering Willy with his mistress. That Bernard should be the one to propel this element of the plot into motion is of course the heart and soul of the scene; the person Willy had least expected to succeed, he now understands all too clearly, is directly in control of his destiny.

In Epps's production, Bernard, sporting the requisite briefcase and tennis racket, was powerfully linked to the cacophony of contemporary critical discourses regarding white male hegemony and the various means by which it is reproduced. Looking for all the world like the youngest member of the proverbial old boys' club, Bernard embodied in this context not only the rewards of disciplined work, as perhaps Miller had intended, but precisely the privileges of being both white and male in the United States. Here Epps's focus was clear: Bernard and Willy sparred as icons in a microcosmic simulation of the American social order: white versus black, rich versus poor, oppressor versus oppressed.

In the pivotal Boston scene that followed, this focus was extended to incorporate an examination of the role of gender and sexuality in the American racial equation. With the casting of Willy's mistress as a white woman, the scene elaborated directly on the various taboos associated with interracial dating and how desire is driven at times by the allure of an exotic Other. Following his meetings with Howard and Bernard, Willy's pursuit of a white woman as an alternative to his black wife appeared in this context to be motivated by his insatiable longing for status and respect in the culture of his oppressors. His affair, as a result, signified less a desperate transgression of exhausted marital boundaries than a concerted attempt to identify, affiliate, and become one with the signs of white male authority. Thus, while The Woman functions in Miller's text primarily as an eroticized object onto which Willy displaces his existential anxiety, in Epps's production, she was additionally objectified as a racially constituted trophy, which Willy believed he deserved and had won. It may be that, of all of Epps's revisions, the representation of a black Willy Loman getting dressed after sex with an anonymous white woman in a hotel room far from his home most provocatively recontextualized *Salesman* within the particular culture of the Guthrie and its audience. Here, it could not be denied that the production had fundamentally destabilized the text and opened it to a greater range of interpretive possibilities than it alone seemed capable of generating.

Redemptive Dialogue

In *Sally's Rape*, Robbie McCauley and Jeannie Hutchins, a white performer, collaborated in a highly visual, nonlinear narrative of the life of McCauley's great-great-grandmother Sally, a slave who was raped by her white master solely to breed cheap field hands. By openly negotiating in their performance a variety of tense physical and discursive spaces constituted by their racial and cultural differences, McCauley and Hutchins challenged spectators to do the same with the play itself: to confront, in personal terms, their relationships to both the represented and actual histories of the rape of an African American slave woman. In short, the predominantly white audience was asked to question the extent to which it had been complicit in Sally's rape and, finally, to articulate the terms of its complicity—or resistance to it— in a postshow dialogue with McCauley and Hutchins.

The pivotal scene in *Sally's Rape* had McCauley standing on an auction block, stripped naked, embodying her great-great-grandmother, while Hutchins led the audience in chanting, "Bid 'em in! Bid 'em in!" Then, in an attempt to understand McCauley's emotions, tangled in the representation of Sally's emotions, Hutchins climbed onto the auction block herself and began to slip out of her own dress. However, just as she was about to complete the action, she stopped, slowly pulled her dress back on, and stepped down. The moment required little elaboration: Sally, McCauley's great-great-grandmother, had no choice; Hutchins did, and she refused to be degraded.

The postshow dialogues began there. McCauley and Hutchins brought chairs to the stage, invited reactions from the audience, sat, and waited. More traditionally staged productions at Penumbra, such as those of August Wilson's plays, have seldom explored the relationship of black theater to white audience as directly as *Sally's Rape*. As moderator of the postshow dialogue, McCauley sought to tactfully draw out of the audience the precise terms and conditions of its affiliation with the play. The following comments emerged in several postshow dialogues in January 1995 and are representative of differing modes of interactive discourse generated in the roughly hour-long sessions.[21]

On one night, a black woman began emotionally: "This play is serious. I mean, it got to me, you know? Black women back then had to keep their heads on straight." McCauley was appreciative but pushed the discussion. "How do people survive?" she asked. "Partly we find out where we come from, no matter how hard it is." Another black woman objected to the nude scene on the grounds that it was degrading to black women. McCauley, having heard the criticism before, acknowledged the validity of the woman's feelings, then explained that she used nudity to shock in order to more powerfully convey her great-great-grandmother's lack of options, her isolation. The audience nodded; the subject was dropped.

No white spectators contributed to this exchange. Was their silence a gesture of respect, a polite acknowledgment of their exclusion from the subject of black female identity and the politics of its representation? Or was it a numbed PC silence, fueled by fear of rhetorically transgressing vague but immutable borders, of appearing to be intolerant? While the texts of such silences are elusive, their cultural contexts are perhaps less so. Erika Thorne, for example, a Twin Cities "diversity and antiracism consultant," reveals just how conveniently a white audience's silence in the face of black theater may be theorized. In response to theater critic Jayne Blanchard's review of *Everlasting Arms* by Rebecca Rice, another Penumbra production (May 1996) soliciting a high degree of audience interaction, Thorne writes:

> Here is Jayne Blanchard. She's a European-American who shows little evidence that she has worked to school herself in the culture and life reality of citizens of color, and she attempts to critique a piece that powerfully embodies the contemporary experience of an African American woman raising a son in our racist culture. . . . You can't critique art from others' culture.[22]

Thorne, who is white, concludes that Blanchard should have been "honest and realistic about her ability to write well about the event, and simply bow[ed] out." While Thorne does not specify on which aspect of Blanchard's review she bases her complaint, it may be that she found Blanchard's conclusion, likening the interactive play to "more of a community outreach program or grief ritual cloaked in the trappings of abstract theatre," sufficiently egregious as to warrant comment.[23] However vague her argument with Blanchard, Thorne's implicit warning to white spectators of black theater is: if you are not black, or if you lack appropriate "diversity and antiracism" training, keep quiet. The silence this predictable position enforces is a form of compensatory deference, trading the discursive potentials of McCauley's project for a mute liberal posture.

On another night, a white man referred to the case of Thomas Jefferson, who while president had several children with a slave who was also named Sally. Picking up the thread, another white man added that, to his knowledge, "Jefferson apparently loved her." McCauley came as close to anger as she would get on this evening. "I'm harsh with that because of slavery," she replied. "I know what rape is during slave time, and I call that rape. If there was so much romance, why didn't Jefferson marry Sally and change history? My great-great-grandmother had children by the master, and to her that was supposed to have been something. But it was rape." Following a brief silence, the man squirmed; the audience applauded.

The collision and collusion of black and white histories in the exchange and the manner in which they were focused by McCauley's anger was a clear threshold. On the one hand, McCauley had encouraged white spectators to test the limits of their compassion for Sally by engaging in discussion. On the other hand, her attempt to correct the respondent's consciousness of Jefferson ironically wound up inhibiting such tests, insofar as the audience signaled its desire to defer to her authority and to reprimand the respondent with a rousing round of applause. Perhaps this was not what McCauley had intended, that a liberal audience should rally so uncritically behind her. For, if such forms of disingenuous deference can be rationalized as socially virtuous, all that can be said of the white man who claimed that "Jefferson apparently loved [his slave]" is that he failed to provide appropriate compensation.

Later in the discussion, a white woman revealed that, while researching her family's history, she had discovered she was related to a wealthy slave owner, who had allegedly raped his slaves. She talked about how guilty the discovery had made her feel, as if her own blood was contaminated by her ancestor's sins. Laughing nervously, she drew McCauley's attention to the irony of what she regarded as their coincidental meeting: McCauley's ancestor was a slave who had been raped; her ancestor was a rapist of slaves. She continued by thanking McCauley, indicating she understood just how difficult it was for her to talk about slavery given her own resistance to dealing with it "from the other side, as it were." McCauley listened carefully, then thanked the woman for her contribution. "Slavery has affected us all so deeply," she said. "It's a painful past, but you can't throw it away and forget it. This country was built on African slave labor, on Indian land, and we're all living with that history. How can we all admit that and talk to each other about it?" Indeed, it appeared to be just what the white woman had done. She had openly and honestly admitted her complicity in the birth of a nation constructed via the systematic oppression of people of color, and she was willing to talk about it. She had gone as far, in fact, as to infer a possible link between her family and Sally's rape. For the moment, it appeared that no more direct admission of complicity and sincere expression of guilt could exist in a dialogue about race than this.

Beyond a Liberal Audience

"Guilt makes us afraid for ourselves and so generates as much self-preoccupation as concern for others," declares Shelby Steele. "The nature of this preoccupation is always the redemption of innocence, the reestablishment of good feeling about oneself." In this sense, Steele argues, guilt ultimately promotes selfishness as it pushes us "to put our own need for innocence above our concern for the problem that made us feel guilt in the first place." Thus, guilt also generates a pressure to escape the guilt-inducing situation. Steele concludes:

> When selfishness and escapism are at work, we are no longer interested in the source of our guilt and, therefore, no longer concerned with an authentic redemption from it. Now we only want the *look* of redemption, the *gesture* of concern that will give us the appearance of innocence and escape from the situation.[24]

To what extent were whites in the audiences of *Death of a Salesman* and *Sally's Rape* engaged in pursuing such a look and gesture? While it is perhaps likely that some hoped their presence and contributions to postshow dialogues would, in fact, exonerate them, maintain their innocence, or fulfill a gesture of concern for African Americans, as Steele suggests, it is just as likely that the productions redeemed the innocence of others by enabling them to escape an immediate and troubling identification with a black Willy Loman, or with McCauley and the represented and actual histories of her great-great-grandmother's rape. In this respect, Steele—like Giroux, D'Souza, and others critical of contemporary liberalism—articulates a greater degree of tension in the white liberal subject than do overdetermined media stereotypes, yet he fails to provide a theory for a liberal theater audience that does not ultimately reproduce the hegemony of dominant culture.

If Lee's observations about the failure of white audiences to come to a better understanding of African American culture after three decades and more of liberal individual and institutional support for the black performing arts are thus, for the most part, accurate, such a theory is needed. The hypocrisies of white liberalism in contemporary America are more complicated, more detrimental to the development of a coherent multiracial politics, than ever, particularly, as I have suggested, in the theater. A theory for a liberal audience must therefore be founded upon the premise that the hierarchies of white privilege and racism are interlocking and provoke deep and complicated reflection on the tenability of the liberal subject. Further, it must, most importantly, indicate a practice that exposes, rather than recapitulates or reinvents, racism. As the responses of white audiences to African American theater productions in the Twin Cities reveal, the difficulty in developing such a practice hinges not on a lack of good intentions but on the insidious ways many liberal whites seem overtaken by the guilt of white privilege. At the Guthrie and Penumbra, this guilt frequently causes whites to doubt that white people have the authority to talk about race, to doubt that whites are a race, and to conclude that all whites can really do is listen. Such doubts are debilitating and lead to the creation of an audience that has neither knowledge of its principles nor any intention of putting them into service. As Edward Abbey cautions, "Sentiment without action is the ruin of soul."[25] To move beyond this audience is thus to acknowledge that the once-invigorating liberal creeds seem exhausted, that toleration has failed to provide a sufficient basis for cross-cultural understanding and respect, and that, ironically, an intractable sense of guilt associated with privilege should not be alleviated but should be interrogated continually, as a vital source of energy for racial healing in America.

NOTES

1. Quoted in Pete Hamill, "Spike Lee Takes No Prisoners," *Esquire* (Aug. 1991): 26.

2. David Spitz, *The Real World of Liberalism* (Chicago: University of Chicago Press, 1982), 214.

3. Penumbra Theatre, "Audience Profile," Oct. 1997.

4. Shannon Jackson used the term "muddy" to describe the relationship of liberal "talking" and "walking" in "Performance and Deterritorialization: White Privilege, Gender, Pedagogy," a paper presented at the American Society for Theatre Research annual meeting in Pasadena in Nov. 1996. I am grateful to Jackson for sharing this paper with me and for her comments on my work.

5. LeRoi Jones, *"Dutchman" and "The Slave Ship"* (New York: William Morrow, 1964), 36.

6. William Grimes, "An Impassioned Debate on Black Theatre," *Minneapolis Star Tribune* (2 Feb. 1997): F9.

7. For discussion of how the 1996 elections defined liberalism through attacks on Wellstone in Minnesota, see "The Last Living Liberal," *Economist* (19 Oct. 1996): 31; and David Corn, "No Holiday for the Busman," *Nation* (21 Oct. 1996): 15.

8. Shelby Steele, "How Liberals Lost Their Virtue over Race," *Newsweek* (9 Jan. 1995): 41.

9. Charles E. Silberman, *Crisis in Black and White* (New York: Vintage/Random, 1964), 3.

10. Eugene Nesmith, "What's Race Got To Do with It?" *American Theatre* (Mar. 1996): 12.

11. Lou Bellamy, letter, 9 Aug. 1996. Bellamy originally sent this to Peter Vaughn, theater critic for the *Minneapolis Star Tribune*, to clarify Penumbra's position on color-blind casting.

12. Linda Reed, *Simple Decency and Common Sense: The Southern Conference Movement, 1938–1963* (Bloomington: Indiana University Press, 1991), xxv–xxvi.

13. John T. Kneebone, *Southern Liberal Journalists and the Issue of Race, 1920–1944* (Chapel Hill: University of North Carolina Press, 1985), 220–222.

14. Henry A. Giroux, *Border Crossings: Cultural Workers and the Politics of Education* (New York: Routledge, 1993), 116–117.

15. Dinesh D'Souza, *The End of Racism* (New York: Free Press, 1995), 528–531.

16. Jackson n. 2.

17. D'Souza 528.

18. D'Souza 531.

19. At the Guthrie, *Death of a Salesman* ran 19 June–8 Sept 1991; at Penumbra, *Sally's Rape* ran 11 Jan.–5 Feb. 1995.

20. U.S. Department of Commerce, 1990 Census of Population: General Population Characteristics, Minnesota (Washington, D.C.: GPO, 1992), 21.

21. See, for example, Mike Steele, "Dialogue on Difference," *Minneapolis Star Tribune* (26 Jan. 1995): 1E.

22. Erika Thorne, "You Can't Critique Arts from Others' Cultures," *St. Paul Pioneer Press* (22 July 1996): 5.

23. Jayne M. Blanchard, " 'Everlasting Arms' Embraces Deep Emotions," *St. Paul Pioneer Press* (1 June 1996): 5D.

24. Shelby Steele, *The Content of Our Character* (New York: St. Martin's, 1990), 84–85.

25. Quoted in Terry Tempest Williams, "Edward Abbey," *Outside* (Oct. 1997): 140.

Part II

Cultural Traditions, Cultural Memory, and Performance

5

Deep Skin

Reconstructing Congo Square

JOSEPH R. ROACH

I believe it to be a fact that the colored people of this country know
and understand the white people better than the white people will
ever know and understand themselves.

James Weldon Johnson

French historian Pierre Nora distinguishes between "places of memory," the
modern repositories of social memory that range from monuments to theme
parks, and "environments of memory," the predominantly oral systems of
cultural transmission in traditional societies. Among the several stimulating
problems raised by such a distinction is its segregation of one kind of people
from another. On the one hand, Nora imagines the literate yet increasingly
amnesiac inhabitants of the modernized *lieux de mémoire*, who patronize
stunted, artificial shrines to ethnic and national identity; on the other, there
are the old folks back home in the *milieux de mémoire*.[1] In *Cities of the Dead:
Circum-Atlantic Performance*, I proposed some alternatives to Nora's theories
of memory based on the model of intercultural performance. Such an approach
interrogates the familiar dichotomy of literacy and orality: it acknowledges
that speech and writing have produced one another interactively over time;
further, it imagines people who are possessed of various modes of communication living together at the same time, even—now and then, here and
there—in the same place at the same time. I found these to be the conditions
prevailing in the performance-saturated interculture of New Orleans, and I
attempted to demonstrate the ways in which that city "performs as a simu-
lacrum of itself, apparently frozen in time, but in fact busily devoted to the
ever-changing task of recreating the illusion that it is frozen in time."[2]

Fundamental to the character of this complex and often contradictory
enterprise is the self-renewing energy of African American performance

traditions. They continuously and powerfully frustrate linear narratives and positivist histories, Eurocentric fables in which the popular fiction known as the dominant culture requires the segregation of the dead from the living—as well as speech from writing and "facts" from "myths"—in order to identify itself with a spurious modernity. This is not limited to New Orleans, although it makes itself starkly visible there. One of the most important challenges facing all scholars in theater and performance studies today is how to do justice to the centrality of African American contributions to cultural life in the United States. In terms of the performing arts, beginning but not ending with jazz and modern dance, African American forms and those derived from them constitute the mainstream, not the margin, and their history as such has only begun to be written.

Writing that history is complicated, as are so many of our most worthy national projects, by skin. Skin is the principal medium that has carried the past into the present in the city of New Orleans and elsewhere, a continuing odyssey mapped by the sinuous track of *Plessy v. Ferguson* through the heart of America. Skin has been and continues to be not only a document but also a performance, persisting as such notwithstanding the courageous resistance of many unwilling participants in the bogus and cruel expansion of its meanings. These meanings metastasize differences that are only skin deep into what I am calling *deep skin*, a melanoma of the imagination: skin deepens into the cancer of race when supposed inner essences and stereotypical behaviors are infected by it in the collective fantasies of one people about another. The malignancy of deep skin usually begins with a blank space or a kind of erasure, which empties out the possibility of empathetic response, but this cavity quickly fills with bizarre growths. First, deep skin becomes invisible; then, after the passage of time—the twinkling of an eye is all that is required—it alone remains visible.

The consequences of deep skin are easy to deplore, difficult to escape. They complicate the writing of history, especially the history of a practice as evanescent as performance, because the authors of eyewitness accounts and other documentary sources on which historians depend were distracted from the cultural productions they observed by the skins not only of the performers but also of the witnesses. Among the skin tones in the sources I have studied most carefully, whiteness is at least as stubbornly intractable as nonwhiteness because, as "the unexamined norm against which all differences are measured," it is more likely to remain unacknowledged, "transparent," however deeply its diseased roots may be embedded in the mind of the beholder.[3] Historians cannot remind themselves too often that when it comes to skins, deep whiteness depends for its meaning on deep nonwhiteness. This disavowed dependency raises the stakes of deep skin for those who consider themselves white. No matter how compelling the performance might be, the skin of the nonwhite performer deepens until art can be reduced to nature: one man's structure of musical temporality becomes another man's natural rhythm. The works are thus denuded of their context in a particular culture and consigned to a limbo of essential skin.

For these and many other reasons, the history of African American performances must include their living memory, not only in the restrictive sense
of formal reconstructions of classic works (although that is necessary and
important) but also in the expansive sense of experiencing what Nora calls
"environments of memory." The implications of this inclusiveness for historians of performance are powerful. The built environment and dynamic
human geography of the circum-Atlantic cityscape itself becomes a perfor-
mance/document, unfolding at once as a scripted text (permanent paths,
borders, nodes, landmarks) and as an acoustical, kinesthetic event (markets,
parades, street music, carnivals). Valuable for their own sake, these events
also provide a context (and often an inspiration) for the works of individual
artists framed by more conventional performance venues. As the jazz virtuoso
Louis Armstrong said about growing up in the streets of New Orleans: "Yeah,
music all around you."[4]

It is, in fact, the New Orleans historical site now named after Armstrong
that provides a concise case study of the struggle of memory and history in
the crucible of performance.

As a consultant on a documentary film project called *Spirit Tides from Congo
Square*, I was recently called upon to make suggestions about how to "recon-
struct" Congo Square. With initial funding by the Ford Foundation and
produced by author Jason Berry, the project has provided an occasion for a
practical test of the mediation between history and memory in representing
the African diaspora through performance. The name of Congo Square appears in virtually every account of the retention of Africanisms in American
culture and in most histories of jazz. Scholars know with as much certainty
as positive history can prove that, on this small plot of ground, slaves gathered
at carefully regulated times to sing and dance in a variety of musical styles,
including ones based on African or Afro-Caribbean forms (figure 5.1). The
"slave dances" continued well into the nineteenth century, and the square
became a celebrated tourist destination as well as a popular spot for Sunday
recreation by the locals. Although musicologists have failed to find positive
evidence of direct links between Congo Square and jazz, the belief that such
links did exist is strong in local tradition, reinforced in recent times by the
incorporation of the site into Armstrong Park and the location of the "Jazz
and Heritage" radio station WWOZ nearby. In the words of the *Spirit Tides*
project grant application:

> Congo Square occupies mythical status in New Orleans history. From the
> 1790s through 1851, a small area along ramparts of the colony, now
> encompassed by Louis Armstrong Park, was the site of Sunday dances by
> slaves. The sustained presence of the dances left a deep mark on the city's
> folkways.[5]

It is in the documentation—and celebration—of those folkways that the
Spirit Tides project has cast its lot. The city is living evidence of its past, not
merely in the built environment but also in the acoustical and kinesthetic
ones. Therefore, the film will contain extraordinary footage and various

Figure 5.1   Slave ring shout, Congo Square, New Orleans. Courtesy Historic
New Orleans Collection, Museum Research Center.

commentaries on the role of jazz funerals, better known to locals as "being
buried with music," in order to demonstrate the enduring power of African
musical and choreographic traditions in daily life today (see figure 5.2). It
will include graphic visual and acoustical accounts of the wave of "crack
funerals" in the 1990s—rites of passage wherein a number of young men,
whose violent deaths were blamed on cocaine-fueled drug wars, were buried
in low-down funk versions of the traditional New Orleans rituals. Supporting
fellow consultant J. H. Kwabena Nketia, director of the International Centre
for African Music and Dance in Ghana, I attempted to summarize the case
for the strategic inclusions of footage of contemporary performances, including dance reconstructions, in the film:

> This strategy foregrounds the problem that most interests me as an his-
> torian of performance: the need to respect memories that remain in pos-
> session of the living who, in opposition to an historic record that has been
> selectively inscribed (and erased), continue to honor their dead as contem-
> poraries. What I am suggesting here is deploying afrocentric as well as
> eurocentric views of history and memory in order to treat this extraordinary
> subject in the depth it deserves. When skeptics ask me about reconstructing
> historic performances, the first question I ask them in return is: What
> makes you think they aren't still going on?[6]

I further suggested that the memorial life of the city, contained in materials
as diverse as George Washington Cable's novel *The Grandissimes* (1880) and
a contemporary debate about street performances, is as relevant to the reconstruction of Congo Square as the more traditional documentary sources.
Above and beyond adding to the quantity of memories, these unconventional
sources suggest that there are better ways of remembering.

Figure 5.2   Alfred "Dute" Lazard funeral, New Orleans (1995). Photo by Michael P. Smith.

In 1997–1998 residents of the increasingly gentrified historic New Orleans French Quarter pushed forward an antinoise ordinance aimed at curtailing the performances of the musicians who entertain passersby in the tourist-filled streets. The law seemed to be aimed especially at the "spasm bands," which tend to draw their membership from teenagers who reside in the predominantly African American community of Treme, which is located across Rampart Street from the French Quarter. Rampart Street, as its name implies, occupies the ground that once accommodated the defensive palisade protecting the fortified colonial city from its enemies without. Today, it separates the French Quarter not only from the residential Treme neighborhood but from Armstrong Park, which commemorates the site of Congo Square, which originally stood just outside the city walls, not far from the cemetery. A city of memory like New Orleans is literally layered with substitutions—palimpsests of adaptive use. In the case of Rampart Street, the palisade gave way to a street, but the street threatens to become a wall once more. A 1998 letter to the editor of the New Orleans *Times-Picayune* proposed just such a retrograde substitution in response to a perceived increase in crimes perpetrated in the French Quarter by youths who then "vanished into Treme." The letter reads in part: "It seems to me that to control criminal activity within the Quarter, the perimeter of the Quarter must be controlled. This means numerous police cars on Rampart at all hours observing and the questioning of suspicious-looking persons." The author goes on to enumerate the characteristics of suspicious-looking persons in rhetoric that clearly differentiates between those citizens whose business it is to know and those whose proper fate it is to be known:

> Let's don't pretend we don't know what a suspicious-looking person is. Anyone who has lived in New Orleans for more than a day knows the characteristics of suspicious-looking persons—walking with apparently no particular destination, constantly looking into cars, traversing the same area again and again, that wild-eyed, drug-crazed predatory look, etc. These people should be questioned and asked for ID.[7]

In an urban pleasure dome notorious for its public drunkenness, bustling drug scene, and aimlessly strolling gawkers, the behaviors described here need not by any means have originated outside the French Quarter. Yet the author calls for a defensive "perimeter" along the precise axis laid down by French military engineers in 1719, replete with armed sentries to challenge the approaching strangers and to repel their attacks. In this letter, the word *skin* need not be spoken because the quality of the bodily movements in the urban space designated speak for themselves. The code remains intelligible enough in the memorial organization of the cityscape that the proximity of the words *perimeter*, *rampart*, and *predatory* alone will suffice to stand in for skin and deepen it into race. Only somewhat more moderately coded rhetoric issued from the mouths of proponents of the antinoise ordinance opposing the "assault" on the French Quarter by members of the Treme brass bands. The story that they are telling is getting very old.

Although it is set at the time of the Louisiana Purchase, George Washington Cable's *The Grandissimes* is written from the authorial perspective shaped by the catastrophe, contemporaneous with its writing, of the collapse of Reconstruction and the rise of the Bourbon Redeemers. In this epoch, which arguably has not yet ended as history and certainly not as memory, the culture of race slavery was itself partially reconstructed by means legal and illegal. Looking back to Jim Crow through *The Grandissimes*, as Cable looked back to the early period of "Americanization" through his reconstruction of remembered events that remained visible in contemporary behaviors, it is possible to imagine the present as a tangled web of consequences through which the past effectively continues to perform itself.

In *The Grandissimes*, memory and history coalesce around a carefully placed reconstruction of Congo Square. Cable published his ethnohistorical research on the subject in *Century Magazine* (Feb. 1886) under the title "The Dance in Place Congo," but his fictional account, which includes an extensive reconstruction of the social and cultural milieu of the surrounding city, is ultimately a more trustworthy guide to the significance of the site. He imaginatively evokes a comprehensive soundscape through his insertion of notated musical examples and his descriptions of the conscious and unconscious listening of many of the novel's characters: "The cathedral clock struck twelve and answered again from the convent tower; as the notes died he suddenly became aware that the weird throb of the African song and dance had been swinging drowsily in his brain for an unknown lapse of time."[8]

Cable is reimagining a moment in time from which living memory has receded, but the acoustical environment of the city, with church bells answering spasm bands, is a tangible reminder that cities endure not only in their buildings but through their performances.

In that regard, architect Benjamin Henry Latrobe's eyewitness account from 1819 generally supports the fictionalized details in *The Grandissimes*. Walking up St. Peter Street in the French Quarter on a Sunday afternoon, Latrobe became aware of "a most extraordinary sound," which he compared to "horses trampling on [a] wooden floor." As he crossed the street where the old rampart had stood and approached Congo Square, he found five or six hundred *"blacks"* (his emphasis as he saw only a few mulattoes). Typically, the Anglo-American city planner first remarked on the skin color of the multitudes, then went on to deplore their noise. The crowd divided itself into many smaller circles. In the middle of each circle, couples or solo dancers performed. Musicians played African drums and stringed instruments, which Latrobe later sketched, and some sang in a language that the architect took to be African. What his untutored ear heard as cacophony—horses stomping on a wooden floor—was very likely a polyrhythmic, call-and-response chorus of drums and voices, the master trope of the musical diaspora. Latrobe responded with disgust, which was intensified by his fear at encountering so many unsupervised slaves together in one place: "I have never seen anything so brutally savage," he concluded.[9] His attitude reflects a frequently noted ambivalence of Anglo-American spectators as they performed their deep skin at the slave dances by telling each other how scandalized they were even as they pushed and shoved to obtain a better view. These spectators were privileged to witness the syncretic production of African and Afro-Caribbean cultural practices, of which the dances were but one aspect, at a key nodal point of a city astride the crossroads of the emerging Atlantic world.

Once the location of Native American corn feasts, the patch of spare ground that became Congo Square began in the eighteenth century as an unofficial marketplace, where African slaves, Indians, and free people of color could mingle with relative freedom, exchange their goods, and recreate themselves. In 1816, it was occupied by a Cuban impresario, Signore Gaetano, who operated his whites-only Congo Circus there for many years. The name of the square might have derived from this Havana-based melange of acrobats, contortionists, and bear baitings. In 1820, a fence was added to control access and contain the crowds. The many different names by which the square has been known recall its contested history: Place des Negres, Place du Cirque, Place Congo, Congo Circus, La Place Publique, Circus Public Square, Congo Plains, Place d'Armes, P. G. T. Beauregard Park (after the Confederate general), and, finally, Armstrong Park.[10] During the 1840s and 1850s, the slave dances dwindled and eventually ceased, but as the square emptied out, smaller spaces in neighborhoods around the city filled with music, dancing, and spirit world practices, which occasioned complaints from the neighbors about the noise.[11] In the composition of the soundscape in an environment of memory, whether shaped by law or by custom, even silence resonates with its own aesthetic and social meanings.

Writing as the Redeemers intensified their efforts to exclude people of color from every aspect of public life and to write them out of history, Cable reconstructed Congo Square in a way that celebrated the African presence in American memory while simultaneously exoticizing it as the locus of bizarre noises and fantastic movements somehow linked to skin:

> It was on a Sabbath afternoon that a band of Choctaws having just played a game of racquette behind the city and a similar game being about to end between the white champions of two rival faubourgs, the beating of tom-toms, rattling of mules' jawbones and sounding of wooden horns drew the populace across the fields to a spot whose present name of Congo Square still preserves a reminder of old barbaric pastimes. On a grassy plain under the ramparts, the performers of these hideous discords sat upon the ground facing each other, and in their midst the dancers danced. They gyrated in couples, a few at a time, throwing their bodies into the most startling attitudes and the wildest contortions, while the whole company of black lookers-on, incited by the tones of the weird music and the violent posturing of the dancers, swayed and writhed in passionate sympathy, beating their breasts, palms and thighs in time with the bones and drums, and at frequent intervals lifting, in that wild African unison no more to be described than forgotten, the unutterable songs of the Babouille and Counjaille dances, with their ejaculatory burdens of *"Aie! Voudou Magnan!"* and *"Aie Calinda! Dance Calinda!"* (*The Grandissimes* 189)

This fictional account synthesizes the details Cable assembled in his *Century Magazine* article. Although many subsequent authorities have quoted his descriptions of the slave dances without questioning Cable's methods, both Johnson, in his definitive article on Congo Square, and S. Frederick Starr, in his biography of composer Louis Moreau Gottschalk, draw skeptical attention to the novelist's use of Médéric Moreau de Saint-Méry's *Déscription topographique de l'Isle Saint-Domingue* (1797) and *De la danse* (1801).[12] These sources describe African-descended dances in Haiti, and Cable appropriated some of their particulars into "The Dance in Place Congo" and *The Grandissimes*. But why not? In opposition to the racial polarity championed by the Redeemers, Cable's goal was not to exalt the seamlessness of origins in a pristine local culture but to comprehend its ethnic profusion: many Haitian refugees, free and slave, arrived in New Orleans after the dislocations of the revolutionary period, while smugglers defied the ban on importation and brought in slaves directly from Africa. Eyewitnesses to the dances in Congo Square variously report slaves playing drums, gourds, reed pipes, cow horns, violins, banjo-like stringed instruments with African gods carved in the handles, marimbas, horses' jawbones, triangles, tambourines, and cremonas. They note costumes of animal hides, fringes, ribbons, percale dresses, silk sashes, and "Turkish" turbans of many hues. They observe dancers from at least four distinct tribal groups, some with filed teeth, keeping their distance in separate circles.[13] This reminds the unaware that no one arrived at a New World destination from a monolithic place called "Africa" but rather from one or more particular cultures on the circum-Atlantic rim.

In *The Grandissimes*, Cable takes advantage of the poetic license of fiction to evoke memories that history too often undervalues. That is what makes so compelling his careful placement of the Congo Square scene just before the climactic moment of the capture, torture, and death of the semimythical maroon Bras-Coupe. In Cable's terms, this character claims a direct link to Africa, but, like the dancers in the square, he embodies its memory in a series of diasporic substitutions:

> His name, he replied to an inquiry touching that subject, was _____
> _____, something in the Jaloff tongue, which he by and by condescended to render into Congo: Mioko-Koanga, in French Bras-Coupe, the Arm Cut Off. . . . He had made himself a type of all Slavery, turning into flesh and blood the truth that Slavery is maiming. (*The Grandissimes* 170–171)

The blanks in Cable's text record in print a lapse of living memory, but in the space created by the absence of the words in the "Jaloff tongue," another African name stands in, only to be succeeded, in the process of memory as substitution, by a French translation of the "Congo" name and then by an English translation of the French. Colonial slave importation to French Louisiana drew heavily on the peoples of Senegambia, and the Wolof (Djolaufs) of that region were regarded with special favor because of their bearing and aptitude.[14] The historic Bras-Coupe, "the greatest Bamboula dancer ever to shake the earth in Congo Square," whose slave name was Squire, became a folk hero to slaves and a figure of awe and dread to slaveholders, who remembered him as the "Brigand of the Swamp" after he "gathered a band of renegade slaves and led them in nocturnal raids on the plantations in the neighborhood."[15] Although it was widely believed that bullets passed right through his body without effect, he was finally killed in July 1837, and his corpse was publicly displayed. Cable juxtaposes his version of the story of the death of Bras-Coupe to his reconstruction of Congo Square. In each instance, the memory of Africa is displaced by substitutes that stand in for the romantic but fugitive original.

With the depth of their white skins at stake, eyewitnesses and commentators on the memory of Congo Square stress its violence. Even the liberal Cable does so. In part, this simply exemplifies an ignorant response to complex performance events by observers whose literacy blinds them to the techniques of oral transmission through performance. They misrecognize the bodily memory of restored behavior as spontaneous, "uncontrolled" expression. In 1826, Timothy Flint of Massachusetts published an account of a journey down the Mississippi to New Orleans. He included a valuable description of a slave dance, which clearly made a deep impression on this New Englander's imagination:

The great Congo-dance is performed. Every thing is license and revelry. Some hundreds of negroes, male and female, follow the king of the wake, who is conspicuous for his youth, size, the whiteness of his eyes, and the blackness of his visage. For a crown he has a series of oblong, gilt-paper boxes on his head, tapering upwards, like a pyramid. From the ends of those boxes hang two huge tassels, like those on epaulets. He wags his head and makes grimaces. By his thousand mountebank tricks, and contortions of countenance and form, he produces an irresistible effect on the multitude. All the characters that follow him, of leading estimation, have their own peculiar dress, and their own contortions. They dance, and their streamers fly, and the bells that they have hung about them tinkle.[16]

Flint does not locate the source of the procession, which resembles in most details a traditional New Orleans "Second Line" parade or jazz funeral, but the descriptive phrase "Congo-dance" might point back in the direction of Congo Square. Perhaps what is most significant about this passage, however, is that the procession, with its "license and revelry," its tintinnabulations, and its vibrant choreography, has spilled out into the streets. In defiance of the laws against slave assembly (other than in Congo Square on Sunday afternoons), the procession follows a king, whose dark visage, framed by fantastic headwear (see figure 5.3), leads the "multitudes" onward like a flag. Predictably, Flint finds the skin not only dark but also deep: "The negro is easily excitable, and in the highest degree susceptible of all the passions."[17]

Deep skin has yet to relinquish its hold over the construction of the past. The future is uncertain. A key strategy for scholars is to demonstrate both the historical and contemporary roles of African American performance genres. The most intense debate among the *Spirit Tides* consultants centered on the difficulty of interpreting (and even the propriety of using) the "crack funeral" footage. Details of physical movement, musical style, and ritual practices informed the discussion, which resembled a panel of English professors of different theoretical persuasions engaging one another over a contested close reading of a difficult text. Some were fearful that the explicitness of the material, which included a grieving mother dancing with abandon on the coffin of her murdered son and scores of chanting teenagers spraying beer over the casket, would "reinforce negative stereotypes" of African Americans. In the cultural thrall of deep skin, that is not a trivial concern. Traditionalists lamented the decline of the old jazz funerals and interpreted the abandonment of some of their more stately features as evidence of "social decay." Apologists for the crack funerals celebrated the astonishing adaptability of the venerable rituals to accommodate themselves to a contemporary crisis in the community.

I thought that the sincere misgivings of the traditionalists could best be answered by citing Cable, Flint, Latrobe, and others who beheld the rites of African American memory in the nineteenth century and found them licentious or barbaric. At an Afro-Catholic interment in 1819, Latrobe stood aghast at the spectacle of children pounding on a wooden coffin lid with

Figure 5.3   Chief Victor Harris. Spirit of the Fi Yi Yi. Photo by Keith Calhoun.

human bones, adding their din to the "noise and laughter," which had "become general by the time the service was over."[18] But the service was not over. One of its most important prerequisites consisted of the ritual moment that is now called "cutting the body loose," which sets off a wave of lively music and motion, a celebration of death as a means of joyously affirming the continuity of the community on the occasion of marking the passing of one of its own. The crack funerals revered this tradition in their own way.

What is needed at this moment is a heightened awareness of the city of New Orleans—and other American cities—as a repository of perform-ances of great beauty and world historic significance of which every citi-zen can be proud. African-descended traditions are central among these forms. Cable's novel owes much of its best material to the pervasive presence of African performance traditions, a revealing instance of the collaboration of literate and oral techniques in the transmission of culture. Can Congo Square be reconstructed without perpetuating the canard of deep skin? If Rampart Street becomes a wall again, hope dwindles. But if the old street can be reclaimed as a path between the past and the present by appropriating it for jazz processions everyone can join, then the odds improve. In this contest between places and environments of memory, the name "Congo Square" has come to represent not only the preservation of inspiring memories of Africa and the diaspora but, even more important, the revitalization of African ways of remembering. If they were to grow into general use, chances are that all peoples would come to know and understand themselves better as a result.

NOTES

1. Pierre Nora, "Between Memory and History: *Les Lieux de Mémoire,*" *Representations* 26 (Spring 1989): 7–75.

2. Joseph R. Roach, *Cities of the Dead: Circum-Atlantic Performance* (New York: Columbia University Press, 1996), 180.

3. Kwame Anthony Appiah and Henry Louis Gates, Jr., "White Skin, White Masks," in "The White Issue," *Transition: An International Review* 73 (n.d.): 5.

4. Louis Armstrong, "Growing Up in New Orleans," in *New Orleans Stories,* ed. John Miller (San Francisco: Chronicle, 1992), 26.

5. Jason Berry, "Spirit Tides from Congo Square," Planning Conference, 6–7 Mar. 1998.

6. Letter to Jason Berry, 19 Mar. 1998, summarizing the panel discussion on *Spirit Tides from Congo Square,* involving Samuel Floyd, Gwendolyn Midlo Hall, Jerah Johnson, Sybil Kein, J. H. Kwabena Nketia, Bruce Raeburn, Michael Smith, Michael White, and Les Blanc.

7. New Orleans *Times-Picayune,* 11 July 1998.

8. George Washington Cable, *The Grandissimes,* ed. Michael Kreyling (New York: Penguin, 1988), 96. Subsequent citations of this edition will be given in the text.

9. Benjamin Henry Latrobe, *Journals, 1799–1820: From Philadelphia to New Orleans,* ed. Edward C. Carter II, John C. Van Horne, and Lee W. Formwalt (New Haven, Conn.: Yale University Press, 1980), 203–204.

10. Jerah Johnson, *Congo Square in New Orleans* (New Orleans: Louisiana Landmarks Society, 1995), 34.

11. Henry A. Kmen, *Music in New Orleans: The Formative Years, 1791–1841* (Baton Rouge: Louisiana State University Press, 1966), 228–130.

12. Johnson 38, n. 42; Frederick Starr, *Bamboula! The Life and Times of Louis Moreau Gottschalk* (New York: Oxford University Press, 1995), 41.

13. Johnson 37–40.

14. Gwendolyn Midlo Hall, *Africans in Colonial Louisiana: The Development of Afro-Creole Culture in the Eighteenth Century* (Baton Rouge: Louisiana State University Press, 1992), 40–41.

15. Lyle Saxon, Edward Dreyer, and Robert Tallant, *Gumbo Ya-Ya: A Collection of Louisiana Folk Tales* (1945; reprint, Gretna, La.: Pelican, 1988), 253.

16. Timothy Flint, *Recollections of the Last Ten Years, Passed in Occasional Residences and Journeyings in the Valley of the Mississippi* (Boston: Cummings, Hilliard, 1826), 140.

17. Flint 139.

18. Latrobe 302.

6

"Calling on the Spirit"

The Performativity of Black Women's Faith in
the Baptist Church Spiritual Traditions and
Its Radical Possibilities for Resistance

TELIA U. ANDERSON

Here, in this here place, we flesh; flesh that weeps, laughs; flesh
that dances on bare feet in grass. Love it. Love it hard. Yonder they
do not love your flesh. They despise it. . . . Love your hands! Love
them. Touch others with them, pat them together, stroke them on
your face 'cause they don't love that either. You got to love it, you!
And no, they ain't in love with your mouth. Yonder, out there,
they will see it broken and break it again. What you say out of it
they will not heed. What you scream from it they do not hear. This
is flesh I'm talking about here. Flesh that needs to be loved. Feet
that need to rest and to dance; backs that need support; shoulders
that need arms, strong arms I'm telling you. . . . Saying no more,
she stood up then and danced with her twisted hip the rest of what
her heart had to say while the others opened their mouths and gave
her the music. Long notes held until the four-part harmony was
perfect enough for their deeply loved flesh.[1]

I ask no favors for my sex. I surrender not our claim to equality. All
I ask of our brethren is, that they will take their feet from off our
necks, and permit us to stand upright on that ground which God
designed us to occupy.[2]

I grew up in a Baptist church where people knew how to get the spirit. You
never knew when the woman next to you would get the spirit, and in an
instant, she would no longer be Mrs. Evans, or your best friend's mother, or
your own mother, but Spirit and not answerable to any call other than that

of God's. You could only move out of her way so that she could sway, jump, and roll on down the aisle. Calling on the spirit was serious business; moved by the rhythm of the music, the hollering of the choir, and the stamping of the preacher, practically every Sunday a woman would "fall out," shouting and writhing with the power of the Holy Ghost. As a child, I was terrified that I would "catch" it, too. In truly holy churches not just women but children also caught the spirit. I was at once mystified and repelled by this force, which caused women to raise themselves from their seats, to forget who or where they were, to jump up and down with skirts raised (discarding all conventions of modesty), to leave infants to fend for themselves in pews, to shout, and to speak in unknowable languages. I was awed by the free reign such a woman had; no one tried to get her to stop or even to restrain her. A woman in the spirit was left alone to have her personal time with God ("My God," "Can't nobody tell me about my God"); and if her visitation interrupted the authority and privileged space of the preacher, so be it. By the time I viewed this phenomenon as an adult, I had begun to realize that a black woman's most powerful weapon against the devastating effects of patriarchy both within and outside of the church is her internal connection with the divine.

In this article, I will explore how black women, through "calling the spirit" (also known as "getting happy," "shouting," or "stomping"), operate a radical Africanist performance strategy that accesses and enacts a personal and corporeal divine authority, which challenges church patriarchy. Although this practice is not exclusively the domain of women, it is one that achieves its fullest expression and vibrancy when engaged by the mostly female congregation of the black church. By extension, I will also show how black women adapt this strategy of resistance to less-hallowed venues as well and, in so doing, prove false the traditional European dichotomy of "sacred" and "secular" in a phenomenon through which black women's bodies and spirits signify, indeed, augur beyond their immediate, present circumstances. Although the church may be the most sanctified arena for the evocation and the "catching" of the Holy Ghost and may even be considered the primary source for this expression, the Spirit, and the call of such, is not exclusively accessed in the Lord's House or, at least, not as this moniker is typically understood; rather, the Spirit surges from within bodies and minds consecrated to this holiness language and performance. Those who are not bound to the conventions and strictures of their singular, present reality may be open to receiving the call.

The unfortunate dialectic of sacred-profane has hindered a holistic examination of black religious practices in the past and, perhaps, still does. I will attempt to bridge (or, at least, avoid replicating) this stubborn schism by reasserting the fluidity of the boundaries of the black church and, particularly, the theatricality of black women's expression, irrespective of venue or environment. With black women's voices, bodies, spirits, and minds as movable orchestration, black women can set up "church" anywhere. In addition, drawing upon the work of discursive black female scholars, I will examine black women's spectacular glossolalic performances in which indecipherable words of faith sound the most holy triumph of spirit over oppression.

Calling on the Spirit

Quoting Antonio Gramsci in his treatise on African American revolutionary Christianity, Cornel West notes, "Any political consciousness of an oppressed group is shaped and molded by the group's cultural resources and resiliency as perceived by individuals in it."[3] Although the exigencies of the slave trade and three centuries of captivity did not permit the cultural preservation of captured Africans and instead brought about the total and complete destruction of an overwhelming number of their cultural resources, "one of the most durable and adaptable constituents of the slave's culture" was her religion.[4] The openness and adaptability of African faiths to syncretism made them the healthy provenance of charismatic forms of worship, which are still found in the United States and in the African diaspora. Black people sustain an impressive tradition of African worship, from rites of possession to the identification of a personal, corporeal relationship with the divine.[5]

The origin of this tradition easily traces to Africa from whence captives brought their religious traditions and beliefs. However, as emphasized by Albert J. Raboteau and other black religious scholars, the African expressions of religious faith and worship are not so much "retentions" of old rituals as revisions and adaptations born from the intervention of and interrelation with white, European Christianity. Evangelical Protestantism of the eighteenth and nineteenth centuries and, in particular, the revivals, permitted and encouraged emotional, charismatic expressions of religious passion. In the conversion to Christianity, the African religious heritage of the slave survived through adaptation.[6] Raboteau tells us:

> Despite the prohibition of dancing as heathenish and sinful, the slaves were able to reinterpret and "sanctify" their African tradition of dance in the "shout." While the North American slaves danced under the impulse of the Spirit of a "new" God, they danced in ways their fathers in Africa would have recognized.[7]

Soon, converted African slaves began setting up their own Christian churches amidst virulent and frequently violent opposition from some whites. Almost invariably, early black churches were under the watchful eye of a white pastor, and the later ones operated under the threat of restrictions.[8] As has been documented and revealed by Raboteau, the black ministry rejected the obedience training disguised as religious catechism proffered by white slave masters and clergy. Instead, slave ministers held secret meetings in the woods (or gullies, ravines, thickets—"hush harbors"),[9] where they would preach sermons to fellow slaves.[10] They readily seized upon interpretations of the Bible that condemned the existence of slavery: "They'd pray, 'Lord, deliver us from under bondage.' "[11] Using scriptural texts as weapons, some slave preachers even led revolts throughout the South.

Irrespective of its numerous doctrinal affiliations, the black church in its myriad manifestations countered white brutality and degradation of African Americans with, to borrow from Cornel West's usage, a "prophetic" vision of black triumph over their oppressors. Survival by slaves depended largely on their resisting the white supremacist project, which, among other oppressions, cast them as grotesquely inferior beings without redemption. By helping to steer the way to black freedom and by nurturing and supporting one of the most crucial spaces of resistance and rejuvenation of African American people—the black church—black women are, in large part, responsible for the cultural and spiritual survival of their people.

However, the black church has a long-standing tradition of gender inequality, in which black women have been unceasingly embattled. Historically, black male leaders of the church have insisted upon adopting the resolutely patriarchal ministry of their white Christian forebears, even as they strove to purify the white theologies of abject racist instruction. It is the peculiar irony of the black church that, while scores of its members (of various denominations) actively transformed an analysis of black oppression into an ethic of black liberation, the churches continued to reinforce the dominant culture's sexual hierarchy, solidly installing black men in the upper ranks of the church's schema of privilege and power. As a result, black women have been almost completely consigned to the position of subordinate. Women, particularly in the nineteenth-century black Baptist churches, were not allowed to become clergy, pray publicly, or attend business meetings in the church. And African Methodist and Episcopal churches were no more progressive about extending equal ecclesiastical rights to women; for years, many of these churches segregated church seating by gender: men in front, women in back.[12]

In *Righteous Discontent*, Evelyn Higginbotham asserts that black Baptist women's organizations mobilized support for equal treatment of men and women in the church and expanded the social and political realm of the Baptist church: "Indeed, one could say that the Black Baptist Church represented a sphere for public deliberation and debate precisely because of women."[13] Ten thousand black women attended the Baptist Women's State Convention in 1890, and "Women's Day" church services owe their genesis to this momentous event.[14] Still, women faced an arduous battle for acceptance in the church. The first National Baptist Convention in 1895, which brought together the largest group of black Americans ever assembled, religious or secular, emphasized the needs and leadership of black men in the church over that of the majority of black women, who buttressed their efforts. Although black clergymen certainly recognized that women's active participation in the church helped them toward their goal of racial self-help and self-reliance, they nonetheless refused to modify male-oriented traditions to allow women their voice. Black men embraced the values of the larger American society, seeking to provide themselves with "full manhood rights," while relegating women to a separate and unequal status.[15]

Like their male counterparts in counteracting Christian rationalizations for slavery, black women in the National Baptist Convention used scriptural texts to "validate, support, and legitimate their exhortations for equality."[16] Black women also held meetings in their homes to minister to each other. In her dissertation on black female ministry of the nineteenth century, Gloria Davis Goode documents the histories of African American women "who viewed themselves as itinerant ministers, but who were not regarded as such by their male counterparts nor recognized by church congregations."[17] Although the development of women's organizations is significant, and Higginbotham takes issue with an overemphasis on the "exceptional" female congregant and/or minister, this chapter is more concerned with the behavior of black females on the micro level of the church. The experience of at least one of these "exceptional" women sheds light on the everyday practice of resistance by less-noted black women in the church.

Sometime between 1803 and 1810, by moving with the spirit in church, Jarena Lee became the first female preacher of the African Methodist Episcopal church. Previously, Lee had met with Richard Allen, the founder of the African Methodist Episcopal church, and urged him to allow her to preach a service in his church. Although relatively liberal with regard to women parishioners at that time—Allen allowed women to hold prayer meetings and to exhort the unsaved—he would not agree to a woman leading a sermon. At first, Lee conformed to Allen's wishes; after a short period, however, she performed her faith as called by the Holy Spirit before hundreds of witnesses:

> Unrestrained in a church service in which the Spirit moved her, she leaped to her feet and expounded on the preacher's text. Instead of admonishing her, Allen, the bishop, stated that he believed that she was called to preach as much as any of the preachers present.[18]

In her autobiography, Jarena Lee recalled the moment of her catching the Spirit: "During this the minister was silent, until my soul felt its duty had been performed."[19] Many would-be female preachers adopted Lee's method of gaining the attention of the congregation by standing up in the middle of a clergyman's sermon and starting to preach. Women seized the moment during any brief pause that the minister took, whether to catch his breath or to collect his thoughts. Preaching spontaneously before a large congregation became a tactic that women used against church officials who denied them legitimate access to preaching. Theirs was an especially effective performance because ministers did not wish to suffer the embarrassment of asking someone to cease praising the Lord in church. Furthermore, women were not often admonished for this activity because it was believed that the Holy Spirit had come upon them, and therefore they were not personally responsible for disrupting the service. Ministers of churches (who naturally opposed the threat to their power and authority) had their doubts about the veracity of the claims by these female devotees of the Spirit, but the strong tradition of an experiential, personal relationship with the divine in the African American community persuaded most people to believe. Says Goode, "To these spiritual women, real-life experiences were worth more than rigid doctrine and speculative theory because no one could deny the validity of another's personal testimony based on first-hand knowledge."[20] Once a woman performed in this "guerrilla" fashion, if the congregants seemed to appreciate her message, she may have been allowed to preach a sermon of her own.[21]

Unfortunately, the steadfast hierarchy of gender in the black church persists. It is still inconceivable in most black churches for a woman to lead worship services, to baptize, or in many cases, to even enter the pulpit. Even though black women's monumental importance to the black church can hardly be overstated, an ecclesiastical glass ceiling still exists. Black women abundantly occupy roles such as ushers, nurses' aids, missionaries, assistants, choir members, cooks, Sunday school teachers, and secretaries in the church, but rarely, if ever, do they break through to assume the roles of bishop, pastor, leader, deacon, steward, trustee, general officer, or director. Although black women currently make up, on the average, two-thirds to three-quarters of black church membership, the church patriarchy is not willing to relinquish privilege and is reluctant to share power in any official capacity with its overwhelmingly female congregation. Nonetheless, women of the church constantly issue challenges to this authority, tapping a well of Africanist cultural methodologies—dancing, singing, shouting—to forge a personal relationship with God. Women call on the spirit, witness, speak in tongues, lay on hands, heal, dance in praise, and sustain the communal spirit of others.

To be sure, the black charismatic church is already a delineated performance venue in which pastor and congregation engage in a spirited performance, which undulates with rhythm, poetry, spectacle, and dance. The pastor is a virtuoso of theatrical technique, letting his vocal timbre, dramatic gestures, and palpitations assist in the dramatic development of his sermon. Most of the formal elements of the church are created around his performance, including when and how the choir sings, the musicians' surreptitious playing underneath his voice to signal the end of the sermon, the call to worship, and the call to the altar. Furthermore, the preacher adopts and holds his position with a text that legitimates and *scripts* his power: the Holy Bible. Says Raboteau, "The Bible is more than a source of texts; it is the single most important source of language, imagery, and story for the sermon."[22]

However, in the charismatic spiritual tradition, women do not allow the preacher the last word. Women subvert the scriptocentrism of the holy space by emptying the text of predetermined meaning and filling it with an organic, physical significance, which reinterprets and redefines its original "objectivity." Though the preacher decides on the entirety of the service, based on—and improvised from—the Bible, women of the congregation push and pull at the rhythm, pace, and meaning of the preacher's presentation with their own performance modalities. Women do not passively regard from their pews; rather, they embellish and complete the words of the pastor. The preacher may provide the text, but the ratification of the Word depends on the vocal and bodily affirmation of the women. Preachers demand and depend upon vocal and bodily feedback. The preacher's delivery of the Word is interrupted and indeed clarified by the shouts of women who say, "Go 'head and preach, sir," "What you say," "Tell it," "Hallelujah," "Amen," "Take your time, man," "Can I get an 'Amen'?" and "You don't hear me!" A service is not complete without this antiphonal collaboration, commonly known as "call and response" but perhaps more properly termed "call and call."

Women also initiate calls and give commands to the preacher, who answers them. Moreover, because they are not bound to preach the gospel, women are free to improvise on the sermon, highlighting those phrases that resonate the most with their own particular theospiritual objectives. These women partially grasp the reins of control over the presentation of the holy Word and, to some degree, appropriate the stage space. Once totally embodied in the Spirit, women actually jump up and down, shout, cry, dance around their pews, and then dance around the church, rupturing the predetermined logic or rationale of the preacher. Once begun, these women are not stopped. Because she is now apotheosized in the spirit, male authority is unable to control her.

In "Beyond the Text: Toward a Performative Cultural Politics," Dwight Conquergood asserts:

> Performance acts as an oppositional practice to hegemonic texts. The borderlines between texts and performances, literacy and orality are highly charged and determined within concrete, historical configurations of power. [Yet performances] are transgressive. Performance recuperates from the text oppositional force, some resistance to the textual imperialism. . . . Performance remains an interruptive Other.[23]

As Conquergood notes, black women's spiritual performance opposes and interrupts the dominant canonical text and acts as a lever, which decenters and destabilizes the scriptural authority of the Word. The performance contributes to a participatory physiospiritual dialogics, which "unsettles valorized paradigms and insists upon immediacy, involvement, and intimacy as modes of understanding."[24] In the conscripted space of the church, black women engage a repertoire of performance practices, which locate and overlay personal meaning onto the textual sanctioning of worship.

Calling on the Spirit, women challenge the doctrinal authority of the preacher and the Word, writ as such, reifying its meaning with their flesh. The women interrupt and break the rhythm of the sermon, telling their own stories in the space of the Word and inserting their witness into the dynamics of the message. At the same time, women physicalize the spaces within the church, stretching conscripted spaces, which limit or define worship. In the sacral space, women resist the linearity and polarity that dichotomize preacher and congregation. When women catch the Spirit at the end of a service, it is not unusual for a preacher to descend from the pulpit in order to stomp, kick his feet, or spin around, twirling his heavy robes in centrifugal fashion, gathering momentum as he moves. In this moment, pastor and parishioner are cocelebrants in an ecstatic performance, which decidedly shifts the focal point of the sermon from the male-controlled altar to the female-inhabited spaces of convergence below. This liturgical mise-en-scène demonstrates the countervailing energy that subtly though defiantly constructs its own critical devices. An exploration of black women's performance of the spirit shatters the Cartesian illusion of mind-body dichotomy, simultaneously mixing affective and exegetical modalities of worship into vast, swirling, energized localities. Through a sacred channeling of Scripture and Spirit, these women vibrate with a gynopomorphic reading of the holy, irrevocably altering the charge of the worship experience.

Performance and Authenticity

A natural consequence of the consideration of the fusion of corporal and spiritual mechanisms in the practice of getting happy is the necessity to examine the role of sexuality in praise. More than one female worshiper has communicated her sexual attraction for a pastor by lifting her skirts high and sashaying down the aisle in exaggerated spiritual fervor. But besides the attraction between pastors and churchwomen, sexuality pervades the direct call from above as well. One black woman whom I interviewed spoke about having a personal, sensual relationship with Jesus, and many regard Him as a lover or spouse in their lives. The familiar response "Nobody but Jesus" echoes from the mouths of black women, as they deflect inquiries about their love lives or the fathers of their children. Indeed, the Bible itself encourages a spiritual sexuality, configuring the Christian church as the "bride of Christ," who waits patiently for the bridegroom to return and open the door of his private chambers.[25] In the Baptist church especially, the sermon, with the steady, pulsating rise of emotion to a heightened catharsis and resolution parallels sexual intercourse.[26] To be "erotically honest," as urged by Michael Dyson in his essay "The Black Church and Sex," the sexual component of religious worship is not foreign to various denominations of the black church, which have evolved from an African heritage that does not strictly demarcate the sacred and the profane, the spiritual from the corporal.[27] (Or, as Dyson puts it, the "holy and horny.")[28] Undoubtedly, some pastors act in bad faith around their sexuality and abuse their power over their female (and, perhaps, male) congregants, a point that fully arrests Dyson's attention in "The Black Church and Sex."[29] He describes an unsettling personal experience in which a fellow pastor inquired after a pretty, excitedly devout sister in the front pew, who distracted his holier attentions with her "shouting and jiggling" during the height of his sermon.[30]

However, more compelling than the dynamics of sexual conquest between black men in power and black women subordinates in the church is the question of how black female worshipers exercise control over this aspect of their performance in the spirit and how they register control over the duality of being both in communication with the divine and fully conscious of their influence over their immediate environment. Although presumably the Holy Spirit is present throughout the service, the performance of it abides by the structure and ritual of the larger performance of church. It almost never occurs in the early part of the service—during devotional prayer or the welcoming of visitors. Some women and men may call out during these times, but the sustained shouting is reserved for some point during the height of the sermon or near the conclusion. If a woman becomes particularly excited and moves as though she may injure herself or others, other women (ushers or nurses' aids) will come to stand near her, guiding her away from objects or people, if necessary, but never interrupting or attempting to curtail her journey in the spirit. Most times, however, this is unnecessary. In my observations of women getting happy, very few have harmed themselves or others. I have seen a woman jump up and down with a tiny infant bouncing in her arms; when the deacons approached her, she handed over the child without missing a beat in her rhythm.

Being conscious of one's performance, however, makes it no less true or authentic; cultural performances are both imitation and "real."[31] This is a signpost of a traditional understanding of performance: an actor is completely engrossed in the emotions of his character and yet acutely aware when he is not standing in his light or when he must pause to wait for audience laughter. Because of the importance placed on charismatic worship in the black church and the almost compulsory nature of speaking in tongues in the Pentecostal denomination, it is natural that some may mimic or go through the motions of an experience that is not prompted on the visceral level. Although this may be true in some cases, it would be incorrect to assess the performance of black women in church as "fake" or only for the sake of garnering attention from the pastor; like the stage actor, they are also desirous of influencing the environments within which they perform. At the same time, it is critically important to accept that the experience of the spirit is the undeniably central phenomenon of calling on the spirit. As Lisa Wolford emphasizes in her essay on Shaker women and possession ritual, ineffable matters must be understood on their own terms and not phobically reinterpreted in a philologocentric manner. One must accept alternate reality as social fact.[32]

The Sacred Within

Speaking in tongues, or glossolalia, first practiced by the apostles on the day of the Pentecost, is one of the most sublime of performative rites in the black church, practiced by only the most holy. This experience is the sine qua non of Pentecostalism but also serves members of other denominations of black people. Women who speak in tongues are messengers filled with the Holy Spirit, uttering a divine immanent language. As "God's mouthpiece," they speak an untranslatable and inimitable tongue. Speaking in tongues represents the presence of God and signals one's election to a higher holy space. In this way, a woman speaking in tongues rivals the presence and the authority of a preacher who, at least initially, relies upon the efficacy of a written, static text. By virtue of the fact that the sound of hearing someone speaking in tongues is so compelling, women who speak in tongues detract attention away from the pulpit. Although there is no prohibition against a preacher speaking in tongues or catching the spirit, typically the onus to preach the Word and to "rationally" lead obviates his engaging in an ecstatic experience during the service that would hinder his clarity and focus. Therefore, women dominate this most precious and spectacular manifestation of the spirit, and they use its rare ontological insight to heal themselves and their community.[33] In this state, many women lay their hands on the afflicted, symbolically or actually curing them of their diseases. The woman herself undertakes a sort of eschatological journey, going to a place beyond her present, objective reality and then returning, unable to describe it. Again, male leadership does not intercede in the performance of this holiness language. She communicates directly without an intercessory and returns from that state unassisted. God is most often pictured, imagined, and spoken about as male (and white, for that matter)[34] in traditionally theological terms, but, when speaking in tongues, women as representatives of the presence of God substitute their own flesh in the void. The presence of God (the Word) within their bodies makes black women the Word, as in "in the beginning was the Word and the Word was with God and the Word was God." Their bodies mediate the Word and metonymically *become* the Word, thereby reenacting the miracle of the "Word made flesh" in every performance. No longer engaging in even antiphonal collaboration, women speaking in tongues operate from their own script and are separate from the rest of the congregation, including other people speaking in the ecstatic language. This phenomenon is not just transcendent but is a transgressive act, which reforms and recontextualizes the idea of church. These women rewrite the text in performance, subverting the scriptocentrism of the Bible and its mores to speak directly to, from, and for God.

In her essay "Speaking in Tongues: Dialogics, Dialectics, and the Black Woman Writer's Literary Tradition," Mae Gwendolyn Henderson interprets the "interlocutory or dialogic character" of black women's discursive written performance as an exemplary condition of "speaking in tongues." Taking the reader through such signature texts of black female authorship as Zora Neale Hurston's *Their Eyes Were Watching God* (1937) and Toni Morrison's *Sula* (1974), Henderson forges a link between these rites of spiritual and literary passage. Henderson states that black female writers' negotiation of their characters and the self-inscription of black female experience demands "disruption, rereading, and rewriting" of the literary canon as it simultaneously bends the existing forms for conventional expression, making it possible for black women writers to breach discourse with "the other(s)." More significantly, expanding Bakhtin's notion of "inner speech," Henderson asserts that black women's literary glossolalia indicates and reflects an internal dialogue, which engages the "plural aspects of self that constitute the matrix of black female subjectivity."[35]

According to bell hooks, "[d]eveloping a feminist consciousness is a crucial part of the process by which one asserts radical black female subjectivity."[36] Hooks stresses the importance of black feminists aligning themselves with a larger feminist movement and of "reading, studying, and engaging in critical pedagogies" in order to acquire the knowledge needed to confront and challenge sexism. Also, hooks tells us that a necessary part of self-actualization is learning about those black women "who have dared to assert radical subjectivity."[37] Although she makes strong arguments for the need of black women to come together in a collective of feminist struggle, hooks ignores the plurality of epistemologies to which black women have access. One need not merely look inside a book or conduct an interview to gain information about feminist agency; the knowledge also lies within. The tools for radical transformation are not externally realized. Neither is the struggle a unilateral event. Says hooks, "Bombarded with images representing black female bodies as expendable, black women have either passively absorbed this thinking or vehemently resisted it."[38] However, the example of black women in the church demonstrates the multifaceted nature of resistance that does not fit neatly into either category. Black women's power must be understood as coming from a spiritual (and internal) as much as an intellectual, emotional, and physical place. The power of the "oppositional" gaze, which looks to resist, may not only look "out" to others but "in" to God, within ourselves. The multiplicity of black women's experiences requires a more flexible model to accommodate our complexity.

Kimberlé Crenshaw arrives closer to the mark in this regard in her analysis of how "Anita Hill's status as a black female—at the crossroads of gender and race hierarchies—was a central feature in the manner in which she was (mis)perceived."[39] With regard to black women's unique status, Crenshaw asserts a concept of "intersectionality." Black women are at once subjected to the oppressive hierarchies of sexuality and race, a unique position that is, in some ways, "unassimilable into the discursive paradigms of gender and race domination." Black women, therefore, want for a means by which to relate the totality of our experiences as black women.[40] Because of our intersectionality, black women are outside many of the mainstream realms of political resistance, including those of and by other black people. Moreover, instead of just being doubly burdened, African American spiritual women are triply burdened by virtue of their being black, female, and *in the church*.

The practice of glossolalia undoes the aforementioned uncomfortable matrix of identities by removing the individual from the margins of a dominant demarcation to a personal, divine place outside the configurations of known speech. If black women's howling or moaning is a prediscursive linguistic "disruption," awaiting entry into proper language,[41] speaking in tongues (like scat, rap, and other xenoglossa) is one of the most powerful forms of postdiscursive speech that black women employ to disrupt the continuity of known speech and to travel beyond the boundaries that restrict black women's agency. Says Henderson:

> As gendered and racial subjects, black women speak/write in multiple voices—not all simultaneously or with equal weight, but with various and changing degrees of intensity, privileging one *parole* and then another. One discovers in these writers a kind of internal dialogue reflecting an *intrasubjective* engagement with *intersubjective* aspects of self, a dialectic neither repressing difference nor, for that matter, privileging identity, but rather expressing engagement with the social aspects of self ("the other[s] in ourselves"). It is this subjective plurality (rather than the notion of the cohesive or fractured subject) that, finally, allows the black woman to become an expressive site for a dialectics/dialogics of identity and difference.[42]

Henderson's model for this process is centrifugal, one that passes through a series of progressions that signify "intervention, appropriation, and revision." Henderson's ideal exemplifies what may be the aim of spirit praise in the form of speaking in tongues—while combative, it does not exist merely in unilateral opposition to oppressive gender practices in black churches, but it is also a multifaceted, creative engagement of power, which varies its modes of resistance and does not rule out collaboration. This "collaborative resistance," as I pose it, allows black women to confront destructive frameworks in stages of combat that do not rule out self-transformation in the process. The collaboration comes from the women joining their voices and bodies in the same pattern of rejoice and from their uniting of their "intersubjective" selves. Henderson's interlocutory interpretation of black women's experience prepares the way for an integrated understanding of black woman's self, "selves," and community. The personal God embraced by black women in the spirit also involves their sisters and brothers. Asserts James Cone, "The 'I,' then, who cries out in the spirituals is a particular black self affirming both his or her being and being-in-community, for the two are inseparable."[43]

This adaptive and collaborative model of resistance unites with that of a long history of blacks withstanding white supremacist attacks on their cultural practices. Historically, our black foremothers and forefathers adapted African religion and religious expression in order to survive, indeed thrive, in places hostile or indifferent to black exigencies for spiritual affirmation and prayer. And, as many blacks before the nineteenth century were denied the privilege to assemble before God or to openly congregate for prayer and worship (after having our more charismatic, public, African forms of worship outlawed), we learned to make our homes the temples of God and turned our diversions into opportunities for fellowship. The most important marker of God was the self and not an institutional structure, whether physical or psychic:

> By seeing themselves in the context of sacred time and sacred space, African Americans in bondage were able to invoke the presence of God anytime

and anyplace. Worship was not limited to a church; it could take place in the fields, by a campfire, or when the individual was alone during the day. The sacred time and sacred space created by African Americans in bondage helped keep them permanently in contact with god.[44]

I have seen a woman get to "shouting" on a bus; I know that the ecstatic performance that occurs inside the church is carried outside afterward, and parishioners can sometimes get the Holy Ghost while in their cars. Black women carry the experience of calling on the spirit with them into all of their activities.

By intervening, appropriating, and revising, blacks have withstood many assaults against their spiritual practices and cultural memory. In fact, the means by which black women and men shout has evolved from previous complex and varied modes of calling on the divine, in particular the ring shout practiced by African slaves of the eighteenth and nineteenth centuries in the South.[45] In this African ritual of praise, slaves would walk or dance around in a circle (or "ring") outdoors, chanting, singing prayers, and stomping their feet until they became entranced and began to shout with the "working of the Spirit."[46] However, white clergymen paled at the sight of the "heathenish" ring shout and eventually banned the practice completely. Once confined to square, contained, and linear space within wooden churches, where a ring shout or any kind of circular configuration of people was impossible, the ring shout went "up."[47] The appropriation of this new ritual stage along with the intervention of blacks who had the creative genius to revise the outward form of their religion to ensure the survival of the sacred rite helped form bonds in the new world. And now, on a spirit-filled Sunday in a black church, you can find women and men sending their praises upward, feet and legs jumping upward, hands lifted upward, heads tilted and voices calling upward, defying but at the same time incorporating the linear grid of pew, aisle, sacristy, and European ritual practices.[48]

Womanist Spirituality

A crucial aspect of black women's worship tradition, then, is that church is as much a verb as a noun. Black women *church*. As modern day apostles, they speak to and from the church within themselves. Church is a process, a performance that is common to many black denominations, whose similarities outweigh their differences. Emilie Townes speaks to this issue in her book *In a Blaze of Glory*:

> Womanist spirituality is not grounded in the notion that spirituality is a practice separate from who we are moment by moment. It is the deep kneading of humanity and divinity into one breath, one hope, one vision.[49]

Black women can and do have church anywhere: in beauty parlors, in the street, on the dance floor, around the kitchen table, in conversations with other sisters. The heightened emotion, the charismatic tongue, the jubilant laughter, the moan, or the shout—"Girl! Lord, don't you know!"—all point to a charismatic calling of the spirit. In Lorraine Hansberry's *A Raisin in the Sun*, Mama goes to church right at home, intoning the gospel on her knees and invoking the spirit to set right what has drastically and ineluctably gone wrong. Playing the role of preacher, Mama attempts to cure her daughter's agnosticism, making her repeat antidotally, "In my mother's house there is still God. In my mother's house there is still God. In my mother's house there is still God."[50] Black women embodied the roles of wife, sister, daughter, and mother, combined them with a *personal* spiritual experience of God in Christ, and understood themselves to be ministers in their homes.

A black woman's witness is a potent mechanism, which achieves its efficacy in the mutability and portability of her instruments: her body and her voice. Black women perform their faith in a discursive milieu that does not heed the parameters of time or space. Spirit is wherever they take it. In church, this performance with its singing and shouting gets its fullest expression. However, the spirit of resistance functions outside of institutional worship in a more public and secular declaration of self and identity. Because of their personal connection with the divine, black women's calling the spirit occupies a place of disclosure, rather than a place of reference. It is, as African religious scholar Marta Morena Vega describes, "evidence of the sacred within."[51] I would argue that one of the most sacred spaces in which sisters of the spirit resist oppression is on the dance floor. Whereas in church they shout, on the dance floor they lift their arms and shake their bodies in a different version of praise dancing, which affirms their joy in the spirit. Black women's spirit call, even in secular practice, defies and counters hegemony, reclaiming a space of identity and resisting representations of themselves in public discourse.

In secular space, too, black women's cultural performances, as much as evoking a transcendent model, evoke a transgressive one, which breaks through sedimented meanings and normative traditions, plunging us back into the vortices of political struggle. From Josephine Baker's audacious banana dance to Judith Jamison's frenetic dance *Cry* to Janet Jackson's bogeling to MC Lyte's "ruffneck" strut to Anna Deavere Smith's speaking in multiple tongues, black women subvert the prescribed order by invoking the church attainable within their individual bodies. Some of these performances are problematic with regard to the commodification and objectification of black women's bodies in a white supremacist, capitalist media, but that is precisely the point. Although black women may not crush the vise of racism through dance, shouting, and the like, by calling on the spirit in whatever idiom, they subvert the totality of its hold. It is not that black women are completely free to perform as they wish within a given hegemonic arena, but rather that they communicate with a force beyond their particular circumstances to salute the divinity within that propels and energizes their performances.

As Toni Morrison so beautifully illustrates in the passage that began this essay, black women have called on the spirit in dark, retiring places to sustain themselves, their families, and their communities. Baby Suggs urges her congregation to *perform* their affirmation, transcending the dual markings of color and gender to attain an agency of the highest order—by discovering the divine in themselves. In *Righteous Discontent*, Higginbotham cites the development of women's organizations within the church as responses to the growing hostility toward and debasement of black women.[52] Defending their names, these women resisted grotesque depictions of black women as mammies, whores, sapphires, and tragic mulattoes. Today, we see the recalcitrance of such name calling in the proliferation of bitches, hos, and welfare queens, sounded from detractors as discursive as black rap artists to white politicians. The defiance to love our own flesh and nurture our own spirits, as depicted by Baby Suggs's invocation, is as incumbent upon us now as a century ago.

A defining moment, which compelled me to work on this chapter, occurred during one of the last times I joined my mom for church. The little girls of this Pentecostal church, from the ages of about six to eleven, were doing a praise dance before the sermon began which was designed to show their devotion to God and their purity and faith to the congregation. As the girls ran in their white dresses and white socks through the aisles of the church, they became more and more entranced until, finally, one little girl, the smallest one, caught the spirit. As an elder woman in the church grabbed and held this small, shaking body in her arms, she prayed, "Dear God, protect these young bodies that the devil may not take them." Watching, I realized that this was an invocation against violations of the flesh and the spirit within, whether they be racism, sexism, or other forms of physical violence. The right to possess one's own body is a new achievement for black people but especially for black women, whose legacy of slavery included rape and forced motherhood in addition to auctions, beatings, lynchings, and segregation. The practice of loving one's body and consecrating it to the spirit *is in itself* a radical practice. By calling on the spirit in whatever context, black women reterritorialize and decolonize the space prescribed for them. Perhaps Ntozake Shange puts it best in her play *for colored girls who have considered suicide/ when the rainbow is enuf*, "I found God in myself and I loved her. I loved her fiercely."[53] In this physiospiritual truth lies a manifesto of freedom.

NOTES

1. Toni Morrison, *Beloved* (New York: Signet, 1991), 108.
2. Elizabeth Clark and Herbert Richardson, eds., *Women and Religion: A Feminist Sourcebook of Christian Thought* (New York: Harper & Row, 1977), 208.
3. Cornel West, *Prophesy Deliverance! An Afro-American Revolutionary Christianity* (Philadelphia: Westminster, 1982), 71.
4. Albert J. Raboteau, *Slave Religion: The "Invisible Institution" in the Antebellum South* (New York: Oxford University Press, 1978), 4.

5. It is important to understand, as Iain MacRobert articulates in his essay "The Black Roots of Pentecostalism," that Africans brought as slaves to the Americas did not arrive tabulae rasae "nor did forced acculturation totally eradicate their primal religious beliefs." Timothy E. Fulop and Albert J. Raboteau, eds., *African-American Religion: Interpretive Essays in History and Culture* (New York: Routledge, 1997), 299.

6. We must bear in mind that, as Raboteau has urged us, these are not static Africanisms, or retentions, but an adapted, "transformed" religious practice, which has its roots in African orthodoxy. Raboteau, *Slave Religion*, 4.

7. Raboteau, *Slave Religion*, 72.

8. Raboteau, *Slave Religion*, 143.

9. Raboteau, *Slave Religion*, 215.

10. When a slave worshiper caught the spirit in these secluded environments, the others would "quickly stop the noise by placing their hands over the offender's mouth" so as not to be detected by anyone. Raboteau, *Slave Religion*, 215.

11. Raboteau, *Slave Religion*, 217. This is a quotation from a former slave. From B. A. Botkin, ed., *Lay My Burden Down: A Folk History of Slavery* (Chicago: University of Chicago Press, 1945), 27.

12. Gloria Davis Goode, "Preachers of the Word and Singers of the Gospel: The Ministry of Women among Nineteenth-Century African Americans," Ph.D. diss., University of Pennsylvania (1990), 164.

13. Evelyn Higginbotham, *Righteous Discontent* (Cambridge, Mass.: Harvard University Press, 1993), 121–122.

14. Higginbotham 62.

15. Higginbotham 3.

16. Higginbotham 135.

17. Goode 8.

18. Goode 169.

19. Goode 223.

20. Goode 239.

21. Goode 284. Another black female preacher of this era, Julia Foote (who was ordained in 1898), began her ministry after an experience in which she fell to the floor unconscious, was carried home, did not eat or drink for twenty hours, and saw visions. Another black female minister, simply known as Elizabeth, was moved to preach after moaning, praying, and having visions in which the savior came to talk with her. Zilpha Elaw became "resplendent with light" after having a vision, and when she awoke, she found hundreds of worshipers weeping from the Holy Ghost. Jarena Lee herself, before approaching Richard Allen, experienced a prayerful trance in which she found herself in her yard, standing with arms outstretched, without having any conscious memory of arriving there (Goode 245).

22. Albert J. Raboteau, *A Fire in the Bones: Reflections on African-American Religious History* (Boston: Beacon Press, 1995), 143. 143. However, it is true, as Raboteau also asserts, that the black preacher must be known not just for the Word but for the Word as performed. See Raboteau, *A Fire in the Bones*, 142.

23. Dwight Conquergood, "Beyond the Text: Toward a Performative Cultural Politics," paper presented at the Future of the Field Performance Studies Conference at New York University, Mar. 1995.

24. Conquergood.

25. Black women are not unique in this. The pervasive use of sexual imagery in possession cults has been demonstrated by I. M. Lewis in his important work, *Ecstatic Religion* (New York: Routledge, 1989).

26. Pentecostal churches, although just as charismatic if not more than Baptist churches, appear to have a more cyclical structure and less of a steady rise to climax. In the Pentecostal worship experience, the congregants sometimes get the spirit during the early part of the service, something that is relatively rare in the black Baptist church experience.

27. At the Performance Studies Conference at Northwestern University in 1996, actress Joni Jones explained that her work with Yoruba women showed her the importance of a sexual receiving of the spirit. She said that one cannot receive possession with one's legs closed. One must be sexually open for it to happen.

28. Michael Eric Dyson, *Race Rules: Navigating the Color Line* (New York: Vintage, 1996), 100.

29. Although I appreciate Dyson's critique that black churches do not expressly explore sexuality and that it is time for an honest and direct address of sex in the black churches, I do not agree that black churches are in particular crisis with regard to sexual repression. On the contrary, black churches go a long way to channel this pent-up sexual arousal during the actual service so that inappropriate and destructive venting of this energy is greatly deterred, if not alleviated. Dyson, 100, *passim*.

30. In the course of writing this chapter, I was apprised of a situation in which a particularly handsome middle-aged preacher drew so many women into the spirit with skirts flying high that his wife threatened to leave him. He decided to leave the church instead.

31. This borrows from Judith Butler's notion of performativity. See her *Gender Trouble: Feminism and the Subversion of Identity* (New York: Routledge, 1990), and *Bodies That Matter: On the Discursive Limits of "Sex"* (New York: Routledge, 1993).

32. Lisa Wolford, "Here Mother Leads Me: Ecstasy and Order in Shaker Women's Cultural Performance," paper delivered at the Aug. 1998 conference of the Association of Theatre in Higher Education in San Antonio, Texas.

33. Again, because men typically make up such a minority of the congregation, one is much more likely to find a woman taking up this spectacular practice, but this is not to say that men do not do it.

34. As any foray into a traditional black Baptist church will reveal, not only whites but blacks, too, have pictured God as white. Until recently, romantic portraits of a wan, pallid Christ adorned the walls of most of the sacristies and the stained-glass windows. This was true even in the homes of many Christian blacks. Although this is gradually changing, with some ministers hanging pictures of a black Christ or God within the body of the church or the pulpit, the furor that such an action provokes is evidence of black Christians' internalization of a white God. In my own black Baptist church, the placing of a portrait of a black Jesus was so offensive to some of the elder members of the church that they made a public protest, and some ceased to attend. In my mother's church, where there is a growing young population, the transition from a portrait of a white Jesus to a black one was more smooth. In his provocative book, *Is God a White Racist?* (Boston: Beacon, 1998), William R. Jones asserts that many blacks see God as white because, if God were black, then black suffering would cease.

35. Mae Gwendolyn Henderson, "Speaking in Tongues: Dialogics, Dialectics, and the Black Woman Writer's Literary Tradition," in *Changing Our Own Words: Essays on Criticism, Theory, and Writing by Black Women*, ed. Cheryl A. Wall (New Brunswick, N.J.: Rutgers University Press, 1989), 17–18.

36. bell hooks, *Black Looks: Race and Representation* (Boston: South End, 1992), 57.

37. hooks 56.

38. hooks 65.

39. Kimberlé Crenshaw, "Whose story is it, Anyway?: Feminist and Antiracist Appropriations of Anita Hill," in Toni Morrison, ed., *Race-ing Justice, En-gendering Power: Essays on Anita Hill, Clarence Thomas, and the Construction of Social Reality* (New York: Pantheon, 1992), 403.

40. Crenshaw 404.

41. Henderson 35.

42. Henderson 36–37.

43. James H. Cone, *The Spirituals and the Blues* (Maryknoll, N.Y.: Orbis, 1995), 61.

44. Clarence Taylor, *The Black Churches of Brooklyn* (New York: Columbia University Press, 1994), 5.

45. Raboteau, *Slave Religion*, 68–75. Although Raboteau acknowledges that some scholars believe the ring shout to have only occurred in the Sea Islands of South Carolina, he submits compelling evidence that this practice was actively engaged all over the South.

46. Raboteau, *Slave Religion,* 68–69.

47. I thank Elmo Terry-Morgan, Artistic Director of Rites and Reason Theatre in Providence, R.I., for this observation.

48. There are numerous examples of such adaptations. An interesting one is *capoeria*, a martial arts system developed by African slaves in Brazil: once outlawed by masters who feared their physical power, slaves adapted their practice fights to appear like dancing (Robert Farris Thompson, lecture at Yale University, 1989). The ring shout itself was an adaptation of an earlier form:

> The shout is a fusion of two seemingly irreconcilable attitudes toward religious behavior. In most of Africa, dance, like singing and drumming, is an integral part of supplication. . . . In the Euro-Christian tradition, however, dancing in church is generally regarded as a profane act. The ring-shout in the United States provides a scheme which reconciles both principles. The circular movement, shuffling steps, and stamping conform to African traditions of supplication, while by definition this activity is not recognized as a "dance."

Raboteau, *Slave Religion*, 339–340.

49. Emilie M. Townes, *In a Blaze of Glory: Womanist Spirituality as Social Witness* (Nashville, Tenn.: Abingdon, 1995), 139.

50. Lorraine Hansberry, *A Raisin in the Sun*, in *Black Theatre, USA*, Vol. 2, James V. Hatch and Ted Shine, eds. (New York: Free Press, 1996), 116.

51. Marta Morena Vega, lecture at St. Paul Community Baptist Church, Nov. 1997.

52. Higginbotham 192.

53. Ntozake Shange, *for colored girls who have considered suicide/when the rainbow is enuf* (New York: Macmillan, 1977), 63.

7

The Chitlin Circuit

HENRY LOUIS GATES, JR.

The setting was the McCarter Theatre, a brick-and-stone edifice on the outskirts of the Princeton University campus. On a hot, sticky evening in June 1998, 500 members of the Theatre Communications Group—all representatives of serious, which is to say nonprofit, theater—gathered for their eleventh biennial national conference. The keynote speech was being delivered by August Wilson, who, at fifty-one, is probably the most celebrated American playwright now writing and is certainly the most accomplished black playwright in this nation's history. Before he said a word, the largely white audience greeted him with a standing ovation.

That was the conference's last moment of unanimity. For here, at this gathering of saints, the dean of American dramatists had come to deliver an unexpected and disturbing polemic. American theater, Wilson declared, was an instrument of white cultural hegemony, and the recent campaign to integrate and diversify it had only made things worse. The spiritual and moral survival of black Americans demanded that they be given a stage of their own. They needed their very own theatres the way they needed sunlight and oxygen. They needed integration the way they needed acid rain.

Wilson told his Princeton audience, in a quietly impassioned voice:

> There are and have always been two distinct and parallel traditions in black art: that is, art that is conceived and designed to entertain white society, and art that feeds the spirit and celebrates the life of black America. The second tradition occurred when the African in the confines of the slave quarters sought to invest his spirit with the strength of his ancestors by conceiving in his art, in his song and dance, a world in which he was the spiritual center.

That was the tradition Wilson found to be exemplified by the Black Power Movement of the sixties and its cultural arm, the Black Arts scene. Revolutionary Black Arts dramatists, such as Ed Bullins and Amiri Baraka, were models for authentic black creativity, Wilson maintained, and he placed himself in their direct line of descent.

"His speech was shocking and it was thrilling," recalled Ricardo Khan, the president of the Theatre Communications Group and the artistic director of the country's premier black repertory company, the Crossroads Theatre in New Brunswick, New Jersey. Wilson is light-skinned, with sparse hair and a close-cropped beard: to some in the audience, he brought to mind Maulana Karenga ("Black art must expose the enemy, praise the people and support the revolution"); to others, Ernst Blofeld ("Hot enough for you, Mr. Bond?"). The black members of the audience started glancing at one another: heads bobbed, a black-power sign was flashed, encouragement was murmured: "Go ahead, brother," "Tell it." Many white audience members, meanwhile, began to shift uneasily, gradually acquiring an expression compounded of pain and puzzlement: *After all we've done for him, this is how he thanks us?* The world of nonprofit theatre is tiny but intense, and, as soon became clear, Wilson's oration was its version of the Simpson verdict.

In the conversational ferment that ensued, almost every conceivable question was given a full airing: Did Wilson's call for an autonomous black theater amount to separatism? Did race matter to culture and, if so, how much? Was Wilson's salvific notion of the theater—and his dream of a theater that would address ordinary black folk—mere romantic delusion? In the course of much high-minded hand wringing, practically the only possibility not broached was that a black theater for the masses *already* existed—just not of an order that anybody in the world of serious theater had in mind.

What attracted the greatest immediate attention was Wilson's unqualified denunciation of color-blind casting. To cast black actors in "white" plays was, he said, "to cast us in the role of mimics." Worse, for a black actor to walk the stage of Western drama was to collaborate with the culture of racism, "to be in league with a thousand naysayers, who wish to corrupt the vigor and spirit of his heart." An all-black production of *Death of a Salesman*, say, would "deny us our own humanity."

Not surprisingly, Wilson's stand on this issue has found little acceptance among working black actors, dramatists, and directors. Lloyd Richards—Wilson's long-time director and creative partner—has never thought twice about casting James Earl Jones as Timon of Athens or as Judge Brack in *Hedda Gabler*. Wole Soyinka, Nigerian playwright and Nobel Laureate, staunchly declares, "I can assure you that if *Death of a Salesman* were performed in Nigeria by an all-Eskimo cast it would have resonances totally outside the mediation of color." What's more surprising is that many stars of the Black Arts firmament are equally dismissive. "If O. J. can play a black man, I don't see any problem with Olivier playing Othello," Amiri Baraka says, with a mordant laugh. And the legendary black playwright and director Douglas Turner Ward claims that many of Sean O'Casey's plays, with their ethos of alienation, actually work better with black actors.

But the dissent on color-blind casting was almost something of a footnote to Wilson's larger brief—that of encouraging the creation of an authentic black theater. As he saw it, the stakes could not be greater. Black theater could help change the world: it could be "the spearhead of a movement to reignite and reunite our people's positive energy for a political and social change that is reflective of our spiritual truths rather than economic fallacies." The urgency of this creed led to a seemingly self-divided rhetoric. On the one hand, Wilson maintained that "we cannot depend on others," that we must be a "self-determining, self-respecting people." On the other hand, this self-sufficiency was to be subsidized by foundations and government agencies.

If Wilson's rhetoric struck many of his listeners as contradictory—seeming to alternate the balled fist and the outstretched palm—the contradictions only multiplied upon further investigation. August Wilson, born Frederick August Kittel, is in some respects an unlikely spokesman for a new Black Arts Movement. He neither looks nor sounds typically black—had he the desire, he could easily "pass"—and that makes him black first and foremost by self-identification. (His father was a German-American baker in Pittsburgh, where he grew up.) Some see significance in this. The estimable black playwright OyamO, né Charles Gordon, says, "Within our history, many people who are lighter—including the very lightest of us, who can really pass—are sometimes the most angry."

Nor has it escaped comment that Wilson failed to acknowledge his own power and stature within the world of mainstream theater: his works debut at major Broadway theaters, and the white critical establishment has honored them with a cascade of Pulitzer, Drama Desk, and Tony awards. The black experimental playwright Suzan-Lori Parks, whose works include *Venus* and *The Death of the Last Black Man in the Whole Entire World*, says, "August can start by having his own acclaimed plays premiere in black theatres, instead of where they premiere now. I'm sorry, but he should examine his own house." One historical luminary of black theater charges that Wilson himself is the problem to which he purports to hold the solution: "Once the white mainstream theatre found a black artistic spokesman, the one playwright who could do no wrong, the money that used to go to autonomous black theatre started to dry up."

And yet, on closer examination, sharply drawn lines of battle begin to blur. Wilson's oration provoked a swingeing rebuttal in *American Theatre* by Robert Brustein, who is the artistic director of the American Repertory Theatre, the drama critic for the *New Republic*, and a long-time sparring partner of Wilson's. Brustein charged Wilson with promoting subsidized separatism: "What next?" he asked. "Separate schools? Separate washrooms? Separate drinking fountains?" With Anna Deavere Smith—herself a paradigm of casting beyond color—serving as the moderator, the men continued their debate Monday, 27 January 1977, in New York's Town Hall. Critic Paul Goldberger, writing in the *New York Times*, went so far as to declare that "this is shaping up to be the sharpest cultural debate" since the Mapplethorpe controversy. You would never guess that Brustein and Wilson are in complete agreement on the one subject that agitates them most: the disastrous nature of the donor-driven trend to diversify regional theaters. Brustein dislikes the trend because he believes that it supplants aesthetic considerations with sociological ones. Wilson dislikes it because, as is true of all movement toward integration, it undermines the integrity and strength of autonomous black institutions.

He has a point. George Wolfe, the producer of the Public Theatre, singles out the Lila Wallace–Reader's Digest Fund as having been "incredibly irresponsible" in this regard. He goes on to explain:

> It has created a peculiar dynamic where, you know, there was a struggling black theatre that had been nurturing a series of artists and all of a sudden this predominantly white theatre next door is getting a couple of million dollars to invite artists of color into its fold.

(To be sure, the officials at the Lila Wallace Fund have also given money to black companies like the Crossroads.) But Wilson wants to take things another step and create black theaters where they do not currently exist. He believes that any theater situated in a city with a black population of more than 60 percent should be converted into a black theater. White board members and staff would be largely retired in order to ensure what he believes to be a cultural and moral imperative: art by, of, and for black people.

Unquestionably, Wilson remains in the grip of a sentimental separatism. (I will own that it has an emotional grip on me, too, just a rather attenuated one.) He says he has a lot of respect for the "do for self" philosophy of the Nation of Islam; in the early seventies, he was briefly a convert although mostly in order to keep his Muslim wife company. He is a man who views integration primarily as a destructive force, one that ruined once vital black institutions. He thinks back fondly to an era when we had our own dress shops and businesses, our own Negro Baseball League. This segregated, pre–*Brown v. Board of Education* era was, he will tell you, "black America at its strongest and most culturally self-sufficient." From his perspective, separate-but-equal, far from being a perversion of social justice, is an ideal to which we should aspire.

It is one thing to hear this view espoused by Minister Louis Farrakhan and quite another to hear it advanced by August Wilson, a man as lionized as any writer of his generation. It represents a romantic attempt to retrieve an imaginary community in the wake of what seems to be a disintegration of the real one. One of the functions of literature is to bring back the dead, the absent, the train gone by; you might say that cultural nationalism is what happens when the genre of the elegy devolves into ideology, the way furniture might be kilned into charcoal.

Certainly, the brutal reductionism of August Wilson's polemics is in stark contrast to his richly textured dramatic oeuvre. Wilson first came to prominence in the mid-1980s, with his fourth play, *Ma Rainey's Black Bottom*, which director Lloyd Richards was able to move from the Yale Repertory Theatre to the Cort Theatre on Broadway. There, Wilson's dramatic and verbal imagination galvanized critics, who heralded a major new presence on the American stage. With *Ma Rainey*, an ambitious and still ongoing cycle of plays came to public notice. Wilson's aim is to explore black American life through plays set during each of the decades of the century; most are situated in a black working-class neighborhood of Pittsburgh. *Joe Turner's Come and Gone* (1986), for example, takes place in 1911 and deals with the sense of cultural loss that accompanied the Great Migration; *The Piano Lesson* (which received the Pulitzer in 1987), set during the Depression, uses a dispute over an inherited piano—once the possession of a slave owner—to show that the past is never quite past. In *Fences* (a 1990 Pulitzer), which opens in the year 1957, the grandiloquently embittered Troy Maxson is a former Negro League baseball player, who now works as a garbage man; the trajectory of his life has made a mockery of the supposed glories of integration.

Wilson's 1990 play, *Two Trains Running*, takes place in a Pittsburgh luncheonette in the late sixties:

WOLF: I thought [the jukebox] was just fixed. Memphis, I thought you was gonna get a new jukebox.

MEMPHIS: I told Zanelli to bring me a new one. That what he say he gonna do. He been saying that for the last year.

If you are black, you cannot rely on the Zanellis of the world, as the characters in the play learn to their detriment. But a great deal more than race politics is going on here. An unruly luxuriance of language—an ability to ease between trash talk and near-choral transport—is Wilson's great gift; sometimes, you wish he were less generous with that gift, for it can come at the expense of conventional dramaturgic virtues, like pacing and a sense of closure. Even when he falters, however, Wilson's work is demanding and complex—at the furthest remove from a cultural manifesto.

But if Wilson's avowed cultural politics are difficult to square with his art, they come with a venerable history of their own. In 1926, W. E. B. Du Bois, writing in his magazine, *Crisis*, took a dim view of "colored" productions of mainstream plays (they "miss the real path," he warned) and called for a new black theater, for which he laid down "four fundamental principles":

The plays of a real Negro theatre must be: (1) *About us*. That is, they must have plots which reveal Negro life as it is. (2) *By us*. That is, they must be written by Negro authors who understand from birth and continual association just what it means to be a Negro today. (3) *For us*. That is, the theatre must cater primarily to Negro audiences and be supported and sustained by their entertainment and approval. (4) *Near us*. The theatre must be in a Negro neighborhood near the mass of ordinary Negro people.

What would such a theater look like? Wilson, of course, directs us to what may seem the most plausible candidate: the dramatic art of the Black Power era. That moment and milieu bring to mind a radicalized, leatherclad generation forging its art in the streets, writing plays fueled by the masses' righteous rage: revolutionary art by the people and for the people. That is certainly how the illuminati liked to represent their project. Baraka's manifesto on "The Revolutionary Theatre" provides a representative précis:

What we show must cause the blood to rush, so that prerevolutionary temperaments will be bathed in this blood, and it will cause their deepest souls to move, and they will find themselves tensed and clenched, even ready to die. . . . We will scream and cry, murder, run through the streets in agony, if it means some soul will be moved.

Theater, precisely because of its supposed potential to mobilize the masses, was always at the forefront of the Black Arts Movement. Still, it is a funny thing about cultural movements: as a rule, they consist of a handful of people. (The aesthetic, the constructivist, and the futurist movements were devoted largely to declaring themselves, self-consciously, to be movements.) And, by the late sixties, it was clear that the vitality of Black Arts drama had come to center upon two New York–based theaters: the Negro Ensemble Company (NEC), based downtown, under the direction of Douglas Turner Ward, and the New Lafayette Theatre, based in Harlem, under the direction of Robert Macbeth. Here was the full flowering of genuine black theater in this country, the kind that would raise consciousness and temperatures, that promised to make us whole.

"Populist modernism," a phrase coined by literary scholar Werner Sollors, characterized the regnant ethos of that time and place—its aspiration to an art of high seriousness, which would engage the energies of the masses. But between the ideals of modernism and those of populism, one or the other had to give. OyamO—who, like many more senior luminaries of the Black Arts Movement (Baraka and Ed Bullins among them), was affiliated with the blacker and artier New Lafayette—recalls that the Harlem theater's high-flown airs were accompanied by paltry audiences. "There was a condescending attitude toward this community, buttressed by the fact that it was getting five hundred grand from the Ford Foundation every year," he recalls. And the NEC was similarly provided for. This is not to say that worthy and important work was not created in these theaters: it was. But these companies do provide a textbook example of how quickly beneficence becomes entitlement, and patronage a paycheck.

So, the dirty little secret of the Black Arts Movement was that it was a project promoted and sustained largely by the Ford Foundation. Liberal-minded Medicis made it; in the fullness of time, they left it to unmake itself. Bullins, one of the principals of the New Lafayette, remembers how that particular temple—a magnificent structure on 137th Street, which the Ford had converted from a movie house with the help of some tony theatrical architects—was destroyed. He describes a meeting between a visiting program officer from the Ford Foundation and the theater's board. The visitor noticed that there were no women on the board, and he asked about their absence. Bullins both laughs and groans when he recalls, "And then some great mind from Harlem, an actor, spoke up and said, 'Oh, no, we don't need any women on the board, because every thirty days women go through their period and they get evil.' Then and there, I saw one million dollars start sprouting wings and flapping away through the door."

These days, of course, all nonprofit theater is starved for cash. And black theaters are already out there, as someone like Larry Leon Hamlin could tell you. Hamlin is the artistic director of the National Black Theatre Festival, and by his count there are perhaps 250 regional black theaters in the United States, about forty of which are reasonably active. Of course, most of Wilson's own plays gestated at places like the Huntington Theatre Company or the Yale Rep before they were launched on the Great White Way. I asked Wilson about this apparent contradiction. He explained that the Negro Ensemble Company had fallen into decline by the early eighties: "It was not doing work of the quality that we deserve, and there's no theatre that's since stepped into the breach." Wilson can sound as if he were boycotting black theaters for artistic reasons, which is why some people in the black theater world cannot decide whether he is their savior or their slayer. "I do good work," he says, his point being that his plays deserve the best conditions he can secure for them. And, among white theaters, he says:

> The rush is now on to do anything that's black. Largely through my plays, what the theatres have found out is that they had this white audience that was starving to get a little understanding of what was happening with the black population, because they very seldom come into contact with them, so they're curious. The white theatres have discovered that there is a market for that.

The fact that part of Wilson's success is owed to the appeal of ethnography is precisely what disturbs some black critics: they suspect that Wilson's work is systematically overrated along those lines. "August is genuinely very gifted," Margo Jefferson, one of those critics, says:

> Whites who don't know the world whereof he writes get a sense of vast, existential melodramas, sweeping pageants, and it's very exciting, with his insistence always that these people onstage are the real and genuine black people. What happens with whites is that the race element is signalling them every minute, "You know nothing about this, you're lucky to be here."

So, if you are looking for a theater of black folk, by black folk, and for black folk—a genuinely sequestered cultural preserve—you will have to cross the extraordinary dramas of August Wilson off your list. Nor would the Black Arts scene, for all its grand aspirations, qualify: the revolution, it is safe to say, will not be subsidized. You could be forgiven for wondering whether such a black popular theater really exists. But it does, and, if populist modernism is your creed, it will probably turn your stomach. It is called the Chitlin Circuit, and nobody says you have to like it. But everything in God's creation has a reason, and the Chitlin Circuit is no exception. Perhaps OyamO brings us closest to comprehension when he despairingly observes an uncomfortable truth: "A lot of what they call highbrow, progressive, avant-garde theatre is *boring the shit out of people*." Not to put too fine a point on it.

The setting now is the Sarah Vaughan Concert Hall—built in 1925 as a Masonic temple—on Broad Street in downtown Newark, New Jersey. It is a chilly, overcast Sunday afternoon, closing in on three o'clock, which is when the matinee performance of Adrian Williamson's play *My Grandmother Prayed for Me* is supposed to begin. In every sense, we are a long way from the Princeton campus, the site of the despondency-drenched Theatre Communications Group conference (TCG). On the sidewalk, patrons are eating grilled sausages and hot dogs. Older people make their way inside with the assistance of wheelchairs or walkers; younger ones strut about and survey one another appraisingly. There is much to appraise. These people are styling out, many of them having come from church: you see cloudlike tulle, hatbands of the finest grosgrain ribbon, wool suits and pants in neon shades. Women have taken care to match their shoes and handbags; men sport Stetson and Dobbs hats, *kente* cloth cummerbunds and scarves. There is a blue velvet fedora here, electric blue trousers there, a Superfly hat and overcoat on a man escorting his magenta-clad wife. Bodies are gleaming, moisturized, and fragrant; cheeks are lightly powdered, eyes mascaraed. Broad Street is a poor substitute for a models' runway, but it will have to do until the theater doors open and swallow up this impromptu village. There are nearly 3,000 seats in the hall; within several minutes, most of them are occupied.

The Chitlin Circuit dates back to the 1920s, when the Theatre Owners Booking Association brought plays and other forms of entertainment to black audiences throughout the South and the Midwest. Although it had a reputation for lousy pay and demanding scheduling—its acronym, TOBA, was sometimes said to stand for "tough on black asses"—it was the spawning ground for a good number of accomplished black actors, comics, and musicians. TOBA proper had gone into eclipse by the decade's end, yet the tradition it began—the disparagingly named Chitlin Circuit—never entirely died out. Touring black companies would play anywhere: in a theater if there was one (sometimes they booked space on weekends or late at night, when the boards would otherwise be vacant) or in a school auditorium if there was not. Crisscrossing black America, the circuit established an empire of comedy and pathos, the sublime and the ridiculous: a movable feast that enabled blacks to patronize black entertainers. On the whole, these productions were for the moment, not for the ages. They were the kind of melodrama or farce—or, often, both—in which nothing succeeded like excess. But the productions were for, by, and about black folks, and their audience was not much inclined to check them against their Stanislavsky anyway.

You do not expect anything fancy from something called the Chitlin Circuit. Wilson—by way of emphasizing the irreducible differences between blacks and whites—had told the TCG members that "in our culinary history we had to make do with the . . . intestines of the pig rather than the loin and the ham and the bacon." The intestines of the pig are the source of the delicacy known as chitlins; it is a good example of how something that was originally eaten of necessity became, as is the way with acquired tastes, a thing actively enjoyed. The same might be said of the Chitlin Circuit, for the circuit is back in full flush and has been for several years. Black audiences throughout the country flock to halls like the Beacon Theatre in New York, the Strand Theatre in Boston, and the Fox Theatre in Atlanta. Those audiences are basically blue collar and pink collar and not the type to attend traditional theater, Larry Leon Hamlin adjudges. But, as the saying has it, they know what they like.

The people behind the shows tend not to vaporize about the "emancipatory potentialities" of their work or about "forging organic links to the community": they would be out of business if black folks stopped turning up. Instead, they like to talk numbers. Terryl Calloway, who has worked as a New England promoter for some Chitlin Circuit productions, tells me about plays that have grossed $20 million or more. "It's no joke," he says gravely.

"Good afternoon! Are you ready to have a good time?" This is the master of ceremonies, warming up the Newark crowd. The play that ensues is a now-standard combination of elements; that is, it is basically a melodrama, with abundant comic relief and a handful of gospel songs interspersed.

So what have we turned out to see? It seems that the grandmother—stout of body and of spirit—is doing her best to raise her two grandsons, as their mother, Samantha, has fallen into crack addiction and prostitution. (When we first see Samantha, she is trying to steal her mother's television in order to pay for her habit.) The older boy, Rashad, is devout and studious, but the younger one, Ein, has taken up with bad company. Today is the day that he and his best friend, Stickey, are to be inducted into the Big Guns, a local gang headed by Slow Pimp. When Stickey is killed on the street by a member of a rival gang, Ein sets out, gun in hand, to avenge his death. What is a grandmother to do? Well, pray, for one thing.

Artistically speaking, *My Grandmother Prayed for Me* makes "Good Times" look like Strindberg. The performances are loud and large; most of the gospel is blared by said grandmother with all the interpretive nuance of a car horn. So broad, so coarse, so over-the-top is this production that to render an aesthetic evaluation would seem a sort of category mistake, like asking Julia Child to taste test chewing tobacco. But it deals with matters that are of immediate concern to the Newark audience, working class and middle class alike: gang violence, crack addiction, teenage pregnancy, deadbeat dads. For this audience, these issues are not *Times* op-ed page fodder; they are the problems of everyday life, as real and close at hand as parking tickets and head colds. It is also true that black America remains disproportionately religious. (Count on a black rap artist—gangsta or no—to thank Jesus in his liner notes.) So that is part of it, too.

On my way to the Sarah Vaughan Concert Hall, I bumped into Amiri Baraka, who, when he learned my destination, gave me a gleaming smile and some brotherly advice: "You're about to step into some deep doo-doo." Maybe he is right, and yet I find myself enjoying the spectacle as much as everybody else here. "You lost faith in the church, abandoned your kids, and I even heard you were prostituting," the grandmother tells her daughter. "Let me tell you something. Them drugs ain't nothing but a demon." Samantha's response: "Well, if they a demon, then I'm gon' love hell." People laugh, but they recognize the sound of a lost soul. So the two fabled institutions of the inner city, the pusher and the preacher, must battle for Samantha's soul. There is a similar exchange between the good son and the one going bad:

RASHAD: Those boys you hang with ain't nothing but a bunch of punks. All y'all do is run around these streets beating up on people, robbing people, our black folks at that. . . .

EIN: If we so-called punks, why we got everybody scared of us? I'll tell you why because we hardcore. We'll smoke anybody that get in our way.

RASHAD: Hardcore? . . . Ain't a thing you out there doing hardcore. Let me tell you what hardcore is: hardcore is going to school, putting your nose in a book getting an education. Hardcore is going to church trying to live your life right for the Lord. Hardcore is going to work every day, busting your behind providing for a family. Look around you. Grandma provided all of this for us, and she pray for us every day. Now that's hardcore.

This doubtless is not what Wilson has in mind when he speaks of the spiritual fortification and survival that black drama can provide. All the same, the audience is audibly stirred by Rashad's peroration, crying out "Hallelujah!" and "Testify!" The subject of racism—or, for that matter, white people—simply never arises: in the all-black world depicted on stage, the risks and remedies are all much closer to hand. That is one puzzle. Here is another: If theater is dying, what do we make of these nearly 3,000 black folks gathered in downtown Newark? The phenomenon I am witnessing has nothing in common with *Tony 'n' Tina's Wedding*, say, or dinner theater in Westchester, which offers *Damn Yankees* over a steak and two eggs. It is true that black audiences have always had a predilection for talking back at performances. But more than that is going on in this theater: the intensity of engagement is palpable. During some of the gospel numbers, there are members of the audience who stand up and do the holy dance by their seats. However crude the script and the production, they are generating the kind of audience communion of which most playwrights can only dream.

In *My Grandmother Prayed for Me*, the deus ex machina is pretty literal. When Ein sets off to seek vengeance, his grandmother and brother go in search of him, joined by Samantha, who—having been visited by an angel in the shape of a little boy—has seen the light. ("It was this voice, Mama, this voice from Heaven. It told me that Ein and Rashad need a good mama.") The curtain rises on a gang-infested project. It appears that Ein, too, has seen the light and laid down his gun. "I know I haven't had the best things in life," he tells Slow Pimp defiantly, "but God gave me the best grandmother in the world." Slow Pimp does not take his defection well, but it is Rashad who catches the first bullet. Next, Slow Pimp turns his gat on the meddling grandmother. She prays for divine intervention and gets it. The gun jams; Slow Pimp is struck by lightning; the angel raises Rashad from the ground. The audience goes wild.

Nobody said it was high culture, but historically this is what a lot of American theater, particularly before the First World War, was like. Other "ghettoized" theaters, for all their vibrancy, also ignored many of the criteria for serious art—not least the Yiddish theater, a center of immigrant Jewish life in New York at the end of the nineteenth century and the beginning of the twentieth. Former *New York Times* theater critic Frank Rich says:

> What we think of as the Yiddish theatre today was essentially popular entertainment for immigrants. There were what we'd now think of as hilarious versions of, say, *King Lear*, in which Lear lives. Or there were fairy tales, about an impoverished family arriving on the Lower East Side and ending up on Riverside Drive living high on the hog.

(There was also, he notes, an avant-garde Yiddish theater, based largely in the Bronx, but that is a different, and more elevated, story.)

The fact that the audience at the Sarah Vaughan Concert Hall is entirely black creates an essential dynamic. I mentioned elements of comic relief: they include a black preacher greedy for the grandmother's chicken wings; a randy old man trailing toilet paper from a split seam in the back of his pants; the grandmother herself, whose churchliness is outlandishly caricatured; endless references to Stickey's lapses of personal hygiene. All the very worst stereotypes of the race are on display, larger than life. Here, in this racially sequestered space, a black audience laughs uninhibitedly, whereas the presence of white folks would have engendered a familiar anxiety: *Will they think that's what we're really like?* If this drama were shown on television—in any integrated forum—Jesse Jackson would probably denounce it, the NAACP would demand a boycott, and every soul here would swap his or her finery for sandwich boards in order to picket it. You do not want white people to see this kind of spectacle; you want them to see the noble dramas of August Wilson, where the injuries and injustices perpetrated by the white man are never far from our consciousness. (It should be mentioned that there are far more respectable and well-groomed versions of gospel drama—most notably Vy Higgenson's *Mama I Want to Sing* and its progeny—that have achieved a measure of crossover success, serving mainly as vehicles for some very impressive singing. But they are better regarded as pageants, or revues, than stage plays.) By contrast, these Chitlin Circuit plays carry an invisible racial warning sticker: for domestic consumption only—export strictly prohibited.

For the creators of this theater, there are other gratifications to be had. "I've never made so much money in my life as I made when I did the forty or so cities we did on the Chitlin Circuit," James Chapmyn, one veteran of the circuit, tells me. And Chapmyn was not even one of the top grossers. "The guy that did *Beauty Shop* probably grossed $15 to $25 million in the Chitlin Circuit," he says. "These plays make enormous money."

Chapmyn is a blunt-featured, odd-shaped man, with a bullet head and a Buddha belly. He's thirty-six, and he grew up in Kansas, the son of a Baptist minister. He tells me that he fell out with his father in his early twenties. "He was adamant in teaching us to stand up for who we are, and who I am happens to be a black gay man. He taught me to tell the truth," Chapmyn says, but adds that his father changed his mind when his son came out. "I just wish you had lied," the minister told his son. A resulting disaffection with the church—and a spell as a homeless person—impelled him to write a play for which he has become widely known: *Our Young Black Men Are Dying and Nobody Seems to Care* (1990). His experience with the Chitlin Circuit was decidedly mixed but still memorable.

Chapmyn, like everyone else who has succeeded on the Chitlin Circuit, had to master the dark arts of marketing and promotion and to do so while bypassing the major media. He genially explains the ground rules:

> What has happened in America is that you have a very active African-American theatre audience that doesn't get their information from the arts section in the newspaper, that doesn't read reviews but listens to the radio, gets things stuffed in their bulletins in church, has flyers put on their car when they're night-clubbing. That's how people get to know about black theatre. Buying the arts section ain't going to cut it for us. That audience is not interested in the "black theatre," and the black-theatre audience is not interested in reading that information. We use radio quite extensively, because in our community and places we've gone, African Americans listen to radio. In fact, there's kind of an unspoken rule on the Chitlin Circuit: if a city doesn't have a black radio station, then the Chitlin Circuit won't perform there.

But the Chitlin Circuit has a less amiable side; indeed, to judge from some of the tales you hear, many of its most dramatic events occur off stage. The inner-city version of foundation program officers are drug dealers with money to burn, and their influence is unmistakable. Chapmyn says:

> They do everything in cash. At our highest point, I know that after we all got our money, we were still collecting in the neighborhood of $100,000 a week. That was cash being given to us, usually in envelopes, by people we didn't know. It was scary. . . . When I was in that circuit, I dealt with a lot of people who didn't have anything but beeper numbers, who would call me with hotel numbers, who operated through post-office boxes, who would show up at the time of the show and most of the time take care of me and my people very well.

Not always, though. Chapmyn recounts:

> In one city, I think we did three shows, and the receipts after expenses were $140,000. My percentage of that was to be $65,000. I remember the people gave me $5,000 and told me that if I wanted the rest I'd have to sue them.

He ended up spending the night in jail. "I was so mad I was ready to hurt somebody," he explains. "Somebody is going to tell me that they got my $60,000 and they ain't going to give it to me? I think I flipped a table over and hit somebody in the face."

Larry Leon Hamlin, too, becomes animated when he talks about the sleazy world of popular theater. He tells me:

> Contracts have been put out on people. If you are a big-time drug dealer, it's like, "These plays are making money, and I've got money. I'm going to put out a play." That drug dealer will write a play who has never written a play before, will direct the play, who has never directed a play before. They get deep with guns.

James Chapmyn says he dropped out of the circuit because of the criminal element:

> Here I am doing a play about all the things killing African-American men, chief among those things being the violence and the drugs, and I'm doing business with people who are probably using the money they make from drugs to promote my play. I had a fundamental problem with that.

Chapmyn, plainly, is a man with a mission of uplift. By contrast, many other stars of the Chitlin Circuit have the more single-minded intent of pleasing an audience: they stoop to conquer.

That might be said, certainly, of the most successful impresario of the Chitlin Circuit, a man named Shelly Garrett. Garrett maintains that his play *Beauty Shop* has been seen by more than 20 million people, that it is the most successful black stage play in American history, and that he himself is "America's number one black theatrical producer, director, and playwright." Shelly Garrett has never met August Wilson; August Wilson has never heard of Shelly Garrett. They are as unacquainted with each other as art and commerce is said to be. (Except for *Fences* and *The Piano Lesson*, both of which were profitable, all of Wilson's plays have lost money.)

Garrett is a handsome man in his early fifties, given to bright-colored sports coats and heavy gold jewelry, and there is about him the unquiet air of a gambler. He was born in Dallas, Texas, worked there as a disk jockey, and later moved to Los Angeles to begin an acting career. He made his debut as a dramatist in 1986, with *Snuff and Miniskirts*. It played in the Ebony Showcase Theatre in Los Angeles for about six weeks. The following year, he staged *Beauty Shop*. After running on and off in Los Angeles, that show went on tour, and, as Garrett likes to say, "The rest is history." Garrett had his audience in the palm of his hand and his formula at his fingertips; all that was left was for him to repeat it with slight variation, in plays like *Beauty Shop Part 2, Living Room, Barber Shop*, and *Laundromat*.

"It reminds you of the old commedia dell'arte stuff," OyamO says of Garrett's approach to theater. "But it's black, and it's today, and it's loud." He also makes the obvious remark that, "if a white man was producing *Beauty*

Shop, they would be lynching it." Still, what Shelly Garrett does has a far better claim to be "community theater" than what we normally refer to by that name.

Garrett's dramatis personae are as uniform as restaurant place settings. The parts invariably include a mouthy fat woman, a beautiful vamp, a sharp-tongued and swishy gay man, and a handsome black stud, who will ultimately be coupled with the fat woman. Much of the dialogue consists of insults and trash talk. Other options and accessories may be added, to taste, but typically there is a striptease scene and lots of Teddy Pendergrass on the mixing board. The gay man and the fat woman swap gibes—"play the dozens"—during lulls in the action.

Although Garrett's plays adhere to pretty much the same situational and narrative template, they are not dashed off. Garrett tells me, "I might rewrite a show forty times, and I take so much time with them and the rehearsals and the delivery of the lines that I just run actors crazy. I run them nuts. But then, at the end, when they get their standing ovation, they love me." A strained chuckle: "Takes them a long time to love me, but finally they do." Garrett prides himself on his professionalism, which lifts him far above the cheesier theatrical realm where drug-pusher auteurs and shakedown artists might freelance. And there is something disarming about his buoyant, show-me-the-money brand of dramaturgy.

Garrett is not the product of anyone's drama workshop; he comes from a world in which "the method" refers to a birth-control technique. He has seen almost no "legitimate" theater, even in its low-end form: "I'm embarrassed to tell people that I've never even seen *The Wiz*. On Broadway, I've seen *Les Miz*, *Cats*, and—what was that black show that had Gregory Hines in it?" His shows play to ordinary black people—the "people on the avenue," as Wilson wistfully puts it—and if these shows are essentially invisible to the white mainstream, so much the better. "I have things in my show that black people can relate to," Garrett declares. "If you're sitting in that audience and something is happening on that stage that you can absolutely not relate to, why are you even there?" Why, indeed?

In *Beauty Shop*, Terry (conservative, pretty) is the proprietor of the hair salon; Sylvia (sexy), Margaret (fat), and Chris (gay) are stylists; Rachel (tall, well-dressed) is a customer.

TERRY: Barbara Dell! Is that man still beating her?

SYLVIA: Punching her lights out! It must have been a humdinger 'cause her glasses were *real* dark!

TERRY: Well, if she's stupid enough to stay there with him, she deserves it!

RACHEL: I have never understood why a woman just takes that kind of stuff off of a man.

MARGARET: I can't understand a man raising his hand to hit a woman!

CHRIS: I guess you wouldn't. What man would be *brave* enough to hit *you?*

Despite outrageous caricature, it does not seem quite right to call these plays homophobic. The gay characters may be stereotyped, but so are all the others. The bigots are not treated charitably, and the queen is always given the last word. "You are an embarrassment to the male gender, to the Y.M.C.A., the Cub Scouts, Boy Scouts, U.S. Army, and . . . Old Spice!" a customer tells Chris in the course of a steadily escalating argument. Chris replies, "Now what you *need* to do is go home and have a little talk with your *mother!* I wasn't *always* gay, I *might* be your *daddy!*" Politically correct it is not, but neither is it mean-spirited. At the end, the fat woman is rewarded with a desirable man. And, occasionally, there are even monologues with morals, in which philandering males are put in their place by right-on women.

First and foremost, though, Garrett is a businessman. His production company moves along with him; he refuses to fly but he has a bus that is fully equipped with fax and phone. He is known for his skill in saturating the black press and radio stations. He is also known for the money he makes selling merchandise like T-shirts and programs. He can tell you that his average ticket price is $27.50, that he rarely plays a venue with fewer than 2,000 seats, that a show he did in Atlanta netted about $600,000 a week. (For purposes of comparison, the weekly net of hit "straight" plays—like *Master Class, Taking Sides*, and so forth—is typically between $100,000 and $200,000; the weekly net of hit musicals like *Miss Saigon, Les Misérables*, and *Sunset Boulevard* is usually in the neighborhood of $500,000.) In New York, Garrett's *Beauty Shop* had weekly revenues of more than $800,000, and that was for an eleven-week run, during which the show sold out every week but one. Garrett remembers the time fondly: "They put me up at the Plaza in New York. First black to ever stay at the penthouse of the Plaza. And I was there for three weeks—the penthouse of the Plaza!"

To most people who both take the theatrical arts seriously and aspire to an "organic connection" with the black community, Garrett is a cultural candy man, and his plays the equivalent of caries. Woodie King, Jr., of New York's New Federal Theatre (which has had unusual success in attracting black audiences for black theater), expresses a widespread sentiment in the world of political theater when he describes Garrett as "an individual going after our personal riches." He says, "It's not doing anything for any kind of black community. It's not like he's going to make money, then find five deserving women writers and put on their work. It's always going to be about him." It is clear that, for dramatists who view themselves as producing work for their community but who depend for their existence on foundation and government support, Garrett is an embarrassment in more ways than one.

"Artistically, I think they're horrible," the Crossroads' Ricardo Khan says of the Chitlin Circuit's carnivalesque productions:

> I don't think the acting is good, I don't think the direction is good, I don't think the level of production is good. But I don't put them down for being

able to speak to something that people are feeling. I think the reason it's working is that it's making people laugh at themselves, making them feel good, and they're tired of heavy stuff.

But his political consciousness rebels at the easy anodyne, the theatergoer's opiate. His own work, he says, aspires to raise consciousness and transform society. He sounds almost discouraged when he adds, "But people don't always want that. Sometimes they just want to have fun."

Nobody wants to see the Chitlin Circuit and the Crossroads converge. But there is something heartening about the spectacle of black drama that pays its own way—even if aficionados of serious theater find something disheartening about the nature of that drama. So maybe we should not worry so much about those Du Boisian yardsticks of blackness. That way lies heartbreak, or confusion. Wilson and his supporters, to listen to them, would divvy up American culture along the color line, sorting out possessions like an amicably divorcing couple. But, I insist, Wilson's polemics disserve his poetics.

Indeed, his work is a tribute to a hybrid vigor, an amalgam of black vernacular, American naturalism, and high modernist influences. (In the history of black drama, perhaps only Baraka's 1964 play *Dutchman* represents as formidable an achievement, and that was explicitly a drama of interracial conflict. By contrast, one of Wilson's accomplishments is to register the ambiguous presence of white folks in a segregated black world—you see them nowhere and feel them everywhere.) There is no contradiction in the fact that Wilson revels in the black cadences of the barbershop and the barbecue, on the one hand, and pledges fealty to Aristotle's poetics, on the other. Wilson may talk about cultural autarky, but, to his credit, he does not practice it. Inevitably, the audience for serious plays in this mostly white country is mostly white. Wilson writes serious plays. His audience is mostly white. What's to apologize for?

By all means, let there be "political" art and formalist art, populism and modernism, Baraka and Beckett, but let them jostle and collide in the cultural agora. There will be theaters that are black—and Latino and Asian and what you will—but, all told, it is better that they not arise from the edicts of cultural commissioners. Despite all the rhetoric about inclusion, I was struck by the fact that many black playwrights told me they felt that their kind of work—usually more "experimental" than realist—was distinctly unwelcome in most black regional theaters. Suzan-Lori Parks reminds me that she did not grow up in the 'hood: "I'm not black according to a nationalist definition of black womanhood. . . . We discriminate in our own family." As a working dramatist and director, George Wolfe—who, in the spirit of pluralism, says he welcomes all kinds of theaters, ethnically specific and otherwise—admits unease about the neatly color-coded cultural landscape that Wilson conjures up. "I don't live in the world of absolutes," Wolfe says. "I don't think it's a matter of a black theatre versus an American theatre, a black theatre versus a white theatre. I think we need an American theatre that is of, for, and by us—*all* of us."

You may wonder, then, what happens to that self-divided creed of populist modernism: the dream of an art that combines aesthetic vanguardism with popular engagement, the elevated black theater for which Wilson seeks patronage. "People are not busting their ass to go and see this stuff," OyamO says bluntly, "and I keep thinking, if this stuff is so significant, why can't it touch ordinary people?" There is reason to believe that such impatience is beginning to spread. Indeed, maybe the most transgressive move for such black theater would be to explore that sordid, sullying world of the truly demotic. Ed Bullins, the doyen of black revolutionary theater, regales me with stories he has heard about Chitlin Circuit entrepreneurs "rolling away at night with suitcases of money," about the shadowy realm of cash-only transactions. But the challenge appeals to him, all the same.

So, brace yourself. The Ed Bullins to whom Wilson paid tribute—as one whose dramatic art was hallowed with the blood of proud black warriors— now tells me he has been thinking about entering the Chitlin Circuit himself. Call it populist postmodernism. Somehow, he relishes the idea of a theater that would be self-supporting, one that did not just glorify the masses but actually appealed to them. Naturally, though, he would try to do it a little better. "The idea is to upgrade the production a bit, but go after the same market," he says eagerly. Now, *that* is a radical thought.

8

Audience and Africanisms in August Wilson's Dramaturgy

A Case Study

@@

SANDRA G. SHANNON

In what is perhaps one of August Wilson's earliest published interviews following the sudden notoriety thrust upon him by the Broadway success of *Ma Rainey's Black Bottom*, he told Kim Powers about his aspirations for his next work, *Joe Turner's Come and Gone*: "My idea is that somewhere, sometime in the course of the play, the audience will discover these are African people. They're black Americans, they speak English, but their worldview is African."[1] Although Wilson's designs for what was shaping up to be the third play in his proposed ten-play series seemed clear enough, this early articulation of his dramatic agenda, posited in 1984, continues to be the source of problematic issues for a specific segment of the American theatergoing public. That is, many of them subscribe to the fantasy-driven and ridiculously fallacious American melting pot theory still embraced by diehard conservatives such as Robert Brustein.[2] Often woefully naive and culturally uninformed, this group regards any effort on Wilson's part to demonstrate that "these are African people" as an attempt to promote separatism and to wage a somewhat arcane and contradictory cultural war against a country into which they have assimilated and prospered.

At issue then—as it has been for centuries—is an imperialist world view that automatically relegates Africa to the margins in matters regarding aesthetics while foregrounding Eurocentric ideals. An extension of this tendency to privilege one culture over another is also prevalent among black theater audiences, in general, and among August Wilson's audiences, in particular, most noticeably manifesting in the refusal or inability on the part of spectators and critics alike, white or black, to recognize the African in African American. Though often advanced in the guise of sophisticated theater reviews or passed off as informed intellectual discourse, the tendency to devalue another culture's aesthetic principles while waving the American flag and advocating Euro-American standards is a dangerous one, which needs to be exposed for what it is. Nigerian playwright, professor, and critic Wole Soyinka argues in his important work *Myth, Literature, and the African World*, "When ideological relations begin to deny, both theoretically and in action, the reality of a cultural entity which we define as the African world [and] to sublimate its existence in theirs, we must begin to look seriously into their political motivation."[3] In what is perhaps the most cogent recent articulation of this Western tendency to negate and denigrate African cultural ideologies, Benny Sato Ambush goes to the heart of the matter in his essay "Culture Wars," which was published in *African American Review*'s Winter 1998 special issue on black theater. He observes:

> This living in at least two worlds while claiming an African-derived identity which refuses to abandon itself by assimilation into mainstream Euro-centric culture is befuddling for many whites who, because of the privilege their white skin carries, have not had to negotiate such dualities.[4]

Adding to this, Brenda Gottschild argues, "We desperately need to cut through the convoluted web of racism that denies acknowledgement of the African part of the whole."[5] Building on Gottschild's observation, this essay will demonstrate the African presence in August Wilson's plays.

A close examination of Wilson's confident prediction that his audiences "will discover these are African people"[6] reveals his pervasive tendency to privilege memory over history in his work and, by so doing, establish a closed communication system within a group unified by "blood's memory." As Pierre Nora notes in "Between Memory and History":

> It [memory] remains in permanent evolution, open to the dialectic of remembering and forgetting, unconscious of its successive deformations, vulnerable to manipulation and appropriation, susceptible to being long dormant and periodically revived. . . . Memory, insofar as it is affective and magical, only accommodates those facts that suit it. . . . Memory is blind to all but the group it binds.[7]

Regarded as such, certain moments in African American history are filtered through Wilson's memory and recovered on stage through performance. The spectator's ability to acknowledge and identify with Wilson's Africa through performances that respond to memory rather than history depends heavily upon how effective are the actors' portrayals of "gestures and habits, in skills passed down by unspoken traditions, in the body's inherent self-knowledge, in unstudied reflexes and ingrained memories."[8]

In addition to those who view the African American as an exclusively American product whose affinities with Africa are, for all intents and purposes, irrelevant, there is another issue: certain critics "just don't get it." That is, the inability (or unwillingness) to recognize the African memory in its rhythms, rituals, and other signifiers, which are conveyed in the dramatic texts as well as in the performances of Wilson's work, seriously impedes the critic's ability to understand their full import. On one level, Wilson's plays, such as *Joe Turner's Come and Gone, The Piano Lesson*, and, to some extent, *Ma Rainey's Black Bottom, Fences*, and *Seven Guitars*, provide enough narrative structure and cross-cultural appeal to engage most audiences. However, on another, the African subtexts and the use of memory in his plays more often than not go unnoticed and are, perhaps, dismissed as directorial flourishes rather than acknowledged as components integral to the play's inherent message. Journalist Bill Moyers, for example, challenged Wilson to bring more into focus this blurry zone between his notion of an Africanist agenda and what his audiences should infer from its implementation in select plays. His pointed questions—"What happens when you get in touch with that African sensibility?" and "What does it mean to go back to Africa?"[9]— situate the concerns and misconceptions around how this aesthetic manifests and operates in Wilson's plays.

Getting in touch with an African sensibility is, Wilson believes, a crucial first step that African American artists must take in order to reorder, deconstruct, and make sense out of a world not of the African American's making. It entails the simultaneous acts of rejection and subversion of Western aesthetics by rhetorical and performative means in order to create space in this new world—also known as *America*—to realize the African nexus of his identity. Wilson likens this process to "[searching] for ways to reconnect, to reassemble" (*JT* xi).[10] Moreover, the concept of "getting in touch with an African sensibility" suggests that this mental responsiveness to Africa already exists within today's African American audiences, yet, for many, this sensibility lies dormant, existing only on a subconscious level, or is even suppressed by denial or ignorance of its current relevance. The job of Wilson as playwright, then, is to tease out this suppressed African consciousness. In his dramatic texts, this process entails the manipulation of language to evoke familiar symbols, scenarios, and potentially recognizable Africanisms for contemporary readers. In performance, this process entails, for the spectator, aural and visual stimuli for reconstructing Africa, such as utterance, ritual, suggestive movement and gesture, and stage machinery.

Closely associated in meaning to Moyers's question "What happens when you get in touch with that African sensibility?" is the other question, which, apparently, is the source of confusion for him and for others who "just don't get it": "What does it mean to go back to Africa?" Although the two questions seem to express essentially identical concerns, the second invites a careful scrutiny of the Africa that Wilson constructs on stage for the modern African American audience, an Africa that is quite different from the Africa that exists for them as a geographically and historically distant continent. The former is a material presence; the latter is a spiritually embodied idea. Hence, in order to follow Wilson's agenda, it is necessary to situate his concept of Africa within the rhetorical and spiritual contexts of his dramatic universe. Wilson is the first to concede to the impracticalities associated with a too-literal interpretation of his back-to-Africa agenda. He explains:

> If you take these people [African Americans] back over to Africa, they'll walk around trying to figure out what the hell's going on. There's no way that they can relate to that. But the sensibilities are African. They are Africans who have been removed from Africa, and they are in America four hundred years later. They're still Africans.[11]

Contrary to those who would argue that African Americans do not have a separate and distinct culture, Wilson argues in his plays that "Africanisms did survive the Middle Passage."[12]

In addition to introducing new African space to allow for an African sensibility, Wilson also constructs a new African, who announces his or her presence on stage in ways not possible in the traditional, mainstream sense of the dramatic text. Frequently, this "African" is not immediately recognizable to modern audiences, accustomed as they are to simplistic sound bites and prepackaged images. The ability to recognize any of Wilson's characters as African is bound intimately with the acquisition of an African sensibility; the spectator must, for example, suspend preconceived notions associated with Western logic and accept an African world view. John Conteh-Morgan's concept of "objective materialism" offers help in understanding such potentially overwhelming experiences in the play:

> Traditional African drama does not really depend on the outcome of a plot action, neither is it dependent on character portrayal. Characters are identifiable visually. In this respect the important factor is . . . the sheer power and expressiveness of the [performers'] stage presence and acts. . . . Meaning is not prosaically represented in words alone but . . . finds "objective materialization" in movement, gesture, and sound.[13]

What, then, is the profile of Wilson's reconstructed New World African? What does it mean to be African? And what is this reconfigured dramatic space, which he calls Africa, like in performance? The answers to these key questions form the basis for this study. Thus, attention must be paid to the impact of these new constructs upon the modern audience, African American or otherwise.

For August Wilson, discovering, claiming, and foregrounding his own African identity fuels both a personal and professional odyssey. Due to childhood circumstances in his native Pittsburgh—which involved a wayward German father, a strong-willed and industrious mother, a house full of siblings, and limited financial resources—Wilson had no choice but to fashion his identity from the culture surrounding him and to define his manhood according to terms dictated by his fate. Pittsburgh's Hill District informed the playwright's African American mother, Daisy Wilson, as did her recollections of her southern past, reinforced by the sights, the sounds, the smells, the language of her life. By extension, the sensibilities of this predominantly black urban environment influenced Wilson. Wilson and many of the people he knew and grew up with had grandparents or great-grandparents from the South, and, in some instances, they were aware of actual slave ancestors. Thus, for the young Wilson, who came of age in an era preoccupied by the concepts of cultural nationalism espoused by Malcolm X and Elijah Muhammad as well as by the Black Arts and Black Power movements, Africa became his center of gravity and a symbol for his mother's dominant heritage, a heritage that he wholeheartedly embraced.

At any given performance of an August Wilson play, it has become commonplace to see a largely white, middle- to upper-class audience pack the houses. For me, the question arises: Must white audiences—or Asian audiences, or Latino audiences, or African audiences, for that matter—see, understand, and appreciate the same African contexts that Wilson creates? Is their experience of a play such as *Joe Turner's Come and Gone*, for example, somehow lessened if, for whatever reason, they do not see what is so African about Herald Loomis? Or, if they cannot relate to the African rhythms resurrected in the Juba, do they miss the true meaning of the play? Also, do they miss out on the full meaning of *Seven Guitars* because they see Hedley in a strictly literal sense? I realize that implicit in my line of questioning here is the simplistic notion that only African Americans can understand August Wilson. However, the issue I raise is not one of audience exclusivity; instead, it is one of the performance's communicative ability. A more appropriate question may be: How do Wilson's plays and performances actualize the African presence he seeks?

Joe Turner's Come and Gone (set in 1911) and *The Piano Lesson* (set in 1936) feature Wilson's efforts "to achieve the preservation of black African identity through theater performance in terms that are quite reminiscent of ritual theater."[14] Wilson's Africa also emerges in less conspicuous ways and to a lesser degree in other plays, such as *Ma Rainey's Black Bottom* (set in 1927), *Seven Guitars* (set in 1948), *Fences* (set in 1957), and *Two Trains Running* (set in 1969). The remaining play in Wilson's current repertoire—*Jitney!* (set in 1971)—noticeably lacks African signifiers both in its text and in its performance. In fact, Wilson admits in a recent interview that when *Jitney!* was conceived and written in 1979, he had not yet adopted an artistic agenda that advanced an African presence:

> I don't think it's [African sensibility] there. Here again, it's eighteen years ago. I've become more different. I became more conscious of what I was doing and wanting to do—to the extent that I determine the way the characters act and the way that they talk.[15]

It stands to reason, then, that Africa looms largest in Wilson's plays that are set in close temporal proximity to the slave and preslave historical eras; the African presence assumes a more subtle tone in plays that are set closer to the present. Hence, one may discern a correlation between the level of difficulty Wilson's audiences experience seeing, understanding, and appreciating his renditions of Africa with his plays' evolution from the Reconstruction era to the Harlem Renaissance and Great Depression to the Civil Rights and Black Power years to the decade of racial integration and the Vietnam War. Distanced by time, censored by racism, buttressed by an oral tradition, and muted by amnesia—selective or otherwise—the historical past of African Americans now largely resides in memory. That collective memory or "blood's memory," has become for him a dramatic landscape, a site of reconstruction, a space that allows him to redefine African Americans' identities through the reimagination of their history. In his ground-breaking theoretical study, *Scars of Conquest/Masks of Resistance: The Invention of Cultural Identities in African, African-American, and Caribbean Drama*, Tejumola Olaniyan defines this same space between memory and history by calling it "an empowering post-Afrocentric space, a space that calls to and radically revises the colonialist, triumphalist narrative of European modernity."[16]

The failure to comprehend Wilson's Africanist agenda has manifested in several forms, and one early indication may be traced to the lackluster reception that *Joe Turner's Come and Gone* received during its Broadway run in 1988. Despite his confidence about the play's potential to mirror the Africanness in his characters, *Joe Turner* fared much worse on Broadway than have other Wilson works. I have noted elsewhere that Broadway audiences were not impressed. In fact, the play had a comparatively short season (27 Mar.– 26 June 1988) at the Ethel Barrymore Theatre. This lack of enthusiasm, I contend, was due not so much to the absence of a celebrity among its cast (as in *Fences*) or to the play's heavy tragic weight but to the play's difficult premise. Many audiences found Wilson's psychic protagonist and mystical flourishes over their heads and left the theater more confused than enlightened.[17]

What was it that spelled doom for Wilson's second play to reach Broadway in four years? In 1984, *Ma Rainey's Black Bottom* had been an unequivocal hit. However, this time, Wilson's work was greeted by a tougher audience— one apparently not impressed by spending an evening at the theater perplexed about the playwright's lessons on being Africans in America. Lloyd Richards, who directed *Joe Turner*, the epic drama of post-Reconstruction African Americans searching for their personal and collective identities while held up at a boardinghouse in Pittsburgh, warded off speculations that the play floundered because its cast did not include a star. He explained in a *New York Times* interview that confusion about *Joe Turner* was due to "the depth and difficulty of the play" and admitted that it "was a much more mystical play than *Fences*, a much more challenging play. . . . It took you deeply into a place where you had never been before. It made you work, and there are people who go to the theater who don't like to work."[18]

One might argue that the short life of *Joe Turner* on Broadway was a commentary on August Wilson's creation of a "closed" performance. That is, *Joe Turner* "anticipate[d] a very precise receiver and demand[ed] well-defined types of 'competence' (encyclopedic, ideological, etc.) for their 'correct' reception."[19] In this sense, the relatively short run of the play was inevitable, given the history of Broadway audiences' lukewarm reception of African-based dramas about black life. But also, I contend, the play did not fare well because the mainstream audience was reluctant to leave its established comfort zone of cultural awareness to examine life—even temporarily—from another's perspective. In order "to do justice to the African presence," Brenda Gottschild favors such a reversal in the dominant point of view. She conjectures, "What if we were to stand on our heads and assume that our American culture is African-rooted, so that the European elements could be regarded from an Africanist perspective?" She sees this revisionist approach of viewing "European elements . . . from an Africanist perspective" particularly useful in communicating the sometimes unconscious exercises in cultural imperialism.[20]

Joe Turner's Come and Gone serves as a paradigm, illuminating the problem between author and critics. Despite Wilson's admission that *Joe Turner* is his favorite play, it was reviewed harshly by critics who just did not get it—the playwright's infusion of Africanisms, that is. Herald Loomis, the darkly clad, brooding tenant at Seth and Bertha Holly's Pittsburgh boardinghouse, bears the brunt of this negative criticism. Those theater critics who detest his character argue that Loomis's "violent rebirth [does not make] dramatic sense," that his religious vision is "so obliquely written, it seems more like an LSD flashback," that his character is "closed mouthed and near crazy," that "the playwright—or Jesus—had struck him with a bolt of lightning," and that "we're left grappling for symbolic explanations and metaphysical justification for his behavior, the knife he wields, and the blood he sheds."[21] This catalog of complaints about Charles Dutton's (Yale Repertory Theatre) and Delroy Lindo's (Broadway) portrayals of Loomis reveals how utterly confounded and ill-equipped these critics were to make sense of the play. Director Lloyd Richards's attempts to convey Wilson's stage note that Loomis is "a man driven not by hellhounds that seemingly bay at his heels, but by his search for a world that speaks to something about himself" were lost on these critics.[22] In fact, Richards saw early on that Loomis would pose problems for audiences and was relatively successful during the play's journey from Yale to Broadway in convincing Wilson to alter the play in order to clarify the character's uncertain motivation and open-ended fate.[23]

The denunciations of Loomis's character are commonplace among those whose sensibilities remain blind to Wilson's Africanist agenda. Nevertheless, as one professor of African literature notes, "Afro-American mythology is not 'strange,' but a common, natural part of life."[24] Viewed according to certain principles of African ritual performance, Dutton and Lindo situate their characters outside the logic of Western thought and within the realm of African sensibility, where "symbolic movements and actions, stylized gestures, patterned dances, and even speech which is molded into a variety of fixed forms, formulaic expressions, and tropes" are expected to be understood as means of communication.[25] Loomis's morbid attire, sullen countenance, ominous narratives of archetypal dimension, and shocking scenes of self-scarification allow each particularity to enter his realm. Thus, without knowledge of African rituals, superstition, religion, or music, which continue to inform Africans in America, audiences are forced to assess Wilson's work using awkward yardsticks that contain little, if any, relevance to Wilson's intentions.

Understanding the actions, gestures, and motivations of Herald Loomis is the toughest challenge of any *Joe Turner* audience. To regard the ominous intruder as an embodiment of Africa requires careful attention to his role in the play. Loomis's prevailing sense of disorientation underscores the degree of devastation he has suffered in the wake of an imposed seven-year work detail, which separated him from his family and, by extension, from his cultural base. When viewed through the lens of an African sensibility, Loomis personifies the aching consciousness of millions of slaves, who were uprooted from their homelands, forced into subjugation, eventually emancipated, and ultimately set out on the road to fend for themselves. He also mirrors the suppressed anxieties of contemporary African Americans, who are haunted by this indelible past. However, despite these African-based perspectives, what has prevented modern audiences and critics alike from regarding Loomis as the conscience of Africa are numerous signals that, in their eyes—and according to Western logic—may be construed as evidence of possible derangement rather than as clues to his symbolic importance. To audiences who experience the play but lack African sensibility or cultural sensitivity to Wilson's agenda, Loomis's nightmares, convulsions, fits of anger, shocking displays of blasphemy, haunting attire, and foreboding appearance impede their understanding of Wilson's loftier regard for his dignity as an African. Still, the majority of the negative assessments that have been compiled by theater critics reveals their ignorance of Africanisms and cultural prejudice and confirms a degree of laziness and shortsightedness regarding cultural differences.

Not only have Herald Loomis's Africanist meanings easily gone unnoted or misconstrued in *Joe Turner*, but other manifestations of this aesthetic have the potential to remain obscure to those insensitive to the culture revealed in the performance text. These include, for example, the tenants dancing the African-based Juba; the conjure man, Bynum, killing pigeons in Seth's garden and relating the tale of Shiny Man; Miss Mabel's ghost actually appearing before the child Reuben; and Loomis claiming to experience atavistic visions of the Middle Passage and, ultimately, inflicting a wound upon his body. Each of these episodes is steeped in African ritual and lore as well as in symbolic aspects of African Americans' slave past, and, taken together, they underscore how the play can operate as a closed performance.

I was witness to intense reactions to one of August Wilson's closed performances when he visited Howard University in September 1995 to participate in an open forum at the Ira Aldridge Theater. During the question-and-answer session, a white woman rose from the predominantly African American audience and admitted that she was unable to observe anything African about the characters in a production of *Joe Turner's Come and Gone*, which she had recently seen, and asked that the playwright expand upon this aspect of the play's premise. Immediately, her question transformed the dynamics of the Howard University audience from collegial and respectful to belligerent and defensive. Before Wilson could address her question, several vocal responses to her statements erupted from the crowd, as if, by admitting her difficulties, she had somehow insulted this particular audience, who evidently had no problems recognizing and accepting the likes of Herald Loomis, Bynum Walker, and Martha Pentacost as Africans. Once the audience had recovered from the initial impact of this woman's query, Wilson responded—not to why she had difficulties seeing Africa but to what, according to his agenda, the play should have revealed to her. In terms quite similar to those he expressed in the interview with Moyers, Wilson explained:

> We are Africans who have been in America since the seventeenth century. We are Americans. But first of all, we are Africans. . . . We have different philosophical ideas and attitudes, different values, different ideas about style and linguistics, different aesthetics.[26]

I cannot recall ever having witnessed a writer, a playwright, a musician, or a dancer being placed in the awkward position of having to explain why a particular member of an audience did not get their meaning. Neither can I recall any artist directly responding to such an honest though artistically intrusive query. Frankly, had Wilson answered this woman's question as forthrightly as she had posed it, he would have likely offended her. In effect, what she wanted to know was how could a white woman sit through a theatrical performance of *Joe Turner*, sharing the same space as African American spectators, and totally miss that the people on stage were Africans? What she revealed instead was that she—like other spectators of various races and cultural backgrounds who share her struggle—had not grasped the manifestations of the Africa that Wilson's plays embrace in performance. These Africanisms do not announce their presence with drum beats, colorful costumes, or expressive dances. Neither are they conveyed in native African tongues. Hence, recognition is not instantaneous or automatic to all members of the audience.

Had Wilson chosen to respond to the woman more directly, his answer might have been, "You don't get it because the play was not intended for you" or "You don't get it because you lack the necessary African sensibility." As if to avert such a scenario, Wilson simply repeated his assertion that these characters were undeniably African and left her to conjecture her own meaning from this.

The imaginary African masks that the Charles family dons in Wilson's *The Piano Lesson* (1988) are less implicit and thus less atavistic than those attempted in *Joe Turner's Come and Gone*. With the notable exception of *New Republic* critic Robert Brustein—whose well-known and widely proclaimed rejection of Africanist ideologies prompted him to denounce the play as "the most poorly composed of Wilson's four produced works"[27]—critics and audiences sensitive to the implications of the play, for the most part, do get it. That they comprehend the ties that bind African Americans living in 1936 Pittsburgh with their slave ancestors is due largely to the clearly didactic message of the play's principal symbolic image: a piano, more than a century old, carved with "African" symbols. Wilson is also more effective in convincing his audiences that the Depression-era Charles family, which has put its roots in Pittsburgh, is actually composed of Africans living in America. Wilson clarifies the ambiguities that he leaves open in *Joe Turner*. In *The Piano Lesson*, he relies upon the speeches of a single character, Doaker Charles, to reveal the crucial narrative of the family's history, which has remained locked in the piano. Conversations dominated by the sage uncle of the family create clear connections between Africa then and Pittsburgh now as he carefully delineates the experiences of his parents and grandparents: "See, now . . . to understand why we say that . . . to understand about that piano . . . you got to go back to slavery time. See, our family was owned by a fellow named Robert Sutter" (*PL* 42). As self-appointed griot, he keeps Africa ever in his family's psyche as well as in the consciousness of the play's audience.

A significant number of critics charge that *The Piano Lesson* is overwritten, devoid of action, repetitious, chatty, excessive in characterization, and (before Lloyd Richards was able to convince Wilson to add an extra scene to answer the unresolved question of the piano's final owner) lacked a resolution.[28] In addition, more than a few regard the supernatural intrusion of the ghost of Robert Sutter as an artificial and forced device.[29] On stage, this spirit announces its presence through the tinkling of the piano's ivory keys, the rustling of Berniece's curtains, and the frightful stares and screams of those who come upon it. Its presence is also confirmed in a physically exaggerated wrestling match, during which it proves a fitting rival for the frantically swinging, punching, tumbling Boy Willie. Thus, for many, Wilson's Africa hinges more upon the piano's profound nonverbal visual message while the supernatural addition of a ghost is relegated to the category of special effects.

Yet, just as the Charles family cannot so easily extract Sutter from the piano, Sutter's place in the Africa that Wilson reconstructs in *The Piano Lesson* must be contended with as well. Although paradoxical in nature, Sutter, the white relative of slave owners who bartered away Berniece's and Boy Willie's ancestors for a piano, is an inextricable part of the Charles family's Africanist past. As such, he is also part of the slave-owning colonialism in Africanist memory. Despite the baggage his ghost brings to the 1936 setting, he remains, until exorcised, a part of the African portrait that Wilson summons to the stage and recreates. Like the painful memories that plague Herald Loomis, Sutter's presence must be acknowledged before it can be understood and overcome.

For audiences of *Seven Guitars*, another one of Wilson's closed performances, the ability to recognize Africa and Africans is far from unanimous. The play has been written off as a disappointing hybrid offspring of Wilson's previous plays. From *Ma Rainey*, it inherits the ambitious though tragic blues musician; from *Joe Turner*, *Two Trains Running*, and *Fences*, it inherits the offbeat mystic; and from *The Piano Lesson*, it inherits a credible manifestation of the spiritual world. For example, in *Seven Guitars*, Hedley, the tubercular Jamaican sandwich vendor, perplexes *New York Times* reviewer Vincent Canby to the extent that he calls him the "most troublesome" aspect of the play's Broadway performance.[30] Hedley does not fit into a conventional scheme of

Western drama. The character is, therefore, "unimportant" and deserves some neatly summarized and witty dismissal by critics—in this case the appellation "idiot savant."[31]

But, despite the dismay of those who question Hedley's relevance to *Seven Guitars*, Wilson has remained faithful to his initial conception of this character as a modern-day reflection of Africa. Prior to the start of rehearsals at the Goodman Theatre late in 1994, he told interviewer Tom Creamer:

> Specifically, the character Hedley may carry inside him the largest African response to the world with his concept of the messiah, with the understanding that there's a necessity for the messiah. In that sense he may be the one who carries the political awareness that blacks are not free and are oppressed. . . . Hedley may be the most African of the characters.[32]

Wilson's views of Hedley as "most African" are antithetical to those who deem him dramatically unworthy and point to the void between what the playwright intends and what certain audiences simply fail to understand. On stage, Hedley's severely stooped posture, his labored walking, and graying hair visibly suggest a man in the twilight of his life, a man whose years have revealed for him many of life's secrets, which he now feels compelled to impart. His desires to father a male child with the sensuous southerner and to get money from the self-taught trumpeter, Buddy Bolden, to build a plantation further underscore Africanist inclinations. However, despite this deceptively uncomplicated view of Hedley, his character, like those of Gabriel (*Fences*) and Hambone (*Two Trains Running*), requires more sophisticated understanding from the "culturally handicapped" audience in order for the African stories to have any serious impact. While the effects of alcohol, dementia, and various other mental impairments understandably lessen the credibility of such characters, Wilson insists that any honest reflection of African American culture must include the stories of these marginalized individuals who, he argues, impart the most useful knowledge of African cosmology, memory, and continuity. As such, Hedley is an example of an Africanism in its most basic, most Wilsonian form.

Although the black and white high school students who shared the audience with me at the spring 1997 Center Stage production of *Seven Guitars* found much to keep their attention for the three-hour performance, many looked dazed as they entered the lobby following the final curtain. A few broke the silence by recalling instances of humor as if to suppress thoughts of the gruesome, bloody images of Hedley slashing the throat of a neighbor's rooster followed soon by a similar bloodletting gesture inflicted upon Floyd Barton. They also chose to keep to themselves their immediate thoughts about a man obsessed with receiving money from a long-dead musician to buy a mythical plantation so that "the white man not going to tell me what to do no more" (*SG* 24). The entire experience prompted me to ask, "What is a teenager in 1997 (or any audience member, for that matter) to make of these images?" What level of knowledge do we need in order to comprehend such a profound performance? As I watched this group exit the theater, I was convinced that *Seven Guitars* had seriously shaken them. However, none spoke of Hedley or of Africa in their bewilderment.

The confused teenagers seemed to lack both the language and the cultural sensitivity needed to articulate clearly an understanding of what they had just experienced. This, of course, is saddening and problematic, for it strongly suggests that primary and secondary educational institutions are grooming another generation of callous, apathetic, and culturally ignorant critics and adult theatergoers to take the place of those now thriving in our adult populations. How are plays of the black experience (or any other experience other than white American) taught in these classrooms? Clearly, without knowledge of African-based rituals and without awareness of the nuances of African American history and culture, these youths—soon to become adults—will remain stunned, speechless, and unable to make sense out of much of what they see.

Perhaps because the symbolic backdrop of Africa lies so much in the distance in *Ma Rainey's Black Bottom*, L. Kenneth Richardson (who directed the Center Stage production of *Ma Rainey* during the fall 1990 season) chose to compensate for this absence in Wilson's 1930s play by adding an African mime dancer. Sensing that Wilson's play had somehow reneged on his agenda by not endowing a more imposing African presence, the director apparently took it upon himself to add the Africanist dimension. At select moments during the course of the more than three-hour performance, an embodiment of African consciousness appears on stage, gesticulating half in the shadows to ensure that the image of Africa remains present. Yet, much to the chagrin of the capacity audience on the night I attended, this "tinkering," as it has been called,[33] was overkill. *Washington Times* critic Hap Erstein concurred: "It [the performance] certainly doesn't need an added symbolic character that Mr. Richardson calls Spirit Dancer, a high-stepping, tribal-minstrel apparition to pop out on occasion and accentuate the obvious with his mute echoes of the action."[34] Interestingly, while Erstein's review of the play may have mirrored some of the audience's sentiments, his argument is significantly weakened by his failure to stipulate his meaning of "obvious" within the context of this performance. Moreover, his reasoning does not extend to the next logical step: a clear explanation of what the African dancer does convey. As is often the tendency of culturally uninformed critics, words can become smoke and mirrors, behind which there is frequently little substance.

Despite popular rejection of this appended device, I believe that the African embellishments made by director Richardson were in accord with August Wilson's Africanist agenda. Richardson's idea was to bridge the gaps he anticipated in the largely white audiences' ability to understand Wilson's African undertones. What the African mime dancer offered the Center Stage audience was an invitation to view the performance they had just seen within an African context informed by an African sensibility. From this site, the motivations, actions, and eventual fates of the characters took on more culturally specific meanings. Although silent, the dancer, who was garbed in

African headdress, mask, and beads, communicated with his body that Ma, her band, and her two associates occupy the same space as their ancestors; moreover, the dancer drew attention to the fact that the characters should call upon their ancestors as they try to find their way in the racist America of the late 1920s. As a result of their refusal to set aside Western logic, the audience and critics, once again, opted to reject and dismiss as flawed this Africanist symbol.

For the most part, observing the characters of *Ma Rainey's Black Bottom* as Africans seems to be less important for Wilson in this play, which hinges upon a black man's more immediate concerns for survival in the racist recording industry of the late 1920s. Wilson must have realized that a too-aggressive demonstration of an African presence could overshadow other, equally pressing issues, including survival in a more modern environment. Furthermore, it stands to reason that, as his repertoire of plays moves chronologically toward the 1990s, Africa's presence must correspondingly assume more subtle forms. More important than establishing an African context in *Ma Rainey* is an emphasis upon the band's current sorry predicament, upon Ma's refusal to become a victim, and upon Levee's deferred dream. One might argue that getting to the root of each of these concerns involves going back to their African connections, but this is not an immediate concern for spectators, whose attention is focused upon the surface conflicts of the play. While Africa resonates in the persons of Herald Loomis and Bynum Walker in *Joe Turner* and in the etched-upon piano in *The Piano Lesson*, in *Ma Rainey's Black Bottom,* African sensibility becomes the subject of a built-in counternarrative, at the center of which Wilson places Toledo, the philosopher-pianist and eventual victim of homicide.

In Toledo, August Wilson creates a character who possesses exceptional potential to effect positive change among his people, yet he is never really able to rise to the occasion. This reflects the tradition of the revolutionary antihero popularized in Amiri Baraka's characters Walker Vessels (*The Slave*, 1964) and Clay (*The Dutchman* 1964). Toledo is apparently the only literate and educated band member, yet he focuses his attention upon belittling Levee's intellect and pontificating pseudointellectual rhetoric about African sensibility. When asked for marijuana, for example, he uses the occasion to ostentatiously display his grasp of African concepts: "That's what you call an African conceptualization. That's when you name the gods and call on the ancestors to achieve whatever your desires are" (*MR* 32). At this moment in the play, Toledo's wisdom is not received well by the group, which deems it to be irrelevant to their present circumstances.

As antihero, Toledo forms a counternarrative, which underscores a misguided African sensibility. His nonwarriorlike demeanor and his seemingly pretentious African idealism place him in opposition to Wilson's pronouncement that these characters are African. Toledo fails to use his knowledge of Africa to assist his comrades in transcending their dead-end conditions; instead, he flaunts it before them as evidence of his superior intelligence. Understood in these terms, his death becomes the supreme payment he must render to appease the gods, for he has failed them. Outside of this African-based logic, Toledo's death may be perceived as the last link in a causal chain of major disappointing events, which frequently culminates in black-on-black violence. His death comes at the hands of Levee, an individual who has witnessed his mother's rape and his father's murder and who has been duped out of his song lyrics—all acts perpetrated by white men. But, rather than focus his rage on the real oppressor, Levee makes Toledo his target.

Africa also finds indirect or built-in expression in the music *of Ma Rainey's Black Bottom*. The actors of the Center Stage production—coached by composer Olu Dara to "become" musicians for this performance—negotiate their own musical tunes during the mock rehearsal sessions they hold while waiting for Ma. In addition to their blues tunes, distinctly African sounds permeate the production to convey the potentially explosive emotional undercurrents of the male band members' separate and collective fates. In a combined mixture of rhythmical blues guitars, trumpets, and flutes, Dara attempted to infuse the play with Africa's presence by "[underscoring] various narrative passages, including a deft blues tune that accompanies August Wilson's text, a ballad Rainey sings to her tired, hurting feet."[35] Taking his cues from his "cultural ancestors in Africa and Mississippi,"[36] Dara conjured up a musical recipe for *Ma Rainey* made up of ingredients from his own cultural past. In addition, Dwight Andrews, Wilson's principal musician, whose long-time role has been to select and fine-tune the musical accompaniments for the plays, also locates Africa in the music by looking inward for the necessary inspiration. He stresses "how people hear" in determining the most appropriate music for the contemporary audience. That is, he sees as his mission not merely trying to create what Ma may have sounded like in the 1920s but determining how to modify her music to permit the modern audience an opportunity to go from patting their feet to comprehending the profound narratives of these characters' lives.[37]

A restaurant in Pittsburgh in 1969 is perhaps one of the least likely settings to introduce African-inspired characters. On the surface, Wilson's *Two Trains Running* appears to be the farthest removed from Africa, yet, just as in *Joe Turner's Come and Gone, The Piano Lesson, Ma Rainey's Black Bottom*, and *Seven Guitars*, Wilson tries to convince audiences that, in this play, too, "African-isms did survive the Middle Passage."[38] The play presents a close look into the lives of black people who come regularly to commune about their despair in a Pittsburgh restaurant slated for demolition. The characters are a diverse group, and several story lines compete for emphasis, ranging from the battle of the restaurant owner to get a fair price from the city for his business to a fragile yet poignant romance between an ex-convict, Sterling, and the restaurant waitress, Risa.

Because *Two Trains Running* is the most historically distant from Africa to date, Wilson's toughest challenge is evoking a sense of an African presence in modern audiences. Previous experience seems to have taught him that the African connection must be subtly conveyed. No doubt in order to elicit the attention of the 1990s audience, which, I contend, has become somewhat numbed by the impact of special effects offered by electronic media, Wilson, in response, sought to modify his presentation of African sensibilities. As a result, the most prominent image of Africa in *Two Trains Running* is a 322-year-old woman, who never appears on stage. The Africanist embodiment is unmistakably signified in Methuselah-like Aunt Ester, the neighborhood faith healer and confidante. While her age is the historical equivalent of the number of years Africans have been in America, her character, like memory, defies exactness and, in fact, encourages belief in otherworldliness. Moreover, since she is never present on stage, Aunt Ester embodies the collisions of history and memory. Her looming presence in the minds of the characters strongly suggests that she is a force with which Memphis Lee's clients must reckon. Her absence from the stage facilitates her role as the distant voice of Africa, but her spiritual presence influences the behaviors on stage. She must be sought after to give counsel and solace and her patrons must act on the faith she supplies rather than on the logic of Western rationalism. We realize that she has absorbed centuries of cultural knowledge and strength, which she imparts on a pay-as-you-go basis. Although Ester never appears on stage, the *idea* of her presence is highly significant to Wilson's neo-Africanist agenda. According to Wilson, "we have [in Aunt Ester] a tradition to re-member and fall back on."[39] Her ubiquitous presence in the minds and conversations of the characters is very much analogous to the modern and practical role that Wilson wills between Africa and his contemporary African American audience. Like the image of Africa, she need not surface as a literal or visible presence in the play in order to affect the well-being of her followers in Memphis Lee's Home-Style Restaurant. Instead, though absent, she raises the consciousness of the characters and the audience in subtle but profound ways. She is the link, through thought and memory, to ancestral roots. She is kept alive in the minds and imaginations of the characters and the audience, and as long as they believe she can be of service to them, the African presence hovers over us all.

Such is the ideal African world view that Wilson sketches in *Two Trains Running*, yet as in each of the previous plays discussed, the ideal does not always coincide with the real. When viewed through the lens of an Africanist aesthetic, what is so often classified by certain critics as "muddled" and "out of control," becomes significant in *Two Trains Running*. If, for example, one considers Brenda Gottschild's assertion that "African-based cultural forms and practices in the Americas . . . have signposts that differentiate them from European-based forms and practices,"[40] we will have a more solid basis for critiquing African-based works, such as those of August Wilson. When, for example, we observe Aunt Ester from a spiritual rather than material per-spective, we enter the African cosmology that Wilson intends. What appears as "muddle" is redefined as ritual; what is taken for "out of control" is reinterpreted as Africanist expressivity; what is absent from the stage becomes present in the body; and what is seen as devoid of plot will be reconsidered as the flexibility of the griot, the African storyteller roots. Similar enlight-enment on differences too automatically perceived as weaknesses in *Two*

Trains may result upon acknowledging Gottschild's well-informed description of what shapes African performance. She notes:

> Another example [of opposing African and European elements in American culture] lies in African "dilemma" tales that illustrate a principle of contrariety, open-endedness, or living with opposition, without the necessity of resolution or closure. These are stories that end with a question or call for a discussion, rather than a solution.[41]

Mainstream critics who adhere to single standards of excellence need to acknowledge the cultural signatures of other peoples and values. On those who continue to question how much of this is African and how much is loss of control, Paul Carter Harrison pins the label "sociological explication[s],"[42] and he attributes such misunderstanding to widespread indoctrination by contemporary modes of thought:

> Lost, for example, is the aesthetic appreciation of discontinuity—rather than linear continuity—as a rhythmic device in the expressive modes of African socialization, including the polymorphic orchestration of off-beats, counter beats, and breaks in music and storytelling, and the visual tension of asymmetrical patterns woven in West African Kente cloth and the African-American quilts of the rural south.[43]

What several of the play's critics claim to be plotless, motiveless, snail-paced performances, Harrison redefines as "a polymorphic orchestration." That is, the unpredictable rhythms and patterns throughout *Two Trains* correspond to the discordant nature that is so prevalent in an African aesthetic.

Fences (set in 1957) features muted African presence different from any others discussed here. As may be deduced by the play's Pulitzer Prize–winning status and the widespread popularity of the domestic drama in both theaters and anthologies, audiences as well as readers connect with the characters and see themselves in the process. Moreover, the numerous universal emotions evoked in *Fences* make it a play that crosses boundaries of time, age, race, gender, and culture. The major story line does not limit itself to a symbolic African landscape. Instead, it involves a garbage collector's war waged against himself, his coworkers, and his family for missing his dream of playing major league baseball.

The play, however, reveals an African presence in basic albeit subtle fashion. Troy Maxson's war-injured brother, Gabriel, whose mental condition leads Gabriel to believe that he is Archangel Gabriel and that he sees Saint Peter on a regular basis, is the conduit through which Wilson transmits an African sensibility in *Fences*. It is not coincidental that Gabriel is both mentally challenged and spiritually gifted, as he joins a number of similar Wilsonian characters whose sensitivity exceeds those around them, even if their mental capabilities do not. As Gabriel attempts to blow his trumpet at the end of the play to signal to Saint Peter to open the Pearly Gates for his brother, he introduces another dimension of *Fences* heretofore unseen; he enters a spiritual realm believed to be inhabited by his African ancestors, where the sound of his horn is, in fact, quite audible. Here again, Wilson subverts Western logic and interrupts the play's naturalistic premise by stepping outside of the borders defined by Eurocentric conventions.

Despite the best Africanist defense, however, this ending seemed to be an awkward attachment for Broadway producer Carol Shorenstein, who threatened to fire Lloyd Richards if he did not clip Gabriel's final gestures. She failed to see the significance of Gabriel's ending and feared it would cause doom for *Fences* in New York. Her decision went beyond personal taste; her reservations also mirrored those of regional theater audiences, which could not decipher Gabriel's "slow strange dance" (*F* 101), his awkward attempt to sing, and his failed efforts to blow his horn for Saint Peter. After months of haggling among Wilson, Richards, and Shorenstein, the three finally made no changes to the script. As a result, Wilson's agenda remained intact, despite efforts by those unfamiliar with his objectives.

The gaps that exist between Wilson's presentation of Africa on stage—in performance and in dialogue—and his audiences' ability to comprehend its depths are not without reason. Filling in these gaps, however, requires honest, conscientious, and willful work on the part of critics and audiences (and producers). Given the playwright's personal quest to negotiate his own African-German heritage, the problematic presence of Africa in his work parallels his maturing awareness of the importance of Africa in claiming his cultural background. Many of Wilson's white critics have been less than kind in their dissecting analyses of such devices, however, revealing evidence of a disturbing lack of cultural sensitivity exacerbated by a refusal to consider any other standards of excellence than their own. We must move beyond one-dimensional critiques, which fail to acknowledge cultural diversity and the plethora of cultural contributions.

August Wilson realizes a crucial and revolutionary role for Africa in his works. No longer can the portrayal of negative stereotypes, such as those that plague *Ma Rainey*'s Levee ("You don't see me running around in no jungle with no bone between my nose" [32]) or *Joe Turner*'s Seth ("that heebie-jeebie stuff" [2]), define Africa for contemporary audiences. In order to advance beyond this, we must recognize what Wole Soyinka refers to as "a prescriptive validation of African self-apprehension," what Paul Carter Harrison refers to as the "African continuum," what Tejumola Olaniyan refers to as "empowering post-Afrocentric space," what Brenda Gottschild refers to as "revisionist thinking,"[44] and what August Wilson consistently refers to as "blood's memory." The stage, as it has done historically, presents enormous opportunity to effect change, and Wilson is in the forefront of playwrights who are experimenting with performance techniques to usher in a new activist-artistic era. In the initially unexplained convulsions of Herald Loomis, in the lively Juba dance of his fellow tenants, in the bloodletting and chanting rituals of Bynum and Hedley, and in the sage advice of the 322-year-old Aunt Ester, Africa is summoned on stage.

1. Kim Powers, "An Interview with August Wilson," *Theater* 16 (1984): 53.

2. Robert Brustein has been August Wilson's long-time adversary, harshly criticizing the playwright as well as the former dean of the Yale School of Drama and Wilson's former director, Lloyd Richards, for using the Yale Repertory Theatre as a steppingstone for Wilson's plays before they proceeded to Broadway. Brustein is director of the American Repertory Theater at the Loeb Drama Center, professor of English at Harvard, and drama critic for the *New Republic.*

3. Wole Soyinka, *Myth, Literature, and the African World* (Cambridge: Cambridge University Press, 1976), xi.

4. Benny Sato Ambush, "Culture Wars," *African American Review* 31 (1998): 582.

5. Brenda Gottschild, *Digging the Africanist Presence in American Performance* (Westport, Conn.: Greenwood, 1996), 3.

6. Powers 53.

7. Pierre Nora, "Between Memory and History," in *History and Memory in African American Culture* ed. Geneviève Fabre and Robert O'Meally (New York: Oxford University Press, 1994), 285–286.

8. Nora 289.

9. Bill Moyers, *A World of Ideas* (New York: Doubleday, 1989), 172–174.

10. Following is the key to the list of play abbreviations used in this chapter:

F	*Fences*
JT	*Joe Turner's Come and Gone*
JY	*Jitney!*
MR	*Ma Rainey's Black Bottom*
PL	*The Piano Lesson*
SG	*Seven Guitars*
TT	*Two Trains Running*

11. Quoted in Moyers 172.

12. James V. Hatch, review of *Digging the Africanist Presence in American Performance*, by Brenda Gottschild, in *African American Review* 3 (Fall 1997): 540.

13. John Conteh-Morgan, "African Traditional Drama and Issues in Theater Performance Criticism," *Comparative Drama* 28 (1994): 12.

14. Amadou Bissiri, "Aspects of Africanness in August Wilson's Drama: Reading *The Piano Lesson* through Wole Soyinka's Drama," *African American Review* 30 (1996): 111.

15. August Wilson, interview by author, tape recording, Baltimore, 25 Apr. 1996.

16. Tejumola Olaniyan, *Scars of Conquest/Masks of Resistance: The Invention of Cultural Identities in African, African American, and Caribbean Drama* (New York: Oxford University Press, 1995), 139.

17. Sandra G. Shannon, *The Dramatic Vision of August Wilson* (Washington, D.C.: Howard University Press, 1995), 133.

18. Mervyn Rothstein, "Round Five for the Theatrical Heavyweight," *New York Times* (15 Apr. 1990): H8.

19. Marco De Marinis, "Dramaturgy of the Spectator," *Drama Review* 31 (1987): 103.

20. Gottschild 6.

21. This series of exaggerated and off-base assessments of Herald Loomis's physical

bout with the demons of his past come from the following reviews: David Richards, "The Tortured Spirit of 'Joe Turner,' " *Washington Post* (9 Oct. 1987): B1, B12; David Stearn, " 'Turner' Comes to a Near Halt," *USA Today* (29 Mar. 1988): 4D; and M. A. Scherer, " 'Turner' Never Comes at All," *Evening Capital* (13 Oct. 1987): B10.

22. *JT* 14

23. During *Joe Turner*'s rehearsal for the 1986 production at Yale, Wilson, Richards, and several observers noted that the script ended with a lingering question as to whether Herald Loomis "finds his song." What audiences needed, according to Richards, was a more emotionally rewarding catharsis after Loomis's frustrated search for his wife for much of the play. Yet it was not until Wilson sat through several intensive rehearsals of the play that he discovered a solution for Loomis's unsatisfying depiction: "I came up with the idea of ending the first act with him on the floor unable to stand up. When he stands at the end, you can read that as him finding his song." For more on the process of revising *Joe Turner*, see Tom Killens, "Black Theater Triumphant: A Dynamic Duo from the Yale Repertory," *The World and I* (Dec. 1987), 236–239.

24. Bissiri 99.

25. Ibid.

26. Moyers 172.

27. Robert Brustein, "The Lessons of 'The Piano,' " *New Republic* (21 May 1990): 29.

28. To learn more about the process of revising *The Piano Lesson*, see Irene Backalenick, "Fine-Tuning *The Piano Lesson*: An Interview with Lloyd Richards," *Theater Week* (16–22 Apr. 1990): 1–19.

29. Dwight Andrews, telephone interview by author, Emory University, Atlanta, 28 Aug. 1997.

30. Vincent Canby, "Unrepentant, Defiant Blues for Seven Strong Voices," *New York Times* (28 Mar. 1996): C32.

31. Ibid.

32. Tom Creamer, "Men with Knives and Steel and Guitar Strings': An Interview with August Wilson," *On Stage* 9 (Goodman Theater Series, 1994–1995): E3.

33. Hap Erstein, " 'Ma Rainey' Triumphs over Racism, Director," *Washington Times* (8 Oct. 1990): E3.

34. Ibid.

35. Stephanie Shapiro, "Olu Dara and All the World's Music," *Evening Sun* (16 Oct. 1990): D1.

36. Ibid.

37. See select reviews in Sandra G. Shannon, "Annotated Bibliography on Works by and about August Wilson since 1992," in *May All Your Fences Have Gates: Essays on the Drama of August Wilson*, ed. Alan Nadel (Iowa City: Iowa University Press, 1994), 230–266.

38. Hatch 540.

39. William K. Gale, "August Wilson's Vision of Light at End of the Tunnel," *Providence Journal-Bulletin* (6 Apr. 1990): D5.

40. Gottschild 7.

41. Ibid., 8.

42. Paul Carter Harrison, "August Wilson's Blues Poetics," in *August Wilson: Three Plays* (Pittsburgh: Pittsburgh University Press, 1991), 295.

43. Ibid.

44. Soyinka xii; Harrison 292; Olaniyan 139; and Gottschild 6.

Part III

Intersections of Race and Gender

9

Black Minstrelsy and Double Inversion, Circa 1890

ANNEMARIE BEAN

MISS JOHNSING: Is that you, Dinah Dewdrop?

DINAH: It am.

MISS J: And how do you find yourself, this evening?

DINAH: I ain't been lost, as I knows on, Miss Johnsing.

MISS J: I mean, Dinah, how is your health? How do you *feel*?

DINAH (*shaking her head*): I's sorry to say, Miss Johnsing, dat I's a leetle *off color* dis night.

MISS J: That is a melancholic fact, Dinah.

TOPSY: 'Pears like we's all on us a bit shady, dis ebenin'![1]

The above exchange comes from *Jolly Joe's Lady Minstrels*, a minstrel guide "written, compiled, and edited in the sole interest of cheerfulness from the most jovial sources, and arranged with a particular eye to the needs of FEMALE NEGRO MINSTRELS."[2] *Jolly Joe's Lady Minstrels* was published in 1893, a significant moment in the history of nineteenth-century American blackface minstrelsy,[3] as there was an increasing number of professional and amateur white minstrel guides published, including Frank Dumont's *The Witmark Amateur Minstrel Guide and Burnt Cork Encyclopedia* (1899) and *The Boys of New York End Men's Joke Book* (1902).[4] Minstrel guides were virtual compendiums on how-to-make-a-minstrel-show, with short introductory essays on the history of minstrelsy, front- and back-of-the-book advertisements for fright wigs and burnt cork makeup, and instructions on the form and material of minstrelsy. *Jolly Joe's Lady Minstrels* is a typical example, offering directions on costumes and makeup and a section on "Specimen Jokes, Stories, and Conundrums."

Not only were the amateur minstrel guides detailed lessons on how to be a minstrel, they also served the additional purpose of telling the reader how to be an Other, in the classical Homi Bhabhan sense of Othering as an ambivalent act of love and subjection.[5] The opening exchange between Dinah Dewdrop, one of the end women (the others are Sukey, Rosy, and Topsy), and Miss Johnsing, the interlocutor, is significant as a representative example of these lessons in Otherness as outlined in the 1890s minstrel guides. Miss Johnsing speaks in mannered words and diction; Dinah answers her questions in an interpretation of black dialect. The conversation concerns Dinah's health. "How is your health?" Miss Johnsing inquires. Dinah replies, "I's a leetle *off color* dis night." The emphasized observation "off color" is meant to set up the first laugh for the audience, which the comic character Topsy delivers: " 'Pears like we's all on us a bit shady, dis ebenin'!" Topsy, a character borrowed from Harriet Beecher Stowe's *Uncle Tom's Cabin* (1852), uses color as a mark of social inclusion, for the minstrels and the audience know that everyone onstage is blackened by burnt cork, not by race. The wink to the audience is based in the mutual understanding that we (the performers) are different from you (the audience) but only because we (the performers) are putting on a show, an act, a minstrel show in blackface. This knowledge— that everyone is "shady," but no one is truly "black"—is an important distinction in deriving pleasure for the white audience and white performers. The joke material on the minstrel stage can be said to display, as Sigmund Freud identifies, "the most social of all the mental functions that aim to yield pleasure."[6]

The first characteristic that is standard to minstrelsy jokes is comic material about color. With the increase in amateur minstrel publications, such as *Jolly Joe's Lady Minstrels*, in the 1890s, color or, more specifically, changing one's color for the amusement of yourself and others had become more and more popular and accessible to the larger public. Amateur performers exercised their abilities to change their color because they could, and because the allowability for and humor of "blacking up" had been amusing since minstrelsy's beginnings in the late 1820s.

I would like here to clarify what I will call the *performance of color* in minstrelsy. My employment of *color* rather than *race* or *ethnic group* is derived from the usage of the minstrels themselves: they were presenting a body literally colored, blackened, and sociologically defined by white culture. In the oft-quoted 1903 words of W. E. B. Du Bois: "The problem of the twentieth century is the problem of the color-line,—the relation of the darker to the lighter races of men."[7] Du Bois makes the distinction that what has been problematized in the nineteenth century, as it continued to be in the twentieth, is the space where colors confront each other. Du Bois marked a line as this space of encounter; minstrelsy designated the popular stage as the locus of color contention.

Minstrelsy was not an ethnography-based performance, nor was it based in any way in the authentic presentation of African American cultural life. There is significant discussion that some of early minstrelsy was based in direct contact between white minstrel performers and African Americans, which can be traced most notably in the adaptation of the West African instrument of the banjo by white minstrels. Ultimately, it was not a concern of the minstrels to present a race with a culture, but rather, to present a color, as in "This is how people of this color act." As is well documented, the "color" of blackness would designate a race inferior in mid–nineteenth century anthropological papers, which were supported by highly questionable scientific conclusions based on measurements of head size, for example.[8] Showing a knowledge of the tenor of the times, blackness (most often), Chineseness, Native Americanness, Japaneseness, Irishness, and Dutch/Germanness were used by white minstrels to entertain audiences through well-established types of humor and nostalgia.[9] At best, these stereotypes limited the range of images of those ethnicities in minstrel performance; at worst, they contained and constricted them.

In addition to performing color, beginning in the 1840s, white male minstrels used gender as a transgressive space of performing Otherness. The mutability of color coupled with the changeability of gender furthered the white minstrels' promotion of color and gender as being primarily theatrical and of entertainment as a type of mimicry or mimesis, an "almost, not-quite" relationship with the subject, the African American woman. When, around the 1840s, white minstrels performed African American women to illustrate satisfaction or disappointment in an African American male-female relationship (often the material of blackface minstrelsy songs), they wrote songs similar to "Miss Lucy Long":

> I've come again to see you,
>> I'll sing another song,
> Jist listen to my story,
>> It isn't very long.
> Oh take your time Miss Lucy,
> Take your time Miss Lucy Long.
> Oh! Miss Lucy's teeth is grinning,
>> Just like an ear ob corn,
> And her eyes dey look so winning
>> Oh! would I'd ne'er been born.
> If she makes a scolding wife,
>> As sure as she was born,
> I'll tote her down to Georgia,
>> And trade her off for corn.[10]

Blackface minstrelsy songs about the relationships between African American men and women were called wench songs; the female impersonators who would perform the songs were the "wenches." Ultimately, the lyrics established the types of African American women portrayed. In the example of the several versions over thirty years of the comic love song "Miss Lucy Long," probably the first wench song, we can observe a genealogy of the portrayal of African American women by female impersonators in white minstrelsy. At every stage, the title character of the song is always warned by her lover to behave as a good wife, or she will be sold or abandoned.[11] She responds to his words by grinning, her teeth as white as snow, speechless. In *Love and Theft*, Eric Lott notes that no one has been able to prove that the early wench actually sang in the sketches that included her as a character; rather, she became the "lyric and theatrical object of the song" and of the entire theater arena.[12] The female impersonator, therefore, was established as a thoroughly contained and constrained African American woman.

Given the history of female impersonation in minstrelsy, it is intriguing to consider how the performances of color and gender continued once white women were allowed to participate in minstrelsy. White women negotiated their colorized and genderized space in several ways. First, they used white womanhood as a contrast to black womanhood. Second, they presented the woman's body in an inverse of female impersonation by performing as white men. By the time of the amateur minstrel movement in the 1890s, full-scale participation and acceptance of women onstage in professional minstrel shows was established. Women had been appearing as performers and audience members since the post–Civil War era in concert saloons and variety halls, where "leg shows," extravaganzas such as *The Black Crook*, and Lydia Thompson's burlesquing British Blondes were featured.[13] On the minstrelsy circuit, Gertie Granville performed with Tony Hart, her husband, beginning in 1882, often with both spouses playing female roles (see figure 9.1). There is a photograph of Hart in blackface drag gently reprimanding Granville, who is dressed as a Little Eva character, the popular young heroine of *Uncle Tom's Cabin*.[14] The circa 1882 photograph captures a moment in the continuum of gender impersonation in blackface minstrelsy. Hart, a white man costumed as an African American woman, poses with his wife, a white woman dressed as a white child with an oversized doll. Hart is very much in the low-comedy Funny Old Gal role of white minstrelsy, recalling the comic Dame character in burlesque.[15] He wears dark Victorian-era women's clothing over his big frame; a wig is piled high on his head; and his face and arms are blackened. Granville is dressed as girlishly as possible; she wears a knee-length, light-colored dress that exposes her legs; and her blonde hair is loose and flowing. Both performances of color and gender exhibit the limits of transgression imposed on women of the popular stage at this time. Hart, the epitome of white minstrelsy's comic female impersonator, shares the stage with minstrelsy's—and the American popular stage's—future female presence: the childlike, ultrafeminized girl-woman with nice legs.

Returning to the excerpt that opened this chapter, the character of Dinah Dewdrop could be costumed similarly to Tony Hart, with one exception. *Jolly Joe's Lady Minstrels* was written for white women to portray African American women. In fact, white women on stage transgressing racial boundaries was encouraged in *Jolly Joe's Lady Minstrels* by the implied endorsement of an African American man, Jolly Joe, whose face is grinning on the cover. In the 1890s, the female body on the popular stage had expanded possibilities compared to her counterpart earlier in the century. One of those areas of expansion was to represent the female body in the form of a male body:

Figure 9.1   Tony Hart and Gertie Granville (n.d.). Courtesy Harvard Theatre Collection, Houghton Library.

> It was in the early [18]90s that the male imps [impersonators] started to give an honest impersonation. The gals with fine shapes naturally showed off men's clothes in a way that no man ever could.[16]

In a chapter entitled "She-He's and He-She's," former vaudevillian Joe Laurie, Jr., expresses great admiration for the work of male impersonators in turn-of-the-century vaudeville. Laurie implies that male impersonation did not develop out of a need for male partners on the vaudeville stage but rather from a desire for the audience to see women's "fine shapes" in closely tailored men's clothes. During her performance as a male impersonator, as she sang and played instruments, flirted, and danced with female partners, the woman's body could always be reassuringly seen through a shapely veil, albeit of masculinity.

In my considerations of minstrelsy's use of the performances of color and gender as a means of entertaining and sentimentally transporting its audiences, I have been intrigued by the recent work of Susan Gubar on what she terms "racechange." White minstrels, Gubar notes, performed a racechange in blackface, which began the American use of the black Other in a commodity fetish relationship.[17] Gubar notes that, unlike the commonly used term *passing*, which has been used to describe the act of "passing for white" by light-skinned African Americans in a quest for less discriminatory lives, a racechange is a much more expansive notion of "the traversing of racial boundaries, racial imitation or impersonation, cross-racial mimicry or mutability, white posing as black or black passing as white, pan-racial mutuality."[18] In the case of minstrelsy, however, there has been little discussion so far about the transgression of gender paralleling the performance of color on the stage. In effect, one could both further complicate and support Gubar's argument marking white minstrelsy as an example of racechange with substantiation of how white minstrels portrayed African American women on the minstrelsy stage: a "race and gender change." The commodity fetishism that occurs in white minstrelsy when we also consider gender impersonation therefore becomes doubled in its meaning and scope.

There were also minstrelsy performers who chose to change their color, although it would seem not to be necessary to do so: African American minstrels. Active primarily during late minstrelsy,[19] they tapped into a desire by American audiences to laugh at performances of color and gender. When African American minstrels accessed the popular entertainment stage, they eventually changed the words, jokes, and look of minstrelsy,[20] but they also maintained its premises of performing color and performing gender for the amusement and nostalgia of their audiences.

A report in the *New York Clipper* in 1858 states that a "colored opera troupe" performed vocal and instrumental songs in the Queen's Concert Rooms in London. "The personal appearance of the parties was extremely ludicrous, but they sang well, and many of their melodies and songs are 'taking,' and likely to become favorites," the writer concludes.[21] The first black minstrels probably existed as early as the 1850s, although it was not until after the Civil War that black performers, including minstrels, were prevalent on the American popular stage.[22] Initially, black minstrelsy tapped into the successful elements of white minstrelsy: "ludicrous" appearance, well-executed music, and catchy tunes. As was the case in white minstrelsy, the skills demanded in black minstrelsy were multiple: black minstrel and vaudeville star Tom Fletcher recalled, in his book *100 Years of the Negro in Show Business*, "In those days you were not hired or even considered in show business unless you could sing, dance, talk, tumble or play some instrument in a brass band."[23] Despite the demanding artistic requirements, African Americans clamored for the few spots available in black minstrelsy groups; in 1894,

2,000 African Americans applied for forty minstrelsy slots in a new troupe.[24] The appeal of the minstrelsy stage to African American performers and audiences needs to be examined more closely. Thomas Riis suggests that the oral culture elements of "exaggeration and [the] grotesque" integral to minstrelsy appealed to the African-based culture of African Americans.[25] What can be said is that minstrelsy offered opportunities for both trained and untrained musicians and performers on a grand scale. As James Weldon Johnson, a former black minstrel, reflected on minstrelsy's mixed legacy, he wrote on its dualistic nature in African American cultural production:

> Minstrelsy was, on the whole, a caricature of Negro life, and it fixed a stage tradition which has not yet been entirely broken. . . . Nevertheless, these companies did provide stage training and theatrical experience for a large number of coloured men. They provided an essential training and theatrical experience, which, at the time, could not have been acquired from any other source. Many of these men, as the vogue of minstrelsy waned, passed on into the second phase, or middle period, of the Negro on the theatrical stage in America; and it was mainly upon the training they had gained that this second phase rested.[26]

A glance at the names of the early black musical performers and composers, those of Johnson's "second phase"—Bert Williams, George Walker, Will Marion Cook, J. Leubrie Hill, Paul Laurence Dunbar, Jesse Shipp, Bob Cole, J. Rosamond Johnson, and James Weldon Johnson himself[27]—offers a sense of the creative potential fed by black minstrelsy. I am not suggesting that minstrelsy provided the only means to the end of performance, as it has been noted by many, including Johnson, that African American performers were successful far from the minstrelsy stage. Instead, with the participation of black minstrels, minstrelsy can be said to have given American culture two legacies: one of creativity and one of resilient stereotypes. Ultimately, there was a certain pride in the African American population at the popularity of the college-affiliated singing troupes, such as the Fisk Jubilee Singers and the Hampton Singers, and "our own colored minstrels earn[ing] honorable reputation and some money."[28]

With the advent of their popularity came the return, at least performatively, of the "Negro" back to the plantation. Offering "trueness" and "realness" by the very nature of the fact that they were not just "acting black" but *were* black, the black minstrels advertised themselves as authentic. To prove this assertion, they restaged old minstrelsy classics out of vogue before the Civil War. The two rival black minstrelsy troupes, Haverly's Colored Minstrels and Callender's Consolidated Colored Minstrels, featured plantation scenes par excellence; at one point, Haverly's even exchanged minstrelsy's opening formation of a semicircle for a full-scale staging of a plantation scene in the South.[29] Ironically, the black minstrels became overdetermined in their "niggerness" precisely at the moment that they were achieving greater visibility as performing artists. They, in all likelihood, were building upon the popularity of the slave dramas of the earlier part of the century, such as

Darling Nelly Gray (1856), William Wells Brown's *Escape; or, A Leap to Freedom* (1858), and the many versions of *Uncle Tom's Cabin* being performed simultaneously throughout the country in the 1850s,[30] as well as upon the touring company combinations of the Hyers Sisters, Anna Madah and Emma Louise, who toured in the 1870s and 1880s and featured songs such as the following, written by white minstrel songster Charles A. White expressly for Emma Hyers:

> Oh golly, aint I happy!
> De Yankee's day hab come;
> I hear de shout of freedom,
> I hear dar fife and drum;
> Dar's gwine to be a smash-up
> Dis chile is gettin' shy,
> She'll leab de old plantation,
> Old cabin home, good-by.[31]

As Thomas Riis notes, emancipation is seen in this song to be a mixed blessing.[32] Similar in its nostalgia to many white minstrelsy songs, "Good-by, Old Cabin Home" permits the urban audiences of minstrelsy to locate the South as a place of structured contentment, where people knew their place and were relatively happy with their designation. The revitalized use of the plantation scenario by African American minstrelsy troupes differed from the early white minstrelsy use of the plantation in its ambivalence. As in the case of the song "Good-by, Old Cabin Home," African Americans lamented leaving their southern homes but leave them they did.

In these theatrical southern worlds of African American minstrelsy, does gender receive the same type of ambivalent performance as color? In a word, yes. Female impersonation was present in black minstrelsy, according to Robert C. Toll, as were all aspects of white minstrelsy: "black 'sweet' singers, graceful prima donnas, refined dancers, pompous interlocutors, and wise-cracking endmen."[33] Yet I have found little documentation that suggests that the female impersonator in black minstrelsy was central to the entertainment of the primarily black audiences. As Toll, Henry Sampson, Mel Watkins, Thomas Riis, James Weldon Johnson, and Eileen Southern have pointed out, African Americans who attended black minstrel shows were of the working class and familiar with laughing at stereotypes because they were based in comedy, not in realistic portrayal.[34] The white female impersonator, especially as the prima donna in late minstrelsy, based her performance in believability, similar to contemporary female impersonators.[35] It is possible that black minstrelsy audiences chose to see actual light-skinned African American women as the "leg show" elements of the black minstrelsy show, rather than those who were mimicking femaleness (see figure 9.2).

Black minstrelsy blended into black musical revues and vaudeville, so it is somewhat difficult to discern a continuum in terms of gender impersonation from white to black minstrelsy. However, it seems that female impersonation of the prima donna type was not performed by any of the major black

Figure 9.2   The Smart Set (1901). Courtesy Hatch-Billops Collection.

minstrels, including Sam Lucas, Billy Kersands, Ernest Hogan, Tom Mc-
Intosh, or Tom Fletcher. This contrasts with white minstrelsy, where such
notables as George Christy and William Henry Rice regularly portrayed
highly dressed and stylized mulatta women. I have found evidence of one
comic female impersonator in black minstrelsy, Andrew Tribble.[36] Tribble,
who may or may not be the cross-dressed male in figure 9.2, seems to have
excelled in playing female comic roles. He was born in 1879 in Kentucky,
and his first role on stage was as a "pickaninny." When he reached adulthood,
he left the stage and married, but he returned to performing in Chicago in
1904. Tribble worked in a music hall and was subsequently hired to work at
the famous Pekin Theatre, where Robert Motts had established a highly
regarded resident company of African American actors, which included, at
various times, Charles Gilpin, Flournoy Miller, and Aubrey Lyles.[37] It was
at the Pekin that "Tribble slipped on a dress and the audience screamed at
his performance."[38] Bob Cole, J. Rosamond Johnson, and James Weldon
Johnson saw him there and cast him in their second work, *The Shoo-Fly
Regiment* (1906). Tribble, about five feet, four inches tall, constructed the role
of Ophelia Snow: "a single-minded woman, careless, kindly, tough, and above
all desirous for an affair of the heart just the same as her sisters blessed with
more beauty."[39] "Ophelia, the Village Pride," wrote another reviewer, "was
exceedingly well done. All must give it to Tribble, he is the goods. His
characterization was great."[40] Tribble would repeat variations on this role
throughout his career. Another character Tribble cross-dressed for the show
was Sis Hopkins, cited by one reviewer as "the most interesting feature of the
cast."[41] Another hit of the show was a comic romantic duet that Tribble sang

with Matt Marshall, entitled "Who Do You Have?" It was, in the words of one reviewer, "screamingly funny, and as well rendered as anything which has been seen here in many moons."[42]

Tribble was also in the next Cole and Johnson production *Red Moon* (1908). His reviews for this production were not as favorable as the ones for *The Shoo-Fly Regiment*, possibly because Tribble was performing a low-comedy character, who was ill-suited for a "show [that] seem[ed] to be above such parts."[43] Tribble appears to have been caught on the cusp of the movement from vaudeville to black musical show/revue, although he does perform similar cross-dressed characters in *Shuffle Along* (1921) and *Put and Take* (1921).[44] Tribble also worked with The Smart Set, the Eddie Hunter Company, the J. Leubrie Hill Company, and the Miller (Quintard) and Slater Company before his death in 1935.[45]

In his female impersonations, Tribble seems to have relied on the comedic elements solely. He was not presenting the prima donna character of white minstrelsy, whose allure was in the convincing portrayal of her realness. Tribble, and probably other female impersonators in black minstrelsy yet to be rediscovered, brought the performance of color and gender of minstrelsy into a realm of being "screamingly funny" for the audiences, which included both African American women and men; his performances were about "us"— African American men and women and their relationships—not about "them." His legacy is almost certainly alive in twentieth-century comedians such as Flip Wilson, whose smart-talking Geraldine character was immensely popular on his television variety show (1970–1977).[46] The comedy of Wilson's gender impersonation was similar to Tribble's in that it based itself in the social and political satire of gender. This type of humor was similar to that used by white minstrels in comic female impersonation and achieved like results: a determined break from the constraints imposed by gender roles in society and a political comment on the increasing ambivalence of men about the changing social roles of women.

In addition, black minstrelsy commented on white minstrelsy's performances of color and gender by narrowing the scope of female impersonation. Gender impersonators such as Tribble were primarily comic in purpose and did not in any way thrive on the ambivalence of whether or not Tribble was truly a man or a woman. Tribble, in his "screamingly funny" female portrayals, both expanded the importance of humor in his performances and neatly contained the oft-present dual purpose in white minstrelsy of denigrating the subject of the performances—African American women—and the vehicle of the performance: his own African American male body.

Further extending the ways in which African American gender impersonation inverted the performance of color and gender of African Americans as constructed by white minstrelsy are performances of African American male impersonation. After the Hyers Sisters broke the gender barrier, all-black musical shows, such as *The Creole Show*, put on by Sam T. Jack's Creole Company in 1890–1897, and *Darkest America* (1896), departed from and depended on the minstrelsy format, featuring plantation scenes as well as original songs and dances.[47] *The Creole Show* is also significant as it was the first show that employed a large number of African American women performers. Extravaganzas with burlesque elements, complete with songs called "minstrel spirituals" (combining elements of the most popular forms of African American entertainment, minstrelsy and concert singing), and musical revues toured the country. African American female minstrels performed male impersonation during this active period of the 1880s and 1890s.

As noted previously with the African American male minstrels, gender impersonation can be seen as an inversion of the performances of color and gender that were developed by white minstrels. First, the male African American minstrels did only comic female impersonation; they did not continue the tradition of high-style drag developed by the male prima donnas of the white minstrelsy stage. Second, the women of African American minstrelsy featured a small faction of performers who donned male costume and played male roles. These performances by the African American minstrels inverted (and, in the case of the women, double inverted) the notions set up by white minstrelsy: that the African American male body was deformed, overdetermined, and emasculated and that the African American female body was highly sexualized and whorish. When performed by African American female minstrels, gender impersonation doubly inverted the representations of blackness rendered by white minstrelsy. White minstrelsy stereotyped African American women as comic and/or whorish; African American male impersonators chose to perform their female selves through maleness, thereby eradicting any connection with the stereotypes previously generated. African American male impersonators' double inversion of color and gender directly tapped into the anxieties that the dominant culture had about African American women and men. By changing the nature of those characterizations, black minstrelsy, in effect, negated their "coloring" and asserted themselves as a race with first, a proud history, and second, an exciting present. African American performing artists could impressively participate, in numbers higher than the percentage of blacks in the general population, and electrify their audiences with new notions of what a black man or woman performer was capable of on stage.

I have become intrigued by a small, vibrant group of African American female minstrels and vaudevillians who worked from the 1890s to the 1910s, some of whom performed male impersonation. Black female minstrels inverted the blackened-up female impersonators' characterizations of black women in two ways. First, although they were women, they did not play only women; they showed that their bodies were suited to playing both genders and to subverting the dominance of minstrelsy's containment of the black female body as fixed, unmoving, and confined to the two categories of mulatta or mama. Second, they reclaimed minstrelsy's black dandy characterization (overly dressed, urban black male) by reinscribing him into a sophisticated "race man" worthy of the upcoming Jazz Age. Strutting in top hats, twirling canes, and dancing in elegantly choreographed numbers, black female minstrels playing black men and women performed a counternarrative to white minstrelsy's violent portrayals of African American relationships. It is impossible to know if the black female minstrels, especially the male impersonators, actively pursued performing this race and gender inversion of white minstrelsy; however, I would like to approach their work by distinguishing, theoretically at least, their performances as social commentaries on the racist and sexist images of black men and women, which were the staple material of white minstrelsy. By contrasting the gender impersonation of white minstrelsy with these inverted portrayals, African American minstrels manipulated the rules of performance established by white minstrelsy. Their performances of color and gender were doubly transgressing, and they changed the scope of what transgression on the minstrelsy stage had been thus far.

African American male impersonators commented on their times and turned inside out the performance history of stereotypical characterizations of African American men and women on the popular stage. During this late stage of minstrelsy (which was evolving into vaudeville), there were several African American women minstrels who specialized in male impersonation. They included Florence Hines (active in the teens and twenties); Ida Forsyne (Howard) (b. 1883–d. early 1980s); Alberta Whitman of the Whitman Sisters (b. 1888–d. 1964); and Aida Overton Walker (1880–1914). It will come as no surprise to anyone who has studied nineteenth-century African American popular entertainment that there is little extant material available, especially on women performers. Through the use of primary and secondary sources, I have attempted to construct the beginnings of a performance history of these African American minstrel/vaudeville performers. However, my primary goal is to present their performance of male impersonation as a counterbalance to several portrayals in white minstrelsy. The male impersonations performed by these women seem to have reflected upon the dandy character popular in white minstrelsy. Emasculated, overly dressed, urban, and ineffectual, the black dandy in white minstrelsy was a "Dandy Jim from Carolina" (1843), more concerned with his ridiculous appearance than anything else. The African American women gave a different spin to the dandy character when they made him into a Jazz Age sophisticate, resplendent in black topcoat, tails, twirling a cane and donning a top hat.

One of the best examples of the sophisticated image of black maleness as performed by black female minstrels is the male impersonation of Alberta (or "Bert") Whitman (see figures 9.3 and 9.4). Describing the Whitman Sisters troupe on 12 February 1910, the *New York Clipper* stated:

> The Whitman Sisters and Billy Kersands' vaudeville company play Lagman's Theatre, Mobile, Alabama. The Whitmans include Mabel, manager; Essie, contralto soloist; Alberta, prima donna; Mattie (adopted sister); and Baby Alice. They are assisted by the boy comedian Thomas Hawkins, who replaces Willie Robinson; William Loften, comedian; and Walter Smith, trap drummer. Billy Kersands is assisted by his wife, Louise, and B. E. Edwards, tenor soloist.[48]

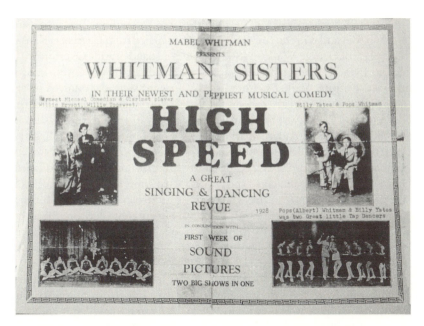

Figure 9.3 "The Whitman Sisters in Their Newest and Peppiest Musical Comedy, *High Speed*" (1928). Courtesy Hatch-Billops Collection.

Figure 9.4 "The World Famous Whitman Sisters" (1928). Courtesy Hatch-Billops Collection.

Alberta Whitman was a male impersonator throughout her successful career on the vaudeville circuit. The Whitmans hailed from Lawrence, Kansas (birthplace of George Walker, 1872?–1911, husband of Aida Overton Walker and Bert Williams's partner) and were the daughters of a well-known minister. Despite Walker's efforts, the Whitmans were not allowed to become professional until after their schooling, which included five years at the New England Conservatory of Music. They first worked with their father on an evangelical tour, and then Essie and Mabel formed an act called the Danzette Sisters in 1899–1900. In 1900, the Whitman Sisters Novelty Company began its career as a group in the Augusta (Georgia) Grand Opera House. Their mother managed the group at that time; by 1904, Mabel took over the management, and they changed the group's name to the Whitman Sisters New Orleans Troubadours. Their debut in New York in 1906 was with the encouragement of Will Marion Cook. They worked the Keith and Proctor, Poli and Fox, and Theatre Owners Booking Association (TOBA) circuits, as well as most theatrical houses. They were truly successful by 1910, occasionally reconfiguring themselves so that several sisters could work independently. Known for their talent and beauty, "These bright, pretty mulatto girls . . . have wonderful voices. . . . The sisters play banjo and sing coon songs with a smack of the original flavor. Their costuming is elegant; their manner is graceful and their appearance striking in a degree as they are unusually handsome," wrote one Alabama reviewer early in their careers.[49] Often billed as a "coon" act, the Whitmans added boy dancers Willie Robinson and "Pops" Whitman (Alice's son) in the '20s; the latter was billed as a child prodigy. A "Befoh De Wah" act was reviewed in 1907; in it, the Whitmans seem to have parodied the plantation scenes so necessary to early black minstrelsy.[50] At this point in vaudeville, the Whitmans were credited with giving the audience a performance "quite different from what we have learned to expect when a Negro turn is announced."[51]

The information about Alberta Whitman is sketchy beyond the facts of the company as a whole. According to photos, she seems to have performed duets with her sister Alice in the clothes of a well-dressed black man of the period, complete with hat and cane. Unlike the rest of the Whitmans, I have found no documentation regarding what Alberta did after the company broke up in the 1930s. Mabel died in 1942, Essie in 1963, Alberta in 1964, and Alice in the 1970s.[52]

Alberta Whitman is one of the most intriguing examples of male impersonators. In figure 9.4, she presses herself against her flapper-costumed sister Alice on the right side of the flyer; on the left side, also with Alice, she sits in a tuxedo with her legs open and her arms spread confidently, while Alice crosses her legs and clasps her hands on top of them. This flyer, from 1928, was augmented by someone who typed, "Bert Whitman, dresses in Man's Suit. Bert Whitman is a woman." Bert Whitman presented her audiences an African American woman who broke out of the stereotypes of both African American men, as caricatured by the dandy, and women, as demonstrated by the white female impersonators; she developed a performance of color and gender that directly inverted her white male predecessors' performances of color and gender.

Primary or even secondary material on other male impersonators is even more elusive than that on Alberta Whitman, but what exists is equally interesting. Florence Hines was called the American Vesta Tilley, after the popular British male impersonator.[53] A review of Richards and Pringle-Rusco and Holland's *Big Minstrel Festival* in 1899 remarked: "As a male impersonator, Miss Hines is fine."[54] Hines also performed in *The Creole Show* (1890–1897). The format was similar to a minstrel show, and Hines, as a male impersonator, was the interlocutor, surrounded by women in a semi-circle (pre-dating a similar performance by Aida Overton Walker and the Porto Rico Girls discussed later in this essay).[55] At one time, Hines also played one of three Conversationalists, who were dressed in male attire.[56] In *The Ghost Walks: A Chronological History of Blacks in Show Business, 1865–1910*, Henry T. Sampson lists Hines in many shows through the teens and twenties, but I have been unable to find any additional biographical data on her.

Another African American woman who performed male impersonation was Ida Forsyne. Forsyne (b.1883–d.early 1980s) was known for two roles during her career: Topsy (she was billed as Topsy throughout her tour of Europe in 1906–1914) and as a Russian dancer.[57] Her big break had happened in 1899, when she was billed with the Black Patti troupe, with which she appeared in *Dreamland* as "Kaffir queen, dressed in a shade of green" and was reviewed as having "danced 'Maiden of Timbuctoo,' quite as fascinating as ever."[58] She also worked with The Smart Set in 1903 and had a solo in Will Marion Cook's *The Southerners* (1904). Apparently, she began to find difficulty working in the teens and twenties, possibly because stage work was often reserved for light-skinned women. Therefore, she took a job as Sophie Tucker's maid in 1920–1922 and was paid $5 a week. In 1927, Forsyne again worked on the TOBA circuit with Bessie Smith. One of her last known jobs in show business was a role in Oscar Micheaux's *The Underworld* (1935).[59] As a member of the Negro Actors Guild's executive board, Forsyne remained active beyond her years as a performer.[60] The most common photo of Ida Forsyne, included in Milton Meltzer and Langston Hughes's black entertainment book, sports a caption stating that she taught Jerome Robbins how to choreograph the cakewalk.[61] The photo features her in male costume similar to that worn by Alberta Whitman. And, like Bert Whitman, Forsyne exudes male-associated confidence in her photo, with a cane on her arm and her legs spread wide.

Aida Overton Walker (also known as Ada Overton) was one of the greatest performers to bridge the performance gap between black minstrelsy and vaudeville. Unlike the previously mentioned African American male impersonators, there have been several excellent articles written exclusively on Walker and her signature dance, the cakewalk.[62] Walker began her career with the concert singer Sissieretta Jones, known as the Black Patti, and her Troubadours. She met George Walker, her future husband, and his comedy partner, Bert Williams, when they all posed for photographs for a trade card sponsored by the American Tobacco Company in 1898. Williams and Walker were pioneers in introducing ragtime to their vaudeville work, and Aida Overton helped them introduce the cakewalk, a dance reminiscent of slave mockery of white society, which was then used by the white minstrels in their frenetic walkarounds.[63] During her short lifetime, Aida Overton Walker became the principal delineator of the cakewalk, but she also was responsible for all of the choreography of the Williams and Walker revues. As a result, she contributed to the changeover from the "coon" show to black musical revues, as dance was as integral to the work of Williams and Walker as was the music and comedy.[64]

An exceptional example of male impersonation was the pinch-hitting role performed by Aida Overton Walker upon the advanced illness of her husband George Walker, during the extended run of *Bandanna Land* (1907–1909). Centered around the character of a minstrel show player named Skunkton Bowser (played by Williams) and his partner, Bud Jenkins (played by Walker), *Bandanna Land* featured routines similar to minstrelsy interlocutor and endmen setups and a cakewalk as well. This old minstrelsy material was reconfigured by Williams, Walker, Aida Overton Walker, Jesse Shipp, Alex Rogers, and Will Marion Cook.[65] In February 1909, Walker began stuttering and forgetting his lines, symptoms of his illness of syphilis. Aida Overton Walker had prepared for this moment by practicing George's role in costume, spawning several cartoons. Walker never saw his wife perform "Bon Bon Buddy," his signature song.[66]

After Walker's death in 1911, Aida Overton Walker mostly worked as a choreographer, but sometimes she continued to impersonate males. At a 1913 benefit, she appeared with the Porto Rico Girls and the Happy Girls:

> As a fitting finale, Miss Walker, in male attire, rendered several old favorite selections, reinforced by the female members of the Porto Rico Girls and the Happy Girls act. When the curtain descended, Miss Walker stood out in bold relief, with the girls forming an effective background. The picture was a pretty one.[67]

As with the male impersonation of Florence Hines in *The Creole Show*, Aida Overton Walker is surrounded in this performance by African American women. The African American woman on stage, therefore, was marked as *either* male (Walker) or female (the Happy Girls). Black femaleness was malleable, not fixed or contained.

It is certainly possible, given the proliferation of black male impersonators in vaudeville, that these women were deftly performing one of many stock roles. Of course, that could also be said for the female impersonators in white minstrelsy. African American male impersonators inverted a theatrical playing out of dominance, turning over and around the assertion of power by the white male. They challenged the gendered metaphor that they inherited from white minstrelsy on a small but significant scale. The importance of their challenge is related to the performances of white male impersonators in

British vaudeville such as Vesta Tilley, Annie Hindle, Ella Wesner, Blanche Selwyn, and Bessie Bonehill,[68] who reconstituted women's bodies and marked them as almost male, as opposed to hyperfeminine. Also, when discussing male impersonation in black minstrelsy and vaudeville, it is important to consider the practical matter of the staging and material. African American female minstrels may have portrayed African American males for practical reasons based in available personnel. The Whitman Sisters often staged plantation scenes, as were popular in the late days of minstrelsy, and Alberta may have chosen to portray a male to round out the domestic drama. However, once the company enlarged, Alberta continued to play male characters, even though the company included grown men and boys. Florence Hines seems to have chosen to perform her male impersonation throughout her long career, and Ida Forsyne must have done male impersonation at least once, according to pictorial documentation. And, as has been stated, Aida Overton Walker donned male attire in performance even when she was no longer substituting for her husband.

Unfortunately, any legacy left by the male impersonator in African American minstrelsy and vaudeville is not as prevalent as white minstrelsy's tragic mulatta or the infantile black man. The theatrical legacy that minstrelsy has left continues to require that the woman on stage—especially the black woman—carry the fantasies of the social order. However, there have been African American women performers who have taken on the act of double inversion—restaging the bodies of the African American woman and man through male impersonation. Consider Josephine Baker, who, in one famous photograph, is tuxedoed, with top hat firmly and attractively placed to complement her smile. In Phyllis Rose's biography of Baker, the caption attached to this picture is "No more bananas." Rose refers to Baker's famous dance, in which the costume consisted solely of a skirt made of bananas,[69] and she acknowledges in this caption a legacy of the African American male impersonators. Baker, like her foresisters, chose to approach her sexuality on her own terms, reforming and expanding the potential of her image through her body beyond what the audience expected of her as an African American woman on the popular stage.

If we return now to the historical moment of *Jolly Joe's Lady Minstrels*, we can see that, at the same time that this and many other amateur minstrel guides were defining for readers how to "be black" by speaking in a nonsensical dialect and by wearing fright wigs and burnt cork make-up, African American minstrels were showing audiences that minstrelsy was just a show, a pretense, a *performance* of color and gender rather than a presence of African American culture, even when performed by African Americans. White minstrelsy came close to defining how the minstrelized black body should sound and appear, but it did not succeed in its latent desire to contain and constrict. This attempt to define the African American staged black Other was thwarted by the nuanced, rebellious, skilled, and, in the case of the African American male and female impersonators, doubly inverted performances of restaging. Ultimately, what African American minstrels created was a new form of theater based in the skills of the performers, not in their ability to conform to stereotypes.

NOTES

1. Mrs. H. M. Silsbee and Mrs. J. B. Horne, *Jolly Joe's Lady Minstrels: Selections for the "Sisters"* (Boston: Walter H. Baker, 1893), 7.

2. Ibid., cover.

3. For the purposes of this chapter, *blackface minstrelsy* or *minstrelsy* is minstrelsy performed by either whites or African Americans. *White minstrelsy* is minstrelsy performed by whites, and *black minstrelsy* is minstrelsy performed by African Americans.

4. Frank Dumont, ed., *The Witmark Amateur Minstrel Guide and Burnt Cork Encyclopedia* (Chicago: M. Witmark, 1899), and Anon., *The Boys of New York End Men's Joke Book* (New York: Frank Tousey, 1902). For an in-depth discussion of the social values contained in minstrel guides and other nineteenth- and twentieth-century publications, see Brooks McNamara, " 'For Laughing Purposes Only': The Literature of American Popular Entertainment," in *The American Stage: Social and Economic Issues from the Colonial Period to the Present*, ed. Ron Engle and Tice L. Miller (New York: Cambridge University Press, 1993), 141–158.

5. Homi Bhabha, "The Other Question: Stereotype, Discrimination and the Discourse of Colonialism," in Bhabha, *The Location of Culture* (London: Routledge, 1994), 66–84.

6. Sigmund Freud, "Jokes, Dreams and the Unconscious," in *Jokes and Their Relation to the Unconscious*, trans. James Strachey (New York: Norton, 1960), 179.

7. W. E. B. Du Bois, *The Souls of Black Folk*, in *Three Negro Classics*, ed. John Hope Franklin (New York: Avon, 1965), 221.

8. In the early twentieth century, Franz Boas put an end to the notion that there exists racial hierarchy, noting that every race has its own variance of body types, languages, and cultural production. See Roger Sanjek, "The Enduring Inequalities of Race," in *Race*, ed. Steven Gregory and Roger Sanjek, (New Brunswick, N.J.: Rutgers University Press, 1994), 1–17.

9. See Robert C. Toll, "Social Commentary in Late Nineteenth-Century White Minstrelsy," in Toll, *Blacking Up: The Minstrel Show in Nineteenth-Century America* (New York: Oxford University Press, 1974), reprinted in *Inside the Minstrel Mask: Readings in Nineteenth-Century Blackface Minstrelsy*, ed. Annemarie Bean, James V. Hatch, and Brooks McNamara (Middletown, Conn.: Wesleyan University Press, 1996), 86–110.

10. Eric Lott, *Love and Theft: Blackface Minstrelsy and the American Working Class* (New York: Oxford University Press, 1993), 160.

11. The lyrics printed are from 1842, according to Lott 160. Lott also excerpts an 1848 version (160). An 1843 version of "Miss Lucy Long" appears in Hans Nathan, "The Performance of the Virginia Minstrels," in *Dam Emmett and the Rise of Negro Minstrelsy* (Oklahoma City: University of Oklahoma Press, 1962), reprinted in Bean et al. 38–39. Robert B. Winans notes the full lyrics of the 1842 version excerpted by Lott in his article "Early Minstrel Show Music, 1843–1852," in *Musical Theatre in America: Papers and Proceedings of the Conference on Musical Theatre in America*, ed. Glen Loney (Westport, Conn.: Greenwood, 1984), reprinted in Bean et al. 151.

12. Lott 160.

13. Laurence Senelick, "Boys and Girls Together: Subcultural Origins of Glamour Drag and Male Impersonation on the Nineteenth-Century Stage," in *Crossing the Stage: Controversies on Cross-Dressing*, ed. Lesley Ferris (London: Routledge, 1993), 90.

14. The novel *Uncle Tom's Cabin* was adapted for the stage in hundreds of productions across the United States and around the world from the mid-1850s to the turn of the century. See Thomas Riis, "The Music and Musicians in Nineteenth-Century Productions of *Uncle Tom's Cabin*," in *American Music* 4, no. 3 (Fall 1986): 268–286.

15. Laurence Hutton, *Curiosities of the American Stage* (New York: Harper & Brothers, 1891), 157. For a further description of female impersonation in American white minstrelsy, see Annemarie Bean, "Transgressing the Gender Divide: The Female Impersonator in Nineteenth-Century Blackface Minstrelsy," in Bean et al. 245–256.

16. Joe Laurie, Jr., *Vaudeville: From the Honky-Tonks to the Palace* (New York: Henry Holt, 1953), 93.

17. Susan Gubar, *Racechanges: White Skin, Black Face in American Culture* (New York: Oxford University Press, 1997), 45.

18. Ibid., 5.

19. "Early minstrelsy" is defined from the purported (as opposed to documented) first minstrelsy performance of "Jumpin' Jim Crow" by T. D. Rice c. 1828 to the beginning of the Civil War in 1860. "Late minstrelsy" is defined as post–Civil War minstrelsy. Both definitions are mine, culled from various sources, such as Lott, and Toll.

20. See Marian Hannah Winter, "Juba and American Minstrelsy," *Dance Index* 6 (1947), reprinted in Bean et al. 223–244; Eileen Southern, *The Music of Black Americans* (New York: Norton, 1971), 4–24, 100–104, 259–270; Southern, "The Georgia Minstrels: The Early Years," *Inter-American Music Review* 10, no. 2 (1989), reprinted in Bean et al. 163–175; Winans, 141–162; Mel Watkins, "Slavery," in *Watkins, On the Real Side: Laughing, Lying, and Signifying—: The Underground Tradition of African-American Humor* (New York: Simon & Schuster, 1994), 45–79; and Richard Kislan, *Hoofing on Broadway* (New York: Prentice Hall, 1987), 12–23.

21. *New York Clipper* (31 July 1858): n.p.

22. Toll 195; Southern, *Music of Black Americans*, 259.

23. Tom Fletcher, *100 Years of the Negro in Show Business* (New York: Burdge, 1954), 53.

24. Toll 219.

25. Thomas Riis, *Just before Jazz: Black Musical Theatre in New York, 1890–1915* (Washington, D.C.: Smithsonian Institution Press, 1989), 6.

26. James Weldon Johnson, *Black Manhattan* (New York: Da Capo Press, 1991), 93.

27. John Graziano, "Sentimental Songs, Rags, and Transformations: The Emergence of the Black Musical, 1895–1910," unpublished manuscript, 211, possession of the author.

28. *New York Globe* (3 May 1884): n.p.

29. Toll 205.

30. Riis 7–8.

31. Ibid., 9–10.

32. Ibid., 10.

33. Toll 251.

34. Toll 195–233; Henry T. Sampson, *Blacks in Blackface: A Sourcebook on Early Musical Shows* (Metuchen, N.J.: Scarecrow, 1980), 1–20; Watkins 104–133; Riis 3–28; Johnson 94–125; and Southern, *Music of Black Americans*, 259–270.

35. Esther Newton, *Mother Camp: Female Impersonators in America* (Chicago: University of Chicago Press, 1979), 5.

36. Most of the evidence I have found on Tribble is cited by Henry T. Sampson, *The Ghost Walks: A Chronological History of Blacks in Show Business, 1865–1910* (Metuchan, N.J.: Scarecrow Press), 1988, and Sampson, *Black in Blackface*. However, serious questions have been raised as to the accuracy of Sampson's newspaper and broadside citations in terms of dates and issues. Wherever possible, I have double-checked Sampson's data; however, given the scope of his research, this has not always been feasible. The questioning of Sampson's work is not about the quotes, which are probably accurate, but rather about exact dates and locations.

37. Sampson, *Blacks in Blackface*, 280.

38. Sampson, *The Ghost Walks*, 434.

39. Ibid.

40. Ibid., 394.

41. Riis 134.

42. Sampson, *The Ghost Walks*, 363.

43. Ibid., 394.

44. Bernard Peterson, Jr., *A Century of Musicals in Black and White* (Westport, Conn.: Greenwood, 1993), 282.

45. Sampson, *Blacks in Blackface*, 436.

46. Watkins 20–21; 523–525.

47. Sampson, *Blacks in Blackface*, 4.

48. *New York Clipper* (12 Feb. 1910).

49. Sampson, *The Ghost Walks*, 245.

50. Ibid., 386.

51. Ibid., 445.

52. Eileen Southern, *Biographical Dictionary of Afro-American and African Musicians* (Westport, Conn.: Greenwood, 1982), 401.

53. Laurence Senelick, "The Evolution of the Male Impersonator on the Nineteenth-Century Popular Stage," *Essays in Theatre* 1, no. 1 (1982): 39–40.

54. Sampson, *The Ghost Walks*, 183.

55. Riis 12.

56. Peterson 136.

57. Fletcher 177; Sampson, *Blacks in Blackface*, 364.

58. Sampson, *The Ghost Walks*, 288.

59. Sampson, *Blacks in Blackface*, 366.

60. Mary Mace Spradling, *In Black and White: Supplement* (Detroit: Gale Research, 1985), 162.

61. Langston Hughes and Milton Meltzer, *Black Magic: A Pictorial History of the Negro in American Entertainment* (Englewood Cliffs, N.J.: Prentice-Hall, 1967), 73.

62. See Richard Newman, " 'The Brightest Star': Aida Overton Walker in the Age of Ragtime and Cakewalk," *Prospects: An Annual of American Cultural Studies* 18 (1993): 465–481; and David Krasner, "Rewriting the Body: Aida Overton Walker and the Social Formation of Cakewalking," *Theatre Survey* 37, no. 2 (Nov. 1996): 67–92.

63. Newman 466–467.

64. Riis 113–124.

65. Ibid., 117.

66. Ann Charters, *Nobody: The Story of Bert Williams* (New York: Macmillan, 1970), 123. Aida Walker began performing her husband's role in *Bandanna Land* in

early 1909, during the Williams and Walker Company's second New England tour. George Walker grew ill during the tour and never recovered. He died in 1911. Aida performed "Bon-Bon Buddy" for approximately three months, from February to April.

67. Eric Ledell Smith, *Bert Williams: A Biography of the Pioneer Black Comedian* (Jefferson, N.C.: McFarland, 1992), 165–166.

68. Senelick, "Evolution of the Male Impersonator," 30–44.

69. Phyllis Rose, *Jazz Cleopatra: Josephine Baker in Her Time* (New York: Doubleday, 1989), 97.

10

Black *Salome*

Exoticism, Dance, and Racial Myths

DAVID KRASNER

[The black female] is there to entertain guests with the naked image of Otherness. They are not to look at her as a whole human being. They are to notice only certain parts. Objectified in a manner similar to that of black female slaves who stood on the auction blocks while owners and overseers described their important, salable parts, the black women whose naked bodies were displayed for whites at social functions had no presence. They were reduced to mere spectacle. Little is known of their lives, their motivations. Their body parts were offered as evidence to support racist notions that black people were more akin to animals than other humans.[1]

Absence and Presence in Early Modern Black Dance

Though black women played a pivotal role in the development of modern choreography, dance scholars have largely ignored their contributions. Roger Copeland, for instance, maintains that the "founding mothers" of modern dance are a corps of elite white dancers: Isadora Duncan, Loïe Fuller, Ruth St–Denis, Doris Humphrey, and Martha Graham.[2] Helen Thomas adds Maud Allen to the pantheon of "major forerunners of American modern dance,"[3] and Elizabeth Dempster identifies Duncan, Fuller, St–Denis, and Allen as choreographers who developed "a decisive and liberating break with the principles and forms of the European ballet."[4] According to Jane Desmond, St–Denis, Fuller, and Duncan are "always cited" as "the three 'mothers' of modern dance,"[5] while Mark Franko affirms the popular idea that Duncan was the "founding mother" of modern dance, responsible for the "organic society" that challenged the "Victorian experience of female culture."[6]

Notwithstanding their accomplishments, labeling early twentieth-century white dancers alone as the "founding mothers" of modern choreography is a limited view. By ignoring, among others, Dora Dean, Josephine Baker, Katherine Dunham, Florence Mills, Judith Jamison, and Pearl Primus, African American women are barred from the historical record. Yet the evidence is unequivocal: black women contributed significantly to the origins of modern dance. Lewis Erenberg maintains that during the early twentieth century, social dance, which originated in black communities, "began making [its] way out of . . . special enclaves and into upper-middle-class life."[7] In addition to social dancing, black women, as this essay will demonstrate, also choreographed "classical" modern dance.

Despite the fact that black Americans, as Ann Douglas asserts, "have contributed more to popular culture in proportion to their numbers than white Americans,"[8] black female choreographers have received little attention. The absence of black women in dance historiography comes as no surprise; Brenda Dixon Gottschild observes that the "historical, systematic denial and invisibilization of the Africanist presence in American culture" have extended itself into virtually every field.[9] Thomas DeFrantz asserts that, for black dancers, the absence of attention to African American performances has "contributed to the historical displacement of dance created by African-American[s]."[10] Katrina Hazzard-Gordon similarly laments the exclusion of black contributions, saying that despite a sizable body of literature on dance, "none of it has focused on the sociohistorical context from which African-American secular social dance has emerged."[11]

It is not my intention to dwell on the reasons for the paucity of black female representation in dance historiography, although a lengthy treatment of this topic would surely deepen our understanding of how and why black women came to be excluded.[12] Here, I will examine the significance of Aida Overton Walker's *Salome* performances in 1908 and 1912. In examining Walker's choreography, we shall discover how Walker negotiated her creativity within a complex period. Rooted in her choreography is the expression of the black woman's struggle, a struggle to gain control over her representations by adapting, absorbing, and challenging the prevailing stereotypes of the period. Neither Walker's choreography nor her response to stereotypic caricatures were uniform; however, investigating how Walker dealt with the slippery slope of identity and subjectivity will, I hope, prove revealing.

Modernism, Primitivism, and Black Dance

> Why do they see a colored woman only as a gross collection of desires, all uncontrolled, reaching out for their Apollos and the Quasimodos with avid indiscrimination?[13]

During the 1910s, dance enjoyed enormous popularity. Lewis Erenberg observes that, during this period, the increase of dances "with such exuberantly unpretentious names as the turkey trot, Texas tommy, bunny hug, monkey hug, lame duck, fox trot, and tango" helped to give social dancing "the appearance of a mania."[14] Ann Wagner adds that changes in urban life and class distinctions "fostered the unprecedented popularity of dancing between 1910 and 1914." Working-class women and men, Wagner maintains, "tended to frequent the new public dance halls, and members of the middle and upper classes enjoyed the growth of cabarets after 1910."[15] Despite the racism of the time, enthusiasm for dance encouraged whites to look to black culture for examples of modern choreography.

As a result of both the emerging interest in dance and the rise of stereotyping of blacks during the early twentieth century, black culture took shape as a resistance to and appropriation of racism. According to Mark Reid, black culture has surfaced "within and around the competing tensions," which yielded the desire "to appropriate, negotiate, and resist mainstream American and European cultures."[16] In his designation of Booker T. Washington as "the quintessential herald of modernism in black expressive culture" circa 1895, Houston A. Baker, Jr., maintains that Washington maneuvered through Jim Crowism and racist stereotyping by "crafting a voice out of tight places."[17] The notions of "competing tensions" and "tight places" were certainly applicable to the conditions facing black female modern dancers, who had to contend with a host of stereotypes. K. Sue Jewell avers that culturally induced images of black women as mammy or jezebel "are at the very foundation of the problem of African American women's limited access to societal resources and institutions."[18] In her 1925 contribution to *The New Negro*, Elise Johnson McDougald makes the point clear: black women, she observes, realize "the shadow" that looms over them; instead of signifiers indicating African American beauty, "the grotesque images" of Aunt Jemimas on streetcar advertisements, she says, "proclaim only an ability to serve, without grace of loveliness."[19] For black women dancers, the deck was clearly stacked: stereotypes often prevented them from enjoying success even during a period of newfound interest in dance. Notions of sexuality in dance worked to reinforce the negative image of black women as primitive and inferior.

Historically, black people were bartered on the auction block as specimens of "primitive" physicality. This attitude of display and fascination did not recede following the demise of slavery; blacks continued to be mythologized as hyperlascivious and sexually debased.[20] In addition to minstrelsy and white folklore depicting black males as sexual predators and black females as permissive, stereotyping gained further ground during the late nineteenth century as Anglo-Europeans put more stock in the social sciences of the time. Art historian Richard Powell reminds us that, for white ethnographers of the late nineteenth century, the inferior status of black peoples in the Western hemisphere was evidence that "all blacks were cut from the same coarse 'biologically-determined' cloth."[21]

At the turn of the century, social Darwinism found a new way of packaging racism. It was argued that a duality in human species pitted (advanced) white civilization against (primitive) people of color. For ethnologists, Western advances in science and technology suggested that other races were still clinging to a primitive past. According to Colin Rhodes, "By insidious reasoning, tribal societies were often not even credited as emerging civilizations, but as evolutionary cul-de-sac, arrested in their development at some nebulous point in the past, at once contemporary and ancient." As a consequence, African Americans could be viewed as "the sociological 'missing link,' preserved, living examples of the 'childhood of humanity.' "[22] Primitivism began to represent a number of aesthetic and cultural myths—demonism, fauvism, masks, voodoo, cannibalism, exoticism, eroticism—which evoked images of unrestrained sexuality, wildness, and passion. Building largely on Enlightenment and, specifically, Rousseauian celebrations of the natural innocence of the "noble savage," racial ideology gained further prominence in the early twentieth century owing to the rise of what Marianna Torgovnick calls the "primitive trope." According to Torgovnick, the so-called primitive is represented as a series of childlike tropes, a combination of our wild selves and subconscious forces, which are "libidinous, irrational, violent, dangerous."[23] Primitive peoples were allegedly in tune with nature's harmony. The primitive trope allowed for the reduction of black culture to either inferiority or idealization; primitives may be childlike and violent, but they may also be "noble savages." Hayden White emphasizes the point when he states:

> Savages were *either* a breed of super animals (similar to dogs, bears, or monkeys), which would account for their violation of human taboos and their presumed physical superiority to men; *or* they were a breed of degenerate men (descendants of the lost tribes of Israel or a race of men rendered destitute of reason and moral sense by the effects of harsh climate).[24]

Either way, people of color were caught in a culturally manufactured double bind, relegated to the lowest rung of the evolutionary ladder, yet looked to as a source of visceral entertainment as well.

Despite negative stereotyping, primitives were thought to enjoy a closer relationship to subconscious impulses, childish innocence, and sexuality. In an increasingly mechanized world, primitivism, rooted in simple "nature," offered an alternative to urban life. Primitivism emerged as a reaction to an increasing alienation from an industrialized world, what Robert Coles and Diane Isaacs call a "cultivating primitivism," which served as an alternative "to modern technological society," which shaped the primitivist cult into "artistic themes, images, and symbols."[25] Primitivism supported artists and social theorists who attempted to inculcate simple values to a culture suffering from industrialization and dehumanization. This led to a "fetishization" of the primitive: primitivism's relation to the supposed early evolutionary stages of human development afforded Western culture a sense of superiority to other groups while simultaneously observing the roots of evolution. According to Harold Isaacs, white ethnographers, despairing over the lack of "nobility" in modern white civilizations, began to search for it in "primitive black savagery." But there was more underlying their motives: a reach for what Isaacs calls the "primeval mysteries, the jungle depths," and "the Freudian 'id' personified in the naked black man in his natural state and setting."[26] Jeffrey Weeks underscores the hypersexuality embedded in primitivism, maintaining that sexuality presented the black person "as lower down the evolutionary scale than the white: closer to the origins of the human race; closer, that is, to nature." As a consequence, the attraction of the primitive, Weeks maintains, was based on a "subliminal feeling that the people there were indefinably freer of the constraints of civilization."[27]

During the late nineteenth and early twentieth centuries, primitivism offered whites an alternative to puritanical mores. If American Victorians of the 1870s and 1880s delineated societies as either civilized or savage and divided races according to black and white, then American modernists of the early twentieth century enjoyed the distinction by exoticizing blacks. Primitivism evolved into myth, often referred to as Orientalism, with the common thread being the symbolically sexualized representation of the nonwhite body. Sander Gilman's essay on the iconography of female sexuality maintains that the perception of the prostitute "merged with the perception of the black" and that this perception created the "commonplace" notion that the so-called primitive black woman "was associated with unbridled sexuality."[28] African American women symbolized the exotic, erotic, and sexually lascivious. For many white men, they represented an image of foreignness and a "colorful" panacea for an overworked, over-industrialized culture looking to spend its disposable income on entertainment.

The vertical arrangement of ethnicities—whites on top, others on the bottom—created as a part of new taxonomies, was not only demeaning, but it allegedly placed blacks closer to impulse, spontaneity, and nature. In 1930, psychologist Carl Jung warned that the "inferior man exercises a tremendous pull upon civilized beings who are forced to live with him, because he fascinates the inferior layers of our psyche, which has lived through untold ages of similar conditions." As Jung put it, to "our subconscious mind contact with primitives recalls not only our childhood, but also our prehistory." He goes on to say that it "would not be difficult to see that the Negro, with his primitive motility, his expressive emotionality, his childlike immediacy, his sense of music and rhythm, his funny and picturesque language, has infected American behavior."[29]

By the twentieth century, primitivism became a catchall phrase defining blacks. Not only were African Americans identified with primitivism, but the implication was that primitivism was an artistic attribute. The notion emerged that black writers, performers, and artists were "real," capable of expressing a racial uniqueness that incorporated authenticity, amateurism, and primitivism. The combination of alleged authenticity and primitivism validated the abilities and talents of African Americans. By the 1910s, the amalgamation of amateurism, primitivism, and atavism into a unified concept of black art, literature, and performance took root; by the 1920s and 1930s it became conventional wisdom. Black people were perceived to have greater access to the subconscious, behave more "authentically," and were more in touch with their spiritual and sensual nature than whites. No matter how manipulative and misleading, the alleged validity of these ideas afforded some African American artists and performers an opportunity to take advantage of the situation. For many, primitivism provided an entry into mainstream culture. Left with little choice but to conform to inaccurate and exaggerated representations or be denied opportunities, some black artists, writers, and performers accentuated the so–called jungle rhythms of black art in order to accommodate the demands of their white audiences. White patrons, eager to associate with what they perceived to be the "real thing," paid for black entertainment. For black women, the problem of sexism added to the racism of the time, making it difficult for black female artists to find creative outlets that went beyond the limitations of stereotyping.

The assumption that black women are "primitive"—sexually obsessed and erotically out of control—is undoubtedly a canard. The falsification involves the attempt to subordinate racial groups for controlling purposes. In response to primitivism, the black middle class eschewed depictions of black sexuality. The early twentieth century began as a period of "racial uplift," in which the black middle class, among other things, forged a campaign against erotic displays. Evelyn Brooks Higginbotham explains that, given their limited access to educational and income opportunities, many black women at the time "linked mainstream domestic duties, codes of dress, sexual conduct, and public etiquette with both individual success and group progress."[30] Club movements, church organizations, and other middle-class collectives during the early twentieth century developed what Hazel Carby calls the "policing" of the black woman's body, a rejection of any indication of sexuality in favor of self-restraint ethics, social service, and church participation. According to Carby, "the denial of desire and the repression of sexuality" became commonplace for many black writers and intellectuals during the early twentieth century.[31] Kevin Gaines notes that the racial uplift ideals of the time were presented as a form of cultural politics "in the hope that unsympathetic whites would relent and recognize the humanity of middle-class African Americans."[32] Showered with sexual and racial stereotypes, black women campaigned for respectability and moral authority. For example in 1904, Fannie Barrier Williams wrote that the black woman's "grave responsibility" to maintain bourgeois respectability was essential because "the Negro is learning that the things that our women are doing come first in the lessons of citizenship; that there will never be an unchallenged vote, a respected political power, or an unquestioned claim to position of influence and importance, until the present stigma is removed from the home and the women of the race."[33] We see, then, that black female dancers faced additional prejudices fostered by bourgeois values within the black community itself.

Yet, however much primitivism carried the stamp of inferiority, the primitive trope was also used by many to promote an aesthetic. No excuses will be ventured on behalf of primitivism; it was part of a racist ideology and must be seen as such, contributing to a mendacious epistemology of racial identity. Moreover, dancing's eroticism, which is fostered by the male gaze, adds to the already reified and objectified female body. Luce Irigaray reminds us that investment in the gaze "is not privileged among women as it is among men." For Irigaray, "The eye [*L'oeil*], more than the other senses, objectifies and masters." Given the ability of the gaze to distance and control, the "predominance of the gaze [*du regard*] over smell, taste, touch, sound, has brought about an impoverishment of corporeal relations."[34] By objectifying women, the gaze enables the dominant society to turn sexuality into a commodity. Black women once again become bartered flesh to be observed and mastered.

Still, it is important to understand the significance of primitivism. Simply put, since black women were mythologized as oversexed, many white and black males were attracted to their stage performances. Many dancers, black and white, exploited the notion of "fetishized" sexuality to varying degrees for commercial gain. The fact that certain performers took advantage of prevailing ideas can neither be ignored nor absolutely condemned. Those living in communities and circumstances where biases restrict advancement cannot always depend on the ethical high ground for sustenance; to survive, oppressed people often realize that only a diverse and sometimes compromising mode of existence can offer the hope of material subsistence. It is easy to dismiss dancers who capitalized on primitivism as exploitative by their capitulation to racist neologisms; it is more difficult to accept the fact that the oppressed must often turn adverse conditions to their advantage. Hazel Carby observes that there is "a touchiness among feminists about representing black women as complex." For Carby, "[P]eople are happier if you portray [black women] as morally superior because of suffering or victimization." But in doing so, Carby asserts, feminist scholars "deny their complexity, their dangerousness, their refusal to be policed."[35] This is not to say that critiques of primitivism are invalid. Instead, critiques ought to be broad enough to include observations on how oppressed people made innovative use of the narrow frames allotted them.

Caught between competing urges to express creativity and to thwart the stereotype, black female choreographers were simultaneously under scrutiny for their erotic movements and under pressure to choreograph according to the current vogue. It is perhaps for this reason that Josephine Baker, rejecting American morality, departed for Europe. Wendy Martin points out that once Baker arrived in Paris in the 1920s, she secured her status by creating a *danse sauvage*, which "played with the paradigm of the black exotic."[36] Free from Puritan morality, Baker exploited a European primitivism that was no less racist; it was simply less inhibited. Baker was not, however, the first choreographer to come to grips with the primitive trope. Aida Walker not only endured the idea of primitivism in America; she continued to choreograph within an American cultural framework replete with racial codes. Walker negotiated a minefield of representations while simultaneously developing a unique choreography.

"Barefoot Classical Dancer" and
Middle-Class Respectability

It took a long time for the disreputable creativity of black artists to climb down from the plinth of primitivism and natural spontaneity and win a different status as modern art.[37]

Aida Overton Walker's objective was to lift black women's choreography into the modern world. At a time when black women were compelled to rein in their expectations and bridle their imaginations, Aida (sometimes spelled Ada) Walker (1880–1914) did the opposite. During her career she made her presence felt in several ways: she was an accomplished cakewalker, teaching the cakewalk to elite, white society; she established herself as the highest paid and most popular female actress, singer, and dancer of the Williams and Walker vaudeville company; she choreographed all of the Williams and Walker shows, including *In Dahomey* (1902–1905), *Abyssinia* (1905–1907), and *Bandanna Land* (1907–1909); and she was considered one of the brightest stars on the vaudeville stage. Despite the overwhelming presence of the male stars in her company—the famous comedian Bert Williams and her husband, George Walker—she managed to gain recognition as a consummate performer during the first decade of the twentieth century.[38]

Walker sought recognition as a consummate choregrapher, and to this end she joined the *Salome* craze, the vogue of choreography based on the biblical story. Percival Pollard of the *New York Times* dubbed the craze itself "Salomania."[39] Popularized in the United States and Europe by white dancers during the early twentieth century, the *Salome* dance enjoyed great success. By adding it to the Williams and Walker production of *Bandanna Land* Aida Walker challenged the accepted notion that only white women could dance the modern "classics." Nevertheless, she had to suppress the erotic component of her dancing. As a result, her choreography, although notable for its grace, was also known for its propriety. Walker had to be especially careful not to offend black audiences, while she simultaneously refused to succumb entirely to prudery. She affected the bourgeois norms of good taste, which meant she submitted her costume to a regime of concealment and restraint. Yet, she also wore exotic and provocative costumes frequently attributed to modern white dancers. As a well–known member of the Harlem community, Walker was likely to be under considerable pressure to conform to a middle–class society caught up in social propriety and racial uplift, while simultaneously she felt compelled to join her fellow white female dancers by presenting her version of "Salomania." The cultural influences that informed her performance exerted considerable and contradictory pressures, creating a unique style, which, as the following reviews will reveal, might have been misinterpreted as obtuse. On the one hand, she stressed the abstract, hiding her sexuality and casting off the visibility of her body. On the other hand, she emphasized the sensual and exotic, which puts the body in full view. Her dance probably changed often, given the improvisatory nature of her work, the touring circuit she followed, and the demands of each city and town she performed in. Some cities had strict puritanical codes of conduct while others loosened restrictions. The rising imposition of Jim Crow laws also made performing a complicated affair; some cities she toured had lax racial restrictions while others imposed strict curfews and boundaries for African Americans. In other words, sometimes her expressions of sexuality were fully conveyed, while at other times a more modest approach was required. The racial and sexual codes of each city compounded for Walker the difficulties involved in the dance.

Beginning in 1908, versions of the *Salome* dance were performed throughout New York. *Current Literature* reported in October 1908 that there were "no less than twenty-four vaudeville dancers in New York alone who give their interpretation of the daughter of Herodias, and from the Empire City the Salome epidemic is spreading over the rest of the country."[40] Around the turn of the century, the popular figure of Salome epitomized the inherent sensuality and, according to some, perversity of women. Bram Dijkstra writes that Salome became the image "of women as serpents, as brute nature's virgin dancer," whose only reason for existence "lay in the movements of the arms, the legs, of the supple body and the muscular loins, born indefinitely from a visible source, the very center of dance."[41] According to Ewa Kuryluk, Salome represented the archetype "of a terrible femininity and fin-de-siècle femme fatale," but her representation also symbolized "the obscure paradoxes of unconscious desires and fears."[42] For many fin-de-siècle artists, writes Françoise Meltzer, Salome symbolized both "the virgin and the devouress."[43] Salome's popularity was closely tied to what Megan Becker-Leckrone calls the "myth's textual genealogy," in which *Salome* denoted "the conventional notion of fetishism which surrounds the Decadent femme fatale."[44] Elaine Showalter raises the significant point that *Salome* was an important figure in the history of dance because women who danced the role found themselves "conflated with Salome in the public mind and condemned for lasciviousness and perversity."[45] Once marked as a *Salome* dancer, the performer had a difficult time shedding her association with the role.

In addition, Walker had to contend with a parody of her *Salome* dance by her co-star, Bert Williams, in the same show. Williams viewed the *Salome* craze as an opportunity in *Bandanna Land* to burlesque the dance, cross—dressing and imitating the gestures commonly associated with the choreography. This was intended to add levity to the show, but it also had the effect of undermining the seriousness of Walker's intent. Still, Walker introduced her version of *Salome* in 1908, working it into *Bandanna Land*. Despite the implications of her Salome as both femme fatale and primitive, Walker likely considered the dance as the perfect opportunity to align herself with both modern dance and highbrow art. It was highly unusual for a black Broadway show to include modern dance, but Walker was determined to position herself within the establishment of white female modern dancers.

Critical responses to Walker's *Salome* were predictably mixed. The fact that she was a black woman dancing a provocative character probably influenced Walker to downplay the erotic, or so it would appear, judging from the reviews of her choreography which emphasized her modest costume, lack of vulgarity, and gracefulness. According to black theater critic Lester A. Walton, Walker's Salome costume and dance music "all come up to expectation, but in comparison with some of the other dancers Miss Walker's interpretation showed to a disadvantage." For Walton, white choreographers "danced more with their body" than Walker, and this, he notes, led them to be more "vulgar." Walton praised Walker's "desire to make 'Salome' a cleaner dance and void of suggestiveness, but in so doing she gives a version that is mild in comparison."[46] Perhaps because of her restraint, Walker chose to emphasize the dramatic elements over the suggestive in her choreography. For example, one reviewer remarked that in Walker's 1908 version of *Salome*, the

> feet began to move, and the arms to sway, and the limbs to portray the passion of motion. And suddenly, at the height of the mad, intoxicating dance, a curtain was drawn and a ray of light fell on the head of the Baptist. The effect was electric, and so was the vision of the head for the dance. It struck her wild joy as with a blight, crushed her consciousness of power and flung her to the ground in defeat.[47]

In the 1908 version (figure 10.1),[48] her persona is audacious, with her hair projecting an African style and her dress bejeweled and spangled. Her appearance in Boston (figure 10.2),[49] suggests a similar approach: exotic jewelry and defiant stance. At least one Boston reviewer was particularly struck by Walker's creative interpretation and, at the same time, the modesty of her costume. Walker, the reviewer reports, "does not handle the gruesome head, she does not rely solely upon the movements of the body, and her dress is not so conspicuous by its absence." The reviewer praised Walker for "the fact that she acts the role of 'Salome' as well as dances it. Her face is unusually mobile and she expresses through its muscles the emotions which the body is also interpreting, thus making the character of the biblical dancer life-like."[50] Another reviewer commented on Walker's modest costume, writing at the time that her dance "is a very properly draped Salome, but the dance is interesting because of the rare grace and skill of the performer."[51] Still, another critic emphasized Walker's restraint, noting:

> Miss Walker's Salome is something like the others, being more modest, but quite as meaningless. Grace it has in abundance, but most of the weirdness and barbaric grandeur is supplied by the trap man of the orchestra, who beats with vigor upon what we assume to be a large dishpan. There are a few wild figures, and much is made of the sinuous parade which most dancers conceive to have been characteristic of the foul-minded daughter of Herodias, but there is nothing of the hoocha-ma-cooch effect which adds a suggestion of sensuality to the exhibitions of other Salomes.[52]

Even Eighth Avenue Has Its Salome.

Williams and Walker, the Colored Comedians, Have Introduced THE Dance Into "Bandanna Land." Ada Overton Walker Does It, and the Critics Say That She Dances Better than Some of the Salomes That Wear Fewer Clothes.

Figure 10.1 Walker's 1908 version of *Salome*, from a drawing by the artist Moe Zayas in the *New York World* (30 Aug. 1908), metropolitan section, p. 2. Also found in the Williams and Walker file, Billy Rose Theatre Collection, New York Public Library at Lincoln Center, Astor, Lenox, Tilden Foundation.

It is clear from the caricature by Moe Zayas, the photograph, and the reviews that Walker wanted a *Salome* that was more dramatic but less erotic than her contemporaries.

In considering Walker's second, 1912 version of *Salome* (figure 10.3),[53] a comparison can be usefully made between Walker and one contemporary, Isadora Duncan. Although Duncan has received considerable attention, Walker, who continually broke new ground in choreography, has not. Like Duncan, Walker saw herself as a modern classical dancer in a quest for innovative ways of using her body to express her creativity. It is also likely that Duncan's presence in the United States influenced Walker. In her essay "Reconsidering Isadora Duncan and the Male Gaze," Ann Daly writes that, when Isadora Duncan "toured America in 1908, 1909, and 1911, her reputation as the 'Barefoot Classical Dancer' had preceded her from Europe."[54]

AIDA WALKER, WHO
WILL INTERPRET A
DANCE OF SALOME

Figure 10.2   Walker's appearance in Boston, circa Sept. 1908. Clipping file
(1908), Billy Rose Theatre Collection, New York Public Library at Lincoln Center,
Astor, Lenox, Tilden Foundation.

Figure 10.3 Walker's 1912 version of *Salome*, from a drawing in Lester A. Walton, "Miss Walker in Salome," *New York Age* (8 Aug. 1910): 6. Artist unknown.

Daly maintains that, whatever audience expectations of Duncan there were, "they were confounded by [Duncan's] actual performance" and her resistance to current conventions.[55] Daly asserts that "Duncan was one of America's first self-made women. She was constantly re-imagining herself, both onstage and in her interviews."[56]

Much the same can be said of Aida Walker. Before Duncan became famous, Walker re–imagined herself from vaudeville star to cakewalker, and from actress to modern dancer. She was, in fact, a self-made woman at a time when black women had neither power nor agency. Yet she found ways to express her creativity. Her dance, for example, was less entertainment (showing off her legs, for instance), and more artistry. Rather than emphasizing the show of body parts, Walker sought to convey her imagination and emotional conviction as an expression of her aesthetic values and artistic ideas. As the drawing of her 1912 *Salome* choreography shows, Walker, like Duncan, was a "barefoot classical dancer" dressed in a loose-fitting outfit, projecting her swaying arms and feet lightly and with grace. Walker executed her second version in flowing movements in which improvisation and spontaneous emotions were marked features. From the drawings and photographs we can see a departure from her 1908 version. By 1912 she was free of the presence of Bert Williams, who parodied her performance and undermined her interpretation, and she was free of the Williams and Walker Company in general. Since the death of her husband George Walker in 1911, Aida Walker was on her own, performing solo acts that toured throughout the country. After appearing in Bob Cole's production of *The Red Moon* (1909–1910) and nursing her husband during the final year of his life, Walker traveled the United States singing, dancing, and performing comedy. By 1912, she revised her *Salome* dance, making it the unique feature of her one–woman show. The 1912 image portrays her as light, airy, and energetic. Her hands are expressive and her body appears to be in fluid motion. Her costume was similar to the outfits worn by Isadora Duncan—a chemise that flowed—but it also covered much of her body, unlike that of other Salomes. It is conceivable that Walker was attempting to imitate Duncan's performance while adding her own, considerably more modest, interpretation. In Walker's second version, she appears to be rising into the air, in contrast to an earth-oriented, knees-bent, hip-centered choreography of her first version. Her lithe body conveys poise and passion.

Walker clearly crafted her interpretations: the 1908 version incorporates the garish jewelry and Jewish emblems bound up with Salome's biblical representation, while the 1912 image represents Walker in modern dance costume and gesture. In all her representations, there is an impression of individuality and awareness of the current scene; she is presenting her own version of *Salome*, while simultaneously incorporating the interpretations of white dancers. Her dance created a hybrid aesthetic, influenced by race, gender, and current fashion.

Despite Walker's efforts to gain acceptance, her choreography was paid little attention at the time. The reasons have to do with race and emanate not just from the usual expected sources but also from her fellow dancers. White choreographers, particularly Isadora Duncan, deliberately designed their choreography antithetically to the so-called primitivism of black dancers. For example, in her autobiography, Duncan claimed that black jazz rhythm "expresses the primitive savage" and that "the ape-like convulsions of the Charleston," like the "inane coquetry of the ballet, or the sensual convulsion of the Negro," are antithetical to the noblest forms of dance.[57] Elsewhere Duncan notes that, if America had adopted her school and theories of dancing, "this deplorable modern dancing, which has its roots in the ceremonies of the African primitive, could never have become dominant."[58] By incorporating the popular dance of *Salome* into her repertoire, Walker may have been seeking an artistic response appropriate to her white contemporaries.

For several modern choreographers, *Salome* represented modern dance. By dancing *Salome*, Walker sought the legitimacy that a modernist aesthetics might offer. In the summer of 1912, after a sixteen-week tour of her vaudeville show across the Midwest, she returned to New York, where impresario Oscar Hammerstein offered her the opportunity to reappear in the role of *Salome* at his Victoria Theatre on Broadway. In a review titled "Victoria's Show Pleases Crowds," Robert Speare reported that Walker "is the only colored artist who has ever been known to give this dance in public." Walker, he said, "fully lives up to expectations and gives a graceful and interesting version of the dance."[59] *Variety* was less complementary; criticizing Walker for turning her *Salome* into a social Tommy dance, the reviewer reported that the "setting looked real nice, and the music was really pleasant, but Miss Walker isn't going to do herself any good coming into Hammerstein's as 'Salome' with the dance she has been doing for the past couple of years."[60] Commenting on her performance, *Stage Pictorial* noted that Walker may have been influenced by Duncan and others when it reported that Walker "shows that she had studied the part and perhaps had also seen several other women in it. She was good without being great."[61] *Vanity Fair* published a précis to Walker's 1912 production that identified her "pantherine movements" as having "all the languorous grace which is traditionally bound up with Orient dancing."[62] The reference to "Orient dancing" reflected the popularity of Orientalism, which was in vogue as symbolic of exoticism, otherness, and mystery.[63] One reviewer went so far as to consider Walker's *Salome* a revival of ragtime. A "ragtime Salome" by "Miss Aida Overton Walker," reported the *New York Herald*, is the result of "the characteristic dance of her race." Judging from the applause, the reviewer wrote, "the revival pleased the spectators":

> Miss Walker was most effective in her dance when the curtain rose, showing her in Oriental costume standing at the top of a short flight of steps. She was graceful and wore her costume well.[64]

Walker danced in Broadway theaters and major theatrical playhouses throughout the United States. Although there are no extant playbills of her 1912 performance of *Salome* at Hammerstein's Victoria Theatre, the production was probably attended by a crowd eager to witness her interpretation of the sophisticated modern dance. The performance referred to a biblical tale, and Walker's dancing attempted to express a story, a plot, and an aesthetic representation commonly found among modern choreographers of the time.

Creating Dance out of Patchwork Quilts

History is more than the accumulation of new data and facts. It is not enough to simply add a few black women to the existing story and stir.[65]

Walker sought recognition as a choreographer. At a time when black women's expectations were severely limited, Walker knew what she wanted and set out to obtain it. Because of the multifarious influences on their work, she developed her choreography in patchwork fashion, borrowing elements from white dancers, drawing on vaudeville and black traditions of dance, and fusing these together, always with a combination of instinct, reflection, and meticulousness. Every gesture she incorporated into her choreography had double, sometimes triple meanings, and she not only had to weigh the significance of these meanings but also had to consider their ramifications for the image of black women collectively.

The complexities that black women faced have been summed up by Mae Henderson, who writes that, through "the multiple voices that enunciate her complex subjectivity, the black woman writer [and dancer] not only speaks familiarly in the discourse of the other(s), but as Other she is in contestorial dialogue with the hegemonic dominant and subdominant or 'ambiguously (non)hegemonic' discourses."[66] Walker was in contestorial dialogue with the dominant society's established expectations and her desire for creative expression. She chafed against the limitations imposed upon her and sought ways to circumvent, resist, and defy convention. She dared to dance what was the domain of white dancers, crossing the racial divide and with it courageously encountering all the dangers such crossings implied. Walker struggled against the constant imposition of being the Other: the "black" Isadora Duncan, the objectified sexual object, and the marginalized dancer unrecognized by both peers and critics. As a black female dancer, she remained on the outside.

Yet Walker did not passively accept the limitations that society sought to impose upon her; she fought for legitimacy and the right to perform. She expressed her creativity definitively. In so doing, Walker developed ways of manipulating cultural conventions, what Elizabeth Fox-Genovese calls a manipulation of language and gesture by which black women "speak in a double tongue, simultaneously associating themselves with and distancing themselves from the dominant models of respectability."[67] Walker's career is located in the specificities of the representation of black women's sexuality at the time. She expressed herself in a "double tongue," fearlessly exploiting the notions of primitivism and the exotic; but, for her, there was also the importance of being taken seriously as an artist. Vaudeville actor and writer Salem Tutt Whitney knew Walker and in 1920, six years after her death, he wrote the following eulogy:

Aida Overton Walker was one of the brightest, sweetest, most loveable, sagacious, talented and intelligent women who ever graced the ranks of show business. By force of ability, diligent study, strenuous work, tenacity of purpose and an almost superfluity of talent, she climbed to the topmost rung of the theatrical ladder, without a white or colored peer in her line. And then, she ran afoul of the color line. . . . Where her white sisters flourished she was not permitted to lead, nor would she condescend to follow.[68]

Walker sought to enter the master's house, as it were, of high-brow art and reinvent that art from her own perspective. Despite the lack of recognition and the paucity of raw data, Walker's contribution to modern choreography is significant.

NOTES

1. bell hooks, "Selling Hot Pussy: Representations of Black Female Sexuality in the Cultural Marketplace," in hooks *Black Looks: Race and Representation* (Boston: South End, 1992), 62.

2. Roger Copeland, "Founding Mothers," *Dance Theatre Journal* 8, no. 3 (1990): 6–9, 27–29.

3. Helen Thomas, *Dance, Modernity and Culture: Explorations in the Sociology of Dance* (London: Routledge, 1995), 24.

4. Elizabeth Dempster, "Women Writing the Body: Let's Watch a Little How She Dances," in *Bodies of the Text: Dance as Theory, Literature as Dance*, ed. Ellen W. Goellner and Jacqueline Shea Murphy (New Brunswick, N.J.: Rutgers University Press, 1995), 27–28.

5. Jane C. Desmond, "Dancing Out the Difference: Cultural Imperialism and Ruth Saint Denis's 'Radha' of 1906," *Signs: Journal of Women in Culture and Society* 17, no. 1 (Autumn 1991): 30.

6. Mark Franko, *Dancing Modernism/Performing Politics* (Bloomington: Indiana University Press, 1995), 2.

7. Lewis A. Erenberg, "Everybody's Doin' It: The Pre–World War I Dance Craze, the Castles, and the Modern American Girl," *Feminist Studies* 3, no. 1/2 (Fall 1975): 156.

8. Ann Douglas, *Terrible Honesty: Mongrel Manhattan in the 1920s* (New York: Noonday, 1995), 399–400.

9. Brenda Dixon Gottschild, *Digging the Africanist Presence in American Performance, Dance and Other Contexts* (Westport, Conn.: Greenwood, 1996), 50. Future references to this work will be listed in the text with page number(s) in parentheses.

10. Thomas DeFrantz, "Simmering Passivity: The Black Male Body in Concert Dance," in *Moving Words: Re-Writing Dance*, ed. Gay Morris (London: Routledge, 1996), 107.

11. Katrina Hazzard-Gordon, "Dancing under the Lash: Sociocultural Disruption, Continuity, and Synthesis," in *African Dance: An Artistic, Historical and Philosophical Inquiry*, ed. Kariamu Weish Asante (Trenton, N.J.: Africa World, 1996), 101.

12. What is particularly intriguing is the notion of "founding mother" in the identification of white choreographers. The exclusion of black women from the realm of "motherhood"—sources of original creativity who spawned "children," or followers—deserves critical attention.

13. Marita Bonner, "On Being Young—a Woman—and Colored," *Crisis* 31, no. 2 (Dec. 1925): 64.

14. Lewis Erenberg, *Steppin' Out: New York Nightlife and the Transformation of American Culture, 1890–1930* (Westport, Conn.: Greenwood, 1981), 150.

15. Ann Wagner, *Adversaries of Dance: From the Puritans to the Present* (Urbana: University of Illinois Press, 1997), 255.

16. Mark A. Reid, *PostNegritude Visual and Literary Culture* (Albany: State University of New York Press, 1997), 13.

17. Houston A. Baker, Jr., *Modernism and the Harlem Renaissance* (Chicago: University of Chicago Press, 1987), 37, 33.

18. K. Sue Jewell, *From Mammy to Miss America and Beyond: Cultural Images and the Shaping of U.S. Social Policy* (London: Routledge, 1993), 12.

19. Elise Johnson McDougald, "The Task of Negro Womanhood," in *The New Negro*, ed. Alain Locke (1925; reprint, New York: Atheneum, 1992), 369–70.

20. The debate over sexuality continues; see, for instance, Michael Marriott, "Black Erotica Challenges Black Tradition," *New York Times* (1 June 1997): 41, 42.

21. Richard J. Powell, *Black Art and Culture in the 20th Century* (London: Thames and Hudson, 1997), 24.

22. Colin Rhodes, *Primitivism and Modern Art* (London: Thames and Hudson, 1994), 16.

23. Marianna Torgovnick, *Gone Primitive: Savage Intellects, Modern Lives* (Chicago: University of Chicago, 1990), 8.

24. Hayden White, "The Noble Savage Theme as Fetish," in White, *Tropics of Discourse: Essays in Cultural Criticism* (Baltimore: Johns Hopkins University Press, 1978), 187–188.

25. Robert A. Coles and Diane Isaacs, "Primitivism as a Therapeutic Pursuit: Notes toward a Reassessment of Harlem Renaissance Literature," in *The Harlem Renaissance: Re-valuations*, ed. Amritjit Singh et al. (New York: Garland, 1989), 3.

26. Harold Isaacs, *The New World of Negro Americans* (New York: John Day, 1963), 233.

27. Jeffrey Weeks, "The Body and Sexuality," in *Modernity: An Introduction to Modern Sciences*, ed. Stuart Hall et al. (Oxford: Blackwell, 1996), 378.

28. Sander L. Gilman, "Black Bodies, White Bodies: Toward an Iconography of Female Sexuality in Late Nineteenth-Century Art, Medicine, and Literature," in *"Race," Writing, and Difference*, ed. Henry Louis Gates, Jr. (Chicago: University of Chicago Press, 1986), 248.

29. Carl G. Jung, "Your Negroid and Indian Behavior," *Forum* 83, no. 4 (Apr. 1930): 196.

30. Evelyn Brooks Higginbotham, "African-American Women's History and the Metalanguage of Race," *Signs: Journal of Women on Culture and Society* 17, no. 2 (Winter 1992): 271.

31. Hazel Carby, " 'It Jus Be's Dat Way Sometime': The Sexual Politics of Women's Blues," in *Unequal Sisters: A Multicultural Reader in U.S. Women's History*, ed. Vicki L. Ruiz and Ellen Carol DuBois (New York: Routledge, 1994), 332.

32. Kevin K. Gaines, *Uplifting the Race: Black Leadership, Politics, and Culture in the Twentieth Century* (Chapel Hill: University of North Carolina Press, 1996), 3.

33. Fannie Barrier Williams, "The Club Movement among the Colored Women," in *Voice of the Negro* 1, no. 3 (Mar. 1904): 102.

34. Luce Irigaray, quoted in *Les femmes, la pornographie, l'érotisme*, ed. Marie-Françoise Hans and Gilles LaPouge (Paris: Éditions du Seuil, 1978), 50, my own translation.

35. Hazel Carby, quoted in Phyllis Rose, "Exactly What Is It About Josephine Baker?" *New York Times* (10 Mar. 1991): 2:31, 35.

36. Wendy Martin, " 'Remembering the Jungle': Josephine Baker and Modernist Parody," in *Prehistories of the Future: The Primitivist Project and the Culture of Modernism*, ed. Elazar Barkan and Ronald Bush (Stanford, Calif.: Stanford University Press, 1995), 311.

37. Paul Gilroy, "To Be Real: The Dissident Forms of Black Expressive Culture," in *Let's Get It On: The Politics of Black Performance*, ed. Catherine Ugwu (Seattle, Wash.: Bay Press, 1995), 21.

38. For a history of Aida Overton Walker, see Richard Newman, " 'The Brightest Star': Aida Overton Walker in the Age of Ragtime and Cakewalk," *Prospects: An Annual of American Cultural Studies* 18 (New York: Cambridge University Press, 1993): 464–481; and David Krasner, "Rewriting the Body: Aida Overton Walker and the Social Formation of Cakewalking," *Theatre Survey* 37, no. 2 (Nov. 1996): 66–92.

39. Percival Pollard, "The Regnant Wave of the Sensational Dance," *New York Times* (23 Aug. 1908): 5–7. See also "The Call of Salome: Rumors that Salome Will Have a Free Hand this Season," *New York Times Magazine* (16 Aug. 1908): 4.

40. "The Vulgarization of Salome," *Current Literature* 45, no.4 (Oct. 1908): 437. For information on the *Salome* dance, see Ann Daly, "Isadora Duncan and the Male Gaze," in *Gender and Performance*, ed. Laurence Senelick (Hanover, N.H.: University Press of New England, 1992), 248; Elizabeth Kendall, *Where She Danced* (New York: Alfred Knopf, 1979), 74–90; Elaine Showalter, *Sexual Anarchy: Gender and Culture at the Fin de Siècle* (New York: Penguin 1990), 144–68; and Richard Bizot, "The Turn-of-the Century Salome Era: High– and Pop–Culture–Variations on the Dance of the Seven Veils," *Choreography and Dance* 2, no. 3 (1992): 71–87.

41. Bram Dijkstra, *Idols of Perversity: Fantasies of Feminine Evil in Fin-de-Siècle Culture* (New York: Oxford University Press, 1986), 385.

42. Ewa Kuryluk, *Salome and Judas in the Cave of Sex* (Evanston, Ill.: Northwestern University Press, 1987), 189.

43. Françoise Meitzer, *Salome and the Dance of Writing: Portraits of Mimesis in Literature* (Chicago: University of Chicago Press, 1987), 18.

44. Megan Becker-Leckrone, "Salome: The Fetishization of a Textual Corpus," *New Literary History* 26, no. 2 (Spring 1995): 242.

45. Showalter 159.

46. Lester Walton, *New York Age* (27 Aug. 1908): 6.

47. "Salome Dance Seen in Bandanna Land," *Boston Herald* (6 Sept. 1908): 8.

48. From a drawing in the *New York World* (30 Aug. 1908), metropolitan section, 2.

49. Publicity photo with handwritten mark: *Boston Herald* (3 Sept. 1908): n.p., Billy Rose Theatre Collection (Robinson Locke Collection), New York Public Library at Lincoln Center, Astor, Lenox, and Tilden Foundation. Future references to this collection will be listed as BR.

50. Undated clipping, titled "Boston to Have Dance of Salome," BR.

51. "Bandanna Land," *Boston Globe* (6 Sept. 1908): 2.

52. Unidentified clipping, noted "Chicago" (Jan. 1909), BR.

53. From a drawing in Lester A. Walton's essay "Miss Walker in 'Salome,' " *New York Age* (8 Aug. 1912): 6.

54. Daly 247.

55. Daly 249.

56. Daly 254.

57. Isadora Duncan, *My Life* (New York: Boni and Liveright, 1927), 341, 342.

58. Isadora Duncan, "Dancing in Relation to Religion and Love," *Theatre Arts Monthly* 11, no. 8 (Aug. 1927): 590–591.

59. Robert Speare, "Victoria's Show Pleases Crowds," *New York Telegraph* (6 Aug. 1912), BR.

60. *Variety* (9 Aug. 1912), BR.

61. "A Salome of Color," *Stage Pictorial* (1912), BR.

62. *Vanity Fair* (3 Aug. 1912), BR.

63. For a discussion of orientalism and modern dance, see Desmond, 39–42, and Amy Koritz, "Dancing the Orient for England: Maud Allen's 'The Vision of Salome,' " *Theatre Journal* 46, no. 1 (Mar. 1994): 63–78.

64. "Ragtime Dance for New Salome," *New York Herald* (6 Aug. 1912): 10. There appears to be a discrepancy in the descriptions of Walker's 1912 *Salome*. Some reviewers speak of her "modern" dance costume while others refer to her "Oriental" costume. Walker probably changed costumes frequently during her performances and experimented with various outfits and styles.

65. Darlene Clark Hine, *Speak Truth to Power* (Brooklyn, N.Y.: Carlson, 1996), 56.

66. Mae Gwendolyn Henderson, "Speaking in Tongues: Dialogics, Dialectics, and the Black Woman Writer's Literary Tradition," in *Reading Black, Reading Feminist: A Critical Anthology*, ed. Henry Louis Gates (New York: Meridian, 1990), 120.

67. Elizabeth Fox-Genovese, "Between Individualism and Fragmentation: American Culture and New Literary Studies of Race and Gender," in *American Quarterly* 42, no. 1 (Mar. 1990): 20.

68. Salem Tutt Whitney, "How to Join a Show," *Competitor* 1 (1920): 71.

11

Uh Tiny Land Mass Just Outside of My Vocabulary

Expression of Creative Nomadism and Contemporary African American Playwrights

KIMBERLY D. DIXON

Journeying is as much sideways and in the standing still as it is 'backwards and forwards.'[1]

> *Ham Bone Ham Bone where you been*
> *Roun thuh worl n back a-gain*
> *Ham Bone Ham Bone whatcha do?*
> *Got uh chance n fairly flew.*[2]

African American cultural history includes within it an extensive expatriate tradition. Scholars often foreground the stories of famous African American writers, such as James Baldwin, Richard Wright, and Chester Himes, who left America behind to seek out new homes abroad for themselves and their work and who produced work with themes and stories that frequently reflected their expatriate status. While these writers are deservedly prominent both for their literary merit and for the influence their lives and careers have had on African American and other cultures, their status as representatives of the African American expatriate tradition is misleading. Their common gender and association with a single genre create an image of the African American expatriate writer as being male and a novelist.[3] Furthermore, the fact that these writers' identities as African American expatriates were secured during the 1950s and 1960s leads some scholars to suggest that the African American expatriate tradition died when they did.[4] Perhaps most significant, these histories frame literal, physical migration as the only means of movement and repositioning embraced by African American artists. Certainly, people of African descent—artists or not—have employed literal, physical

212

migration as a method of improving their circumstances, and many continue to do so. There are the examples of Baldwin and others, as well as the historical instances of blacks' mass exodus from the southern United States, the movement from cities to suburbs, and, most recently, the move of many African Americans from the North (back) to southern states. However, the better lesson offered by the African American expatriate tradition is that of movement as an aid to creative expression—or even as the expression itself. Since African American artistic expatriation actually stands as part of a larger pattern of African Americans' continuous migration, the experience of migration is as much a shared cultural memory as an individual experience. As a result, the migratory phenomenon is available even to nonmigratory artists as an element in black history, which can be explored creatively.[5]

The historical fact of African American writers' movement across geographical borders has symbolic resonance, not just historical significance. It is a point of reference in African American cultural history, which all artists—not just expatriates—can incorporate into the form or content of their expression. Correspondingly, analyses of works by African American playwrights should also consider expatriation and other geographical movement as another possible discursive mode. Again, the investigation of an African American's artistic migration is not dependent on evidence of such literal migration in that artist's own life; instead, such an investigation considers evidence in the artist's stories, structures, and characterizations, exploring the presence and expression of creative nomadism in the artist's work.

One contemporary African American playwright whose work demands consideration as an expression of creative nomadism is playwright Suzan-Lori Parks. Parks elicits passionate responses to her distinctive dramaturgy, a style full of nonlinear progressions, distilled language, iconic characters, and abstract settings. Theater audiences seem at once intrigued and frustrated by this playwright's refusal to slip quietly into their erected houses of expectations for theater, particularly their expectations for theater written by African American women. This essay will examine the presence and influence of nomadic themes in Parks's work, not only for the insight that nomadism can offer into Parks's particular dramaturgy but also as a way to begin exploring the viability of the concept of creative nomadism in the analysis of theater by other African American playwrights. The concept will be examined according to two basic measures: movement and homelessness. I have selected these two states of being because they are held in common across the various instances of blacks' continuous migration. In addition, they lend themselves to the simultaneous consideration of both physical/literal states and metaphorical or psychic ones; both "movement" and "homelessness" are easily understood in terms of concrete objects and abstract consciousnesses. Such simultaneity nicely parallels not only the connection between creative nomadism and historical migration but also the combination of literalness and abstraction that is at the heart of theater and performance.

The consideration of Parks's illusions of and allusions to nomadism is in keeping with previous criticism of her work; it, too, assumes a purposefulness to her writing style's complexity.[6] More important, it is a way of examining her plays' combinations of words, sounds, actions, and behaviors by working *with* rather than *against* their kaleidoscopic nature. As Parks herself points out, her works' meanings are ever-shifting,[7] so critical analysis of that work must be similarly nimble. Parks's work reaches the audience member not as a framed painting or even as a picture show as much as the flashing colored horses of a carousel. Standing beyond the gate of the ride, we may detect the occasional horse among the stampede circling by, but we will miss much detail. However, if we are able to stand on the turning platform, we will see their spangled saddles, carved manes, and painted-on eyes. Better still, we will sense each horse's individual vertical movement against our circular one. Finally, in the midst of the music and spinning, we will realize that the supposedly stationary crowd waving us on appears to be moving as well; their stability is actually an illusion dependent on perspective. The concept of African American creative nomadism is one means by which to become riders on that carousel, not onlookers beyond the gate. It encourages us to uncover the richness in Parks's plays by operating from the same logic of movement and homelessness that has played a significant part in African American cultural history, the same logic that Parks explores in her plays.

The nomadism of Parks's work can be understood not only as a product of the migratory history of black people but also as an expression of postmodernism's preoccupation with migration, exile, and shifting identities.[8] Rosi Braidotti's concept of nomadic subjects is one example of this discourse. Although Braidotti's original application involved the female feminist subject, because there is a concern for the intersection of identities at the heart of Braidotti's theory, I believe that it naturally extends to a subject whose gender *and* race identity overtly shape her nomadism. Such a subject is just as likely as Braidotti's original figure to seek to develop new frameworks and images in which to conceive of subjectivity, ones that would recognize the possibilities in supposed contradictions and allow affirmation in a resistant context. Meanwhile, a playwright's cultural production is simply another model for how the nomadic subject employs imagination to act against "the settled and conventional nature of theoretical and especially philosophical thinking" and develop a new epistemology, this time by theatrical and performative means.[9] Parks and others are merely demonstrating their multiple literacies in the languages of stage narrative. In fact, Parks's theater setting is perhaps an ideal one in which to explore nomadic subjectivity because of its abstracted nature. After all, Braidotti describes the shifting and relative nature of the nomadic existence as contributing to a nomadic consciousness, which is based on a transmobility of thought and identity rather than of the physical self:

> Though the image of "nomadic subjects" is inspired by the experience of peoples or cultures that are literally nomadic, the nomadism in question here refers to the kind of critical consciousness that resists settling into socially coded modes of thought and behavior. Not all nomads are world

travelers; some of the greatest trips can take place without physically moving from one's habitat. It is the subversion of set conventions that defines the nomadic state, not the literal act of traveling.[10]

This "critical consciousness" allows the nomadic subject to resist settling and to instead subvert socially coded modes and set conventions. The nomadic subject is an *active* agent, therefore; she is not simply buffeted by social forces, which hold standards the nomad cannot meet, but rather the nomadic subject critically evaluates those standards and rejects them as she sees fit.

Parks's position as a nomadic artist-subject at the close of the twentieth century and the opening of the twenty-first makes her part of the continuing pursuit of new frameworks and images. As only two examples, the feminist theater and black theater movements of the late 1960s and early 1970s were cultural movements that set out to subvert normative conventions in efforts to defend African Americans and women against misrepresentation, denigration, and other attacks found in more established cultural practices. One of the aspects of traditional Western theater that these movements rejected was the structure of dramatic realism; black and feminist theater practitioners argued that this form could neither accommodate the exploration of new identities and consciousness nor incorporate alternative performance modes, both of which were deemed essential to the movements' political agendas of black and women's liberation, respectively.[11] In response, the feminist and black theater movements brought about conceptual and practical changes which continue to circulate more than thirty years later, including their contribution to current expressions of nomadic consciousness in American theater. Therefore, Parks's use of nonlinear narratives and nonstandard English are examples of an artist's individual vision, but they also speak to and from a broader cultural climate, which has been shaped in part by blacks' and women's liberation movements as well as by postmodernist discourse. For example, Parks's use of characters and created moments mirrors both black cultural history and contemporary postmodernism, as well as the intersection of the two. In fact, Parks could be said to be theorizing on—not just reflecting—the relationship of postmodern and African Diaspora discourses through invocations of travel metaphors and psychic displacement and references to blurred points of departure and final destinations.[12]

Ham Bone Ham Bone where you been
Roun thuh worl n back a-gain

Before turning to a detailed examination of Parks's plays, it is necessary to spend some time defining in greater detail the world in which Parks and other contemporary African American playwrights are working. There are three aspects of their identity that potentially affect their expression of a nomadic subjectivity: their status as postmodern, social, and professional subjects. Furthermore, issues of race and gender identity are constant influences in all three of those identities and can further affect their nomadic subjectivity.

Along with their location in a postmodern context, including the aftermath of feminism's and black nationalism's social and cultural movements, contemporary African American artists also exist in a postcolonial environment. Specifically, these artists' nomadic subjectivity is in keeping with postmodern and postcolonial discourse on the renegotiation of positionality by the monolithic West and its subjects. No longer are oppressor-oppressed or self-Other precise or permanent identities. Subjects now frequently resist their disadvantaged position, while the monolith now finds it fashionable to examine its own oppression at the hands of individuals or the social systems at large. Says Una Chaudhuri of these developments: "[H]uman beings can be said to be returning to a nomadic form of existence. . . . 'Who am I' is firmly anchored in a new form of '*where* am I?' "[13] African American women (artists) are not the only holders of this nomadic consciousness, of course, and neither they nor members of other groups are nomadic at all times. Still, Chaudhuri's description suggests a widespread perception of nomadic subjectivity, which may encourage the contemporary African American artist's exploration of her own nomadism. In this climate, identity—even that of a "minority" or "Third World" person, vulnerable to extensive stereotyping—is no longer seen as a concrete essence that transfers unchanged into all settings; now, it is understood as determined in great part by each environment. It is only natural that the artistic identities of contemporary playwrights—their writing styles and their characters' language, behavior, movement—would be similarly affected.

To be sure, an illusion of a "home" and the relativity it brings to our understanding of subjectivity are key to this climate. Liz Bondi describes the modern condition of displacement and continual homelessness as requiring a home as a reference point: "The metaphor of position is deployed to capture both the multiplicity and internal fracturing of identities, while the concept of subject reminds [us] that we still operate with narratives of our individual integrity."[14] A subject's individual integrity is that psychic home from which excursions can be measured.

But again, though it has a wide reach, postmodernism's pervasive instability is particularly powerful for people of color and other marginalized groups for the ways in which it allows the expression of alternative subjectivities.[15] It enables the necessary shift in consciousness away from possibly oppressive established patterns and goals and toward an inclusive, broader view. Gloria Anzaldúa names this a "tolerance for ambiguity";[16] others have named it "awareness of simultaneous dimensions,"[17] "multicultural competence,"[18] or "trying to face (at least) two ways at once."[19] Whatever the term, contemporary African American artists' creative nomadism is the movement among and through social and cultural institutions in much the same way that literal nomadism is movement through well-defined territories in search of food or other resources. The invention of new creative frameworks and images is those artists' search for sustenance for their artistic life in the face of harsh conditions of censorship, ignorance, prejudice, or other restrictive forces. Playwright Ntozake Shange is one of several African American writers to offer an illustration of this in her rebellion against so-called standard English. Shange points to her exploration of other cultures' literature as one way to "escape what I really feel to be one of our [black women writers'] primary prisons, which is the English language."[20] Shange and others have escaped this and other prisons by moving away from the established patterns of some cultural practices and by incorporating others in new or unexpected ways. Their migration within and among those practices results in an ambiguous positionality and a free-moving consciousness.

I want to underscore this potential for freedom in nomadism. The contemporary African American artist's nomadic consciousness should not be thought of negatively, as yet another coping mechanism that is the consequence of the history of African American ostracism from mainstream (white) society. It is not simply another variation on Du Bois's concept of a double consciousness, which is the unfortunate result of warring ideals. Nor is it a handicap in need of correction or compensation, a condition under which the nomadic subject must endure an endless friction. Rather, the nomadic subject frequently enjoys a positive vantage point because of her nomadism, a valid alternative to a traditional subjectivity.[21] Nomadic subjectivity could even be understood as a more evolved and enlightened consciousness.[22] In that understanding, what might otherwise be seen as Parks's confused combination of seemingly mismatched black vernacular English and absurdist theater, for example, can instead be understood as a liberating hybridity. Her complex writing style is not the result of her failure to thrive or to be welcomed in one cultural world or another but of her nomadic negotiation between them. Again, such an interpretation is possible in part because of the overall tolerance for ambiguity in contemporary society. At the same time, it hinges on decades of restrictive definitions of cultures and identities in this country, definitions that first created the illusion of the boundaries that nomadism transgresses. Nevertheless, nomadic subjectivity is now a viable expression of identity, one that contemporary African American artists, such as Parks, employ effectively.

What of race's direct influence on African American artists' nomadic subjectivity? One aspect of their racial identity that can significantly affect their nomadic consciousness is social class.[23] Higher economic class backgrounds—and the educational opportunities that frequently accompany that status—can lead to a worldliness that facilitates a creative nomadism; in a sense, an artist's psychic travel is aided by her knowledge of the geography of the "worlds" of technique and subject matter with which she might create.[24] As alluded to earlier, however, the expression of a nomadic subjectivity was not always seen as potentially beneficial. For example, in his 1950s study of the black middle class, E. Franklin Frazier stated:

> Because of their social isolation and lack of a cultural tradition, the members of the black bourgeoisie in the United States seem to be in the process of becoming NOBODY.[25]

Yet I would argue that many of Frazier's generation of subjects necessarily developed a hybridity and agility in their cultural practices, which enabled them to negotiate between black and non-black worlds. They were becoming "everybody" as much as "nobody." Furthermore, these strategies sowed benefits and consequences that contemporary generations of African Americans are now reaping; the chameleonlike quality, which Frazier interprets as "nobodyness," is the foundation for today's nomadic artist and the creative nomadism of her work. For example, where Frazier blames the education of the black middle class for uprooting those blacks from " 'racial' traditions or, more specifically, from [their] folk background,"[26] the 1960s and '70s saw the development of prominent programs in black studies at the very institutions most likely to attract children of that economic class. This provided these African Americans with exposure—though late and qualified—to Frazier's "racial traditions" and contributed to the formation of a nomadic subjectivity in today's middle class and, therefore, contributed to that same subjectivity in the African American community at large.[27] Quite naturally, this affected cultural production. Trey Ellis describes how the ripple-effect played out in what he calls the "New Black Aesthetic":

> For the first time in our history we are producing a critical mass of college graduates who are children of college graduates themselves. Like most artistic booms, the [New Black Aesthetic] is a post-bourgeois movement driven by a second generation of middle class. . . . We now feel secure enough to attend art school instead of medical school.[28]

Ellis goes on to describe the new generation of middle class African American artists, of which Parks is one,[29] as feeling no obligation to either a Black Arts legacy or a mainstream aesthetic. His discussion of the hybridity in contemporary African American artists' consciousness further illuminates the contemporary African American artist as nomad by showing how social class can help shape nomadic consciousness.

Along with race identity and postmodern context, the nomadic subjectivity of the contemporary African American playwright is also determined by her identity as a writer for theater. Certainly, the kind of literal homelessness common to an American playwright's life (full of comings and goings to various productions, workshops, and readings) is a factor. Beyond that, however, theorists suggest that contemporary authorship and American theater practice are both dominated by an assumption of fractured identity and constant movement. Keith and Pile invoke deCerteau's thesis that every story is one of travel, "a spatial practice,"[30] while Chaudhuri asserts that humankind's return to a nomadic existence has resulted in a modern drama based on "a principle of dispersal, of dissolution."[31] Contemporary writing has—or is seen to have—inherent in it the two basic nomadic elements of movement and homelessness. I stated earlier that postmodernism's ambiguous notions of identity include the renegotiation of social roles and investigation of their constructedness and symbolic force. Accordingly, representations of race and gender in contemporary drama are affected by this climate, and many African American playwrights work to capture the ambiguities with characters who hover somewhere in between, or even outside, traditional categorizations.

At the same time, artists' dramatic representations are also shaped by the gender and racial circumstances surrounding African Americans' literal movement. Historians, including Darlene Clark Hine, have documented how African American men and women had markedly different experiences during the Great Migration of the 1920s;[32] despite changes in social standards, it is likely that there were gender-based differences during other migratory periods as well. Along with these factual influences, there are also social narratives (often myths), which circulate about the mobility of African American women versus nonblack women or African American men. For example, some feminists point to African American women's long history of work outside the home as evidence of their liberated, mobile womanhood (although it was just as often the result of economic need, potentially continuing the women's experiences of racism and sexism). Others argue that contemporary African American women are more successful economically and educationally than African American men because they are thought to be less threatening and are thereby allowed to navigate mainstream American society. In both cases, African Americans' mobility is understood in relationship to both their race *and* gender. Likewise, then, African American playwrights' nomadic subjectivity must also be framed by both factors.

Playwriting as a genre of creative nomadism is also determined by issues of race and gender. For example, the black theater and feminist theater movements, which contributed to today's nomadism, were dominated by black males and white females, respectively. As a result, although contemporary African American women playwrights, such as Parks, clearly have a connection to both eras and the new dramatic forms they encouraged, these playwrights must first rework those movements' reworking in order to define a place for their own creativity. Their nomadic experience as theater professionals is similarly intensified. Some argue that "minority" playwrights, including African American women, are even more transient than others in this age of multiculturalism; there is a market within the regional theater system for such playwrights, so they are constantly shuttled back and forth among theaters' "second stages," festivals, or workshops.[33] Playwright Anna Deavere Smith says of the predicament of black women theater artists:

> It's all well and good if an artistic director says, "I want you to come work here," but it's much bigger than that. It's back to this thing: Are there any *homes* for black women? . . . If we are nomadic, why is it that we are walking and walking and walking and not finding a place to rest?[34]

Dramaturg and critic Sydné Mahone offers some answers in the introduction to her anthology of the work of contemporary African American women playwrights. She describes such playwrights as living in the "hostile" environment of the mostly "white patriarchal institution" of American theater, an environment in which "hostility towards African-American women writers and 'others' has been expressed, not through malevolence, but more dangerously through avoidance and neglect." And yet, Mahone points out, even those few "others" who may manage to thrive in the hallowed halls of mainstream theater may be reluctant to do so, since marginalization is often taken as a sign of true artistry:

> One could argue that [exceptional African American women writers'] very extraordinary qualities justify their 'outsider' status; to include them would somehow compromise or corrupt their integrity, thus diminishing their power to challenge the status quo.[35]

So, one way that contemporary African American women playwrights negotiate between the rock of exclusion and the hard place of assimilation is the proven strategy of constant movement. Deavere Smith attributes black women playwrights' homelessness to gender identity's influence on their craft and on the demands they make of American theater practice. I would argue that it is, in fact, the combination of race *and* gender that influences and demands.[36]

Racegender is a definite factor in the contemporary African American woman playwright's exploration of a nomadic subjectivity, because of both the playwright's identity and the identity representations in her work.[37] It shapes how the basic elements of movement and homelessness are understood by invoking histories and discourses around race or gender that frame them in certain ways. For example, a play that features a black woman on a cross-country trip alludes—purposefully or not—to historical instances of black women's geographic travel, and the circumstances behind those instances are very different from historical instances of black men's, white men's, or white women's travel. Nevertheless, depending on the artist and the particular play, the influence of racegender issues varies: for some, it may serve as the vehicle in the journeys of nomadic subjectivity and consciousness, for others only as accompanying baggage. Parks tends to treat her characters' racegender, like their other characteristics, as emblematic. Regarding gender, she places her characters in superficially conventional roles, such as wife (Black Woman with Fried Drumstick in *Last Black Man*), mother (Mrs. Sergeant Smith in *Imperceptible Mutabilities in the Third Kingdom*), sister (Molly/Mona, Charlene/Chona, Veronica/Verona in *Imperceptible Mutabilities*); husband (Lucius in *Betting on the Dust Commander*), father (Mr. Sergeant Smith in *Imperceptible Mutabilities*), son (Brazil in *The America Play*). Regarding race, Parks's characters often resemble icons of blackness (Black Man with Watermelon, Old Man River Jordan, Queen-Then-Pharaoh Hatshepsut in *Last Black Man*) or nonblackness (Abraham Lincoln–impersonator The Foundling Father in *The America Play*). And yet, because of the surreal nature of Parks's created worlds, her characters seem somewhat removed from social conventions surrounding race and gender. Furthermore, Parks's story lines rarely center around race or gender issues alone. Even in *Last Black Man* and, more recently, *Venus* (two plays that focus on clearly racegendered main characters), Parks skillfully embeds these loaded figures in layered studies of other, seemingly non–racegender-based ideas. Still, at the same time, Parks's treatment of issues such as memory, death, and desire reveals how these issues are shaped by factors like racegender identity.[38] Her work provides an example of the complications that racegender brings to African American artists'—particularly women artists'—expression of that subjectivity.

I have divided the factors in the contemporary African American playwright's creative nomadism into the influences of postmodernism, social class, and profession, with racegender a factor in all three. However, I do not mean to imply a primacy of influences. More likely, any set of forces can move into position at a given moment, necessarily displacing another set. In this way—and true to a nomadic subjectivity—tensions that might otherwise arise through categories' jockeying for a permanent superior position are resolved through a negotiation of perspective. For example, from the perspective of "mainstream American" theater, playwright Adrienne Kennedy's 1960s surrealist psychological dramas could be seen as a move away from the traditional, linear narratives of the few other African American women playwrights recognized at that time by the mainstream, such as Lorraine Hansberry or Alice Childress. From the perspective of the contemporaneous Black Nationalist theater, however, the form could be a departure from the politically overt and macho plays most often associated with the Black Theater Movement. While some might argue that Kennedy's relevance to both streams ultimately makes her relevant to neither, by approaching her work as an expression of a nomadic subjectivity, both perspectives—and possibly others—can be accommodated. Once again, the nomadic subject's creative nomadism must be evaluated according to distance and relationship to a given "home."[39]

Ham Bone Ham Bone whatcha do?
Got uh chance n fairly flew.

Parks offers an appropriate study of creative nomadism and contemporary African American playwrights because of her representative qualities. First, she achieved significant visibility in American theater during the 1990s, moving beyond the status of an "emerging" playwright to enjoy a level of artistic and career maturity. Parks has a distinctive voice among contemporary American playwrights in general, and she resists pigeonholing when grouped with other African American, female, or African American women playwrights in particular. Furthermore, Parks's success has been primarily in mainstream (white- and male-dominated) American theater, and yet her work routinely incorporates issues of African American and female identity. This combination of position and subject matter highlights the function of race and gender in Parks's work and suggests particular consequences for her expression of a creative nomadism. Finally, I consider Parks's work to be, to borrow Sydné Mahone's words, "compelling, thought-provoking and stylistically fresh."[40] Her work demands the spectator's and reader's full attention with an intricacy of language and action that invites second and third interpretations. As mentioned earlier, Parks endures/enjoys somewhat of a reputation for creating works whose meanings are difficult to uncover, although she finds the search for meaning a misguided one:

> I've had so many interviews where someone would say, so what does it mean? . . . That's basically saying, you're being obscure and why don't you tell us what you want, what you really mean, thinking the writer has some sort of agenda that hides somewhere behind or underneath the text or behind the production somewhere. . . . Instead of saying, what does that mean? which is already a sentence that is outside of the play, ask[s] you to fill in some blanks, it means this—that's an equation that's outside of the play. Stick to the play.[41]

Again, an investigation into creative nomadism in Parks's work is one way to reframe ambiguities as dramatic strategy, thereby "sticking to the play." It can help in the move away from a preoccupation with meaning to an occupation with the play experience.[42]

Parks's exploration of nomadic subjectivity is set in worlds of constant movement and change, worlds full of permeable boundaries, which her characters and stories negotiate easily. The two main sets of boundaries that Parks subverts are those of space and time. Parks's exploration of the boundaries of space are best exemplified by her articulation of a Third Kingdom in *Imperceptible Mutabilities in the Third Kingdom (1989);* the Third Kingdom exemplifies one set of characters' condition of movement and homelessness.[43] Character Over-Seer traces the genesis of this condition and the meaning of the play's title: "Half the world had fallen away making 2 worlds and a sea between. Those 2 worlds inscribe the Third Kingdom."[44] This Third Kingdom immediately conjures up images of the "real" so-called Third World and its anonymous inhabitants of color. There, too, the space is hemmed by two worlds: the Old and the New. And, as with the Third Kingdom, in order for Third World inhabitants to reach either of the other two worlds, they must cross geographical, cultural, philosophical, even chronological seas.

Perhaps more than the term *"world,"* however, Parks's Third Kingdom suggests an autonomy in that third space. Although it may be unknown and annoyingly distant to First and Second World on-lookers, the idea of a kingdom implies that it holds a good deal of space, cultures, and beliefs of its own, which its subjects can navigate. Furthermore, the movements and transformations of the kingdom's subject may be imperceptible, but they are real nonetheless. In this formulation, those who brave the sea can no longer be presumed to be trading homelessness for home; Parks's having set an entire play in that homeless space necessarily reverses that presumption. The piece explores the way in which those who migrate from the Third Kingdom are actually leaving a home of homelessness. Such a contradiction is perfectly acceptable within the context of creative nomadism. Says Braidotti, "[N]omadism consists not so much in being homeless, as in being capable of recreating your home everywhere."[45] In *Imperceptible Mutabilities*, Parks not only writes new spaces for her characters but actually reinscribes our notions of the connection between space and the individual inhabitant.

Parks's work also alludes to historical, literal migrations. *Imperceptible Mutabilities* deals most explicitly with the black Atlantic slave trade as a catalyst for Parks's characters' nomadic consciousness, but this and other works also introduce other periods in black migration.[46] Blacks have repeatedly shown themselves capable of recreating their homes wherever they land, and Parks crafts plays that embody that tradition. She preserves her characters' agency even in their state of limbo and thereby champions the freedom of nomadic consciousness.[47] She allows her characters to showcase this liminal space as a valid—though compromised—place in which to exist. She leads us to reconsider African Americans not as homeless residents of a strange land but as nomadic subjects of a different kingdom.

Meanwhile, Parks employs a dramatic strategy of repetition and revision in order to thin conventional boundaries of time. The strategy allows her to create dramatic moments, which are then repeated with just enough variation to demonstrate the tenuous relationship between inertia and change. Says Parks:

> "Repetition and Revision" is a concept integral to the Jazz esthetic [sic] in which the composer or performer will write or play a musical phrase once and again and again; etc.—with each revisit the phrase is slightly revised. "Rep & Rev" as I call it is a central element in my work[48] . . . a text based on the concept of repetition and revision is one which breaks from the text which we are told to write—the text which cleanly ARCS. . . . In such plays we are not moving from A→B but rather, for example, from A→A→A→B→A. Through such movement, we refigure A.[49]

Rep and rev is particularly effective when applied to dialogue: a character's lines may be identical at two different points in a play, and yet in the repetition the audience member or reader is forced to contemplate why the lines were repeated. Part 2: Third Kingdom of *Imperceptible Mutabilities* ends this way:

KIN-SEER: You said I could wave as long as I see um. I still see um.

OVER-SEER: Wave then.

Later in the play, during Third Kingdom (Reprise), the characters repeat the lines, but the scene continues for several more moments in a frenzy of drowning, waving, and sailing away. The changed context gives the identical lines different resonances: a peaceful tableau in Part 2 becomes the image of an oblivious Kin-Seer making a pointless gesture while a detached Over-Seer looks on in the Reprise. As another example, at the close of the first panel in *Last Black Man*, Black Woman with Fried Drumstick and Black Man have this exchange:

BLACK WOMAN: They eat their own yuh know.

BLACK MAN: HooDoo.

BLACK WOMAN: Hen do. Saw it on thuh Tee V.

BLACK MAN: Aint that nice.[50]

This exchange is immediately repeated at the start of the next panel, with revisions; the same words are now spoken between Black Woman and the rest of the ensemble. With that change—and an upper case "HOODOO" for emphasis—the words mutate from a simple performance of misconjugation in Black Vernacular English (BVE), to a performance of a political commentary, quite possibly about media misrepresentation of African Americans as savages and the general population's complacency about it.

As a final example, Parks has drawn an "equation" for *Imperceptible Mutabilities* that shows the outlines of "USA" and of "Africa" with a note to "solve for X." X is represented by a double-headed arrow placed in between the two land masses: "↔."[51] In geometry this symbolizes the space between two points, but the figure also leads the eye back and forth along the arrow's axis never allowing it to rest for too long on one side or the other. Parks's rep and rev gives her audience firsthand experience of nomadic consciousness; time passes, and yet we are brought "back" to an earlier moment—where we started. Or are we? Or are we in both moments at once? And does it matter? The rep and rev technique collapses time and causes the reader/spectator to experience nomadism's constant movement back and forth between different points of being.

Not only are Parks's constructions of time and of space blurred within their own conventional boundaries, but the two sometimes appear to bleed into each other as well. Thus the line "The black man moves his hands.—He moves his hands round. Back. Back. Back tuh that" seems to refer to a movement both back to a position and back to a moment. This, too, echoes blacks' literal nomadic experiences, such as the current trend for northern-based blacks to move "back" to the South, to a "simpler time."

Now (in Parks's collapsed sense of the word), with an environment of shifting time and space established, Parks explores the various aspects of nomadic subjectivity, the nomad's states of mind or ways of understanding the world. First, Parks portrays the nomadic figure at rest, during which he or she exhibits the qualities of double-consciousness and self-reflexivity described by Du Bois, Mitchell, and others.[52] She presents characters who combine self-perception with an awareness of how they are perceived by others; rather than a solely introverted consciousness, Parks's characters also face outward. One manifestation of that outward stance is the way in which Parks's characters speak about themselves. In *Last Black Man*, the central character, Black Man with Watermelon, has a refrain: "The black man moves his hands." With each repetition and accompanying gesture during the play, the character not only demonstrates his self-gaze, but he also shows that he is aware of our and his fellow characters' spectatorship. By speaking in the third person, he has adopted a narrative voice that mimics the point of view of the other characters and the audience, who are all witnessing his action. As the character speaks this line, then, we see his nomadic consciousness at work as he moves between his own psychic space and that of his observers. In other characters, meanwhile, Parks sometimes goes as far as to confine the distance between self and others fully within a character; the character becomes her own spectator:

> KIN-SEER: I was standin with my toes stuckted in thuh dirt. Nothin in front of me but water. And I was wavin. Wavin. Wavin at my uther me who I could barely see. Over thuh water on thuh uther cliff I could see my uther me but my uther me could not see me. And I was wavin wavin wavin sayin gaw gaw gaw gaw eeeeeee-uh.[53] . . . My uther me then waved back at me and then I was happy. But my uther me whuduhnt wavin at me. My uther me was wavin at my Self. My uther me was wavin at uh black black speck in thuh middle of thuh sea where years uhgoh from uh boat I had been—UUH![54]

The last moment in this passage (referring to both literary and geographical meanings of passage) captures the nightmare most nomadic subjects experience at one time or another: the inability to find one's true self amid the different homes and constant movement. In this passage, the character adopts a new perspective only to mistake her for another.

In the midst of their displacements, migrations, and journeys, it is a struggle for Parks's characters to keep sight of the literal or psychic shore. Parks depicts the complications of the African-descended nomad's privileged standpoint, where sight does not necessarily mean vision or understanding, or worse yet, where vision is ultimately thwarted by inadequate language:

> YES AND GREENS BLACK-EYED PEAS CORNBREAD: Whatcha seen hambone girl?
> BLACK WOMAN WITH FRIED DRUMSTICK: Didnt see you. I saw thuh worl.
> QUEEN-THEN-PHARAOH HATSHEPSUT: I was there.
> LOTS OF GREASE AND LOTS OF PORK: Didnt see you.
> BLACK WOMAN WITH FRIED DRUMSTICK: I was there.
> BLACK MAN WITH WATERMELON: Didnt see you.[55]

In these lines, Parks reminds us of the various instances of historical and contemporary black invisibility. Along with these ideas of large-scale societal misrepresentation or omission of a black presence, however, the passage also suggests that similar invisibility is occurring in the relationships between individual people. Parks's characters suggest that, in both contexts, the literal and nonliteral selves are not seen and that the attempt to speak to that gap can be little more than vague and repetitive.[56]

Another of the nomadic subject's states of being that Parks explores is that of immobility. In Part 1 of *Imperceptible Mutabilities*, appropriately entitled "Snails," Parks presents three sisters threatened by an infestation of inertia as well as roaches. (Throughout "Snails," the sisters frantically chase and kill the insects and even summon a pesticide specialist, yet they are "splatting" bugs until the end.) They seem torn between the desire and ability to escape their situation and immobility. Molly/Mona's ability to move is a tangle of contradictions. She quits a job because she cannot speak in standard English—" 'Talk right or youre outta here!' I couldn't. I walked."—yet she cannot leave the apartment: "Once there was uh me named Mona who wanted tuh jump ship but didnt."[57] Charlene/Chona, meanwhile, seems resigned to her inactivity. She states: "Once there was uh woman who wanted tuh get uhway for uhwhile but didnt know which way tuh go tuh get gone. Once there was uh woman who just layed down."[58] Ostensibly, Charlene/Chona's line is a response to Veronica/Verona's asking where Molly/Mona was, but since the quoted line is said several moments after the question is asked and after Charlene/Chona has already given an answer, she seems to implicate herself as well.

Only Veronica/Verona seems to have resolved the conflict between a desire to move and a failure to do so. At the end of the section, she delivers a monologue about her love for animals and how, as a child, she had a black dog named Namib, who refused to behave and eventually ran away. She tells us that, many years later, while working in a veterinary hospital as a euthanasia specialist, she came across another black dog, who presumably was also a wanderer. After putting the dog down, she performs an autopsy "because I had to see I just had to see the heart of such a disagreeable domesticated thing." What Veronica/Verona finds causes her to realize that the source of the nomadic instinct is not a physical abnormality. "Nothing different. Everything in its place. Do you know what that means? Everything in its place. Thats all."[59] This sister has discovered that the condition is undetectable and therefore inexplicable. Through her story, Parks suggests that nomadic subjectivity is more dependent on a certain consciousness than on a physical characteristic. This, too, is in keeping with the tradition of African American migration. Writer James Baldwin explained his decision to expatriate this way: "I left America because I doubted my ability to survive the fury of the color problem here. . . . I wanted to prevent myself from becoming *merely* a Negro; or, even, merely a Negro writer."[60] This is a complaint common to many African American artists, expatriate or not, in Baldwin's time and since. Its prevalence reminds us that the power in an artist's literal or creative migration comes not so much from the arrival at a new location as from ways in which that location allows her to see herself as an artist. Baldwin's comment suggests that the geographical journeying of earlier expatriates was ultimately superseded by the journey of the mind from one identity consciousness to another.

Of course, some characters are not simply incapable of developing a nomadic consciousness but actually resist doing so. In Part 4 of *Imperceptible Mutabilities*, Mrs. Sergeant Smith boasts how she is able to travel by bus to visit her husband on the military base without looking the least bit disheveled: "I was just as proud. 'Ain't traveled a mile nor sweated a drop!' "[61] She repeats her husband's words, a compliment that erases her movement.

True to her commitment to movement, Parks not only presents states or nonstates of nomadic consciousness but also the progression away from inertia. Characters are regularly located within one setting for most of the play, and yet there is frequent talk of someone's recent arrival or imminent departure. As examples, both *Last Black Man* and *The America Play* feature themes of death and dying. In the former, Black Man with Watermelon has endured multiple executions; in the latter, the lead character, The Foundling Father, has died, leaving his wife and son to make their living "keeping secrets for the dead" and attending funerals as a professional mourner, respectively. Parks frames these characters' travel back and forth across the lines of life and death as the ultimate in arrivals and departures. Even as they move, however, Parks's characters continue to question movement's effectiveness as a means of agency for themselves and others. In *Last Black Man*, characters question Black Man's destination after death: "Where he gonna go now that he done dieded? . . . Where he gonna go tuh wash his hands?"[62] Other characters say of their own movement: "There is uh tiny land mass just above my reach. . . . There is uh tiny land mass just outside of my vocabulary."[63]

In fact, one of the most obvious signs of nomadic consciousness in Parks' work is her characters' use of language, particularly of BVE. Parks manages to dismantle the structure of both standard English and BVE so that her characters' written text is filled with jolting (mis)spellings and cryptic notations for sounds, which transform, in performance, into speech that is both natural (punctuated by rhythms, pauses, and vocal interjections) and heightened (able to capture the poetry and potential for layered meanings in natural speech). Parks's description of her use of language speaks to some of the bars and spaces-between-bars of the prison of language that Shange described:

> [H]ow do I adequately represent not merely the speech patterns of a people oppressed by language (which is the simple question) but the patterns of a people whose language use is so complex and varied and ephemeral that its daily use not only Signifies on the non-vernacular language forms, but on the construct of writing as well. If language is a construct and writing is a construct and Signifyin(g) on the double construct is the daily use, then I have chosen to Signify on the Signifyin(g).[64]

Parks's choice to "Signify on the Signifyin(g)" through her characters' language is a move toward what sociologist Paul Gilroy describes as the "liberation of culture, especially language, as a means of social self-creation."[65] In that way, her use of language mirrors her use of time and space: as a means of creative freedom. Braidotti labels such strategic use of language "linguistic nomadism"; within this construction, Parks manipulates the languages of conventional English, BVE, drama's text, and theater's performance to create spaces and propel bodies:

BEFORE COLUMBUS: Back then when they thought the world was flat they were afeared and stayed at home. They wanted to go out back then when they thought the world

was flat but the water had in it dragons of which
meaning these dragons they were afeared back then
when they thought the world was flat. They stayed
at home. Them thinking the world was flat kept
it roun. Them thinking the sun revolved around
the earth kept them satellite-like. They figured
out the truth and scurried out. Figuring out the
truth put them in their place and they scurried out
to put us in ours.[66]

Parks's nomadic subjects are left with a sense of regret over their lost selves
and ambiguous progress; again, we can hear these words in terms of blacks'
various forced and voluntary migrations: "And I whuduhnt me no more and
I whuduhnt no fish. My new Self was uh third Self made by thuh space in
between. And my new Self wonders: Am I happy? Is my new Self happy in
my new-Self shoes?"[67] This element of regret, of questioning whether one is
better off before or after the journey, is the only fitting conclusion that Parks
can offer. It necessarily complicates her portrait of African Americans as
nomadic subjects by underscoring that their movement is not simply a
reaction to outside forces but an implication and consequence of their own
agency. It preserves the value of their fictive nomadism—and thus the value
of Parks's creative nomadism—by revealing the choice inherent in it. As the
above passages demonstrate, nomadism does not promise a positive outcome
or better destination, only their possibility.

Nomadism does promise new times, spaces, and options, however. Parks's
characters may express disappointment with the consequences of their migrations, yet regret does not eradicate the value of having begun the journey.
If anything, it serves as a reminder that the most effective migration must
manage to preserve a connection to a homeplace. bell hooks states that those
nomads who do survive the journey "passionately holding on to aspects of
that 'downhome' life we do not intend to lose while simultaneously seeking
new knowledge and experience" are those best prepared to "invent spaces of
radical openness."[68] By allowing her characters to express regret over their
own nomadism, Parks creates figures who are at once holding on and seeking
new knowledge. They reside in the spaces of radical openness created by their
own nomadic consciousness. I would argue, further, that the nomadism of
Parks's characters reinforces Parks's own nomadism as a contemporary African American woman playwright. Her works operate on stage as open spaces
in which language, plot, and characterization are in a constant state of
movement. Parks's plays shadow the author's own perpetual state of creative
middle passage, then, between the influences of her African American
woman, postmodern subject, and theater artist identities.

Roun thuh worl n back a-gain

So this is not necessarily even an account of travel. For to travel implies
movement between fixed positions, a site of departure, a point of arrival,

the knowledge of an itinerary. It also intimates an eventual return, a potential homecoming. Migrancy, on the contrary, involves a movement in which neither the points of departure nor those of arrival are immutable or certain.[69]

BLACK WOMAN WITH FRIED DRUMSTICK: You comed back.

BLACK MAN WITH WATERMELON: —Not exactly.[70]

Suzan-Lori Parks renegotiates the boundaries of the African American migratory tradition just as she does the boundaries of time and space, form and content. In *Black Looks: Race and Representation*, hooks describes "critical remembering" as a way to interrogate the past.[71] Parks's explorations of the strengths and weaknesses in nomadic subjectivity do indeed recall the history of African American artistic expatriation. At the same time, her efforts are creating a record by which to critically remember contemporary African Americans' nomadic consciousness and African American artists' creative nomadism.

Again, the key is to approach African American artists' nomadism not solely as a makeshift solution to social and aesthetic oppression, the instinctive reaction of a people under attack. Rather, analysis must consider this nomadism as a form of creative agency. Parks has created works too visionary, too invigorating, too much of a theatrical spectacle, and too blessed with humor to be subject to accusations of being aimless and disorderly. At the same time, her works are constructed too carefully to be viewed simply as the product of sheer instinct. The concept of African American artists' creative nomadism offers a way to explore her plays' characteristics critically rather than apologetically, thereby producing more complex, satisfying analysis. Similarly, other African American artists' works, the form or content of which seem to have been made kaleidoscopic or even incoherent by the influences of postmodernism and the artist's compound identities, can also benefit from careful application of the nomadic concept. Through it, critics and audiences alike can better respect, appreciate, even give in to such works' challenges, moving with them rather than trying to clip their wings.

Ham bone ham bone whatcha do?
Got uh chance n fairly flew

NOTES

1. Barnor Hesse, "black to Front and black Again: Racialization through Contested Times and Spaces," in *Place and the Politics of Identity*, ed. Michael Keith and Steve Pile (New York: Routledge, 1993), 179.

2. Suzan-Lori Parks, *The Death of the Last Black Man in the Whole Entire World* (1992), 123.

3. All three of these authors wrote in other forms, including political essays, autobiographies, and even drama, but they are best known as novelists. Also, Baldwin

does complicate this construction of the African American artist expatriate somewhat, by both his longevity and the diverse body of his work. See Ursula Broschke Davis, *Paris without Regret: James Baldwin, Kenny Clarke, Chester Himes and Donald Byrd* (Iowa City: University of Iowa Press, 1986), 3; and Bryan R. Washington, *The Politics of Exile: Ideology in Henry James, F. Scott Fitzgerald, and James Baldwin* (Boston: Northeastern University Press, 1985), 15.

4. See Davis ix; Michael Fabre, *From Harlem to Paris: Black American Writers in France 1840–1980* (Urbana: University of Illinois Press, 1991), 337.

5. An analogous example would be a woman artist's creative exploration of the act of giving birth, although she herself may be childless.

6. See Alisa Solomon, "Signifying on the Signifyin': The Plays of Suzan–Lori Parks," *Theater* 21, no. 3 (Summer/Fall 1990): 73–80; Alvin Klein "About Women, about Pedestals," *New York Times* (31 Mar. 1996): 13, 21. Steven Drukman, "Suzan-Lori Parks and Liz Diamond: Doo-a-diddly-dit-dit," *TDR* 39, no. 3 (Fall 1995); and Alice Rayner and Harry J. Elam, Jr., "Unfinished Business: Reconfiguring History in Suzan-Lori Parks's *The Death of the Last Black Man in the Whole Entire World*," *Theatre Journal* 46, no. 4 (Dec. 1994): 447.

7. Parks describes her plays as "plutonium" because that element "moves . . . is alive" (Drukman 63).

8. This connection to postmodernism also justifies my study's emphasis on conditions of homelessness and continuous movement, rather than on markers of permanence and a completed physical journey. Like the transition from literal to metaphorical expatriation, this emphasis makes the necessary room for broader connections, including the relative and ambiguous nature of terms such as *movement* and *home* in this time of supersonic jets and virtual reality.

9. Rosi Braidotti, "Introduction: By Way of Nomadism," in Braidotti, *Nomadic Subjects: Embodiment and Sexual Difference in Contemporary Feminist Theory* (New York: Columbia University Press, 1994), 4.

10. Ibid., 5. See also Jill Dolan, *Feminist Spectator as Critic* (Ann Arbor: University of Michigan Press, 1988); and Addison Gayle, Jr., ed., *The Black Aesthetic* (New York: Doubleday, 1971).

11. See Jill Dolan, *The Feminist Spectator as Critic* (Ann Arbor: University of Michigan Press, 1988); and Addison Gayle, Jr., ed., *The Black Aesthetic* (New York: Doubleday, 1971).

12. Parks acknowledges many critics' resistance to seeing her as a theorist, however, and attributes it to "what we allow ourselves—we, meaning the world, black people included—what we allow black people to do and one of them is not theory" (Drukman 61). Fortunately, the following scholars challenge this limited permission, exploring ways in which African American (women) have traditionally developed theories through overlooked means, such as artistic expression: hooks, *Talking Back: Thinking Feminist, Thinking Black* (Boston: South End, 1989); Barbara Christian, "The Race for Theory," *Feminist Studies* 14, no. 1 (1988): 67–79; and Patricia Hill Collins, *Black Feminist Thought: Knowledge, Consciousness, and the Politics of Empowerment* (Boston: Unwin Hyman, 1990).

13. Una Chaudhuri, *Staging Place: The Geography of Modern Drama* (Ann Arbor: University of Michigan Press, 1995), 4.

14. Liz Bondi, "Locating Identity Politics," in *Place and the Politics of Identity*, ed. Michael Keith and Steve Pile, (New York: Routledge, 1993), 98.

15. bell hooks states: "Postmodern critiques of essentialism which challenge notions of universality and static over-determined identity within mass culture and

mass consciousness can open up new possibilities for the construction of self and assertion of agency." hooks, "Post-Modern blackness," in hooks, *Yearning: Race, Gender, and Cultural Politics* (Boston: South End, 1990), 28.

16. Gloria Anzaldúa, *Borderlands/La Frontera: The New Mestiza* (San Francisco: aunt lute books, 1987), 79.

17. Edward Said, "Reflections on Exile," in *Out There: Marginalization and Contemporary Cultures*, ed. Russell Ferguson, et al. (Cambridge, Mass.: MIT Press, and New York: New Museum of Contemporary Art, 1990), 366.

18. Ella Pearson Mitchell, "Du Bois' Dilemma and African American Adaptiveness," in *Lure and Loathing: Essays on Race, Identity, and the Ambivalence of Assimilation*, ed. Gerald Early (New York: Penguin, 1993), 266.

19. Paul Gilroy, *The Black Atlantic: Modernity and Double Consciousness* (Cambridge, Mass.: Harvard University Press, 1993), 3.

20. Quoted in Sydné Mahone, ed., *Moon Marked and Touched by Sun: Plays by African-American Women* (New York: Theatre Communications Group, 1994), 325.

21. Paul Gilroy asserts that members of the African diaspora enjoy a privileged standpoint, which is "a response to the successive displacements, migrations, and journeys (forced and otherwise) which have come to constitute these black cultures' special conditions of existence" (Gilroy 111).

22. Similar arguments have been made in feminist camps as women of color have asserted that they can contribute greatly to the efficacy of feminist movements and theory because of their perspective as a "double minority," which requires their negotiation between at least two worlds. See the following for discussions of difference and African American feminism: Elsa Barkley Brown, "African-American Women's Quilting: A Framework for Conceptualizing and Teaching African-American Women's History," in *Black Women in America: Social Science Perspectives*, ed. Micheline R. Malson et al. (Chicago: University of Chicago Press, 1988); Brown, " 'What Has Happened Here': The Politics of Difference in Women's History and Feminist Politics," in *"We Specialize in the Wholly Impossible": A Reader in Black Women's History*, ed. Darlene Clark Hine et al. (Brooklyn N.Y.: Carlson, 1995); and Deborah K. King, "Multiple Jeopardy, Multiple Consciousness: The Context of a Black Feminist Ideology," in Malson et al. Similarly, cultural critics, including Trey Ellis and Greg Tate, argue that contemporary African American artists benefit from a hybridized sensibility, which allows them to employ whichever creative influences they choose, regardless of whether those influences are seen as "black" or not. See Trey Ellis, "The New Black Aesthetic," *Callaloo* 12, no. 1 (Winter 1989); and Greg Tate, "Nobody Loves a Genius Child: Jean Michael Basquiat, Flyboy in the Buttermilk," in Tate, *Flyboy in the Buttermilk: Essays on Contemporary America* (New York: Simon & Schuster, 1992), 231–244.

23. I refer to social class as an *aspect* of racial identity rather than as its own separate category because of how race shapes the expression of social class.

24. Privileges of education and economic status are not unique to African Americans, of course. However, this group's history of oppression and still-complicated presence in this country have caused the notion of privilege to have unique applications as compared to other racial groups. Albert Murray reminds us that African Americans' continued exposure to discriminatory practices has affected our achievement such that the clean class divisions according to income or education level, which are usually applied to white Americans, are impossible for black Americans. See Murray, "The Illusive Black Middle Class," in *The Omni-Americans: Some Alternatives to the Folklore of White Supremacy* (New York: Vintage, 1970), 94–96.

For additional analyses of the particular circumstances of the African American middle class, see Bart Landry's sociological study, *The New Black Middle Class* (Berkeley: University of California Press, 1987); Annie S. Barnes's *The Black Middle Class Family: A Study of Black Subsociety, Neighborhood, and Home in Interaction* (Bristol, Ind.: Wyndham Hall, 1985); and Charles T. Banner-Haley's cultural critique, *The Fruits of Integration: Black Middle Class Ideology and Culture, 1960–1990* (Jackson, Miss.: University Press of Mississippi, 1994).

25. E. Franklin Frazier, *Black Bourgeoisie* (New York: Free Press, 1957), 26.

26. Ibid., 24.

27. Ironically, more than four decades after Frazier's writing, there continues to be the assumption that a true black consciousness is inextricably tied to the cultural and economic status of lower-class blacks.

28. Ellis 237.

29. Parks earned a B.A. at Mount Holyoke College and received her professional training at the prestigious Yale School of Drama.

30. Keith and Pile, 16.

31. Chaudhuri 5.

32. See Darlene Clark Hine et al., eds., *Black Women in United States History: From Colonial Times to the Present* (New York: Carlson, 1990).

33. Mahone describes it as a "purgatory phase," which becomes a "ghetto of multiculturalism" based on a "sharecropocracy model" (Mahone xx).

34. Quoted in Ibid., 359.

35. Ibid., xvi, xvii.

36. Using Said's formulation, Iain Chambers tells us that migrancy is "a form of picking a quarrel with where you come from"; it requires homes, which Said describes as "provisional." I am inclined to think of American theater traditions as provisional homes with which contemporary African American women playwrights are often quarreling through their work and existence as artists. Chambers, *Migrancy, Culture, Identity* (New York: Routledge, 1994), 2.

37. The term *racegender* acknowledges how American ideas about masculinity and femininity have been and continue to be shaped by ideas about race and vice versa.

38. *Last Black Man* is a rich example: the death of the last black man in the whole entire world is framed as a media event through the intermittent interruptions of Voice on Thuh Tee V. His death is significant enough for nine other cultural and historical figures to gather to commemorate it. Even the black man himself has returned from the dead to tell the tale. We learn that the violent death(s) of this fictional last black man echoes the deaths of countless actual black men in world history. His death(s) at once stand(s) in for, and exemplifies, the others. An audience member who does not know the history of black male persecution could still appreciate the ways in which the story moves through time and place, how its language navigates between sound and meaning, how the structure twists and turns in on itself, and how all this functions in an exploration of death and dying. But only by recognizing Parks's allusions to racegender history, as well as her other allusions, can that spectator appreciate the play's full meaning.

39. In *The Politics of Exile*, Washington observes that the American restrictions on African American authorship, which pushed Baldwin to exile himself to Paris, also forced the author "to write America from a distance" (Washington 126).

40. Mahone xvii.

41. Drukman 61–62.

42. Again, Parks is not the only example of a contemporary African American woman playwright whose work displays a connection to nomadic subjectivity. Playwright/performer Anna Deavere Smith's *On the Road* series provides one important instance of nomadic consciousness through its interview-based portraits of various members of a community in conflict. Unlike Parks's work, however, the process of creation and performance—rather than the content of the works—is what ties Smith's pieces to matters of nomadism. Smith's pieces work because of how uncannily she is able to fully embody the different voices of her subjects and how carefully she juxtaposes those different voices in one performance. These effects depend on the illusion—however momentary—of *static, discrete* identities and moments. In fact, the "stories" of *Twilight: Los Angeles, 1992, Fires in the Mirror*, and her other works are based in large part on how the illusion of static identities can lead to conflicts between groups. Parks, on the other hand, assembles characters and stories that revel in the fact that identities and places are highly mobile and integrated. She creates works that inhabit the margins between, thereby demonstrating the sometimes liberatory, sometimes debilitating consequences. Other contemporary African American women playwrights whose works encourage an exploration of their nomadic sensibility include Kia Corthron, Pearl Cleage, Ntozake Shange, and predecessor Adrienne Kennedy.

43. Critic Alisa Solomon argues that Parks shows African Americans "in a perpetual state of middle passage." Solomon, "Signifying on the Signifyin': The Plays of Suzan-Lori Parks," *Theater* 21, no. 3 (Summer–Fall 1990): 79.

44. Suzan-Lori Parks, *The America Play and Other Works* (New York: Theatre Communications Group, 1995), 39.

45. Braidotti 16.

46. For example, *The America Play*, with its Lincoln impersonator and the wife and son who trail behind, suggests blacks' migration to the West in the late 1800s or even the migration of black performers in traveling minstrel shows. bell hooks, "Choosing the Margin as a Space of Radical Openness," in hooks, *Yearnings*, 145–153.

47. See bell hooks, "Choosing the Margin," as a Space of Radical Openness," in hooks, *Yearnings,* 145–153.

48. Is it merely coincidence that Parks's nickname seems to suggest accelerated motion?

49. Parks, *The America Play*, 8–10.

50. Ibid., 109.

51. Ibid., 12. In another essay, Parks references the African concept of time as described by theologist and philosopher John S. Mbiti, in which inhabitants of the past—the dead—can also enter the present (ibid., 5).

52. Solomon argues that, through disjointed narrative and disembodied speech, Parks stages Du Bois's double-consciousness itself rather than staging stories about people struggling with such consciousness (Solomon 74).

53. Glottal stops and wheezes to simulate the sound of strangling or drowning.

54. Parks, *The America Play*, 38.

55. Ibid., 103.

56. Interestingly, this exchange is repeated later in the play (ibid., 123). What was at first a discussion about black female invisibility in a new combination of male and female characters becomes one of male invisibility.

57. Ibid., 26.

58. Ibid., 30.

59. Ibid., 36–37.

60. Quoted in Washington 20.

61. Parks, *The America Play*, 60.

62. Ibid., 111.

63. Ibid., 116.

64. Quoted in Solomon 75. Such double meaning is typical in African American vernacular speech—frequently referred to as signifyin' or signification. Literary critic Henry Louis Gates, Jr., and linguist Claudia Mitchell-Kernan offer classic studies on this subject. See, Henry Louis Gates, Jr., *The Signifying Monkey: A Theory of African-American Literary Criticism* (New York: Oxford University Press, 1988); and Claudia Mitchell–Kernan, "Signifying as a Form of Verbal Art," in *Mother Wit from the Laughing Barrel: Readings in the Interpretation of Afro-American Folklore*, ed. Alan Dundes (Englewood Cliffs, N.J.: Prentice Hall, 1973), 310–328.

65. Gilroy 124.

66. Parks, *The America Play*, 103.

67. Ibid., 39. According to Said, exiles have an "essential sadness" that can never be overcome, and triumphant moments in exile are only doomed attempts to combat the "crippling sorrow of estrangement . . . , undermined by the loss of something left behind for ever" (Said 357).

68. hooks, "Choosing the Margin," 148.

69. Chambers 5.

70. Parks, *The America Play*, 108.

71. bell hooks, "Loving Blackness as Political Resistance," in hooks, *Black Looks: Race and Representation* (Boston, South End, 1992), 19.

12

Attending Walt Whitman High

The Lessons of Pomo Afro Homos' *Dark Fruit*

JAY PLUM

Pomo Afro Homos (Postmodern African American Homosexuals) was a San Francisco–based performance group founded in November 1990 by Brian Freeman, Djola Bernard Branner, and Eric Gupton. The three performers met as part of the support group Black Gay Men United. Among its twenty-some members was the late filmmaker Marlon Riggs, whose 1991 film, *Tongues Untied* (in which Branner appeared and for which Freeman served as executive producer), inspired the trio to form a company. In January 1991, the Pomos debuted *Fierce Love: Stories from Black Gay Life* at Josie's Cabaret and Juice Joint, a performance space located in San Francisco's Castro District that is well-known for producing queer work. That year, the production traveled to Seattle, Chicago, and Los Angeles before the group received an invitation from George C. Wolfe to appear as part of Moving beyond the Margins: A Festival of New Voices at the Joseph Papp Public Theater in New York. *Dark Fruit*, the group's second and only other collaboration, received a workshop production at the Public on 14 December 1991. *Fierce Love* and *Dark Fruit* subsequently toured in repertory throughout the United States and Great Britain over the course of the next four years. Marvin K. White joined the company in 1993 during Gupton's brief sabbatical. The group officially disbanded in 1995 to pursue individual projects.[1]

Although the Pomos' existence as a performance company was short-lived, its contributions to the creation of a black cultural politic no doubt will be long-lasting. The early 1990s witnessed a virtual explosion of cultural activity by gay black artists. This network of politically committed artists working in film, fiction, dance, and theater reexamined the complexities of gay black life and created a sense of community that reinvigorated the more general notion of what political communities can look like. Brian Freeman notes, for example, that *Fierce Love* was a "warm and cuddly show" about the diversity of black gay male lives, whereas *Dark Fruit* is "more about ambivalence and

235

things that are not right within our community and within the larger communities we travel through."[2] Indeed, the seven sketches in *Dark Fruit* ("Aunties in America: Epiphanies 'n Roaches," "Last Rights," "Black and Gay: A Psycho-Sex Study," "Sweet Sadie," "Doin' Alright," "Tasty," and "Chocolate City, U.S.A.") stage a larger conversation about racial and sexual politics in the United States and theater's potential to reimagine how those politics might play themselves out.[3]

Dark Fruit opens with "Aunties in America," an imagined conversation among the black gay characters from three critically acclaimed Broadway productions: Belize from *Angels in America* (1992–1993), Paul from *Six Degrees of Separation* (1990), and Jacob from *La Cage aux Folles* (1983). After describing their respective relationships with Missy Kushner, Missy Guare, and Missy Fierstein, the three figures don kerchiefs to transform themselves into stereotypical mammies. *Dark Fruit* closes with a litany of letters addressed to institutions like the African American church; activist organizations like ACT-UP, Queer Nation, and Gay Men's Health Crisis (GMHC), and cultural figures from Leonard Jeffries and Magic Johnson to Bill and Hillary Clinton. The letters read in "Chocolate City, U.S.A." protest the failure of society at large to acknowledge the presence of black male homosexuality, let alone AIDS as an issue affecting gay black men. At the end of the piece, the Pomos throw the letters into the air as Tina Turner's "We Don't Need Another Hero" plays over the sound system. Together, "Aunties in America" and "Chocolate City, U.S.A." frame the production's larger interest in exploring how representations of gay men generally are marked "white" and how representations of African Americans generally are marked "straight." If gay black men are represented at all, the Pomos suggest, they are usually depicted as stereotypical figures, like mammies.

"Aunties in America" specifically brings a critique of assimilationist politics to the theater, challenging generalizations like literary critic John M. Clum's conclusion in the revised edition of *Acting Gay* that the American theater experienced a "lively renaissance" during the 1990s because of the success of so-called gay plays like *Angels in America*.[4] When *Millennium Approaches* received the 1993 Pulitzer Prize for drama, Tony Kushner heralded the award as a sign that the 1990s marked a "break-through decade" for plays with gay themes: "This is a play about being gay, and I think it's a great thing that the [Pulitzer] jury decided to recognize it in this way."[5] What both Kushner and Clum fail to recognize is that the image of gay culture in *Angels in America* comes at the expense of an Other. Kushner may be correct in claiming that *Millennium Approaches* is a "play about being gay," but the Pomos suggest that it more accurately is a play about being *white* and gay.

In his discussion of *Angels in America*, David Román notes that "of all the major characters, Belize seems to lack an interiority. We mainly see him in relation to the other characters, who are all white, never quite getting a sense of his inner life or outer journey."[6] Belize is a supporting character in *Angels in America*, whose roles as faithful friend, surrogate mother, and nurturing caregiver transform him into what the Pomos might describe as a desexed mammy. Belize, moreover, carries the burden of being the sole representative of racial difference. He sums up his predicament in *Perestroika*: "I am trapped in a world of white people. That's *my* problem."[7] In the published text, the line occurs following a series of recognitions in which Prior identifies Joe as Harper's "gay" husband, and Joe identifies Belize as Roy Cohn's nurse. "We all look alike to you," Belize tells Joe in an attempt to hide behind the mask of racial stereotypes.[8] As staged in George C. Wolfe's production on Broadway, Belize literally hides behind a scarf, which he finally drops to comment on his role in the drama. The act momentarily disrupts the production's flow, but it is quickly smoothed over by the narrative's forward drive.

The Pomos are of the opinion that *Angels in America* fails to examine fully the complexity of difference within its dramatic universe.[9] In his performance as Belize in the Pomos' "Aunties in America," Brian Freeman takes up the mask of racial stereotypes. This time, however, the mask gives the performer license to comment on the whiteness of *Angels in America*. The scene opens with Belize's reenactment of the angel's entrance at the end of *Millennium Approaches*. He then describes the appearance of what, in Kushner's text, represents the divine "Continental Principality of America": "The *last* Miss Ann Angel: white dress, white wings, white halo, white attitude, white everything—looks like a flying igloo. Miss Thing comes crashing through the ceiling."[10] The description points to the whiteness of the angel as well as to the whiteness of *Angels in America* more generally. For example, Paul and Jacob wonder why the angel crashes through the ceiling rather than using the front door. "You know white folks," Belize explains. "Then everywhere you look feathers, plasters, epiphanies, and roaches." Paul asks, "Now who's going to clean that up?"[11] Belize looks at him, not having to answer. After all, they both know white folks.

Through "Aunties in America," the Pomos suggest that whiteness is so pervasive in plays like *Angels in America* that it is rendered invisible as a particularizing quality. If Richard Dyer is correct in claiming that "any instance of white representation is always immediately something more specific,"[12] then Kushner's description of *Angels in America* as a "play about being gay" risks a representation of gay culture in late twentieth-century America in which the Other is reproduced as the Same. Nor is *Angels in America* an isolated example. In her discussion of the W.O.W. Cafe, Kate Davy suggests that the issue of whiteness is endemic to lesbian and gay performance: "Performing sexuality *excessively* as an oppositional strategy . . . depends on racial encoding."[13] Davy argues that lesbian and gay culture reproduces hegemonic structures and values, specifically the values of white middle-class respectability, in part because the constant revaluing of assimilation as the goal of the lesbian and gay cultural movement. As the lesbian and gay movement struggles with the politics of visibility, it must ask what remains invisible in the quest for recognition and respectability.

With "Aunties in America," the Pomos expose the operations of whiteness by talking back to the roles scripted for gay black men by Kushner, Guare, and Fierstein. In effect, to paraphrase Homi K. Bhabha, the act of mimicry becomes an act of menace.[14] In effect, the Pomos respond to the place for gay black men created by Kushner, Guare, and Fierstein. "Missy Kushner has me up there every night reading those kids' asses or wiping their butts," says Belize. "It's all the same to me. In part two I get to wipe Roy Cohn's butt. Find an epiphany in that!"[15] Paul (Djola Branner) similarly finds his fate in *Six Degrees of Separation* lacking as an epiphany, describing himself as "some kind of Hattie McDaniels meets Mandingo biotech fruit." First, he has to feed them, then he has to sleep with them. "Do I look like some anecdote to dine out on to you?"[16] Far worse is Jacob's (Marvin K. White) plight, however. He is trapped in a world of dinner theater productions of *La Cage*, where he is put through a "Butterfly French Maid McQueen" routine eight times a week: "I can live with the eye bugging and noble caretaker nonsense. But, children, it hurts my pride so bad, night after night, to put on heels and have to walk around like the last Steppin' Jungle Bunny Fetchit!" They all agree that "a black drag queen in her first pair of pumps can out sashay/chante Naomi, Cindy, and Claudia."[17] Ultimately, Belize, Paul, and Jacob take solace in their time away from what is sometimes an isolating and lonely existence. "But what we gonna do?" Belize asks. "Quit?"[18] They pause, then laugh in unison.

The resoundingly negative and defiant response to the possibility of quitting reveals a conscious decision on the part of the characters not to retreat but to engage the conditions of their oppression. Like the characters they perform in "Aunties in America," the Pomos confront the images that disempower gay black men and find agency by momentarily seizing control of the discourse. They speak through the figures of Belize, Paul, and Jacob without becoming them or validating the stereotypes their dramatic alter egos represent. The space between these racialized images and their embodied meanings in representation creates a Brechtian distance among spectators that not only forces them to confront their empowerment/disempowerment through such images but also allows them to begin to imagine how difference can transform how we understand identities and communities.

In the gestus of American politics, tensions between difference and sameness historically have manifested themselves in debates about racial integration and segregation and, more recently, in the anti-assimilationist critique of liberation politics found in contemporary queer theory. The political strategies of assimilation and integration are limited to the extent that they are based on a myth of an American common culture that seeks equality through the disavowal of differences. The categories of race, gender, class, and sexuality unarguably are sites of discrimination, but they are also the terms used by disenfranchised groups to mark their presence and to mobilize as communities.

So-called identity politics became an "issue" in the 1990s in large part because of the crisis of agency that black cultural critic Kobena Mercer associates with an:

atomistic and essentialist logic . . . in which differences are dealt with one-at-a-time and which therefore ignores the conflicts and contradictions that arise in relation *within* and *between* the various movements, agents, and actors in contemporary forms of democratic antagonism.[19]

The so-called "Rainbow theory" of multiculturalism feeds a pluralistic impulse in which the categories of identification are predetermined and unchangeable, overlooking the intersection of various factors in the construction of social and political identities as well as the negotiability of any identity claim.

"Aunties in America" takes queer cultural politics to task for the reproduction of hegemonic structures that privilege white men. *Dark Fruit*, however, also challenges an essentialism in black cultural politics found in authenticating claims of masculinity that deny differences within the race.

The virulent masculism and homophobia beneath claims to an "authentic" blackness perpetuate a cycle of internalized racism and sexual alienation among African Americans. In the monologue "Tasty," Marvin K. White explores the effects of internalized racism on the desire of gay black men for one another. White shares the story of his first sexual encounter with another gay black man, an attractive African American executive he met during a temporary assignment at an integrated corporation. Finding themselves working late on a Friday night, the business executive invites White over to his apartment, where one thing leads to another. For White, the sex was the "most powerful experience of [his] life": "I just laid there, my head on his chest, and I thought, my God, how perfect. The act of love. Me and this black man together in this room. The first black man in my life."[20] The elation quickly dissipates, however, when the man's white lover comes home. White gathers his things and leaves, turning down their invitation to stay. On Monday, he receives a phone call from the executive, who apologizes and tells White: "I could never *be* with a black man you know. But every once in a while I need a little taste."[21]

The need for a "little taste" is symptomatic of an internalized racism that denigrates gay black men as sexual objects. Kaja Silverman maintains that, within the mise en scène of desire, identification allows the ego to transform itself into the desired object.[22] If this is the case, then the desire of the African American executive to be with a white lover is an act of disavowal that betrays a desire to be white. Imaginary identifications, however, are also "capable of transforming the ideological import of unconscious desire, or even of pushing the latter in new directions."[23] White, for example, experiences a black man loving another black man as a form of "perfect love." It is this scene, as Marlon Riggs suggests at the end of *Tongues Untied*, that may be "*the* revolutionary act." Black on black love is revolutionary because it defies the claim of whiteness as being *the* object of desire.

Indeed, love between two black men (or two black women) reveals the ways in which race is intimately linked with desire (i.e., race is desire) and challenges an ideology in which racial categories are seen as natural and fixed. At the same time, the expression of desire between two gay black men challenges masculinity's claim to being something more than a social performance. Concerns about a crisis of masculinity actually reveal a deep-seated anxiety, which Bhahba takes as "a 'sign' of danger implicit/on the threshold of identity, *in between* its claims to coherence and its fear of dissolution."[24] When forced to confront the knowledge posed by difference, the rigid codes of masculinity require that difference be denied, disavowed, or (if need be) punished.

Brian Freeman's monologue, "Doin' Alright," is a saturated moment in *Dark Fruit*, which explores the consequences of a virulent black masculinity on gay black men through the lived experience of a black drag queen. Freeman relates his chance encounter at a gay working-class bar in Boston with a childhood friend named Dennis, now a Donna Summer lookalike going by the name Denise. Denise ultimately is killed by the leading cause of death among gay black men. But it is not what you think, he tells the largely white audience during a 1993 performance at New York University. The presumption that Denise died from AIDS complications privileges sexual identification in such a way that it ignores the intersection of sexuality with other factors, like race and class, in the construction of social identities. Denise was killed because she was in the wrong place at the wrong time, and, as Freeman notes: "When you're poor, black, effeminate, and gay, *life is the wrong place at the wrong time*."[25]

Henry Louis Gates, Jr., attributes intraracial violence against gay black men to the sexualized definition of nationalism inherited from the Black Power Movement of the 1960s and 1970s.[26] Within the radical definitions of self and nationhood espoused by the Black Nationalists, masculinity was the unquestioned norm from which any deviation was regarded as a betrayal of the race. Gates notes that Black Nationalism and homophobia are intimately linked in a passage from *Home* in which Amiri Baraka (then LeRoi Jones) states in no uncertain terms: "Most white men are trained to be fags."[27] The sentence casts homosexuality as a "white man's disease" or, more accurately, as a social performance that trains white men how to be white.

Baraka is a key figure in conventional narratives of African American theater history. Larry Neal, for instance, credits Baraka with "radically reordering the internal structure of black theater" with his 1964 play, *Dutchman*.[28] Baraka arguably broke with the conventions of social realism characteristic of earlier African American drama. His was a functional aesthetic "implicitly but very clearly addressed to the radical sector of black sociopolitical consciousness."[29] If *Dutchman* enacts the revolutionary values of Black Power, it does so through a violent, masculinist rhetoric that erases differences within the race. The play displaces stereotypes about the excessive sexuality of black men onto the figure of an oversexed white woman named Lula, who seduces the representative figure of Clay into believing that he can escape a history of social exclusion. Clay, however, cannot escape a history of racial genocide without the violent revolution triggered by the "simple act" of murder.[30] The ritual sacrifice of Clay at the hands of Lula depicts racial conflict in highly sexualized and gendered terms. *Dutchman* clearly distinguishes between an "us" and a "them" in an attempt to remove barriers to social awareness.

While critics applauded *Dutchman* for revealing the violence done to African American men, they were decidedly mixed in their reception of Baraka's *The Toilet* (which opened less than nine months after *Dutchman*'s premiere in 1964). *The Toilet* documents the punishment of a white high school student named Jimmy Karolis, whose love letter to a black male student is intercepted by his friends. The letter is addressed to Foots, the unofficial leader of a group of African American youth. Foots's efforts to convince his friends to cease Karolis's "flushing" lose out to the group's collective need to reinforce its heterosexuality. Indeed, the group is startled to learn that the intercepted letter may have been welcomed by Foots. Karolis reveals an intimacy when he asks the young black man whether his name is Foots or Ray: "Ray, you said your name was. You said Ray. Right here in this filthy toilet. You put your head on me and said Ray."[31] As the group brutally beats him, Karolis insists that "his name is Ray, not Foots. You stupid bastards. I love somebody you don't even know."[32]

Mainstream critics found *The Toilet* disturbing, particularly its profane language and excessive violence. Robert Vorlicky suggests that critics failed to grasp the complexity of the work, pointing only vaguely to race and class as the themes of a play in which "the conflict is less with whiteness than with gender and sexual identity."[33] *The Toilet* arguably stages a crisis of masculinity in which one of the group's own is suspected of not being the "same." That difference needs to purged. The final tableau of the piece is striking, however, and is a curious choice from a playwright who, two years after *The Toilet*'s opening, claimed most white men are trained to be fags. The play ends with Ray returning to comfort the badly beaten Karolis.

Where *Dutchman* and *The Toilet* dramatically illustrate the need to remove barriers to social awareness (even though they risk, at times, the subjugation of other groups), *Dark Fruit* examines the effects of the atomistic and essentialist logic of identity politics on relationships that cross categories of difference. Djola Branner's "Sweet Sadie" tells the story of Branner's troubled relationship with his mother, who emotionally abandoned him as a child and who now suffers from Alzheimer's disease. Branner is seated on a bench for most of the monologue. As he shifts weight and changes poses, the lines between characters blur: Branner's mother becomes his childhood self; his childhood self becomes his adult self; his adult self becomes his mother. Branner's performance realizes a prelapserian moment, when the subject's sense of self is contiguous with his/her environment, staging the "messy space" of identity to mark the failure of the body to secure one's subjectivity. Branner never disappears into his environment, nor does he "become" his mother in the Stanislavskian sense. Their relationship remains in flux. At one point during the piece, Branner steps into the audience to speak in what the stage directions indicate is the voice of the "universal black mother":

You are one selfish and ungrateful man. How could you even think of saying those things about your mama? Have mercy! Blasphemy! That's what it is. She's the one who pushed you from her womb, and you know she did the very best she could. You even changed the name she gave you. What the hell is a "Djola"?[34]

The use of the universal black mother as the interlocutor between Branner and his mother unfortunately risks the reinscription of the trope of the black welfare mother, who becomes the scapegoat for the plight of the black male, as well as the reinscription of a psychological explanation of male homosexuality as compensation for the absence of male role models (read: straight) during childhood. According to these narratives, Sadie's six-year-old son will grow up to be gay because he was fatherless and "abandoned" by his mother during his youth.[35] "I believed for some time that I didn't love her," Branner tells the audience. "This woman who tossed me onto the earth to fend for myself. Who never said, 'I love you.' "[36]

Following his departure from the Pomos, Branner developed the monologue into a full evening. In the expanded version, Branner comments that no one seems able to understand his relationship with his mother, let alone his need to tell his dying mother that he wants to write a performance piece about their lives together. "The pain is only an illusion," he repeats as a mantra throughout the performance. He finally realizes that the pain is only an illusion because beneath the pain, there was love. Both versions of "Sweet Sadie" point to the difficulties of overcoming preconceptions about social positions without falling into stereotypes, as well as to the difficulty of representing something as fundamental as the relationship between a gay black man and his mother outside controlling cultural narratives.

"Sweet Sadie" and *Dark Fruit* more generally suggest that performance can have a role in transforming the ways that identity politics get played out in the United States. Indeed, as Susan Stewart explains, "We will not change the subjective and social terms of representation without a more dynamic aesthetic practice."[37] The controversy surrounding the exclusion of the Pomos from the National Black Theatre Festival (NBTF) in 1991 and 1993 effectively illustrates the power of representation as well as the stakes when certain representations are made to appear. In justifying the exclusion of the Pomos from the NBTF, festival director Larry Hamlin maintained that the Pomos were not invited to participate because the inferior quality of the videotapes submitted by the group made it difficult to evaluate their work. The tapes also were submitted after the application deadline. Freeman insists, however, that the Pomos were "banned" from the NBTF because the homosexual content of their work made them too controversial to be included in Hamlin's "Parade of Stars." Most of the celebrities who attend the festival are invited not to perform but to take part in nightly receptions, which in 1993 included a tribute to Sidney Poitier.[38] It seems that Hamlin has substituted an assimilationist politic for the separatism once espoused by Black Nationalists. But the erasure of sexual difference is an expensive price to pay in representing "community," enacting what Jewelle Gomez characterizes as an internalized oppression and political smugness that leaves everyone in a vulnerable position.[39]

In a 1993 op-ed piece in the *New York Times*, Donald Suggs and Mandy Carter write about an alliance formed between the religious right and conservative churches in Cincinnati, which wanted to prevent social reforms that would secure the rights of lesbians and gay men. Through *Gay Rights, Special Rights*, a videotape produced by conservative groups, which juxtaposes visual images from the black and gay liberation movements, the right has propagated notions that gay rights and black rights inherently conflict. More significantly, the videotape suggests that the call for gay rights is in effect a demand for "preferential treatment" based on the sexual orientation of an elite minority comprised largely of white men.[40]

Politics makes strange bedfellows. Preferential treatment is a charge frequently evoked to denounce affirmative action programs. The failure of gay activists and black religious leaders to look beyond their immediate concerns validates claims that marginalized interest groups are self-serving and, more disturbingly, it prevents them from imagining a revitalized sense of community based on shared struggles. Cathy Cohen concludes that "the process of movement-building [should] be rooted not in our shared history or identity, but in our shared marginal relationship to dominant power which normalizes, legitimizes, and privileges."[41] It is in this way that politics has the potential to make *queer* bedfellows.

Brian Freeman imagines the possibility of a coalitional politic that crosses identity positions in his journey to "Chocolate City, U.S.A." Freeman and his lover travel to the National March on Washington for Lesbian and Gay Rights: For Love and For Life We Are Not Going Back. Quickly losing his companion among the 650,000 marchers, Freeman stands on the sidelines watching various banners pass by. He is moved by the demonstration of solidarity among the groups and particularly by Whoopi Goldberg's compassion and political commitment to issues that touch all our lives. "Today Whoopi Goldberg is beautiful because she has pushed Jimmy Maness, a person with AIDS, the entire length of this March in a wheelchair."[42] Later that day, she asks the crowd at the rally to join her in asking: "How long is it going to take before people get smart, huh?"[43] Goldberg's words and actions resonate because they are based on a shared experience of marginalization that does not reinscribe differences among groups but directs its critique at the institutions of power that inscribe those differences.

Nowhere is this critique more powerfully enacted in *Dark Fruit* than in Freeman's "Black and Gay: A Psycho-Sex Study." According to the program notes from a 1993 performance at NYU, the piece is "adapted 99 percent from an actual 60s pulp/porn pseudoscience novel, *Black and Gay: A Psycho-Sex Study* by Victor Dodson." Dodson serves as the narrator of the piece, presenting a "scientific" lecture (complete with charts and slides of black male nudes from gay pornography) about the ability of gay black men to "adjust normally" to white gay culture:

Our research indicates that the majority of Negro homosexual males seem to prefer sexual relations with Caucasians rather than with members of their own race. Furthermore, many white homosexuals very often prefer their sexual partners to be Negroid.[44]

To support his claim, Dodson presents the dramatized case study of Cliff, a model black student from a single-parent household in Shantytown, who has been bused to a predominantly white high school on the other side of the tracks. Cliff becomes the desired object of a white jock/integrationist named Paul, who wants nothing more than to call Cliff "friend": "How can we hope to change the world, Cliff, if we don't start right here at Walt Whitman High?"[45] At first reluctant, Cliff eventually consents to meet Paul for a "man to man" talk and stroll by the river. The young men quickly give in to their passions, dropping their pants and rubbing their Fruit of the Looms against each other. Here is "a fine example of the seeds of racial tolerance being planted," Dodson concludes.[46]

Walt Whitman is a queer place, as the allusion to the nineteenth-century American poet suggests. The name, however, also has another and equally significant meaning in terms of the representational history of racial politics in the United States. Walt Whitman High School was the setting for the award-winning television series "Room 222." Aired on ABC from 1969 to 1974, the television drama looked at the experiences of students, faculty, and staff at an integrated high school in Los Angeles through the eyes of an African American teacher, whose history class meets in Room 222. Phillip Brian Harper suggests that African American viewers regarded the series as not so much about social integration as about social differentiation among various socioeconomic groups. Aware of the difficulties of representing a single African American community, "Room 222" presented a multiplicity of black subjectivities.[47]

Like "Room 222," "Black and Gay" resists integration as a resolution of racial differences, using theater to frame the contradictions and limitations of its liberal foundation. Walt Whitman is invoked in the performance piece to challenge the claim that integration allows gay men of color to "adjust normally" to a culture defined and controlled by white gay men. Cliff's relationship with Paul is far from equal. When the young men are discovered by Miss Emory, the high school's sex education teacher, Cliff is the one blamed for corrupting the innocent white man. "You can take the boy out of Shantytown, but you can't take the Shantytown out of the boy," says Miss Emory.[48] Paul goes home holding his head in shame, but the consequences for Cliff are more severe. He loses Miss Emory's recommendation for the state's Booker T. Washington Scholarship. That night, Cliff runs away from home to lose himself in the "homosexual jungle they call New York City."[49]

"Black and Gay" effectively demonstrates how social identities and relationships are constructed by the discourses of institutions like education and science. "Viewed as a normative and social force," Steven Seidman writes, for example, "science has the effect of drawing moral boundaries, producing social hierarchies, and creating identities."[50] Just as classic stage realism requires a stable referent to assure the spectator of the "truth" of its representation, science requires a control to produce its sense of "truth" and to obscure the assumptions it makes. "Black and Gay" quotes the institutional discourses of science and education (in the Brechtian sense of the term) to queer the process of normalization that they attempt to ensure. The pseudoscientific language of Dodson's supposedly objective study of black homosexuality is demystified with the camp narrative and the pornographic slides of black male nudes. At one point during the NYU performance, Freeman stepped out of his role as Dodson to respond to the audience's laughter. He suggested that our reactions revealed a familiarity with these photographic images. The moment was a transformative experience in which, as Elizabeth Wright argues in her discussion of the Brechtian comic:

> The spectator's own subjectivity is brought into question along with the representations on the stage; the desires of the body are . . . reached so that it awakens to an understanding of its own socialization and the discovery of its political repression.[51]

The spectatorial gaze becomes an object of the Pomos' performance, and, in much the same way that Robert Mapplethorpe's photographs of black male nudes are as much about the agency of the photographer as they are about the fetishized subjects in the photographs, the spectator is made aware of his/her "seeing" and "being seen." The identity of the spectator is rendered multiple and fractured as my psyche becomes the object of the spectator's eye. And, as the gaze becomes the object of the performance, "I" disappear.

Identification can be an act that appropriates the Other as the same or in which the subject imagines becoming the object of his desire. The subject, however, can also be transformed by an encounter with an Other, depending on the position that he/she takes within that mise-en-scène. Indeed, an identification not *as* but *with* another can reimagine social as well as political relationships. The "I" becomes a "we" in which difference is not assimilated by a common culture but transformed into a radical politic informed for the present as well as the future. In the end, how can I—how can we—hope to change the world if we do not start right here at Walt Whitman High?

NOTES

1. In 1996, Branner toured the United States with *Sweet Sadie*, an expanded version of a monologue originally presented as part of *Dark Fruit*. Between 1997 and 2000 Freeman performed in *Civil Sex* (1997–2000), a performance piece he created through original research about civil rights leader Baynard Rustin.

2. Brian Freeman, quoted in Stephen Holden, "In the Margins of Two Minorities: A Double Fringe," *New York Times* (23 July 1993): C3.

3. My discussion of *Dark Fruit* is based on the performance I attended at New York University's Loeb Student Center, 21 Sept. 1993.

4. John M. Clum, *Acting Gay: Male Homosexuality in Modern Drama*, rev. ed. (New York: Columbia University Press, 1994), 281.

5. Tony Kushner, quoted in Greg Evans, "*Angels* Proves a Box Office Blessing," *Variety* (19 Apr. 1993): 58.

6. David Román, *Acts of Intervention: Performance, Gay Culture, and AIDS* (Bloomington: Indiana University Press, 1998), 213.

7. Tony Kushner, *Angels in America: A Gay Fantasia on National Themes*, part 2: *Perestroika* (New York: Theatre Communications Group, 1993), 93. Emphasis in original.

8. Ibid., 92.

9. Framji Minwalla complicates the function of Belize as the only person of color in Kushner's dramatic universe in "When Girls Collide: Considering Race in *Angels in America*," in *Approaching the Millennium: Essays on Angels in America*, ed. Deborah R. Geis and Steven F. Kruger (Ann Arbor: University of Michigan Press, 1997), 103–117. Minwalla suggests that Belize serves not only as a mouthpiece for Kushner but as his ethical touchstone: "By locating a black man at the ethical center of his fictive universe, and then playing his other characters off him, Kushner makes identity, especially racial and gendered identity, one of the central facets of his drama. Belize occupies that space against which we gauge the ideology, morality, actions— perhaps even the very humanity—of Kushner's other inventions" (104). Minwalla's reading significantly differs from the critique made by Freeman in "Aunties in America." Together, I believe, the two positions illustrate the extent to which *Angels in America* is a culturally rich text that invites discussions of numerous identity positions.

10. Pomo Afro Homos, *Dark Fruit*, in *Staging Gay Lives: An Anthology of Contemporary Gay Theater*, ed. John M. Clum (Boulder, Colo.: Westview, 1996), 323. Emphasis in original. Unless indicated otherwise, all quotations are from the published text.

11. Ibid., 324.

12. Richard Dyer, "White," *Screen 29* (Autumn 1988): 47.

13. Kate Davy, "Outing Whiteness: A Feminist Lesbian Project," *Theatre Journal* 47 (May 1995): 195. Emphasis in original.

14. Tony Kushner, *Angels in America: A Gay Fantasia on National Themes*, part 1: *Millennium Approaches* (New York: Theatre Communications Group, 1993), 118; Homi K. Bhabha, "The Other Question: Difference, Discrimination and the Discourse of Colonialism," in *Literature, Politics, and Theory: Papers from the Essex Conference, 1976–1984*, ed. Francis Barker et al. (New York: Methuen, 1986), 149.

15. Pomo Afro Homos 324.

16. Ibid.

17. Ibid.

18. Ibid., 325.

19. Kobena Mercer, *Welcome to the Jungle: New Positions in Black Cultural Politics* (New York: Routledge, 1994), 289. Emphasis in original.

20. Pomo Afro Homos 338.

21. Ibid. Emphasis in original.

22. Kaja Silverman, *Male Subjectivity at the Margins* (New York: Routledge, 1992), 337.

23. Ibid.

24. Homi K. Bhabha, "Are You a Mouse or a Man?" in *Constructing Masculinity*,

ed. Maurice Berger, Brian Wallis, and Simon Watson (New York: Routledge, 1995), 60. Emphasis in original.

25. Pomo Afro Homos 337. Emphasis added. Another telling moment occurred during the discussion following the performance at NYU when Freeman had to reassure the audience that the reason for Gupton's brief hiatus was not that he was "sick" (as if the only reason a gay man would take a break from performing was that he was HIV-positive).

26. Henry Louis Gates, Jr., "The Black Man's Burden," in *Black Popular Culture: A Project*, ed. Gina Dent (Seattle, Wash.: Bay Press, 1992), 79.

27. LeRoi Jones, "American Sexual Reference: Black Male," in Jones, *Home: Social Essays* (New York: William Morrow, 1966), 216.

28. Larry Neal, "Into Nationalism, Out of Parochialism," in *The Theatre of Black Americans: A Collection of Critical Essays*, ed. Errol Hill (New York: Applause, 1987), 296.

29. Ibid.

30. LeRoi Jones, *Dutchman*, in *"Dutchman" and "The Slave": Two Plays* (New York: Morrow Quill, 1964), 35.

31. LeRoi Jones, *The Toilet*, in *"The Baptism" and "The Toilet"* (New York: Grove, 1966), 60.

32. Ibid.

33. Robert Vorlicky, *Act Like a Man: Challenging Masculinity in American Drama* (Ann Arbor: University of Michigan Press, 1995), 114.

34. Pomo Afro Homos 335.

35. For more on the black matriarch, welfare queen, and other controlling images of black womanhood, see Patricia Hill Collins, *Black Feminist Thought: Knowledge, Consciousness, and the Politics of Empowerment* (Boston: Unwin Hyman, 1990); for an insightful critique of psychological discourses of male homosexuality, see Eve Kosofsky Sedgwick, "How to Bring Your Kids Up Gay: The War on Effeminate Boys," in *Tendencies* (Durham, N.C.: Duke University Press, 1993), 154–64.

36. Pomo Afro Homos 335.

37. Susan Stewart, "The State of Cultural Theory and the Future of Literary Form," *Profession* 93 (1993): 3.

38. For an excellent analysis of the tensions between Freeman and Hamlin, see C. Carr, "Show Me the Way To Go Home," *Village Voice* 17 Aug. 1993): 37.

39. Jewelle Gomez and Barbara Smith, "Talking about It: Homophobia in the Black Community," *Feminist Review* 34 (Spring 1990): 47–48.

40. Donald Suggs and Mandy Carter, "Cincinnati's Odd Couple," *New York Times* (13 Dec. 1993): A17.

41. Cathy Cohen, "Punks, Bulldaggers, and Welfare Queens: The Radical Potential of Queer Politics?" *GLQ: A Journal of Lesbian and Gay Studies* 3, no. 4 (1997): 458.

42. Pomo Afro Homos 340.

43. Ibid.

44. Ibid., 325.

45. Ibid., 329.

46. Ibid., 327.

47. Phillip Brian Harper, *Are We Not Men?: Masculine Anxiety and the Problem of African-American Identity* (New York: Oxford University Press, 1996), 165–66.

48. Pomo Afro Homos 332.

49. Ibid.

50. Steven Seidman, "Identity and Politics in 'Postmodern' Gay Culture: Some Historical and Conceptual Notes," in *Fear of a Queer Planet: Queer Politics and Social Theory*, ed. Michael Warner (Minneapolis: University of Minnesota Press, 1993), 109.

51. Elizabeth Wright, *Postmodern Brecht: A Re-Presentation* (London and New York: Methuen, 1989), 62.

Part IV

African American Performativity and
the Performance of Race

13

Acting Out Miscegenation

DIANA R. PAULIN

Because of the ways that black-white, or interracial, intimate affairs have symbolized both explicit acts of racial transgression and implicit threats to essentialized racial categories in the United States, their representation creates space for complex readings of racial identities. The ambivalent and liminal space in which interracial desire is most frequently represented does not merely complicate race, it functions as a place for more productive and multivalent articulations of black and white subjectivities.

Bartley Campbell's 1882 play, *The White Slave*, demonstrates how representations of (black-white) interracial liaisons in late nineteenth- and early twentieth-century U.S. drama and fiction invoke anxieties about the impact of cross-racial contact, while they simultaneously rehearse the multiple possibilities of these transgressive relationships. In keeping with these ideas, in this chapter, I explore how Campbell's play complicates black and white by "playing out" the possibility of erotic cross-racial relations. At the same time, I consider how the logic of the play's narrative, through a multitude of intricate plot twists and unexpected revelations, undermines the legitimacy of interracial liaisons, thereby helping to minimize their disruptive potential.

By focusing on the explosive and contested space of representation in *The White Slave*, my reading foregrounds historical moments when blackness and whiteness are destabilized. Rather than examining blackness or whiteness as discrete, self-contained categories, I consider how Campbell's historical representation of cross-racial affairs emphasizes the mutual formation of those polarized racial identities. In doing so, my reading complicates and reevaluates current antiessentialist debates about the construction of racial identities; I locate moments in Campbell's historical representation that demonstrate how the interstices created by the intersection of black and white subjectivities not only produce destabilizing racial formulations but also enable us to rethink how race is enunciated in multiple and particular locations.

The White Slave engages in multiple racial performances and depicts race in performative terms. That is, the play presents an interracial liaison that is part of a broader performance—a performance of multiply articulated racial subjectivities, of miscegenation, of hierarchical power relations—which simultaneously challenges and reinforces what it attempts to represent.[1] The contradictions produced by these cross-purposes demonstrate the ambivalence that usually characterizes depictions of interracial encounters. For, while most nineteenth- and early twentieth-century fictional portrayals of cross-racial relationships indicate that they will fail, they also leave many of the conflicting issues and possibilities generated by the liaison unresolved and unexplored. This ambiguity not only complicates these representations of intimate black-white unions, it also provides a starting point for rearticulating the complexity of racial identities that are, more often than not, defined in opposition to each other.

Building on Judith Butler's performative theories, I utilize the notion of performativity to describe the process of historical sedimentation, which naturalizes and reinforces static definitions of black and white subjectivities in the United States.[2] When representations of interracial contact articulate desire that challenges established racial boundaries, they also directly challenge strict definitions of black and white. Although temporary, the potential explosion of the rigid categories of black and white threatens the discursive and social schemata that rigidify these identities. Thus, by identifying particular enactments of interracial desire as performative, this reading interrupts the process of enunciation, which attempts to reinscribe black and white subjectivities into the dominant and regulatory "norms" of racial identification.[3]

This examination links the disruptive impact of interracial representations on racial subjectivity with the contested spaces actualized by performance.[4] Like the productive space of performance, representations of interracial unions allow for a playing out of the complexities of real life in a contained sphere. Similar to staged productions, which invite analyses of the subjects they portray because of the ways in which they frame norms that usually remain unmarked, my reading of this representation of black-white interracial desire reevaluates static definitions of black and white identities by foregrounding the conventions that constitute them.

Although dramatic depictions of lived experience and racial (black-white) identities cannot be collapsed into a catchall category called the performative, particular representations of racial subjectivity can, and often do, demonstrate the different ways in which race is performed. The performative lens helps to focus readings of racial subjectivity on the intersection of race's staged portrayals and lived embodiments.[5] The space in between the constructedness and materiality of racial subjectivity functions as a site in which the symbolic and productive power of performance can be identified and interpreted. The interpretive grid of performance provides a useful strategy for evaluating the significant ways that cultures and societies not only establish "who and what they are" (following Joseph Roach) but also reinvent themselves now and in the future.[6] This articulation of performance reinforces my claim that performed representations of interracial unions allow for a rehearsal of relations that are prohibited in society. Taboo subjects and behavior, such as interracial alliances, are often perceived as less threatening when they are performed or imagined in a staged arena because they can be dismissed as fictional and, therefore, less real. Still, each staged enactment of these historically embedded black-white unions provides space for different possibilities, or what Richard Schechner refers to as "virtual alternatives," which extend beyond the limits of the narratives in which they are produced.[7]

Contextualizing Miscegenation

A brief historical overview of responses to miscegenation in the United States provides a context that promotes layered readings of dramatic representations of cross-racial liaisons. The word *miscegenation*—a derogatory term for cross-racial sexual relations—was popularized in the United States by proslavery journalists David Croly and George Wakeman in 1864. Their inflammatory pamphlet, *Miscegenation: The Theory of the Blending of the Races, Applied to the American White Man and Negro*, purposefully played on the fears of many white Americans by disingenuously advocating interracial marriage and by suggesting that mixed races were superior to "pure" ones.[8] Although cross-racial liaisons were not new, and sexual relations between white planters and their black slaves were tenuously accepted by the dominant society as one of the unfortunate evils of slavery, this sensational document stirred up many anxieties about the negative effects of black and white sexual contact.[9]

Immediately following Emancipation in the United States (1863) and continuing well into the twentieth century, contradictory and competing discourses about miscegenation and "the Negro problem" circulated in almost every realm of society, including politics, the media, academia, popular culture, and science. White supremacists suggested that the innate inferiority of blacks not only caused the failure of Reconstruction but also reinforced the need for segregation and white domination.[10] These racist theories were supported and "documented" in a variety of texts, including John H. Van Evrie's 1864 propagandistic pamphlet, *Subgenation: The Theory of the Normal Relation of the Races; An Answer to "Miscegenation,"* and Alfred P. Schultz's 1908 reactionary study, *Race or Mongrel*, which argued that "the fall of the nations is due to intermarriage with alien stock."[11] Advocates of these racially prejudiced ideologies also supported the notion that sustained contact between whites and blacks would contaminate white society and that whites' only hope for survival was the eventual "extinction"—or, if not extinction, segregation—of the "weaker," in the social Darwinian sense, black population.[12] Many sympathetic whites supported paternalistic policies toward blacks but were quick to disassociate themselves from charges that they were promoting social equality and intimate relations between blacks and whites.[13] Significant portions of the black community also supported anti-miscegenation rhetoric and were proponents of conservative ideologies that promoted racial separation.[14] Although these theories supported racial segregation explicitly and implicitly, they could not erase the fact that a significant percentage of the population lived in bodies that contained "evidence" of miscegenation. Both literally and symbolically, these mixed-race bodies—usually depicted as "tragic" mulattoes, quadroons, or octoroons—represented interracial sexual unions. Despite increased numbers of lynchings and the heightened animosity of whites toward any person who contained even "one drop"[15] of black blood, black-white sexual relations continued to disrupt the dominant discourse, which argued for racial purity and white supremacy.[16]

Re-Viewing *The White Slave*

Bartley Campbell's *The White Slave*[17] is representative of the complex and sometimes contradictory articulations of the tense racial, gender, class, and sexual politics of the late nineteenth-century United States.[18] My investigation identifies moments in the play in which race and interracial unions emerge as both performative and embodied representations of the many anxieties that black-white interracial "transgressions" generate(d).

The following description of *The White Slave* from the *St. Louis Republican* summarizes the play's elaborate plot and provides some insight as to how it was received and understood when it opened in 1882:

> An interesting girl in a Southern home grows up in the belief that she is an octoroon. Under the conditions of this supposed taint of blood she falls as a slave into the hands of a man who would betray her. She has a lover who aids her escape, and the business of the play is chiefly concerned with her perils undergone to avoid degraded bondage and pollution, and incidents which uncover facts that finally prove her to be a white woman.[19]

This melodramatic piece, set on Big Bend Plantation, somewhere in Kentucky, opens with plantation owner Judge Hardin lying on his deathbed saying his final good-byes to his family, friends, and slaves. We quickly discover that his unmarried daughter, Grace, died in Italy just after giving birth to her daughter, Lisa. We also learn that Lisa's biological father, Marquis De Bernaugre, fled to France from Italy, abandoning both mother and daughter. Because Judge Hardin does not want to sully his family name by acknowledging that his daughter had a child out of wedlock (and with a "foreigner," no less), he and his quadroon slave, Nance, bring Lisa back to Big Bend Plantation and pass her off as Nance's octoroon daughter.[20] Despite Nance's pleas for the judge to tell Lisa that she is a "free born white woman" (*WS* 209), he remains silent and threatens to haunt her from the grave if she does not keep his secret.

After the judge's death, his adopted son, Clay Britton, almost loses the plantation because of his gambling debts. In order to save the land, he sells all of the slaves to his disreputable "friend," Bill Lacy. It turns out that Lacy engineered a scheme wherein he encouraged Clay to risk all of his money so that Clay would have to sell most of his grandfather's property in order to avoid bankruptcy. Lacy's underlying motive for befriending and manipulating Clay is his desire to purchase the prized octoroon, Lisa, and force her to become his concubine on his own plantation in Mississippi. Clay, who loves Lisa regardless of her slave status, tries to stop Lacy from buying her and is arrested for interfering with the allegedly legal transaction. Then, Clay breaks out of jail, locates Lisa, and helps her escape from Lacy's plantation. At the climax of the play, Lacy discovers Lisa and Clay fleeing and tries to recapture her just as the steamer on which they are escaping mysteriously catches fire. Miraculously, Clay and Lisa avoid harm by floating to safety on a detached piece of the burning ship. In the final scene, a lawyer hired by the deceased judge's sister-in-law (Mrs. Lee) reveals the truth about Lisa's identity—that she is really white—so that she and Clay can get married, repossess their slaves, and return to Big Bend Plantation.

In addition to this intricate plot full of unlikely coincidences, this piece relies on several of the conventional tragic octoroon tropes, which were well-established by 1882. The most common characteristics of the tragic octoroon/ mulatto narratives were that s/he was handsome and admired by many but alienated from both white and black communities because of her/his tragic difference. Usually, her/his young life ended in an untimely death caused by suicide, murder, or some incurable disease.[21] Besides the obvious similarity to Dion Boucicault's 1859 piece, *The Octoroon; or, Life in Louisiana,* Campbell's play invokes and then transforms many of the conventions associated with this type of "racial melodrama."[22] Several nineteenth-century reviewers made note of their familiarity with the narrative in their responses to the play, asserting that this story was hardly original and that Campbell had obviously "kidnapped" the idea from other depictions of similar subjects.[23] Lisa's role as the tragic octoroon doomed to death not only recalls earlier incarnations of this tradition, it also pre-dates twentieth-century redeployments of a similar figure in works by black writers, such as Langston Hughes's play *Mulatto: A Tragedy of the Deep South*, (1928/1935), Nella Larsen's novel *Passing* (1929), Adrienne Kennedy's play *Funnyhouse of a Negro* (1964), Rita Dove's verse play *The Darker Faces of the Earth: A Verse Play in Fourteen Scenes* (1994), and Dorothy West's novel *The Wedding* (1995).[24]

Like these later writers, Campbell reshapes tragic octoroon/mulatto conventions so that they address the specificities of his contemporary context. His postbellum articulation of miscegenation and his reformulation of its common narrative tropes produce a text that engages contemporary social, political, juridical, and even scientific discourses, which informed readings of his play. Rather than presenting a clearly identifiable stance on current debates, such as racial purity and the future of the United States after "failed" Reconstruction, Campbell's play entices its audiences with references to these explosive issues and reproduces them within the imaginative and somewhat distanced space of the stage. A significant number of reviews from 1882 reiterate this point by claiming that Campbell's main purpose was to appeal to as many people as possible without alienating anyone. For example, an unfavorable review stated that Campbell "is careful to produce nothing that will be caviare to the meanest capacity" and that he

> recognizes the fact that in a high-pressure age like this men who have been at business all day do not want to be bothered with too much thought when they visit the theatre at night. Mr. Campbell, consequently, abstains from giving them anything that might by any chance be provocative of thought, or make any intellectual demand upon an audience.[25]

Another judicious review made the same observation but couched its response in terms that emphasized the play's apparent neutrality, claiming that "there is not the least sectional bias or coloring about it. It is not warped in the interest of section or party."[26] Both reactions suggest that Campbell avoided presenting material in a confrontational or offensive manner in order to please his audiences. They also indicate that he was willing to tone down and revise any potentially controversial issues in order to avoid conflict.

Role Reversal: Whitewashing Slavery

The most evident transformation that Campbell presents in *The White Slave* is his use of a white character to play the role of the vulnerable octoroon. Not only does this revision of the traditional tragic octoroon figure invert that convention, it also indicates that both whiteness and blackness are positions that can be temporarily inhabited and performed in certain situations. Rather than introduce the miscegenated or octoroon body of typical narratives about interracial transgressions, Campbell invokes "pure" white womanhood as the underlying "appeal" that generates Clay Britton's and Bill Lacy's attraction to Lisa; she looks like a white woman and acts like an educated, elite, white lady. Other characteristics also point to her familiarity with the trappings of the landed class. Her speech is highly standardized if not excessively formal. She uses flowery alliterative language throughout the play, which distinguishes her from others, as in her elaborate description of the nights she, Clay, and Nance were marooned on a deserted island after barely escaping from the burning ship. Music accompanies Lisa's lyrical lamentations: "How long and lonesome the night has been—the second we have spent on this desolate island with only a dreary waste of rushing waters in our ears," she bemoans (*WS* 238). Her speech demonstrates a refinement expected only from those of the upper echelons of society. Unlike the other black characters and the nonaristocratic white characters in the play, Lisa does not speak in dialect, which would have been an easily recognizable marker of race and class distinctions.[27]

It is only through other characters' words and gestures, as well as the racial hierarchy that the play establishes, that Lisa's "nonwhite" status is fully recognizable. Both black and white characters respond to her as if she were white (by subordinating themselves to her); this behavior indicates that her almost-white appearance and graceful demeanor diminish any characteristics that other characters or white audience members could associate with her slave status and supposed black ancestry. Black members of Big Bend Plantation reinforce Lisa's ambiguous role by treating her as though she were extraordinary; at the same time, however, they also resist the urge to label her white, at least until it is authorized by her racial unveiling in the final scene of the play.

For upper-class whites, Lisa's elite decorum is unsettling. Mrs. Lee, a white woman of an older generation and a relative of the late judge, articulates this uneasiness when she expresses her disapproval of the late judge's decision to give Lisa "the training of a lady," which "created a great deal of scandal" (*WS* 204). Not only is Mrs. Lee insulted because Lisa has mastered the etiquette of aristocratic white women successfully, but she is also intimidated by Lisa's ability to transgress the boundaries of her lower status. Revealing her own insecurity, Mrs. Lee consistently reminds Lisa that her "drop of African blood" marks her as inferior: "You forget who you are," she admonishes Lisa, "Your white skin and dainty rearing cannot obliterate the fact that you belong to a race of slaves" (*WS* 206). Mrs. Lee's juxtaposition of the terms *dainty* and *slave* both invokes numerous behavioral standards established for elite white women (refinement, chastity, submission to patriarchs) and places them at odds with the roles assigned to slaves (licentious, hard laboring, primitive). Her use of the term *slave* reminds Lisa that her classification as chattel and as black cancels out those intimations that she may belong to the category of (white) lady. Black women, whether or not they performed gentility successfully or even looked white, were still considered part of an inferior class in the 1880s.[28] However, the fact that Mrs. Lee must reiterate Lisa's subordinate role indicates that Lisa's liminal position poses a threat that must be consistently identified and policed in order to maintain the racist hierarchy of the old South.

In contrast, Letty, Mrs. Lee's daughter, suggests that the racist ideas expressed by her mother are inappropriate, at least in those explicit terms, when she scolds her mother for making this type of derogatory remark and consoles Lisa: "She will be sorry some day. Please forget it" (*WS* 207). Here, Letty acknowledges that her mother's position is distasteful; at the same time, she relegates any possible reformation of those bigoted convictions to the distant future of "some day." This difference in thinking between two white women who share the same familial and class status represents a subtle shift in racial rhetoric. Without articulating any overt argument about how to treat blacks, their mild disagreement suggests that a compassionate and civil attitude might be more effective than the reactionary approach of the past. This "kinder, gentler" approach masks the inherent racism and patriarchal structure that continues to keep blacks, among others, in their place without recalling the unpleasant memories of the Civil War and Reconstruction, which both southerners and northerners seemed to want to either deny or forget.[29] Letty's supposedly sympathetic attitude allows her to appease Lisa while simultaneously maintaining her superior position and upholding the status quo.

By avoiding conflict, Letty is also free to focus on solidifying her own position in the social and patriarchal structure. In fact, both Letty and her lover, Jack, seem to represent a different option for white southerners. Neither one of them has inherited property, forcing both of them to forge a new path as "liberated" members of the "new" South. Despite the fact that Letty is aristocratic and Jack is working class, they plan to get married and fend for themselves rather than rely on any inheritance from the old plantation legacy. Both feel that they can overcome their class differences and that Jack should be treated as Letty's social equal. Jack reiterates this point by confronting Mrs. Lee, Letty's mother. In his defense, he declares: "You object to my suit because I am poor; but poverty is not perpetual, and with her love to fight for, I am certain to make my way" (*WS* 218). This claim to self-sufficiency suggests that, now that slavery is a relic, all capable men will be able to reap the benefits of hard work, and the democratic vision can be recuperated.[30] This philosophy was particularly significant because many racists argued that blacks failed to prosper not because of the racist oppressive system but because of their innate inferiority. This unapologetic assertion of the supremacy of white male potential and free-market individualism also distinguishes "honorable" white men from "guilty," predatory, degenerate white male figures, represented by fictional characters like Simon Legree from Harriet Beecher Stowe's *Uncle Tom's Cabin*, whose status and power relied on the racial hierarchy established by the southern plantation economy. It also elevates the former group of white men by suggesting that all blame for the unspeakable practices of slavery, such as the forced sexual liaisons with black women, which produced a large percentage of mixed-raced slaves, should be attributed to this morally deficient group of white men.[31] The placement of all accountability on lower-class white men also evades the issue of white female-black male liaisons, which also threatened the racial and patriarchal order and complicated property inheritance issues.[32] This differentiation between "good" and "bad" white men redeems the virtues of whiteness, patriarchy, and landed-class aspirations, while simultaneously rejecting the corruption associated with the history of slaveholding.

Cross-Racial Performance

Although Campbell's focus on the restoration of white virtue seems to displace anxiety about the history of black-white relations in the South, Lisa's multivalent role continues to invoke these issues. Her indeterminate racial status refuses easy categorization. On the one hand, Lisa could be characterized as a surrogate for black womanhood because she takes on the position of property usually assigned to black slaves. On the other hand, she demonstrates a type of "delicacy," which was equated with upper-class white womanhood in the nineteenth century by such ideological directives as the "Cult of True Womanhood."[33] Lisa moves in between these polarized definitions of womanhood. She also invokes nineteenth-century protofeminist discourse, which frequently conflated the position of white women with the position of slaves.[34] Contemporary white women may have identified with a character like Lisa more readily because she looks and acts like a free-born white aristocratic woman but is treated more like a piece of property than a person. She literally embodies the slave status that white women often used metaphorically to describe their limited rights and second-class citizenship. Still, Lisa's mobility and her reenactment of these historical representations of feminized whiteness and blackness also challenge these definitions in various ways.

Lisa embodies the role of the tragic octoroon temporarily, only to emerge as something else at the end of the play when her "authentic" whiteness is unveiled. However, far from establishing the certainty of her white racial ancestry, her misidentification as an octoroon places both her blackness and her whiteness into the realm of the performative. If her owners and peers impose the category of octoroon on her without any "evidence" of black ancestry, it seems logical that she can also take on the position of a white woman just as easily even if she does possess "one drop" of black blood; there is no "proof" that she is *really* white either. In both cases, she performs the role that is assigned to her rather than producing some authenticating documentation of her genetic makeup. Neither category—black or white—fully contains or confirms Lisa's race; as a result, her performativity, rather than her genetic makeup, constitutes her racial identity.

Whether Lisa is placed into the position of slavery by her grandfather because, for him, blackness masks or incorporates her illegitimacy or whether she is reclassified as white because of her mother's white status, her ability to pass in both situations invites a subtle critique of biologically based racial definitions. However, the fact that she is bought and sold also provides a powerful reminder of the material impact of the position that she has been assigned. Lisa's successful performance as octoroon is buttressed by Judge Hardin's power to place Lisa into that category by his will, literally and figuratively, rather than by any genetically determined proof. His status as patriarch and landowner enables him to govern all the members of his private domain. Additionally, since Judge Hardin is dead, and Nance has been terrorized into remaining silent, Lisa has neither the knowledge nor the authority to contest her slave status.

What complicates this performance even further is that the actress who plays the role of the white-looking and -acting octoroon is actually white. Thus, it is only through the roles established within the framework of the performance, as well as through the audience's familiarity with the racial hierarchy that informs the play's characterizations, that her racial differences are expressed. Moreover, audiences, despite their knowledge of her undiscovered whiteness, would have had to engage in Lisa's temporary status as octoroon, as well as in her eventual emergence as white. These multiple layers of performance help to produce complex readings of race represented both by the character Lisa and by the actress who plays her; as a consequence, audiences would have been compelled to read different markers of blackness and whiteness at different points throughout the performance. It is not until the final scene of *The White Slave* that whiteness and blackness no longer function as liminal and performable parts of Lisa's identity but emerge as fixed identities, always already present in the cultural lexicon.

Foiled Again: Restoring Whiteness, Dislocating Blackness

In addition to fixing her racial identity, the confirmation of Lisa's whiteness at the end of the play is finally what allows her to transcend the boundaries of the traditional tragic narrative that she inhabits. Unlike the typical octoroon figure, who dies tragically at the end of the story, Lisa is allowed to live. By characterizing her role as naturally superior to more conventional representations of fragile octoroons, Campbell prefigures her transcendent whiteness. In contrast to quadroon Nance and octoroon Daphne (Bill Lacy's enslaved concubine), who are abused and condescended to by white men, Lisa remains defiant and self-assured in her interactions with whites and blacks. Her assertiveness differs from the required subservience of other slave women in the play, who are expected to submit to advances from and attacks by white owners and overseers. Even Lisa's romantic advances toward her lover, Clay, are presented as signs of her strength and romantic savvy. This noble characterization of Lisa's actions differs from more conventional and stereotypical representations of black women. If the same behavior were attributed to an identifiably black woman at all, they would most likely be represented as comic or even brutish. Lisa also refuses to become the concubine of a man she does not love, distinguishing herself from many black women, who were forced into sexually exploitative relationships with white men in the slave system. She states: "A woman cannot fall lower than to live with a man she does not love—cannot even respect" (*WS* 228). Here, she establishes a high moral standard, which many black woman were not in a position to meet. This assertion points directly to the vulnerability of the real octoroon character in the play, Daphne. In contrast to Lisa, Daphne is compelled to serve as Lacy's mistress, to endure his constant abuse, and to bear his child.

Unlike her subjugated "sisters," who are forced to inhabit the inferior status assigned to them permanently because they are black, Lisa's temporary and liminal status enables Campbell to characterize her differently. Lisa functions as an effective surrogate for black and white women because she possesses mobility that they will never attain. She can present the tragedy of black women's lives at the same time that her whiteness radically transforms her position. Still, her body functions as a site for all of the transgressive desires that white audiences identified with black bodies. In a sense, what makes Lisa's apparent whiteness more tantalizing is the unidentifiable part of her that has been labeled black. This unmarked blackness also invokes both the "contaminated" status of Daphne and Nance—the actual mixed-race female slaves in the play—and the slave condition of other black characters in the play.[35] Despite the multiple significations that Lisa's symbolic blackness produces, in the end, her "legitimate" whiteness asserts its cultural authority.

Emphasizing the primacy of Lisa's role and the displacement of their own servitude, black characters are more concerned with her suffering than their own. Time after time in *The White Slave*, black slaves break into song and dance or engage in comic dialogues, providing a backdrop similar to a minstrel show. These conventions would have been familiar to contemporary audiences because of the well-established tradition of minstrel performances, which were eventually absorbed by other forms of popular entertainment (musicals, vaudeville) at the end of the nineteenth century.[36] This indirect invocation of stereotypes popularized by the blackface minstrel tradition reinforces essentialized formulations of blackness ("zip coon," contented slave, "yaller gal"), further distinguishing the "authentic" blackness of the other slaves from Lisa's counterfeit representation.[37] Reiterating the frequency with which blacks were placed in the role of objectified spectacle, one nineteenth-century reviewer includes the play's representations of black bodies in a list of common props and trappings characteristic of this type of production. He recalls:

> The action, plots, and counterplots, characters, serious and humorous passages, crowd the scenes of the play. . . . There are plantation scenes and songs, and banjo-playing and dances and the African of every age and shade.[38]

Black characters are conflated into flat stereotypes so that they remain part of the scenery. Campbell contrasts Lisa with this type of black-identified behavior by foregrounding her refined persona, placing her in a transcendent role. In effect, the "blackface" chorus provides the spectacular entertainment and emotional background for Lisa's drama.[39]

This minstrelization of the *real* black characters deemphasizes increasing anxiety about the contaminating impact of free blacks by reducing them to comic and subordinate backdrops.[40] Moreover, none of the black male characters, who were the main objects of alarmist antimiscegenation attacks, ever express any desire for Lisa; they are safely paired off with other black female characters in the play.[41] Their subservient roles indicated that ordinary blacks were willing to maintain their servant status and would not overstep the established racial boundaries. Even the music—sad spirituals or happy banjo strumming—that frames the narrative and interrupts the dialogue helps to widen the gap between the comic entertaining role of the "happy darkies" and the tragic drama of "almost" white Lisa. And, Lisa's "blackface" performance is so muted that her characterization invokes its proximity to whiteness (a kind of whiteface) more than anything else.

Despite this apparent displacement of blackness, its symbolic power still has a disruptive, albeit temporary, impact on the white characters. Because of Lisa's invisible drop of black blood, Bill Lacy is able to purchase her, and Clay Britton is imprisoned for helping her. In fact, once Clay assists in Lisa's escape from Lacy's plantation, he becomes a fugitive like her. He loses the rights afforded white people and enters the realm of slave status, temporarily. This placement of Clay and Lisa into subjugated positions displaces blackness, erases the issue of slavery, and enables white figures to appropriate the burdens of blacks. First, they take on the role of fugitives, which transforms them into mistreated victims. Then, they easily shed this vulnerable position in order to reoccupy their stations as sanctioned white people. Or, as the steamboat captain asserts after a quick appraisal of Lisa's appearance, genteel comportment, and white male companion: "This lady is a genuine white woman!" (WS 236).

The authentication of Lisa's "genuine whiteness" at the end of the play and the restoration of her family property provide a conciliatory resolution, which conventional tragic octoroon narratives did not furnish. The symbolic removal of the contaminating drop of black blood from her body enables Lisa to enter the safe realm of whiteness legitimately. She and Clay occupy their positions as the benevolent masters of the idyllic plantation of the past almost effortlessly. With the legitimacy of their alliance restored, the moral outrage of Lisa's unjust treatment is foregrounded rather than the racist ideology that endorses slavery and prohibits cross-racial unions.[42]

Their newly acquired roles represent a restoration of antebellum racial, gender, and class order in the South. Campbell's play conflates Lisa's miraculous shift from being owned (property) to owning (property holder) with her reclassification as white so that the play's conclusion supports the notion that all possessions, which were confiscated from white landowners during and after the war, should be returned to their "rightful" owners. It also suggests that only a select group of whites, those who have demonstrated their legitimacy and moral aptitude, deserve the rights associated with the position of property holder. The other implication is that blacks, so recently emancipated from the status of chattel, are not yet ready to assume the responsibility of ownership, especially self-governance. Rather than challenging the inherent racism of these patronizing justifications for slavery, this ending reestablishes the legitimacy of the slave system's racial hierarchy and idealizes the benevolent masters of the not-so-distant past. In a sense, blackness is the foil against which whiteness is reasserted.[43] It serves as the literal and symbolic justification for maintaining white hegemony.

This nostalgic recreation of the antebellum racial hierarchy emphasizes the desire of many white (male) Americans to bury the conflicts of the past and to (re)establish their dominant position in the increasingly diversified and competitive U.S. society.[44] Supporting this move, an 1882 review describes the romanticizing effect and "collective amnesia" that Campbell's play produces: "Campbell has gathered up and put in its construction all that is worth saving of the old Southern society and the conditions of plantation life and property in the past and gone slavery system."[45]

All that is *not* worth saving—the actual octoroon character, (Daphne), the threat of interracial desire, the lecherous white male, the immorality of slavery—seems to fade into the background of the play and into the irretrievable memory of the reviewer. In fact, Daphne's and Lacy's fates represent the typical punishment for carrying out intimate interracial affairs: they both die. Bill Lacy murders Daphne because she stops him from preventing Lisa's escape from his plantation; the Sheriff then shoots Lacy for resisting arrest, for interfering with Lisa's rescue, and for attempting to defile Lisa when she was held captive on his plantation. Lacy's punishment punctuates the force behind racial categorization by demonstrating the material impact of Lisa's shift from octoroon to white. When she occupies the position of octoroon, the law supports Lacy's exploitation of her, but when she moves into the category of white, Lacy's predatory sexual advances become criminal. Still, Lisa's status depends on her classification, whereas Lacy's is already tainted by his alliance with a black-identified woman (Daphne) and his overall characterization as morally weak. Unlike Lisa and Clay, Lacy and Daphne represent contaminated bodies, which can neither be cleansed nor recuperated. Lacy and Daphne function as foils to Lisa and Clay because they engage and fulfill the cross-racial desires that Lisa and Clay merely act out. Lacy's ability to express his white male desire for Daphne, the exoticized octoroon, contrasts with the denial and unfulfilled fantasy that his attempted sexual liaison with Lisa represents. Lacy's and Daphne's bodies are contaminated irreversibly because they have engaged in interracial sex and have produced a "miscegenated" child. Their literal and symbolic deaths in the play help to maintain Lisa's purity and to eliminate the cross-racial eroticism that their presence invokes.

Although the other black characters do not die, they do disappear by returning to their prescribed roles as slaves on Big Bend Plantation. One could also argue that the more explosive form of interracial relations— between black men and white women—remains invisible and unspeakable. This would have been pertinent in the 1880s, when racist white southerners used alarmist rhetoric about the danger of free black men raping white women in the South to justify violence against blacks.[46] In fact, this extremely transgressive form of interracial union is arguably what this post-Reconstruction narrative is really displacing. Most white male–black female relationships were not considered bad by slave owners because they reproduced the slave population, according to the law that stated that the condition of the child follows the condition of the mother (they remain slaves). However, white female–black male liaisons were viewed as a direct threat to white southern patriarchal authority, since, technically, those children could share the free status of their white mothers.[47]

Rather than addressing this issue, the narrative circumvents black male–white female liaisons by focusing on the ways in which the crisis of Lisa's misclassification as octoroon gets played out as a competition between the two central white male characters, Bill Lacy and Clay Britton, for ownership of her body. Unlike the slaves and most antebellum white women, Lacy and Clay are authorized to navigate the "marketplace" and all that it represents in U.S. culture from positions of power. As legitimate property holders, their actions, intentions, and right to possess Lisa are never challenged. By refocusing the destabilizing impact of Lisa's counterfeit octoroon status on these white male characters, the narrative formulates the question of Lisa's liminal racial status in terms of white male identity and desire, while it also precludes any articulation of desire between black men and white women.

Even Lisa and Clay's mimetic cross-racial relationship is "whitened" and forced into the background by Lisa's transformation from octoroon to white. The legal status of their union changes along with Lisa's racial classification because she is now permitted to marry Clay legally. This difference from the slaves, whose unions were not authorized by the state, reinforces both the forbidden nature of their earlier alliance and the legitimacy of their current relationship.

Lisa's racial transmogrification from black to white also indicates that the desirability of octoroon women is fueled by a desire for both pure whiteness and exotic blackness. Lisa's character represents this multifaceted appeal for she occupies a different or even "interesting" category, as she's referred to in one of the nineteenth-century reviews, while she simultaneously embodies an idealized model of whiteness. She and Clay enter into a transgressive relationship because she has the status of octoroon but, eventually, she emerges as white, which simultaneously permits and sanitizes the mythos of their cross racial affair. Lisa and Clay's counterfeit interracial encounter replicates and replaces Lacy and Daphne's genuine interracial union, suggesting that Lisa and Clay's enactment of cross-racial love was a performance rather than an actualization of transgressive desire. Moreover, Lisa's role as a tragic octoroon and the desire that she evokes is eventually defused when her contaminated status is removed by the official exorcism of any blackness associated with her body. This symbolic purification of Lisa's body affirms her whiteness and eradicates the threat of the mixed-race body, the miscegenated body.

Unsettling Conclusions

This depiction of the tragic octoroon and the destructive effects of cross-racial relations remains part of the performance and, therefore, indicates that none of the characters necessarily represents realities beyond the stage. However, the performance intersects with lived experiences and provides a powerful reminder that transgressive interracial liaisons and mixed-race individuals exist and create (and experience) similar disruptions in real life.[48]

Despite the triumph of white racial supremacy at the end of the play, the ambiguous performances of miscegenation represented in *The White Slave* attest to the unresolved anxieties that interracial unions and miscegenated bodies generate(d). Even within the context of Campbell's conciliatory play, conventional tropes about transgressive cross-racial liaisons emerge in relation to a broad matrix of historically grounded racial discourse, which informs representations and resists reductive readings. One might also argue that it is only because white male–black female relations were institutionalized and reproduced through the slave system that Campbell's representation is recognizable, imaginable, or acceptable to its viewers.

The ambiguous space between Campbell's safe solution to transgressive interracial desire and the explosive responses surrounding the issue of miscegenation indicate that Campbell's imaginative formulations of cross-racial unions should be read as performative, rather than as accurate depictions of reality. Therefore, it is possible to re-view them in order to better understand the cultural and historical conditions that informed them. By examining the way in which black-white boundaries were never firmly in place in the nineteenth century and were always contested, it becomes clearer how attempts to fix race were and continue to be strategic methods of policing individual lives. This analysis makes more visible the way in which Campbell's representation reconstructs the tragic mulatto and the black-white love-as-impossible conventions in order to reinforce particular ideological impulses, such as post-Reconstruction northern-southern reconciliation, white hegemony, and black inferiority. Reevaluating this representation in terms of its performance and reformulation of those limited narratives is useful in that it offers alternative possibilities, which disrupt reductive articulations of race and interracial desire. Rather than arguing that these historical enunciations of racial complexity merely reinforce contemporary discussions, my interpretation demonstrates how these debates were already being tested and negotiated in late nineteenth-century narratives; it takes into account the intersecting lives and competing histories of those implicated in and by this representation, as well as identifies the layered articulations of black-white subjectivities that it generates.

NOTES

An earlier version of this chapter was presented as part of the Race as a Device: The Performance of Race and Ethnicity in Theatre panel at the 1996 Association for Theatre in Higher Education (ATHE) conference in New York City. I would like to thank Kandice Chuh, Harry J. Elam, Jr., David Krasner, and Yvonne Yarbro-Bejarano for their generous readings and helpful suggestions on this chapter.

1. See Forrest G. Wood, *Black Scare: The Racist Response to Emancipation and Reconstruction* (Berkeley: University of California Press, 1968), 53–79.

2. My application of this theoretical frame intersects with Judith Butler's formulation of performativity, which can be understood as the "reiterative power of discourse to produce the phenomena that it regulates and constrains," in Butler, *Bodies that Matter: On the Discursive Limits of "Sex"* (New York: Routledge, 1993), 2.

3. My use of regulatory norms that are reproduced in mainstream discourse is informed by Butler's discussion of performativity in *Bodies that Matter*, especially in her introduction and her chapter on Nella Larsen's *Passing* (Butler 1–23, 167–185).

4. Here, the term *performance* takes into account social performance and the particularities of organized and/or theatrical performance along the lines of Elin Diamond's theory. In her introduction to *Performance and Cultural Politics*, ed. Elin Diamond (New York: Routledge, 1996), Diamond theorizes:

> Performance . . . is precisely the site in which concealed or dissimulated conventions might be investigated. When performativity materializes as performance in that risky and dangerous negotiation between a doing (a reiteration of the norms) and a thing done (discursive conventions that frame our interpretations), between someone's body and the conventions of embodiment, we have access to cultural meanings and critique. (5)

5. I am indebted to those performance critics whose work has sharpened both the field and my own understanding of performance/dramatic studies, including, but not limited to, Marvin Carlson, Una Chaudhuri, Coco Fusco, Paul Gilroy, Peggy Phelan, Sandra L. Richards, Amy Robinson, and Eve Sedgwick.

6. Joseph Roach argues that performance characterizes the "powerful way in which cultures set about the necessary business of remembering who and what they are . . . of making them into who and what they are, and even into who and what they might someday be." Roach, "Slave Spectacles and Tragic Octoroons: A Cultural Genealogy of Antebellum Performance," *Theatre Survey* 33, no. 2 (Nov. 1992): 168.

7. Richard Schechner, *Performance Theory* (New York: Routledge, 1988), 184.

8. David G. Croly and George Wakeman, *Miscegenation: The Theory of the Blending of the Races, Applied to the American White Man and Negro* (London: Trubner, 1864). See also Wood, 53–79 and George Fredrickson, *The Black Image in the White Mind: The Debate on Afro-American Character and Destiny, 1817–1914* (Hanover, N.H.: Wesleyan University Press, 1987), 171–174.

9. Fredrickson, 171–172, and Eva Saks, "Miscegenation Law," *Raritan* 8, no. 2 (Fall 1988): 42.

10. See Fredrickson 228–255.

11. See Alfred P. Schultz, *Race or Mongrel* (Boston: L. C. Page, 1908), title pg; and John H. Van Evrie, *Subgenation: The Theory of the Normal Relation of the Races; An Answer to "Miscegenation"* (New York: J. Bradburn, 1864).

12. Fredrickson suggests that social Darwinism solidified racist claims that (mixed-race) blacks were physically and intellectually inferior and would eventually disappear as a species. Fredrickson 228–255.

13. See George Washington Cable, "The Negro Question," in *The Negro Question: A Selection of Writings on Civil Rights in the South by George Washington Cable*, ed. Arlin Turner (New York: W. W. Norton 1968), 119–154.

14. Kevin Gaines, in *Uplifting the Race: Black Leadership, Politics, and Culture in the Twentieth Century* (Chapel Hill: University of North Carolina Press, 1996), claims, "For the black South . . . theories influenced by scientific racism and eugenics positing the immorality and degeneracy of mulattoes also provided an additional basis for arguments against intermarriage" (58). He also argues that, for many blacks, racial purity equaled racial respectability and that black responses to interracial unions were related to an overall desire to demonstrate and practice high standards of morality to disprove white accusations of black inferiority (121–125).

15. The "one-drop" rule stated that a person was considered black as long as she contained any percentage of black blood, even one drop. See Gaines 50.

16. For examples of antimiscegenation rhetoric and attacks on blacks, see Ida B.

Wells-Barnett, *On Lynchings: Southern Horrors, A Red Record, Mob Rules in New Orleans*, ed. William Loren Katz (Salem, N. H.: Ayer, 1987).

17. Bartley Campbell, *The White Slave*, in *"The White Slave" and Other Plays, 1882–1909*, vol. 19 of *America's Lost Plays*, ed. Napier Wilt (Princeton, N.J.: Princeton University Press, 1941), 199–248. Subsequent references will be included parenthetically in the text.

18. After the failure of Reconstruction and an attempt to reconcile white America (despite class differences, an increasing immigrant population, competition for jobs, the rise of new industries, westward expansion, political shifts, and a large free black population), race had many competitors to capture national attention and inspire public debate. Robert Toll describes this shift in national issues in his discussion of the history and evolution of minstrelsy performances in *Blacking Up: The Minstrel Show in Nineteenth-Century America* (New York: Oxford University Press, 1974), 125–127, 135, 148, 160–163.

19. "Pope's Theatre—The White Slave," *St. Louis Republican* (24 Oct. 1882): 9.

20. During the 1880s, "foreigners" could easily represent immigrants, who were competing for jobs and diversifying the U.S. population. By removing him from the narrative, Campbell displaces this volatile issue so that neither the characters nor the audience has to address it. Toll discusses the threat of immigrants to the notion of a consolidated (democratic) white male class in *Blacking Up*, 186.

21. Some examples of these texts include William Wells Brown, *Clotel; or, The President's Daughter,* (1853), in *Three Classic African-American Novels*, ed. Henry Louis Gates, Jr. (New York: Random House Vintage Classics, 1990), 3–224; Gertrude Stein, "Melenctha" (1909), in *Three Lives* (New York: Signet–New American Library, 1985), 81–238; Pauline Hopkins, *Contending Forces: A Romance Illustrative of Negro Life North and South* (1899), in *The Schomberg Library of Nineteenth-Century Black Women Writers*, ed. Henry Louis Gates, Jr. (New York: Oxford University Press, 1988); and William Faulkner, *Light in August* (1932) (New York: Vintage–Random House, 1990). For more examples, consult James Kinney, *Amalgamation! Race, Sex, and Rhetoric in the Nineteenth-Century American Novel* (Westport, Conn.: Greenwood, 1985); Judith R. Berzon, *Neither White nor Black: The Mulatto Character in American Fiction* (New York: New York University Press, 1978); and Werner Sollors, *Neither Black nor White Yet Both: Thematic Explorations of Interracial Literature* (New York: Oxford University Press, 1997).

22. Susan Gillman defines race melodramas as those texts that use the excesses of melodrama to "express and explore the ideologies of race and race analysis," which connect the worlds of fact and fiction, imagination and politics. See *The American Race Melodramas, 1877–1915* (forthcoming), 3, and Gillman, "The Mulatto: Tragic or Triumphant? The Nineteenth-Century American Race Melodrama," in *Culture of Sentiment: Race, Gender and Sentimentality in Nineteenth-Century America*, ed. Shirley Samuels (New York: Oxford University Press, 1992), 221–243.

23. For example, in the *Chicago Daily News* of 30 Oct. 1882, the reviewer stated: "Bits of Uncle Tom, The Octoroon, Kit, and The World, and other sensational dramas have been kidnapped, uglified, attenuated, and melted in the Campbellean stewpan, warmed up with the gentle heat of the Bartlean genius" (quoted in Wilt lxxxi).

24. Rita Dove, *The Darker Faces of the Earth: A Verse Play in Fourteen Scenes* (Brownsville, Oreg.: Story Line Press, 1994); Langston Hughes, *Mulatto* (1935), in *Black Theatre USA: Plays by African Americans: The Recent Period: 1935–Today,* rev. ed., ed.

James V. Hatch and Ted Shine (New York: Free Press, 1996), 4–23; Adrienne Kennedy, *Funnyhouse of a Negro* (1964), in Hatch and Shine, 333–343; Nella Larsen, *Passing* (1929), in *An Intimation of Things Distant: The Collected Fiction of Nella Larsen*, ed. Charles R. Larson (New York: Anchor, 1992), 163–276; and Dorothy West, *The Wedding* (New York: Doubleday, 1995).

25. "The White Slave at Hooley's," *Chicago Tribune* (31 Oct. 1882): 7.

26. "The White Slave," *St. Louis Republican* (29 Oct. 1882): 3. For some other examples, see "The White Slave," *Chicago Daily News* (30 Oct. 1882); "The White Slave," *New York Daily Tribune* (4 Apr. 1882); "The White Slave," *New York Dramatic Mirror* (8 Apr. 1882); and "Of the Premiere 'The White Slave,' "*New York Illustrated Times* (22 Apr. 1882). In an interview, Bartley Campbell admitted that he borrowed material from other plays and transformed it for his own purposes:

> I don't mind the charges they make about my cribbing from *Uncle Tom* and *The Octoroon*—see?—because that was just what I did—see? I took the meat out of both—eh?—added a little sauce and spice—eh?—and there you had it see? This morning I'll make some changes where they are needed—see?— cut out some of the talk in the first part and spice her up at the end. "News and Interviews." (*New York Mirror* [8 Apr. 1882]: 7)

27. In *Aristocrats of Color: The Black Elite, 1880–1920* (Bloomington: Indiana University Press, 1990), Willard Gatewood asserts that, like elite whites, blacks were very conscious of decorum and adhered to a strict set of codes (what he also refers to as a "genteel performance"); the use of proper English was one of the most significant indicators that one belonged to "polite society." He states: "Perhaps nothing was so indicative of one's degree of gentility as one's use of language" (143).

28. In *A Voice from the South* (New York: Oxford University Press, 1988), 32, 96, Anna Julia Cooper emphasizes the fact that "Negro women" were not considered "ladies" and that the racial/gender hierarchy that was in place at the end of the nineteenth century distinguished "white ladies" from "colored people" (which included black men and women).

29. After Reconstruction and the Democratic take-over of the South, the rest of the country watched as black civil rights were reversed and white supremacy reigned again in the South. In *America's Reconstruction: People and Politics after the Civil War* (New York: Harper Collins, 1995), Eric Foner and Olivia Mahoney claim:

> Despite its expanded authority over citizens' rights, the federal government stood by indifferently as the Southern states effectively nullified the Fourteenth and Fifteenth Amendments and, beginning in the 1890s, stripped African-Americans of the right to vote. (134)

30. Foner and Mahoney describe the dismantling of black rights during the period after Reconstruction in *America's Reconstruction*, 134–135. This led to more racist policies at the end of the nineteenth century, such as *Plessy v. Ferguson*, and reinforced racist theories that claimed that black inferiority was to blame for inequalities.

31. At the beginning of the twenty-first century, this argument is still relevant in the light of new information about Thomas Jefferson's illicit affair with his young slave Sally Hemmings. Recent DNA evidence linking descendants of Hemmings's family to Jefferson was produced, which indicated that this affair, deemed improbable by many historians, did indeed occur. This evidence that Jefferson engaged in cross-racial sex disrupts his reputation as a model of morally upright (white American)

manhood. See Dinitia Smith and Nicholas Wade, "DNA Test Finds Evidence of Jefferson Child by Slave," *New York Times* (1 Nov. 1998): 1.

32. See Martha Hodes, *White Women, Black Men: Illicit Sex in the Nineteenth-Century South* (New Haven, Conn.: Yale University Press, 1997), for a description of the conflicts and legal battles that arose when descendants of black male–white female unions made property claims.

33. For a useful explanation of this nineteenth-century position, assigned to elite white women by the "Cult of True Womanhood," as well as a thoughtful critique of its claims and contradictions, especially in relation to black women, see Hazel Carby, *Reconstructing Womanhood: The Emergence of the Afro-American Novelist* (London: Oxford University Press, 1987).

34. See Karen Sánchez-Eppler's chapter, "Bodily Bonds: The Intersecting Rhetorics of Feminism and Abolition," in *Touching Liberty: Abolition, Feminism and the Politics of the Body* (Berkeley: University of California Press, 1993).

35. As an argument against intermarriage, both blacks and whites often claimed that a mulatto or any mixed-race individual was corrupt, sullied, and inferior to anyone with "pure" blood (see Fredrickson 173–174, 321 and Gaines 58, 121–25).

36. See Toll 134–55, 263.

37. In *Blacking Up*, Toll explains that white northerners did not have much contact with blacks so their views of blacks were often based on the caricatures they saw in minstrel performances, which were flat types that emphasized the subordinate position of blacks. He also explains that, once blacks were able to perform as minstrels, they were perceived to be more authentic portraits of what blacks were really like rather than performances of black stereotypes (75–78).

38. *"The White Slave," St. Louis Republican* (29 Oct. 1882): 9.

39. The notion of the spectacular element of Campbell's production also raises the question of how this play would have been categorized at the time. More than one nineteenth-century reviewer remarked that his play combined minstrelsy, jubilee singing, drama, sensationalism, and comedy; it included aspects of several different forms of entertainment in order to captivate audiences. Like white minstrel performers, who moved away from black subjects except to present nostalgic plantation portraits, he also deemphasized the racial issue by placing blackness into the background. Whether audiences would have also been familiar with melodramatic conventions or would have anticipated the reconciled outcome of the play, audiences attended these performances to experience both the titillation of something forbidden and the satisfaction of seeing everything returned to its appropriate place. Robert Toll's discussion of the changes in minstrel performances (more lavish, larger companies) supports this claim by indicating that minstrelsy had to compete with other forms of entertainment toward the end of the century (Toll 134–155, 263).

40. The desire to assure whites that blacks were willing to remain in their place was particularly relevant in the 1880s after Reconstruction. Whites from the North and the South did not want contact with blacks, except when they were being entertained.

41. Marriage was not a legal option for slaves, which meant that blacks had no legal recourse for transferring property to their children or to their wives.

42. In the *St. Louis Republican*, the reviewer asserted that Lisa's fate is considered more tragic because she is white and has had to suffer the cruelties of slavery: "The effects of her treatment as a bond woman and beautiful are thus intensified tenfold, and the sympathy for her grows wonderfully strong" (29 Oct. 1882, 3).

43. For an informative discussion of the reassertion of hegemonic whiteness in relation to racial Others (colonizers and postcolonial subjects), see Homi K. Bhabha, *The Location of Culture* (New York: Routledge, 1994).

44. Fredrickson, 198–227.

45. *"The White Slave," St. Louis Republican* (29 Oct. 1882): 3.

46. Many historians assert that the fear of black male–white female relations became more critical after the Civil War and that efforts to control blacks in the South were supported by racist claims that free black men were predators who needed to be controlled. Also, actual relationships between white women and black men threatened the social-economic structure of the white patriarchy because it enabled children of these unions to make property claims after the war (see Hodes 4–6, 19–28).

47. Hortense Spillers, "Mama's Baby, Papa's Maybe: An American Grammar Book," *Diacritics* (Summer 1987): 65–82. In this article, which describes the impact of slavery on black families and bodies, Spillers cites the law *partus sequitir ventrum*, which states that the condition of the child follows the condition of the mother. This law enabled white slave owners to claim any children of female slaves as property, even if the father were free.

48. Hodes documents the destabilizing impact of mixed-race individuals, interracial marriages, and the contradictory and conflicting responses to these liaisons. Her historical examples demonstrate how black-white liaisons challenged and complicated the racial, class, and gender hierarchies at the time these liaisons occurred and, later, when the descendants of these relationships challenged laws that denied them property and other rights. See also Gatewood 177–78 and Gaines 58–59, 121–25 for descriptions of how skin color and the color line complicated intra- and interracial relations in the nineteenth and twentieth centuries.

14

Birmingham's Federal Theater Project Negro Unit

The Administration of Race

TINA REDD

In a social order that is deeply racialized, any policy that invokes race as a sign, a mark of, rather than as grounds for preferential treatment, even where justified, is likely *to be used* to exacerbate racial tensions and divides, to magnify whatever racially characterized tensions and ambivalences there are.

David Theo Goldberg,
Racist Culture[1]

The speed and enthusiasm with which the Federal Theater Project was conceived, organized, and instituted during the late summer and early fall of 1935 is a model of bureaucratic maneuvering. Between August and November 1935, the improbable idea of a federally funded national theater program became a reality. On 14 November 1935, the Works Program Administration (WPA) allocated $6,784,036 to support theater projects in nineteen states for a period of six months.[2] Hallie Flanagan, the Federal Theater Project (FTP) national director, initially envisioned a relief program for unemployed professional actors, which would limit its activities to cities where the majority of those actors resided. New York City, for example, would receive $1.8 million to cover four months' operating expenses while most states received less than half of that to cover the same period. With her program's initial funding secured, Flanagan and her administrative staff began formulating and implementing FTP "units," and in a matter of months, various FTP theater troupes across the country prepared to open their doors to the public.

In October 1935, with a variety of theater projects across the country already underway, Flanagan established an advisory board, which included leaders of the largest theatrical organizations in New York, theater producers, critics, playwrights, and actors. Included in Flanagan's initial mailing to her board was an outline of her goals for the FTP:

> Although the immediate necessity of the project is to put back to work some ten thousand theatre people now on relief rolls, the more far-reaching purpose is to establish them in theatrical enterprises which, we hope, will achieve a degree of excellence, fulfill a need in their communities, and thus become self-supporting.[3]

Flanagan intended to use the opportunity of federal sponsorship to create a nationwide theater network.

Her optimism surrounding the FTP's potential to become a self-sustaining and integral part of community life indicates Flanagan's belief that theater should function as a social institution. Flanagan eagerly courted diversity— racial, regional, and ideological. Her goal was to mirror the complexities of American life while creating a program specific to the needs of individual communities. For Flanagan, an "American" theater would demonstrate diversity as one of the United States's greatest strengths. Her national plan, however, ignored the fact that local policies might inhibit the project's central goals. Representing diversity meant enacting problematic intersections of racial and regional thinking. As a result, Flanagan's nationwide policies became entangled in regional politics, which, in the South, were also the politics of race—although by no means were the project's intentions to overtly challenge existing social mores.

During the early planning stages, black actress Rose McClendon suggested to Flanagan the concept of "Negro" units. Flanagan's background in experimental theater as head of the Theatre Department at Vassar, her exposure to European theater practices and social politics in the 1920s through Guggenheim grants, and, especially, her commitment to socially relevant theater made her a receptive audience to McClendon's suggestion. She agreed that a truly American theater project would need to include African American representation. As a result of their discussion, the Harlem Negro Unit opened on 5 February 1936, with cosponsorship from the National Association for the Advancement of Colored People and the Urban League. The Harlem unit, included in the overall plan for New York City, served as the Negro units' model for a national design. Negro units would specifically address the needs of African American theater workers, while the supposed racially "unmarked" federal theaters would provide an outlet for white artists. Following the Harlem unit's opening in February 1936, Negro units were created in Los Angeles, Chicago, Boston, Newark, Seattle, and Birmingham, Alabama.[4]

Rose McClendon's ideas about the political potential of a Negro theater differed significantly from Flanagan's. In June 1935, just a month before their first meeting, McClendon spoke publicly about the prospects for any successful Negro theater. In a letter to the *New York Times* Drama editor, she remarked:

Now what makes a Negro theater is not so much the use of Negroes as the selection of plays that deal with Negroes, with Negro problems, with phases of Negro life, faithfully presented and accurately delineated. Any other approach is doomed to failure.[5]

The distinction between McClendon's goals for the Negro units and what eventually became institutionalized through FTP practices can best be understood through an examination of the racialized nature of the FTP's administrative framework. While in design FTP implemented Negro units with admirable intentions, in practice the lack of racial discourse—except as an identifying marker for the recruitment of personnel—in the context of the racially stratified United States made the Negro units, in McClendon's phrase, "doomed to failure."

To varying degrees, any of the sixteen Negro units could serve as a model for the process of how a white-centered framework affected the choices for, the criticism and the stereotyping of, and the artistic restrictions placed upon African Americans working in the FTP. The Birmingham Negro Unit, however, is an exceptional study in administrative practices. The very idea of a Negro theater unit in Birmingham, Alabama, met with resistance, even from its sponsors. Segregation and inequality had been the rule in Birmingham since its founding by iron and steel developers in the late 1870s. While the iron and steel industry attracted both black and white workers from the northern mills, it relegated blacks to common labor and promised whites higher grades of employment reserved only for them.[6] Although Birmingham's Negro community supported a small business section within the downtown sector and two small newspapers, Jim Crow statutes governed every aspect of black life in the 1930s. The racial climate in Alabama made every FTP and WPA administrative decision regarding the Negro unit, racially unmarked and marked, suspect. While all Negro units—in the North as well as the South—adhered to racial hierarchies and were segregated, the Birmingham Negro Unit illustrates the ways in which interacting levels of power and bureaucracy discouraged development of Negro theater as a whole.

In Birmingham—a city whose population was nearly half black; where the steel industry, the major employer in the region, had collapsed during the depression, creating significant need for relief; and where local universities and theaters responded enthusiastically with offers of sponsorship—the Negro unit sputtered into existence and stammered out in less than a year. Given the Federal Theater Project's dual goal of providing relief and developing community-based theater, one might expect the Birmingham Negro Unit to be an anomaly. Instead, this Negro unit's history can be extrapolated to more broadly question the effectiveness as well as the effects of a liberal framework in ensuring artistic integrity in a context of ensconced racial biases.

Initially, interest in forming a Negro unit in Alabama was substantial. By the first week of October 1935, Flanagan had sent acknowledgment letters to the heads of the theater departments at Tuskegee Institute and Alabama College. The Birmingham, Montgomery, and Anniston Little Theaters had also expressed interest in sponsorship.[7] News of the FTP's funding spread even beyond academic and theater circles. A woman in Fairhope, Alabama, sent in an extensive proposal, which included "colored people" who would "have their chance through their dance, their song and theater."[8] All proposals adhered to the separation of Negro and white theater stipulated within the larger Federal Theater Project. Whether this separation was a pragmatic resolution to prevailing circumstances or a rationalized response to serving what were perceived as two inherently different communities remains unclear despite the various historical studies written about the project.

The formation of Negro units depended on evidence that professional performers already existed on a proposed location's relief rolls. Evidence of professional activity was nearly impossible to provide in smaller communities, regardless of the communities' interest or need for a unit. Even African American performers in New York were unemployed most of the time. In addition, Negro units required sponsorship by an individual or group already in possession of performance space and production equipment. Categorized as artistic criteria, this restriction required capital before aid. The struggle for decision-making power within the Harlem Negro Unit included black participants because the Negro community in New York City was itself a sponsor for the project. This was not the case in Birmingham.

From the time the initial proposals arrived on Hallie Flanagan's desk in October 1935 to the unit's closing in December 1936, the Birmingham Negro Unit was at the center of a struggle for power among three levels of government-sponsored bureaucracy. At the civic level, Laura Sharp, representing the Birmingham Parks and Recreation Board, wanted a supervisory position within the FTP and funds to build a Negro recreation center where Negro "dramatics" would be included in the activities. Birmingham Parks and Recreation provided access to recreational facilities and educational programs for Negroes, and its board hoped to sponsor the Negro unit. At the state level, in Montgomery, Alabama, Mary Weber, WPA administrator for Women's and Professional Services, assumed the FTP to be yet another works project under her supervision. Weber's office already had a working relationship with the Parks and Recreation Department, and it was her office that informed Sharp of the FTP and its Negro theater program.

John McGee, FTP director for the southern states and one of Flanagan's first administrative appointees, represented the FTP regionally. With an understanding of the FTP's national directives, McGee assumed that setting up a project involved verifying sponsorship and establishing the need for relief among the theater professionals. Alabama was one of six states under his jurisdiction, and he expected the process to move along quickly. Although all three of these individuals, McGee, Weber, and Sharp, sought to procure benefits for Negroes who met the criteria for unemployed theater workers, it became obvious, as their interactions progressed, that they had little else in common. A history of cosponsorship did connect the WPA to the Parks and

Recreation Department; McGee and the FTP, however, held control over a substantial amount of newly directed funding, and this gave him considerable leverage in any negotiations. Although the historically black Tuskegee Institute, with its active drama group, had applied to sponsor the Negro unit, nothing in the records indicates that they were even considered by McGee. Negroes, therefore, were silenced, totally outside of the discussions regarding the unit that was to represent their community.

Of the various letters and proposals that came to Flanagan's Washington, D.C., office in the fall of 1935, none was as ardent as that from Sharp. The Fine Arts Committee of the Birmingham Parks and Recreation Board, of which Sharp was chair, was "prepared to take twenty white and twenty negro [sic] actors [and they] need[ed] to begin with them at once."[9] Weber contacted Sharp once it became official that funding was available for a theater project. In addition to its schedule of activities for white residents, the Birmingham Parks and Recreation Board already actively sponsored recreational activities for Birmingham's Negro community. Weber, in fact, shared Sharp's hope that federal funds could be used to build a Negro recreation center, but establishing a Negro theater was not their ultimate goal. Since Birmingham's white facilities barred Negroes, Sharp and Weber wanted to build black residents a recreation facility of their own.

Flanagan referred Sharp directly to McGee, who had only been on the job one month in October 1935; still, he was already familiar with Birmingham and its racial tensions. After graduating from Grinnell College in Iowa (Flanagan's alma mater), McGee had directed plays at Purdue University before relocating to Birmingham, where he directed the Birmingham Little Theatre. While McGee focused on the artistic and educational goals of the Negro unit, WPA administrators in Montgomery—Weber, in particular—concerned themselves with the more pragmatic problems of providing relief.

Issues of authority were in question from the beginning of the FTP. Federal Theater Project administrators planned an autonomous management structure, ranging from the national to the regional and, finally, to state and local levels. This clashed with WPA authority primarily because the FTP imagined itself independent, while the WPA considered the FTP, like all of the arts projects, directly under its supervision. In September 1935, Flanagan documented her frustration with this arrangement:

> [New projects] are now subject to so many checks in states and districts that the whole affair is assuming the proportions of a colossal joke. Any assistant administrator in any State or locality can now negate or hold up indefinitely any project even if such a project has the approval of the Federal Theatre Director and his Regional representative.[10]

John McGee experienced this negative power of local bureaucracies in Birmingham.

The problems McGee had in establishing a Negro unit in Birmingham resulted in part from the confusing circumstances surrounding the formation and funding of the FTP. In June 1935, less than two months before Flanagan assumed the FTP directorship, WPA director Bruce McClure elaborated on his program's Section for Professional and Service Projects' intention "to concentrate its energies upon an arts program" at the WPA's national conference.[11] These programs—in art, drama, and music—were to be locally sponsored by existing public organizations. A drama program proposed under the sponsorship of the Birmingham Parks and Recreation Board would thus fit the criteria that Mary Weber, as a WPA administrator, found appropriate. Complications in establishing both white and Negro units in Birmingham resulted from McGee and Weber's differing perspectives on how to carry out evolving government policies.

Since Negroes had no input at this stage of the planning process, their concerns and experiences did not receive consideration. In the segregated South, where intolerance of racial interaction had a long and volatile history, racial antagonisms were deeply embedded in all social and political arenas. Despite their acceptance of a "separate but equal" artistic system, white FTP administrators maintained that the project's aesthetic values, artistic creativity, and administrative policies were racially neutral and racially unmarked. Yet, administration of these units, as well as the material that would ultimately be acceptable for Negro units to produce, *was* always racially marked. Race dictated who could be employed and in what capacity by these units. Racial politics may have been an impetus for creating Negro units, but white administration ensured that neither the productions nor the units' artistic strategies engaged meaningful issues of racial identity or politics. White administrators had the power to approve or deny production material, including the representation of race, and, in so doing, invoked white privilege. Negroes constantly experienced injustice as a result of the enforcement of white privilege. The structure of the FTP, however, made it difficult if not impossible to express or challenge such experiences of oppression. For all intents and purposes, the Birmingham Negro Unit was a white endeavor carried out by black participants.[12] This situation was the antithesis of Rose McClendon's vision for a Negro theater.

By the end of October 1935, despite the FTP's hope to begin a Negro project immediately, the Birmingham unit was clearly stalled. McGee wanted to give up on Alabama. The relatively simple plan that FTP administrators had envisioned for a nationwide theater had become tangled in the already established networks of the WPA. McGee faced two levels of WPA resistance. At the first and foremost level was a general disinclination to accept theater as a legitimate relief activity: as recreation, yes, but not as an undertaking that would benefit a community in the same way as a bridge, a building, or any other functional structure. Second, since the city's founding, Negroes in Birmingham had been relegated to the most physically demanding labor for wages consistently lower than white workers. Black "players" earning relief wages was an affront to accepted divisions of labor, and the WPA did not intend to override regional and local racial policies and customs.

In a report titled the "Alabama Situation," McGee remarked that the project stalled, first, because Sharp demanded that she be placed in charge of the Negro unit, a position for which she was "neither technically qualified nor ethically eligible."[13] As chair of the Parks and Recreation Board, Sharp believed she should also have administrative control over the unit. Aware of the existing relationship between Sharp and Weber, McGee rightly concluded that district WPA officials under Weber would not approve the project without the Parks and Recreation Board's sponsorship. McGee pointed out that "six other prospective sponsors, including the University of Alabama, Alabama College for Women, Alabama Polytechnic Institute," and three little theaters were willing to work with the Federal Theater Project.[14] He, however, understood that the WPA worked through existing civic organizations and that WPA officials had already made up their minds, so alternative sponsorship was not feasible.

McGee did, however, have the full backing of his FTP boss in Washington. Dismayed by the bureaucracy and determined to set things straight, Flanagan wrote to her superiors:

> At the present time, the Federal Directors are not directors but are advisors. It is not in such a capacity they were hired, nor is it their intention to continue to function in a position which is at present all responsibility and no power.[15]

The frustrations McGee and Flanagan experienced were only partly due to WPA policy. They were also caught unaware by the local bureaucratic constraints and by racial politics in Birmingham, and, since McGee had spent some time in the South before taking the regional directorship, this is somewhat surprising. Little documentation exists to shed light on what Flanagan thought about the racial tensions already prevalent in the United States or on the heightened state of racial agitation during the depression. Her comments tended to come in the form of questions: Could Negroes in Seattle perform convincingly in the nationwide opening of *It Can't Happen Here*? Could audiences be integrated in the South?[16] Flanagan's plans for establishing Negro units throughout the United States did not account for the social, economic, and political realities of America's black communities. What the Federal Theater Project encountered and helped maintain in Birmingham was institutionalized racism. Her approach—to provide structure at the national level in hopes of allowing for regional, state, and local diversity to meet community needs—seems, in the South, to have backfired.

Of the many letters Sharp wrote to Flanagan in October 1935, one remarked, "The Negro Theatre Project with fifty names and case numbers is ready to be submitted."[17] In January 1936, however, after being told by McGee that the "professional qualifications" of the persons listed were "questionable," Sharp responded by writing directly to the WPA director in Washington, Jacob Baker:

> We realized that we had not a Theatre Project and in making out the Negro Recreational Project we, in no way, stressed the theatrical experience

of the negroes [*sic*] because we had no desire for a negro [*sic*] Theatre Project.[18]

Here, Sharp points to the underlying miscommunication among Weber, McGee, and her. The Negro theater unit, in her mind, was merely a general funding category. McGee, however, assumed that the Negro unit would produce theater with professional standards. Although Sharp's tenacity delayed the project, her actions aimed at procuring funding for several Negro recreational activities. She worked within existing social frameworks as she understood them. McGee, using Harlem as his guide, had certain professional standards in mind, but he had no tangible strategies for instituting professionalism in a community so far removed, in every way, from Harlem.

In November 1935, Weber reevaluated McGee's list of qualified theater personnel for the Negro unit and narrowed his list of twenty-two down to twelve. Her list included only one actor, no singers, a scene shifter, a radio violinist, and a guitar player. According to Weber, she had "attempted to contact several people who were familiar with the situation and all expressed . . . the idea that there are not professional actors and actresses available."[19] At every turn, the very concept of Negro performer, professional or not, came under scrutiny and was subjected to prevailing prejudices, racist perceptions, and biases.

On 26 March 1936, after the Negro unit was finally initiated, McGee wrote, wearied by the experience, to Flanagan's assistant, William Farnsworth, suggesting that "in the light of our various experiences with the Alabama situation, we cancel the project for white workers and withdraw the funds provided there for. The negro [*sic*] project which is in operation should, I think, be continued."[20] The suggestion was ignored. Four days later, a WPA memorandum from Jacob Baker arrived in D.C. It notified Alabama WPA state administrator, Ray Crowe, that Ivan Paul would arrive within the week "to set up the long delayed theatre project for white workers in Birmingham."[21] On 9 April 1936, just over a week after his arrival from New York, Paul received approval for a 25 percent exemption (25 percent of his personnel need not qualify for relief), an exemption common within the FTP.[22] In this instance, however, the FTP granted approval on the grounds that the delay in setting up both the white and Negro units necessitated immediate recruitment of qualified theater personnel. The following day, Paul signed a lease on the Jefferson Theatre, the largest performance space in Birmingham, with special approval wired from Washington, D.C. While the WPA and FTP delayed the Negro unit's opening for more than four months, they pushed the white unit through in two weeks. The telegrams, memoranda, and letters surrounding this administrative action do not indicate specific racial concerns. And yet, WPA and FTP officials not only disregarded McGee's suggestion to cancel plans for the white unit, they managed to cut through months of paperwork. Their haste indicates a perception of racial imbalance and potential unrest if they canceled the white unit and funded the black one. In racially stratified Alabama, a Negro theater without a bigger and better white counterpart was unimaginable.

The speed with which the white project was set up, however, created problems for both units down the line. The Jefferson Theatre's size was a problem. A WPA field agent, after seeing the white unit's third production, *The Spider*, complained that it was less than half full on a good night. In May 1936, more serious problems arose. By the end of the month, delinquent lease payments had accumulated to $600, which Alabama treasury officials refused to pay because the procurement had not been cleared through their offices. In addition to recommendations that the lease be canceled by the end of June and that the white unit be moved to the Birmingham Little Theatre, personnel problems, including the agent cashier's WPA eligibility and the pageant director's "habitual intoxication," prompted WPA officials to suggest that McGee, the regional director, return to Birmingham "as soon as possible."[23] McGee, who was in Little Rock, Arkansas, working on regional business, wrote to Flanagan on 24 May 1936, explaining the situation.[24] Since his original advice to cancel the white unit was ignored, McGee felt that those who had created the mess should resolve it. In his letter, he notified Flanagan that he had "telephoned Mr. Farnsworth," Flanagan's assistant, who approved funding in the first place, and requested Farnsworth "persuade the Alabama treasury officials to pay the amount which is in arrears." The eventual loss of the Jefferson Theatre also affected the Negro unit, which had been given a small space to rehearse there.

While the accomplishments and administrative concerns of the white unit dominate correspondence between the Birmingham FTP and the central office in Washington, D.C., Clyde Limbaugh, a white director and local playwright, who McGee had appointed to run the Negro unit, did attempt to draw the national administration's attention to the work of his Negro ensemble. Limbaugh wrote the Negro unit's first production, *Home in Glory*. He described his play as a "symphonic drama" and told Flanagan that the production garnered notices in both *Harper's* and *Vogue*.[25] Although the production only received three performances, it did draw a reasonable audience. The Municipal Auditorium, where the play was presented, had a fixed seating capacity of 6,000. The stage was 100 feet wide and 55 feet deep. According to Limbaugh, 2,500 people attended the production. Significantly, the play catered to white audiences, the seating was segregated, and the representation tended heavily toward stereotypical depictions of Negroes.[26] While Limbaugh had the best of intentions for the Negro unit, a lack of quality scripts for black actors coupled with his own limited knowledge of Negro experience and a privileged white subject position hampered his efforts on behalf of his black employees.

In early July 1936, Limbaugh wrote to Hallie Flanagan, enthusiastically outlining his plans for the future:

We are just beginning on a small scale and are doing the simpler things first with the idea of "Stevedore," "Porgy" and the bigger things later on.

Through the cooperation of our local Park and Recreation Board and by giving the services of our negro [*sic*] Director we have been able to assemble a choir of 200 voices to assist in the productions here.[27]

Once the Birmingham Negro Unit began, despite Weber's claim that no qualified theater personnel existed, a black choir and director were immediately procured from a community church.

The FTP provided Harold White McCoo, an accomplished Negro choir director, with as much support as the Negro unit director, Limbaugh. The choir performed a weekly half-hour show on a local radio station as well as in every Negro unit production. This practice was not exclusive to Birmingham; in Seattle, a gospel choir was added to the production of *Stevedore* and even the Harlem unit regularly imposed musical interludes upon straight drama.[28] By the 1930s, Birmingham had become a national "center for the development and diffusion of jubilee gospel quartet music." Given the prominence of the steel and iron industry and the experiences of the mines in the black populace of Birmingham, gospel songs and singers began to feature labor themes in their lyrics.[29] Gospel recording artist George Korson toured coal regions between 1928 and 1941 under the sponsorship of the United Mine Workers. He included in his repertoire a union-commissioned ballad that celebrated passage of the National Industrial Recovery Act (NIRA) in 1933. The passion and religious spirit of the gospel music made it a palatable and nonthreatening vehicle for the dissemination of labor messages and political platforms.

Similarly, the fusion of an accepted spiritual endeavor, gospel, with labor concerns proved a successful tactic for the Birmingham Negro Unit. The unit's first production, *Home in Glory*, included eleven spirituals, which were one of the few acceptable ways to express political discontent. Not surprisingly, nearly every Negro unit production employed a choir. Gospel music also ensured white attendance at a production. By the time negotiations for the Birmingham Negro Unit were underway, Marc Connelly's Pulitzer Prize–winning *The Green Pastures* with its gospel music and stereotypical black "heaven" had toured the United States for nearly four years and was about to be released in a film version, with the Harlem Negro Unit's Rex Ingram in the starring role of De Lawd.

Unfortunately, instead of deepening support for the Negro unit in Birmingham, the choir represented the only successful aspect of its work in the eyes of the local WPA. In October 1936, as southern WPA officials began circulating memoranda outlining their concerns about the FTP in their region, one official recommended "that the Negro Unit, set up at insistence of Parks and Recreation Board, be reviewed with the view of shifting emphasis from dramatic to musical productions."[30] Ironically, this WPA official saw the Harlem unit's touring production of the "voodoo" *Macbeth* in Dallas and suggested that Birmingham model itself after that unit's success. When the WPA withdrew funding from the Birmingham Negro Unit at the end of

November 1936, funding for the choir under the auspices of the WPA's recreation program continued.

The Negro unit's second production, Harold Courlander's *Swamp Mud*, opened on 11 July 1936 at the Industrial High School. *Swamp Mud*'s subject matter, chain gangs in Georgia, held significance for Birmingham's Negro community. Chain gangs, the continued presence of forced labor maintained by a corrupt legal system in Birmingham, provided for blacks a visceral connection to the experiences of their parents and grandparents in slavery. Shortly after the city's founding, Birmingham had incorporated a convict-lease system, followed by a scrip system for exchange in company stores. Although both black and white workers revolted against these systems, it was black workers and their families who were systematically deprived of the power to negotiate a fair return for their labor. The institution of the chain gang further enforced free black labor.[31]

The Industrial High School, the venue for *Swamp Mud*, also had historical import. Founded in 1900 as the city's first and only Negro high school, this stone and stucco building covered an entire city block. The high school was the realization of a dream of A. H. Parker, the son of freed slaves, who taught school in Birmingham. Even more significant was the school's location. Situated on 8th Avenue between 5th and 6th streets, it bordered a proposed housing project, Smithfield Court, which was, in 1936, under construction. Included in that proposed project, which would eventually provide shelter for 544 families, was the planned Community Center building. Although the Negro unit was canceled, that building would be completed with WPA funds in 1937. It would contain an auditorium "with a seating capacity of 700 and a stage large enough for concerts and plays" and would be managed "under the supervision of the Birmingham Parks and Recreation Board."[32]

Still, the representation of Negro characters by Courlander in *Swamp Mud* and by Limbaugh in the Negro unit plays that he wrote by no means radically departed from the stereotypical black musicals and primitivistic dramas of the era.[33] In the context of Birmingham's racial history and segregated social structure, any realistic representation of black experience courted controversy. As implied by the title *Swamp Mud*, prior to the Civil War, the territory where Birmingham would eventually be located was known only as Jones Valley, a largely uninhabited area with swamps, cornfields, pines, and dirt used as a source of red dye by local farmers. One social historian, writing in the mid-1930s, pointed out, "Birmingham is a Southern city and now one of the most populous. The word 'Southern' implies a past, a past going back to Calhoun and slavery wealth. Birmingham has no such past."[34] During the 1850s, once the industrial potential of the area was discovered through surveys, which revealed extensive iron and coal deposits, organized efforts to extend rail transport into the area began. Postponed by the war, however, industrial development in Birmingham did not gain momentum until the late 1870s. The aid of northern capital accelerated the process, and as the turn of the century approached, iron and steel created the town of Birmingham.

The rapid increase in both black and white populations at the turn of the century, as Birmingham developed into a major steel town, created a need for company involvement in all aspects of Birmingham's early development, including segregated company housing. As blacks throughout Alabama and some from surrounding states left the restrictive sharecropping system for positions as common laborers, various legislative acts reduced the threat of losing the cheap labor supply. Industrial concerns reacted by stepping up their recruitment campaigns aimed at blacks, and by the turn of the century blacks made up more than 40 percent of Birmingham's population.

The tensions such practices produced were magnified significantly following the First World War, and in the years between the war and the depression, relations between blacks and whites were mediated by a third concern: class. The International Labor Defense's intense campaign on behalf of the Scottsboro Boys, young black teens accused of raping two white women, who later recanted, brought worldwide attention to Birmingham; it also created the misleading public perception that there was a widespread connection between blacks and the Communist party. In 1933, Robert L. Vann's *Pittsburgh Courier* claimed, "Experienced 'agitators' stayed clear of Dixie but . . . inexperienced, idealistic youths were being sent there to suffer."[35] One of those "agitators," Angelo Herndon, was first arrested in Birmingham before moving on to Atlanta, where his subsequent arrest would attract international attention. A suspected connection between Communism and the FTP by the anti–New Dealers in the House and Senate eventually led to congressional hearings and the FTP's loss of funding.

By the 1930s, Birmingham strictly adhered to Jim Crow laws. Not only were neighborhoods segregated, but every aspect of the community was divided along racial lines. Of the city's ten movie houses, two served Negroes; there were no Negro hotels; and in a population that was almost 50 percent Negro, six high schools educated white children, and one high school accepted Negro children.[36] In every way imaginable, the Birmingham to which Federal Theater Project and WPA officials brought relief was racialized, and at every level of the racializing process, white privilege was instituted. The mere inclusion of Negroes within the FTP was problematic in Birmingham, and to bring concepts formulated in postrenaissance Harlem to the deep South was shortsighted on the part of white administrators. Were one to view Negro units solely in terms of productions, longevity, and innovations, much of the information regarding administrative practices that contradicted the FTP's overarching idealistic goals would be missed. In the case of the Birmingham Negro Unit, administrative maneuvering *is* its history; a history from the black perspective, which can only be reconstructed from silence.

As autumn 1936 approached, both the Negro and white units developed plans for the upcoming year. Verner Haldene, who had replaced Ivan Paul as director of the white unit, planned for the first Regional Federal Theatre

Conference to be held 6–8 October 1936. Clyde Limbaugh rehearsed what Haldene described as "by far the most ambitious production attempted by the negro [*sic*] group."[37] That production, *Great Day*, written by a local playwright, M. Wood Morrison, traced the history of the Negro race from 4500 B.C. to the present. According to Limbaugh, the play was "written as it might be seen through the eyes of the Negro himself. His trials and tribulations are brought down to the present day in dramatic fashion."[38] Limbaugh felt the choreography especially notable because it included both "ancient" and "modern" dance. Significantly, it was the first play produced in Birmingham written by a Negro. Haldene described it as "a large production by our colored unit written by a young negro [*sic*] man assigned to our coordinating Project."[39] In October, conference attendees from throughout the southern region watched a dress rehearsal of this Negro unit play, in addition to a white unit rehearsal of Sophie Treadwell's *Machinal*.

The October conference concluded with a reading of *Altars of Steel* by southerner Thomas Hall-Rogers. The action of the play, set in a Birmingham mill recently bought by United States Steel, centered on the struggle between management and labor. The reading alone was said to have made "a profound impression on the assembly" and likely inspired the Atlanta staff to mount a production that spring.[40] After the Birmingham units were closed, the Atlanta white unit would produce *Altars of Steel*, featuring stark and angular scenery by Josef Lenz, twenty-one staged deaths, a workers' riot, and an explosion in the mill.

Written and directed by Clyde Limbaugh, *Mining Town*, the Negro unit's last production, took up similar concerns. The play's theme—racial tensions that test the limits of organized labor—indicates that Limbaugh was sincere in his desire to have the Negro unit work toward producing relevant material, such as Peters and Sklar's *Stevedore*. In mid-October 1936, Hallie Flanagan wrote to Verner Haldene to thank him for hosting the southern conference. Haldene, meanwhile, concerned himself with rehearsals for Birmingham's part in the simultaneous national opening of *It Can't Happen Here*. At the same time, Clyde Limbaugh began rehearsing *Mining Town*. The Birmingham FTP personnel assumed that all was developing smoothly. As far as the WPA was concerned, however, the FTP in Alabama was a fiasco.

At the local level, the Parks and Recreation Board remained involved in sponsoring the Negro unit even though Sharp was not given control over the unit's administration. At the state level, however, Weber continued to campaign against the project in favor of returning to the original idea of a Negro recreational center. In September 1936, Weber wrote to her regional director, renouncing any responsibility for the theater Project:

> We did not approve of the operation of the Theatre project in Alabama, due to the fact that there were very few certified persons who had professional qualifications for the project. As you know, after considerable pressure from Mrs. Flanagan and Mr. McGee, the project was put into operation.[41]

After outlining the scope of the project in Birmingham, paying special attention to the 25 percent relief exemption, Weber concluded, "My recommendation would be a serious investigation of the project as to its justification."[42]

In the following weeks, Malcolm Miller, a WPA field representative, received memoranda from both Frank Bentley and Blanche Ralston, the regional WPA section directors, recommending that the FTP in Alabama be closed. Miller had already made his stand on the relationship between regional WPA concerns and national FTP dictates over the issue of touring theatricals. According to Miller, "No one [could] come into the South without an invitation."[43] He was even willing to carry out Bentley and Ralston's recommendations personally. Bentley substantiated Weber's remarks by claiming that, in addition to unreasonable rental fees for the Jefferson Theatre and a larger nonrelief than relief payroll in some instances, Weber did not receive an invitation to attend the regional conference for the FTP in Birmingham. According to Bentley, Weber had informed him of the upcoming conference, but "she [had] not been notified of this meeting officially."[44] For the WPA, this "clearly indicate[d] the lack of proper coordination between the Federal Director at Washington and the state administration."[45] While the FTP officials now finally believed that the "Birmingham situation" would work within the national FTP framework, WPA officials had no interest in allowing their power to be usurped any longer.

Early in October 1936, the WPA would have its way. Although no materials exist that speak to the experiences of the Negro performers in the Birmingham unit, Clyde Limbaugh's frustration with the unit's sudden close illustrates the vulnerability of the Negro units in the face of white bureaucratic disputes. Limbaugh had already expressed concern for his position as a white director of a Negro unit only four months into the job, when a young black apprentice was sent in to work with him. McGee responded to his concern by reminding Limbaugh of the policy, as it had been formulated in Harlem. "As you know, I am very anxious to place in charge of negro units competent persons of their own race, if and when those people are discovered." He continued, however, by reassuring Limbaugh that "the young man we have asked in there is strictly on trial, and will, for the present, work under your general supervision."[46] On 14 August 1936, administration of the Harlem unit transferred from its white director, John Houseman, to the joint Negro directorship of Harry Edwards, Carlton Moss, and Gus Smith. Limbaugh, no doubt, knew of these changes.[47] That McGee truly intended to follow through with the model for Negro theater established in Harlem illustrates the optimism both he and Hallie Flanagan felt for the Negro units. The fact that few Negro units outside of Harlem were ever turned over to a black director—and none were administrated by blacks—illustrates that optimism is not enough.

Five productions and eight months after it finally opened, the Birmingham Negro Unit closed. Some of the white personnel transferred to Atlanta, where they had the opportunity to work on *Altars of Steel*. Unlike many Negro units, whose black actors and audiences managed to leave traces of their struggles and remnants of their small victories, the Birmingham Negro Unit's history is a study in silence. In arguments to withdraw FTP funding, Congress critiqued the Birmingham Negro Unit and other Negro units as if they were autonomous black artistic endeavors. Yet, interacting levels of white administrative hierarchy dictated personnel, financial workings, performance space, and choices in theatrical subject matter in Birmingham. White administrative hegemony functioned as a form of censorship, silencing black voices.

In her study of the FTP's Negro units, *Blueprints for a Black Federal Theatre*, Rena Fraden asks: "What is the relationship between a national culture and a racial subculture?"[48] The history of the Birmingham Negro Unit suggests that mechanisms operating to maintain racialized subcultures are not necessarily identifiable as racist practices. Significant obstacles in the realization of artistic autonomy for any racially marked group receiving institutionalized patronage are the very mechanisms that outline and sustain racial identity in the first place. The formulations of racial difference and racial identity are, in fact, the problem; the structures enabling these categories necessarily maintain divisions and inequities. The unusual organizational arrangement between the FTP and the WPA created a variety of conflicts, which played out on terrain ranging from censorship to the closing of units, but, in all cases, racial tensions—as the quote that began this article asserts—were magnified. This resulted from using race as a label to identify who should receive funding instead of deeply examining the grounds for funding and from not questioning the validity of racial categorization in the first place.

A history of contention above—and silence below—the story of Birmingham's short-lived Negro unit attests to the problematic nature of artistic patronage in a system of preestablished values that permeate and direct the distribution of resources. Government support for the arts continues to be controversial. If the underlying ideological foundations delineating the racial categorization and artistic expectations of recipients are not examined, we will continue to foster the very divisiveness in the arts that public policies are aimed at diminishing.

NOTES

1. David Theo Goldberg, *Racist Culture* (Cambridge: Blackwell, 1993): 234.

2. Hallie Flanagan, Jacob Baker, and Bruce McClure, 15 Nov. 1935, National Archives and Record Administration (NARA), Record Group (RG) 211.2 AAAA.

3. Flanagan and Arthur Hopkins, 9 Oct. 1935, NARA, RG 211.2 AAAA.

4. In addition, vaudeville units were located in Oakland, Chicago, Boston, and Camden, New Jersey; marionette units were in the District of Columbia and Buffalo; musical revues were performed by the Peoria Negro Unit; and a teaching unit was located in Raleigh, North Carolina. George Mason University Archives, Theatre of the Thirties Collection, Fairfax, Va.

5. Rose McClendon, "As to a New Negro Stage," *New York Times* (30 June 1935): 10:1.

6. See Henry M. McKiven, *Iron and Steel* (Chapel Hill: University of North Carolina Press, 1995).

7. Hallie Flanagan, General Correspondence, Oct. 1935, NARA, RG 69.

8. Letter dated 15 Aug. 1935. NARA, RG 69.

9. Laura Sharp to Flanagan, 1 Oct. 1935, NARA, RG 69.

10. Hallie Flanagan (Davis), *Arena* (New York: Duell, Sloan and Pearle, 1940), 288.

11. William F. MacDonald, *Federal Relief Administration and the Arts* (Columbus: Ohio State University Press, 1969), 512.

12. For a more detailed discussion of white attitudes and control over the Negro units in the South, see John Russell Poole, "The Federal Theatre Project in Georgia and Alabama: An Historical Analysis of Government Theatre in the Deep South," Ph.D. diss., University of Georgia, 1995.

13. John McGee to Lester E. Lang, 7 Feb. 1936, NARA, RG 69.

14. Ibid.

15. MacDonald 512.

16. Flanagan, *Arena*, 120.

17. Sharp to Flanagan, 31 Oct. 1935, NARA, RG 69.

18. Sharp to Baker, 9 Jan. 1936, NARA, RG 69.

19. Weber to Baker, 1 Nov. 1935, NARA, RG 69.

20. NARA, RG 69. William Farnsworth became assistant national director of the Federal Theater Project in Feb. 1936; he took over much of the administrative work from Hallie Flanagan. Formerly, he had served as executive head of the Legitimate Theatre Code Authority.

21. Baker to Crow, 30 Mar. 1936, NARA, RG 69.

22. Ivan Paul to William Farnsworth, 10 Apr. 1936, NARA, RG 69.

23. Frank Bentley to Bruce McClure, 12 June 1936, NARA, RG 69.

24. McGee to Flanagan, 24 May 1936, NARA, RG 69.

25. Limbaugh to Flanagan, 9 Dec. 1936, NARA, RG 69.

26. Poole 146, n. 10.

27. Limbaugh to Flanagan, 8 July 1936.

28. For a detailed history of this production, see Tina Redd, "Stage Race: The Seattle Negro Unit Production of *Stevedore*," *Journal of American Drama and Theatre* 7, no. 2 (Spring 1995): 66–85.

29. Brenda McCallum, "Songs of Work and Songs of Worship: Sanctifying Black Unionism in the Southern City of Steel," *New York Folklore* 14 (1988): 15.

30. Blanche M. Ralston to Malcolm Miller, 12 Oct. 1936, NARA, RG 69, Series 651.312, Alabama.

31. See McKiven 47–52.

32. *Alabama: A Guide to the Deep South*, comp. Writers' Program of the Works Projects Administration (New York: R. R. Smith, 1941), 174.

33. For a more complete discussion of details and the reception to the plays that the unit produced, see Poole 143–168.

34. George R. Leighton, *Five Cities* (New York: Harper and Brothers, 1939), 100.

35. Quoted in Charles Martin, *The Angelo Herndon Case and Southern Justice* (Baton Rouge: Louisiana State University Press, 1976), 52.

36. *Alabama: A Guide*, 174.

37. "Narrative Report of Federal Theatre Project Ending, 15 Sep. 1936," signed by Verner Haldene, NARA, RG 69.

38. Federal Theatre in the South, I, Oct. 1936, George Mason University Archives, Theatre of the Thirties Collection, Fairfax, Va.

39. Verner Haldene to Flanagan, 24 Aug. 1936, NARA, RG 69, Alabama.

40. Ibid.

41. Weber to Blanche M. Ralston, 12 Oct. 1936, NARA, RG 69. (This letter is dated September, with no specific date, it is stamped as received 12 Oct.)

42. Ibid.

43. MacDonald 516.

44. Blanche M. Ralston to Malcolm Miller, 12 Oct. 1936, NARA, RG 69, Series 651.312, Alabama.

45. Ibid.

46. McGee to Limbaugh, 15 Aug. 1936, NARA, RG 69.

47. Philip Barber, New York City FTP Director to All Project Supervisors and Heads of Departments, NARA, RG 69, Philip Barber File.

48. Rena Fraden, *Blueprints for a Black Federal Theatre* (New York: Cambridge University Press, 1996), 204.

15

The Black Performer and the Performance of Blackness

The Escape; or, A Leap to Freedom
by William Wells Brown and
No Place To Be Somebody by Charles Gordone

HARRY J. ELAM, JR.

Throughout African American theater history, African American playwrights, actors, and artists have manipulated the "productive ambivalence" of the black performer to transgress, transcend, and even subvert established racial categories. Performers and performances have effectively challenged racial definitions and provoked audiences to reconsider the sociocultural justifications for racial identifications. Repeatedly, performances have interrogated and exploited the slippage between the meanings of race and its visible signifiers. In this essay, I will explore the subversive potential of the black performer by analyzing two important works from the canon of black theater history: the first play ever published by a black author in the United States, *The Escape; or, A Leap to Freedom* (1858) by William Wells Brown and the 1969 Pulitzer Prize–winning play by Charles Gordone, *No Place To Be Somebody*. Implicitly and explicitly, these works foreground the power of the black performer to renegotiate the meanings of blackness. Significantly, in these plays, the playwrights' use of language functions both to construct and to confront racial categories. Despite obvious differences in time period, in intended audience, and in perceptions of blackness, each of these texts relies on the "productive ambivalence" of the black performer to deconstruct existing racial definitions. In the process, the authors comment on how blackness is conceived and performed both on stage and in life.

By my use of the term *productive ambivalence*, I am appropriating a concept developed by Homi Bhabha in his important article "Of Mimicry and Man: The Ambivalence of Colonial Discourse." Bhabha writes, "The discourse of mimicry is constructed around an *ambivalence*; in order to be effective, mimicry must continually produce its slippage, its excess, its difference."[1] Translated to the theatrical performance, the performer succeeds because of the ambivalence, the excess, the slippage between him or herself, his or her role, and the social implications of that performer and of that role. The audience applauds a performance because it recognizes the performer's *productive* negotiation of this ambivalence.

The solo performer, the singular live body before an audience, heightens this productive ambivalence. The solo performer is always mediating among differing levels of subjectivity, reality, and meaning. She must negotiate among the self as creation, as performing subject, as art object, as real self, and as performed character(s). It is the excess, the slippage between these negotiations that constitute successful performances. Bhabha argues that the ambivalence inherent in the colonial project of *mimicry*— an attempt by the colonizer to remake the colonial subject as "almost the same, but not quite"—produces "an uncertainty which fixes the colonial subject as a 'partial' presence. By 'partial' I [Bhabha] mean 'incomplete' and 'virtual.' "[2] Expanding Bhabha's critique of the partiality of colonial mimicry, the partiality that results from the ambivalence of performance is productive. For the productive ambivalence of the solo performer renders not only the performing subject "virtual" but his gender and race as well. This "incomplete," or virtual, status is critical to the performer's ability to transcend and even subvert the socially patrolled boundaries of race and gender.

What makes black performers and black solo performance affective and effective arenas for the consideration of racial identity is that definitions of race also depend on ambivalences. Race as a signifier is inherently ambivalent. A slippage occurs between the sociohistorical constructions and cultural uses of race and the real, material conditions of oppression and subjugation, which people must endure merely as a result of their racial classification. As Ralph Ellison so eloquently noted in *Invisible Man*, "Now black is . . . an' black ain't."[3] The black performer, visibly marked and read by the audience as "black," enters the stage and negotiates not only the spaces between the stage representation and the social reality but also racial definitions and stereotypes, racial misconceptions, and ambivalences of race.[4] My contention is that, through the productive ambivalence of the black performer, these racialized meanings can be destabilized and possibly even erased. The black performer can purposefully acknowledge and utilize her ambiguous status—as real person, as theatrical representation, as sociocultural construction—to explore, expose, and even explode definitions of blackness. Crucial to these processes is language and how language in performance produces, exceeds, and controls racial representation. In both *The Escape* and *No Place*, the performative interactions of the theatrical language and text with the text of the black performer's own body accentuate the situational significance of race and provoke the audience to reconsider the social, cultural, and historical meanings of blackness.

William Wells Brown, Nineteenth-Century "Performance Artist"

Prior to writing *The Escape* and an earlier, unpublished play, *The Experience; or, How to Give a Northern Man a Backbone* (1856),[5] Wells Brown, an escaped slave, appeared frequently as an orator at abolitionist meetings. As was the common practice of ex-slave lecturers, Wells Brown would begin his address with an apology, which constituted a strategic, racialized, and theatrical device. It served as a disclaimer, freeing Wells Brown from any responsibility for clumsiness in his writing or delivery. Even more important, it allowed the audience to marvel at and to sympathize with his ability to overcome in the face of insurmountable odds. He had escaped slavery and taught himself to read and write, and he now stood before them able to demonstrate a high level of proficiency as an orator. Consequently, the apology positioned the black orator in relation to the institution of slavery as well as in respect to his white abolitionist audience.

The ex-slave oratory itself functioned as a racialized performance in which the former slave performed his blackness. Here, in order to understand the performance of race or race as performative, I am adapting an idea from the theories on gender performativity developed by Judith Butler.[6] In a chapter in *Bodies that Matter* on Nella Larsen's *Passing*, Butler discusses, in a footnote, how the character Bellew could be construed as performing whiteness:

> This suggests one sense in which "race" might be construed as performative. Bellew produces his whiteness through a ritualized production of its sexual barriers. This anxious repetition accumulates the force of the material effect of a circumscribed whiteness, but its boundary conceded its tenuous status precisely because it requires the "blackness" that it excludes. In a sense a dominant race is constructed (in the sense of *materialized*) through reiteration and exclusion.[7]

Butler contends that Bellew's performance of whiteness includes blackness by excluding it. Transferring this performative equation to the situation of the black ex-slave orator, she performed blackness in relation to the whiteness of the audience. She performed blackness with an awareness of how it was excluded and included in whiteness. The black orator performing before a sea of white spectators was extremely conscious of himself as theatricalized "spectacle." Frantz Fanon observes:

> For not only must the black man be black; he must be black in relation to the white man. . . . In the white world, the man of color encounters difficulties in the development of his bodily schema. Consciousness of the body is a negating activity. It is a third-person consciousness.[8]

The third-person consciousness of the black body, of being black in relation to the white world as Fanon describes, was exacerbated by the artificiality and theatricality of the ex-slave oratorical performance. For, although the audience for the ex-slave oratorical performance was generally an audience of the converted, faithful abolitionists, this audience was still susceptible to nineteenth-century attitudes and theories on black inferiority. Antislavery sentiment at this time often exhibited what George Fredrickson terms a "romantic racialism."[9] Romantic racialists, despite a commitment to abolition, continued to exoticize and patronize blacks and to maintain that innate differences existed between the Anglo-Saxon and African races.[10]

Wells Brown wrote *The Escape* not to be staged by a troupe of actors, but to be read by him, in lieu of an oratorical address, at northern abolitionist meetings. *The Escape* depicts a series of events on the fictitious Muddy Creek Plantation owned by Dr. Gaines, which led three of his slaves, Glen, Melinda, and Cato, to escape. By performing a play within the context of the already performative ex-slave oratory, Wells Brown both intensified and reified the theatricality of the event. For Wells Brown, performing a play within the structure of the ex-slave oratorical performance represented an empowering act, an act through which he asserted control over the representational apparatus. Through his theatrical performance, Wells Brown reached beyond the constraints imposed on the genre of ex-slave oratory. Rather than being simply objectified before the abolitionist gaze, Wells Brown placed himself in the subject position as artist, playwright, and performer. Wells Brown's performance of *The Escape* exploited his own exoticization by white abolitionists as well as his own degradation under the horrors of slavery.[11]

When he performed *The Escape*, Wells Brown's body as well as his words represented performative texts. The interaction of the body as text with the traditional mimesis of the text-performance structure is, in a contemporary context, commonly associated with performance art.[12] Examining or contextualizing Wells Brown's performance through a contemporary critical gaze could locate him as an early black "performance artist," a precursor to the work of Anna Deavere Smith.[13] Such a reading of this early modern work is potentially problematic because postmodern circumstances and conditions not only surround contemporary performance art but are elements in its definition. Nonetheless, Wells Brown's solo body in performance, much like Deavere Smith's 1990s solo projects, pushes the boundaries between performance and reality. His public reading of all the characters in the play challenges not only the dynamics and structure of ex-slave oratory but that of traditional theatrical production as well. In an article on feminist performance art, Jeanie Forte observes, "Arguably all performance art, particularly in the early years, evidenced a deconstructive intent."[14] Implicitly recognizing the productive ambivalence of the genre, Forte maintains that performance art foregrounds the problematic relationship between life and art, "between a Renaissance conception of the self and a postmodern subject constructed by cultural practices."[15] Through this process, performance art, she argues, questions, attacks, and deconstructs accepted practices of representation, "knowledge acquisition and accumulation."[16] Clearly, Wells Brown's intent with his live solo performance of *The Escape* was equally deconstructive. In *The Escape*, he articulated the inherent contradictions, hypocrisy, and inhumanity present in the practices of the white slave owners. Through his representation of the slaves, he critiqued the images of blackness promoted by the dominant culture.

The solo performance of Wells Brown, similar to Deavere Smith's critically acclaimed *Fires in the Mirror* (1993) and *Twilight: Los Angeles 1992* (1994), was polyphonic; it represented many voices, both black and white. John Ernest writes, "As the author and the single voice performing all the parts, Brown became a nexus of the various characters he portrayed—white and black, northern and southern, antislavery and proslavery—and of the ideological and social forces that shaped them."[17] Wells Brown's performance was not so much interested in the individual characters as subjects but rather in their statements, their discourse, and how this discourse reflected on the injustices, the inequities, the economics of slavery. Using the concepts of *subjects* and *discourse* theorized by Michel Foucault in *The Archaeology of Knowledge* (French 1969, English 1972), Charles and James Lyons conclude that, in Anna Deavere Smith's theater, the statement or discourse is "not the expression of the subject; the subject is she or he whose position is predicated by the statement."[18] Wells Brown's performance could be similarly interpreted. In his reading performance, Wells Brown did not identify with nor attempt to embody the different characters but, rather, the discourse revealed their subjectivity.

The language that Wells Brown uses to represent the slaves Glen and his wife, Melinda, works against existing stereotypical images of blackness. Their language is free of any association with black or slave vernacular. As Melinda awaits Glen's arrival, she muses:

> It is often said that the darkest hour of night precedes the dawn. It is ever thus with the vicissitudes of human suffering. After the soul has reached the lowest depths of despair, and can no deeper plunge amid its rolling foetid shades, then the reactionary force of man's nature begin[s] to operate, resolution takes the place of despondency, energy succeeds instead of apathy, and an upward tendency is felt and exhibited.[19]

Certainly, this language was not traditionally associated with black speech, with white speech, or with any common speech patterns. Significantly, Glen and Melinda are the only characters in the play who use this language. Their speech patterns distance them from the white characters as well as from the other slaves. Consequently, their linguistic separation from the other characters highlights their difference and invites the audience to focus on their particular plight and exploitation. Yet, Glen and Melinda's dialogue not only places them in isolation, it also connects them with the elevated prose found in European and American romantic melodramas of this period. By constructing Glen and Melinda as subjects through this dialogue, Wells Brown not only destabilizes conventional expectations of "Negro speech patterns," he demonstrates the poetic capabilities of these black figures. Paradoxically, Glen and Melinda perform their blackness through Wells

Brown's appropriation of the flourishes and romanticism associated with white, Victorian aestheticism.

Another level of performing blackness was also at play in Wells Brown's delineation of Glen and Melinda: the performance of Wells Brown himself. By creating this dialogue for Glen and Melinda, Wells Brown was also consciously constructing and performing his own blackness. Wells Brown, aware of his blackness in relation to his white audience, did not want to project his Otherness, but his worthiness of equal stature, freedom, and equal rights. His productive ambivalence as a performer rendered the spectators' readings of him as black ex-slave incomplete. Ernest argues:

> Brown could play his role differently and he could in such a way challenge the terms of the multiply contingent performances of identity on the United States cultural stage. Brown's effort to revise the script of his own cultural performance largely involved redefining himself as a professional lecturer and man of letters rather than a fugitive slave.[20]

Through his performance of *The Escape* and of blackness, Wells Brown intended to displace nineteenth-century perceptions of black intelligence and literary ability.

The language and representation that Wells Brown assigns to the slave Cato stand in stark contrast to those of Glen and Melinda and produce a different image of blackness. While Glen and Melinda speak in elevated prose, Cato speaks in the dialect traditionally and pejoratively associated with the image of the blackface minstrel, which dominated American popular culture at that time. When Dr. Gaines leaves Cato alone in the clinic to tend to the slave patients, Cato responds, "I allers knowed I was a doctor, an' now de ole boss has put me at it, I muss change my coat. Ef any niggers come in, I wants to look suspectable" (*TE* I:2: 38). With his malapropisms and false sense of self-importance, Cato is the embodiment of the comic "darky." This stereotypical icon has been a constant in American representations and conceptions of blackness. Mel Watkins points out in *On the Real Side*, "In America, blackness was associated with humor from the outset."[21] The blackface archetypes presented in this theatrical genre would have been well known to northern abolitionist audiences. In fact, historian Ronald L. Davis argues, "Blackface archetypes fundamentally issued from the imagination of northern whites."[22] In addition, Wells Brown's construction of Cato was consistent with the sentimentalized notions of the childlike, self-sacrificing slave presented in Harriet Beecher Stowe's *Uncle Tom's Cabin*, which had been published six years earlier. The happy and docile Cato appears to fulfill all of his master's requests. When the mistress, Mrs. Gaines, compels him to marry Hannah, a slave woman in love with another man, he willingly complies, despite Hannah's protests. Later in the play, after Glen and Melinda have escaped, Cato goes to their master, Dr. Gaines, and informs him of their flight. Thus, at first, the image of Cato met the expectations of an audience steeped in nineteenth-century literary and theatrical representations of blackness.

And yet, with Cato, Wells Brown subverts the comic slave/house slave stereotype and the romantic racial expectations of this role by demonstrating that even the most seemingly accommodating and docile of slaves still desires to be free. When Dr. Gaines takes Cato north with the slave-catching expedition to assist in the recapture of Glen and Melinda, Cato seizes the opportunity to leap for his own freedom. Consequently, Cato's prior performance of the "happy darky" must be recognized as just that: a performance. He adopts a strategic blackness as a subterfuge or coping mechanism in order to survive on the plantation. Such tactical performances were common in slavery times and after. The mask, the device of a differentiated performance of blackness solely for the white gaze, helped blacks to negotiate the dangers of racism and oppression. In the words of the old slave adage, "Got one mind for white folk to see, 'nother for what I know is me."[23]

Still, because of the purposes of his own black performance, Wells Brown was aware that he could not totally subvert the scopic image, or expectations, of the audience, or he would risk alienating them from the abolitionist cause. Consequently, even after Cato's escape to freedom, Wells Brown has him retain elements of the happy darky performance. Once free, Cato looks to change his name, just as Wells Brown had changed his own name from Sanford, the slave, to William Wells Brown, the free man, after he had escaped. Cato relates his decision to undergo a name change to the audience:

> Well now it is me, an' I em a free man. But, stop! I muss change my name, kase ole massa might foller me, and somebody might tell him dat dey seed Cato; so I'll change my name, and den he wont know me ef he sees me. Now, what shall I call myself? I'm now in a suspectable part of de country, an' I muss have a suspectable name. Ah! I'll call myself Alexander Washington Napoleon Pompey Caesar. Dar, now dat's a good long, suspectable name, and every body will suspect me. (*TE* V:3: 55).

While fulfilling comic expectations, this performance of Cato still exhibits a productive ambivalence and excess. For ex-slaves, who had previously been named by their master, the process of naming carried added importance. Since southern masters often gave their slaves ancient Greek and Roman names, such as Pompey and Caesar, these names were generally rejected by the newly freed blacks as slave designations.[24] Cato, however, joins these slave names with Washington, a name commonly chosen by freed blacks because of its association with the father of the country, George Washington, and connotations of American liberty. Cato calls attention to the process of naming by choosing a name that is both excessive and literally "suspectable," for its excess would draw suspicious attention to him. His comic naming ceremony emphasizes the significance of names and labels to the construction of racial, social, and cultural identity. By representing Cato in conjunction with Glen and Melinda, Wells Brown implies that a commonality of their blackness lies in the desire to be free.

Certainly, between the time of Wells Brown's performances of *The Escape* and the off-Broadway debut of Charles Gordone's *No Place To Be Somebody* in 1969, public conceptions and definitions of blackness had changed significantly (see figure 15.1). And while the previous discussion of *The Escape* noted how playwright Wells Brown actually functioned as a solo performer, the examination of *No Place* focuses on how the playwright, Charles Gordone, constructs a character, Gabe Gabriel, who operates as a solo black performer within the context of the play. Through Gabe, Gordone disrupts the conventions of stage realism and the expectations of black drama of the period, just

Figure 15.1   *No Place To Be Somebody* by Charles Gordone, Public Theatre, New York, 1969, directed by Ted Cornel. Ron O'Neal as Gabe Gabriel, Nathan George as Johnny, Paul Benjamin as Machine Dog. Courtesy Billy Rose Theatre Collection, New York Public Library at Lincoln Center.

as Wells Brown's reading challenged the norms of ex-slave oratory and theater production. *No Place*, like *The Escape*, foregrounds the performance of blackness as meanings of blackness are displaced, replaced, and critiqued. In the decade of the 1960s and into the early 1970s, black artists and activists practiced a different sort of romanticized racialism, which idealized the African roots of African American culture. Black Nationalist paradigms of the period perceived race not as socially constructed but as ontological in its foundations. They imagined an essentialized, organicized blackness. *No Place* is both a critique and a celebration of those romanticized and essentialized ideals. The plot of *No Place* acts as a metaphor for the imagined racial revolution. Johnny Williams, a black bar owner and Harlem hustler, plans to usurp the power of the white crime bosses in Harlem. He exclaims to his friend and alter ego, Gabe Gabriel, "We at war, Gabe! Black ag'int white."[25] Gabe kills Johnny for his exuberance, for his insistence on perpetuating this racial divisiveness.[26]

As the doubling repetition in his name suggests, Gabe Gabriel is a character constructed on excess and ambivalence. Significantly, Gabe is an actor and playwright. As an actor, Gabe is unemployed and perhaps unemployable because of the dominant culture's definitions of blackness. He is repeatedly not cast as an actor because he is too light for black roles and too dark for white ones. Early in the first act, he informs Johnny that, at a recent audition for a musical on slavery, "Stage Manager calls me over. Whispers they're auditionin' the white actors tomorrow" (*NP* I:1: 645). Gabe's casting difficulties, the ambivalence of his visibility, make evident the inherent problems with reading skin color as race.[27] The reductivism of interpreting skin color as race not only limits the castability of Gabe, but in a much broader context, it severely restricts the possible representations of race and racial identity. When the representations of race are reduced to the visible, the invisible determinants of racial identity are ignored. Such essentialism labels all black people solely by their phenotype and does not allow for heterogeneity. One of Gordone's projects in *No Place* is to assail such essentialism through the performance of Gabe.

Throughout the play, Gabe directly addresses the audience and breaks the fourth wall. Gabe proclaims that he is not only a character in the play but the writer of the play. In his opening monologue, Gabe informs the audience:

> Right now I'm working on a play. They say if you wanna be a writer you gotta go out and live. I don't believe that no more. Take my play for instance. Might not believe it but I'm gonna make it all up in my head as I go along. Before I prove it to you, wanna warn you not to be thinkin' I'm tellin' you a bunch'a barefaced lies. An' no matter how far out I git, don't want you goin' out'a here with the idea what you see happen' is all a figment of my grassy imagination. 'Cause it aint. (*NP* I:1: 637)

Gabe claims an intriguing duality: he is creating the play in his head as he goes along and yet the events are real, they are not "barefaced lies" nor "figments of [his] grassy imagination." And, in fact, Gabe's words and actions are not products of his imagination but the result of playwright Gordone's creativity. Through the ambivalent representation that is Gabe, Gordone, the real playwright, purposefully reveals his art and artifice to the audience. By foregrounding the stage character Gabe—who maintains that he is constructing the play as he performs within it and is his own construction—Gordone simultaneously blurs and extends the space between the theatrical illusion and reality.

At key moments in *No Place*, Gabe steps out of the immediate context and action of the play and performs his own "original" poetry for the audience. In these poetic moments, Gabe, the character, functions as a solo black performer. When he acts as solo performer, Gabe situates himself as "speaking subject." He delivers introspective and revealing performances directly to the audience. The conceit of such direct and "personal" performances is that the audience now interacts in a more tangible way with the "real" as the performer engages in a self-articulating, self-reflexive performance. At the same time, a distance between audience and the performer remains. For both audience and performers are still aware that the events within the performance transpire in the realm of the performative and therefore are not real. Moreover, in contrast to the performance of the very real Wells Brown, the audience is aware not only of the performative nature of this encounter but that Gabe himself is performed. Still, the flexibility of Gordone's construction of Gabe—as both character within the story and solo performer outside the plot directly before the audience—enables him to reflect and comment on the action and on race in ways that a position of merely being inside the representation could not afford him. Gordone's creation of this unique, reflective vantage point parallels effects achieved by Wells Brown's eschewing of a conventional abolitionist speech to instead perform *The Escape*. Correspondingly, Wells Brown's polyphonic performance allowed him to express perspectives, to present viewpoints, to address issues of race and slavery in a manner not available to more conventional oratory. In both cases, the playwrights used the productive ambivalence of performance to their advantage.

At the opening of act 2, an "obviously drunk" Gabe appears before the audience and performs a poem. His inebriation is itself a device, a classic and often-repeated theatrical device. When drunk, theatrical figures, their minds and bodies oblivious to their surroundings and the ramifications of their actions, their tongues and inhibitions liberated, reveal their innermost feelings and the truth of their emotions. The device of drunkenness provides Gabe with a particularly ambiguous position of agency. For his acerbic comments on the construction and performance of blackness can be construed and consequently dismissed as the mere rantings and ravings of a drunk. Or, is he lucid? After all, Gabe's drunkenness, like Gabe, is performed. Gabe's poem begins with an old Protestant hymn:

> Whiter than snow, yes!
> Whiter than snow!

Now wash me, and I shall be
Whiter than snow! (*NP* II:1: 663)

Gabe's intonation of this hymn has immediate and significant social and cultural connotations; it conjures traditional Western associations of whiteness with purity and goodness. By having the ambiguously black Gabe perform this hymn, Gordone immediately problematizes the conventional Western binary, which constructs white as good and black as bad with no ambiguity. Gabe/Gordone's project in the body of the poem is to subvert the Manichaean opposition of whiteness and blackness by negotiating the space in between the two, to find a space for his own identity by problematizing essential definitions and thereby questioning and exploding the absolute.

Gabe's poem details how his family attempted to "wash away" the negative stigma of blackness. They:

> moved out of the dirty-black slum!
> Away from those dirty-black people!
> Who live in those dirty-black hovels,
> Amidst all of that garbage and filth!
> Away from those dirty-black people,
> Who in every way,
> Prove daily
> They are what they are!
> Just dirty-black people! (*NP* II:2: 662)

Note that, within the construction of the poem, dirty and black are hyphenated, so that the two are elided in their vocal presentation. This semantic arrangement eliminates the difference between these two adjectives. They become inseparable, part of one identity. Black is dirty. The relationship between black and dirty in Gabe's poem reflects the ways in which poverty and crime have been and continue to be racialized in this country. Terms such as "the poor and underprivileged," "the urban underclass," "the welfare dependents" have become code words that consciously, if covertly, denote blackness or people of color in our New World order. In addition, through this linguistic construction, the attributes *dirty* and *black* are made substantive. Thus, through the pattern of words in Gabe's poem, "dirty-black" becomes inculcated into patterns of behavior, internalized into social attitudes, and manifested in social performances of inferiority. Gabe relates that these "dirty-black people" prove daily "They are what they are! Just dirty-black people!" The theatrical device of linguistic conflation foregrounds the damaging effects of such absolute racial signifiers.

Gabe and his family tried to escape dirty-blackness by moving to a "clean-white neighborhood" that had "clean-white sidewalks" and "clean-white people." In addition:

> We went to schools that had clean-white
> Rooms with clean-white teachers
> Who taught us and all the clean-white

Children how to be clean and white!
(*NP* II:2: 662)

Gabe and his family wanted to perform the privileges of whiteness. However, the poem argues, the social advantages, the performance of whiteness, could not be separated from the "being" of whiteness. Social mobility depended on one being clean and white. Thus, the attempt at "clean-white" access by Gabe and his family was a project doomed to failure. Despite their attempts to wash away their associations with dirty-blackness, they could not remove the racialized meanings that "colored" their bodies.

In the concluding section of the poem, Gabe differentiates himself and his blackness from the dirty urban masses by linguistically Othering and purposefully dehumanizing them. No longer does he denote them as "dirty-black people," but, rather, he refers to them as "dirty-black *Niggers*." Gabe informs the audience:

Most of all! We were safe!
Assured at last!
We could never more be
Like those dirty-black *Niggers*!
Those filthy, dirty-black *Niggers*!
(*NP* II:1: 665)

Gabe's invocation of the term *nigger* is a deliberate tactic of denigration, distancing, displacement, and denial. It can even be perceived as evidence of an internalized racism, which is as pernicious and as damaging as the external variety. Gabe internalizes his rejection by the clean-white world and denies any connection to these "niggers" and his own "niggerness." His inclusive *We*—"We were safe!"—explicitly excludes other blacks and demonstrates his continued victimization by the device of race.

Act 3 of *No Place* again opens with a solo performance by Gabe in which he builds on his earlier considerations of the nature of blackness. In this poem, he repeats the refrain "They's mo to bein' black than meets the Eye!" (*NP* III: 3: 683). This repeated coda again reinforces the notion that blackness cannot be equated with skin color, that there is more to being black than the visible. Here, as in *The Escape*, the language used is critical to the production and meanings of blackness. In black vernacular practices, the verb *to be* denotes a constant state or reiterative behavior: "I be going to church on Sundays." Accordingly, Gabe's use of the phrase *bein' black* emphasizes the permanence of this condition. And yet, the actions, gestures, and behaviors that Gabe describes as "bein' black" are historically, culturally, and socially constructed practices:

Bein' black is like a way ya walk an' Talk!
It's a way'a lookin' at life!
Bein' black is like sayin', "What's happenin', Babeee!"
An' bein' understood!
Bein' black has a way'a making ya call some-

Body a mu-tha-fuc-kah an' really meanin' it!
An namin' eva'body broh-thah, even if you don't!
Bein' black, is eatin' chit'lins an wah-tah
Melon, an' to hell with anybody, if they don't
Like it! (*NP* III:1:683)

Gabe's definitions of blackness satirize black stereotypes and reimagine the connotations of and contexts for performing blackness. Again, Gabe/Gordone's linguistic construction is important. In addition to saying, "bein' black is," Gabe uses the phrases "bein' black has a way" or "is like a way." The implication is that bein' black compels or propels the performance of certain behaviors. This behavior, similar to Cato's adoption of the happy darky performance mask in *The Escape*, acts as a cultural, coping mechanism, a necessary response to the conditions of black existence:

It's all the stuff that nobody wants but
Cain't live without!
It's the body that keeps us standin! The
Soul that keeps us goin! An' the spirit
That'll take us thoooo! (*NP* III:1: 684)

Gabe's discourse on bein' black is also a product of its specific historic moment. By the late 1960s, a momentous movement of black pride and consciousness had emerged. Representations of blackness and black visibility proliferated within American culture. This burgeoning spirit of black consciousness would have contextualized and contributed to the audience experience with and response to Gabe's pronouncements of bein' black back in 1969.[28]

Despite its historical and social context, Gabe's declarations on the collective, essentialized nature of bein' black are purposefully restrictive and reductive. Gordone problematizes the meanings of Gabe's essential pronouncements on bein' black through the symbolic implications of the setting that he constructs for Gabe's performance. As Gabe enters onto the stage from an offstage bathroom, Gordone's stage directions note:

The Table at center has a folded newspaper leaning against a large Molotov cocktail. Its headline reads: "Negroes Riot!" A banner resembling the American flag dangles from a flagstand. Next to the Molotov cocktail is a plate on which rests a black automatic pistol. Beside the plate is a knife and fork. (NP III:1: 663)

The newspaper headline on the table is extremely dramatic: "Negroes Riot!" Within the immediate theatrical context, the headline calls attention to the recurring motif of Gabe's poem, "They's mo to bein' black than meets the Eye." The media's sensationalized representation of blacks solely as rioters denies the complexities of blackness as well as the causes of racial frustration, which lie below the surface "eye," or cursory reading of the newspaper. In addition, the setting, with its black gun and Molotov cocktail, implies another dimension, a profoundly political dimension, to blackness. The gun and Molotov cocktail together with the newspaper headline infer that the exigencies of the current racial climate have prompted a violent response, a different sort of black performance: "Negroes Riot!" The gun and the Molotov cocktail visually signify black revolutionary rage.

Gordone juxtaposes the political constructions and violent manifestations of blackness with the humorous social and cultural constructions of blackness presented in the text. This juxtapositioning implies that there is more to bein' black than rage and rioting. In addition, after Gabe has concluded his poem, he sits at the center stage table and *"Cuts into gun with knife and fork. Finally {he} picks up gun. Bites into it. Chews and swallows. Takes a drink from Molotov cocktail. Wipes mouth"* (*NP* III:1:684). Then, Gabe turns to the black audience members and invites them to participate in this meal. "Bruthas an' sistahs! Will ya jine me!" (*NP* III:1:684) Through this new "call to arms," the "I" that is Gabe deceives the "eye" of the audience and enacts an explicitly ambivalent, black performance. By eating the gun and drinking the Molotov cocktail, Gabe literally internalizes black rage into the black body. This action could be interpreted to mean that violence, the revolutionary imperative, is a critical element of black construction and an internalized essence of bein' black. However, this reading is not supported by the cultural constructions of blackness presented in the text. I would argue that, by swallowing the representations of violence, Gabe demystifies and deactivates their power and authority. The images of revolt are not only consumed by Gabe's black body, they are confuted by the body of Gabe's text and rendered partial or incomplete by his ambivalent performance.

Perhaps conservative, antirevolutionary readings of Gabe's actions and the messages of *No Place* contributed to the play's popularity with white audiences. Unlike more incendiary black plays of the period, such as Amiri Baraka's *Slave Ship* (1967),[29] *No Place* did not advocate the murder of whites nor militant action to overturn the current social system. Significantly, rather than the violent events of *Slave Ship*, *No Place*, much like Brown's *The Escape*, relies on humor and satire. Similar to Brown's forethought in performing *The Escape* at abolitionist meetings, Gordone in *No Place* anticipated white audiences. His play neither attacks nor threatens white spectators as he challenges their perceptions of race. White audiences, in fact, made up the majority of those who originally attended *No Place*. Joseph Papp first produced the play at the Public Theatre in New York in June 1969. It then moved uptown to Broadway, where it won the Pulitzer Prize in 1970. This award and the support of white spectators stand in sharp contrast to Baraka's cultural nationalism and the tenets of the Black Arts Movement of that period. The Black Arts Movement viewed such success in the white commercial mainstream as antithetical to the objectives of revolutionary black theater. The Black Arts Movement proclaimed the black community to be its sole audience and critic. Despite their federal funding, Baraka and the Black Arts Repertory Theater School (BART/s) in Harlem, during the mid-1960s, barred whites, including government officials, from attending their productions.

In his final solo performance, Gabe continues to deconstruct and destabilize racial meanings through his employment of the ambivalence of the black performer. After killing the enraged black hustler, Johnny, Gabe returns for the play's epilogue. He now addresses the audience dressed in drag, as The Black Lady in Mourning. The costume change emphasizes the constructed nature of both gender and race. Certainly, Gabe's drag performance has profound implications for feminist readings. Recent feminist criticism has interpreted male cross-dressing as a misogynistic act that reinforces male privilege. "A man imitates a woman in order to confirm that she belongs to him."[30] Gabe's drag portrayal is encoded with misogyny and male-centrism. For Gabe must become feminized in drag in order to mourn.

Certainly, Gabe's transvestism provides him with even more ambiguity and ambivalence as a performer. Peggy Phelan argues that, for the male drag performer, "Performing the image of what he is not allows him to dramatize himself as 'all.' "[31] Accordingly, Gabe in drag determines that he will "change [his] part over and over again" (*NP* 705) in order to provoke his audience. His final performance is constituted by its historical significations: Gabe argues that black identity is constructed in and through history, that black people are "a people whose identity could only be measured by the struggle, the dehumanization, the degradation they suffered. Or allowed themselves to suffer perhaps" (*NP* 705). Dressed in black with a shroud draped over his head, he references the famous historical images of Betty Shabazz and Coretta Scott King bravely mourning the deaths of their assassinated husbands, Malcolm X and Martin Luther King, Jr. Yet, Gabe in his drag performance also transcends history. He is a harbinger of destiny, who predicts his future as well as that of the audience and the entire black race.

Gabe purposefully conflates endings and beginnings. He mourns "the passing of a people dying into a new life." He proclaims that the "new life" of black people will be a death because it will entail a loss of or disconnection from history. He believes that the revolutionary paradigms of Black Nationalism are not built upon an understanding of the history of black struggle. Instead, they are conceived in and solely concerned with the present and predicated on the disruption of the historic continuum. For Gabe, Black Nationalistic fervor marks a drastic change from the past, and he will "mourn the ending of those years." Through this final performance, Gabe wants to provoke in his audience a consciousness of this passing of history. Significantly, Gordone advances this argument on and through the productive ambivalence of the black performing artist, Gabe.

Conclusions

As is evident in *No Place* as well as in *The Escape*, the productive ambivalence of the black performer informs our understanding of the situational meanings and social constructions of blackness. Both *No Place* and *The Escape* foreground the power of the black performer through his body and language to destabilize the visible. They argue that there is, indeed, "mo to bein' black than meets the Eye." In fact, the invocation of black performers and solo performances works to deconstruct the social or aesthetic structures within which these performances are supposedly situated. Wells Brown's solo performance subverts the conventional format of ex-slave oratory. Gordone's injection of Gabe's poetry and prose disrupts any attempt to read or categorize *No Place* as conventional realism or, even more significantly, as a prototypical black revolutionary drama of the late 1960s. Juxtaposing Gordone's manipulation of the character Gabe with Wells Brown's polyphonic performance of *The Escape* reveals how the power of performance, the dynamic interactions of a singular live body with an audience, can confront and effectively challenge established social and cultural constructions of race.

The transcendent and transformative power, the productive ambivalence of the black performer, has been operative since the earliest black performances in America. Eric Lott in his significant study on blackface minstrelsy, *Love and Theft* (1993), argues that a recognition of the potential subversive agency of the black performer was one important reason for white appropriation of blackface minstrelsy.[32] In the 1980s and 1990s, black playwrights like George C. Wolfe and Suzan-Lori Parks in works such as *The Colored Museum* (1984) and *The America Play* (1990–1993) have employed the productive ambivalence of the black performer by featuring solo black performances that implicitly and explicitly comment on the meanings of race as they explore and explode racial categories. *The Colored Museum* by Wolfe riffs on the ambivalence between the constructedness of blackness and the real sociocultural pressures associated with black existence in America. After symbolically strangling his black rage, The Man in *The Colored Museum* exhibit entitled "Symbiosis" announces that he will engage in a new situational performance of blackness: "Being black is too emotionally taxing. Therefore, I will be black only on weekends and holidays."[33]

Through the language of The Man, Wolfe humorously disrupts the concept that blackness is biologically fixed. The Man intends to both construct and deconstruct his own blackness. There has been and continues to be a historic continuum of black destabilizing performances, which must be recognized. For, as bell hooks argues:

> African-American performance artists have always played a role in the process of collective black political self-recovery, in both the process of decolonization and the imagining and construction of liberatory identities. It has been a space where communities of resistance are forged to sustain us, a place where we know we are not alone.[34]

NOTES

1. Homi Bhabha, "Of Mimicry and Man: The Ambivalence of Colonial Discourse," in his *The Location of Culture* (London: Routledge, 1994), 86.

2. Bhabha 86.

3. Ralph Ellison, *Invisible Man* (New York: Modern Library, 1994), 9.

4. This racialized inscription of the black performer can have a profound effect on so-called nontraditional performances, such as the appearances of Joe Morton as Coriolanus in William Shakespeare's *Coriolanus* or James Earl Jones as Big Daddy in *Cat on a Hot Tin Roof* by Tennessee Williams.

5. The play *The Experience* is listed in some sources as *Doughface*, in others as *Doe Face*. At that time, the term *doughface* was slang for northern preachers, such as those characterized in the play.

6. Judith Butler, *Bodies that Matter* (New York: Routledge, 1993), 12.

7. Butler, 275, n.4.

8. Frantz Fanon, "The Fact of Blackness," in *Black Skins White Masks* (New York: Grove, 1967), 110.

9. George Fredrickson, *The Black Image in the White Mind: The Debate on Afro-American Character and Destiny, 1817–1914* (New York: Harper and Row, 1971), 102.

10. Eric Lott, *Love and Theft* (New York: Oxford University Press, 1993), 34.

11. The theatrical performance that Wells Brown created displaced and yet reinforced the real of his life as a slave on a plantation. Wells Brown based the characters in both *The Escape* and *The Experience* on his own life and modeled the plantation owner, Dr. Gaines of *The Escape*, on his own original owner, Dr. Young. And yet, by theatricalizing real figures and actual life incidents, Wells Brown was able to manipulate their emotional impact. He could shape the representations of both slave and slave masters to meet the didactic purposes of his drama, while he simultaneously remained cognizant of the drama as an artistic medium and the need to "delight" as well as "instruct" his audience. On 28 Apr. 1857, after a reading of *The Experience* in Boston, a reviewer in the *Auburn Daily Advertiser* wrote:

> The play is itself a masterly refutation of all apologies for slavery and abounds with wit and satire, philosophy, argument, and facts, all ingeniously interwoven into one of the most interesting dramatic compositions of modern times.

Unfortunately, given the unpublished status of *The Experience*, we can never verify whether it was "one of the most interesting dramatic compositions of modern times."

12. Elin Diamond, "Mimesis, Mimicry, and the 'True-Real,' " in *Acting Out*, ed. Lynda Hart and Peggy Phelan (Ann Arbor: University of Michigan Press, 1993), 377.

13. Anna Deavere Smith is one of the most important and renowned performance artists of the late twentieth and early twenty-first centuries. She uses interviews with actual persons and real accounts of significant incidents to form the texts of her performances. Her most noted works are *Fires in the Mirror* (1992), an examination of the racial and religious conflagration that arose in Crown Heights, New York (1990) and *Twilight: Los Angeles 1992* (1992), an exploration of the riots and aftermath of the Rodney King decision in Los Angeles (1992).

14. Jeanie Forte, "Women's Performance Art: Feminism and Postmodernism," in *Performing Feminisms*, ed. Sue-Ellen Case (Baltimore: Johns Hopkins University Press, 1990), 251.

15. Forte 251.

16. Ibid.

17. John Ernest, "The Reconstruction of Whiteness: William Wells Brown's *The Escape; or, A Leap to Freedom,*" *PMLA* 113, no. 5 (Oct. 1998): 1109.

18. Charles R. Lyons and James C. Lyons, "Anna Deavere Smith: Perspectives on Her Performance within the Context of Critical Theory," *Journal of Dramatic Theory and Criticism* 9, no. 1 (Fall 1994): 49.

19. William Wells Brown, "*The Escape; or, A Leap to Freedom,*" in *Black Theater USA*, ed. James Hatch and Ted Shine (New York: Free Press, 1974), I:3:39. All subsequent references to this play will be noted in the text.

20. Ernest 1116.

21. Mel Watkins, *On the Real Side: Laughing, Lying, and Signifying: The Underground Tradition of African-American Humor that Transformed American Culture from Slavery to Richard Pryor* (New York: Simon & Schuster, 1994), 83.

22. Ronald L. Davis, *A History of Music in American Life*, Vol. 1, *The Formative Years, 1620–1865* (Malabar, Fla.: Robert Krieger, 1982), 209.

23. Watkins 52.

24. See Herbert G. Gutman, *The Black Family in Slavery and Freedom, 1750–1925* (New York: Pantheon, 1976), 185, 186.

25. Charles Gordone, "*No Place To Be Somebody,*" in *Black Theater*, ed. Lindsay Patterson (New York: New American Library, 1971), III:3:703. All subsequent references to this play will be noted in the text.

26. The repetition evident in the name Gabe Gabriel also demonstrates a conscious excess, like the new name of the former slave Cato in *The Escape*, and Gabe's name also connects him to the Archangel Gabriel from The Bible. He acts, in a manner similar to his namesake, as a beacon, a harbinger of things to come, warning black people and directing their future.

27. See Peggy Phelan, *Unmarked: the politics of performance* (New York: Routledge, 1993), 8.

28. Lisa Kennedy, "The Body in Question," in *Black Popular Culture*, ed. Gina Dent (Seattle, Wash.: Bay Press, 1992), 108.

29. For a discussion of Amiri Baraka's *Slave Ship*, see Harry J. Elam, Jr., *Taking It to the Streets* (Ann Arbor: University of Michigan Press, 1997), 86–100.

30. Phelan 17.

31. Ibid.

32. Lott 6.

33. George C. Wolfe, "Symbiosis," *The Colored Museum* (London: Metheun, 1987), 43. For further discussion of this play, see: Harry J. Elam, Jr., "Signifyin(g) on African American Theatre: *The Colored Museum* by George C. Wolfe," *Theatre Journal* 44:3 (1992): 291–303.

34. bell hooks, "Performance Practice as a Site of Opposition," in *Let's Get It On: The Politics of Black Performance*, ed. Catherine Ugwu (Seattle, Wash.: Bay Press, 1995), 220.

16

The Costs of Re-Membering

What's at Stake in Gayl Jones's *Corregidora*

CHRISTINA E. SHARPE

Everything said in the beginning must be said better than in the beginning.[1]

Re-Membering Enslavement

On Sunday, 2 April 1995, the front page of the *New York Times* featured an article entitled "Bringing Slavery's Long Shadow to the Light." The sub-heading continued, "Blacks Seek Catharsis by Bringing Slavery's Long Shadow to the Light." This article focused on the work of some African Americans to remember the Middle Passage with ceremonies, rebirthings, and other performances in order to transform our individual and community relationships to the living memory of slavery:

> Within the last decade [the] . . . evolution of emotion has been experienced by a growing number of African-Americans, who have begun to re-examine slavery—reflecting upon it in film and music, remembering it through ritual and ceremony, assessing its legacy from universities to neighborhood study groups.[2]

While the article focuses on the fact of the legacy, the ceremonies actually focus on the performance of the legacy of enslavement through specific ritualistic rememberings. bell hooks locates this repetition of oppressive structures with a difference as part of a "strategy of re-enactment [that] has been at the core of African American performance practice."[3] I contend that performativity as a strategy of reenactment is crucial to understanding Gayl Jones's blues novel *Corregidora* as a text concerned with performing the legacies of enslavement. For, as Angela Davis notes, "The blues . . . marked the advent of a popular culture of performance, with the borders of performer and audience becoming increasingly differentiated."[4]

More specifically, *Corregidora* engages concerns of "race," African American collective trauma, and remembrance largely as problems of visuality, reproduction, and memory, which are compelled to be performed. Jones's *Corregidora* works at the tension between a desire for the disappearing nonreproductive performance and the monumental. The problematic of visuality is not a desire for increased visibility: I am not concerned with the multiplication of representations of black people in mainstream visual or textual economies. Rather, Jones and a text like *Corregidora* realize that only in the performance of the ways in which the descendants of enslaved people are constituted can particular traumas be realized and resisted. Jones is concerned with a life in which there is a decision to block the production of new generations in ways that are destructive for the descendants of slaves.

Corregidora is concerned with four generations of women, who struggle to make sense of the violence and traumatic effects of Brazilian enslavement. As we begin *Corregidora*, we are taken into the life and memory of Ursa Corregidora, a blues singer and the third generation of women descended from the Portuguese "slaveowner/whoremonger" Corregidora. Through Ursa's singing the blues within Jones's text, (non) reproductive possibilities are made possible. As Peggy Phelan argues in *Unmarked*, "Performance is the art form which most fully understands the generative possibilities of disappearance. Poised forever at the threshold of the present, performance enacts the productive appeal of the nonreproductive."[5] Part of the power and beauty of the blues performance is that it is transient and not monumental. It lives on in the memories of those who have witnessed it. When Ursa performs, she at first singles out a male member of the audience to sing to; she later reconfigures this and sings to and for a community of men and women, and this change is one way that nonreproductive witnessing is made possible by her blues performances.

The blues articulate the possibilities of nonreproductive remembering; a noncommodifiable working out of historical memory. Largely through rememory, Ursa Corregidora relates her experiences with her ex-husband, Mutt Thomas, her mother and grandmothers, and her (long dead) slave-owning ancestor, old man Corregidora. Through Ursa's life, we also enter into the lives of the previous generations of Corregidora women. From an early age, Ursa is immersed in the process of reproduction; she is told repeatedly that the Brazilian government destroyed the records of enslavement and that she must "make generations" to keep visible the horrors of slavery. In *Corregidora* and in the world, the absence of markers that corroborate memory, in combination with a corresponding emphasis on the visible, often makes women's reproductive bodies the site for reconstituting and reenacting racialized and gendered social and cultural histories. In the absence of Brazilian records of enslavement, the grandmothers insist on inscribing that history on and in their bodies. In their control, bearing witness ceases to be a dynamic activity:

the generations of daughters are supposed to tell the same stories uninf(l)ected by their lived lives. For Ursa, this unchanging same has been particularly devastating: she undergoes a hysterectomy, which makes it impossible for her to leave evidence in the ways that the ancestors demand.[6]

Ursa's performances of her familial histories offer up a space of possibility for re-membering relationships among the descendants of the formerly enslaved. Singing the blues bears witness in a way that disappears, that does not presume the stasis required by Gram's, Great Gram's, and Mama's definitions of "bearing witness." For Ursa and Jones, the blues offer a possible space of intervention: a performance that recedes as it appears. The blues become a guerrilla tactic—Ursa's sometimes oppositional, ever-changing performance against those transmitted oppressions.

Reproducing Poisoned Relationships

Corregidora insists on the necessity of rethinking our emphasis on particular kinds of embodied social memory as a visual marker of or way to witness historical events. It begins a revision of mononarratives of the flesh by attempting to locate remembering in song, rather than by further stigmatizing the body through the reproduction of particular historical moments, like enslavement. *Corregidora* is about overcoming remembering so well that one is consumed by the past.[7] Ursa Corregidora struggles to locate remembering outside of her body because, for the enslaved and the formerly enslaved, such memories have historically and insistently been located within and on the body—the "hieroglyphics of the flesh" during enslavement.[8] As Hortense Spillers writes, "We might well ask if [the] phenomenon of marking and branding actually 'transfers' from one generation to another, finding its various symbolic substitutions in an efficacy of meanings that repeat the initiating moments" (Spillers 67). For the image of branding used by Spillers, one may substitute rape or any other sort of trauma or rupture of the flesh and/or psyche, the intention of which is to produce prolonged and systemic effects. Jones examines the ways that traumas and oppressive structures are enacted upon and later internalized by the enslaved and their descendants and then enacted intraracially.

In *Corregidora*, the generations of women's insistence upon the photograph of Corregidora as the image of "whom to hate" and the process of keeping an unspecified *it* visible function in much the same ways that Spillers's branding describes. They are an insistence both on the possibility of making historical memory visible and on an unchanging notion of what that visible historical memory might look like. The picture of Corregidora that the women possess tells them "what evil look like" (*C* 12), and it does not look like them. For Ursa, initially, anger at being unable to reproduce is directed not at a particular black man or at the unchanging ubiquity of the mothers' stories but at the image of the distant Corregidora. Following Ursa's hysterectomy, Tadpole McCormick (owner of Happy's Bar, where Ursa sings, and her second husband) asks her if she hates "him." Ursa replies: "What my mama always told me is Ursa, you got to make generations. Something I've always grown up with." Tadpole initially says nothing and then insists, "I guess you hate *him* then, don't you?" (*C* 10; emphasis mine). Ursa intentionally (mis)reads the "him" as Corregidora and not Mutt and answers, "I don't even know the bastard" (*C* 10). She continues, stating that all that she has of "him" is a picture and the stories of Mama, Gram, and Great Gram. Their continued insistence upon the ubiquity of this image, the "picture" of whom to hate, is an insistence upon the misrecognition of what has previously been unspoken (intraracial hate and desire) by deferring to a monolithic idea of historical memory. It is also a cloaking of their problems, which functions as a means of keeping them in perpetual recurrence. Ursa says, "I don't even know the bastard" rather than "I didn't even know him," and her attempt to push this moment into the past is betrayed by the grammar of the sentence.[9] Moreover, Ursa does know old man Corregidora; she converses with him, visits with him in her dreams and nightmares; he is reconstituted within her and within all of her relationships. The interaction between Tadpole and Ursa displaces sexual violence onto a powerfully resonant image from the past and refuses fully to examine contemporary violence and silences between black women and black men. It is a refusal fully to examine the complications at stake in any discussion of power and desire. A possible intervention in and explication of inter- and intraracial violence, love, hate, and desire is deflected by deferring to the monolithic, albeit in a particular moment oppositional, historical imperative of hatred that was passed on to Ursa.

Thus, the women-headed households in *Corregidora* reproduce the mothers' stories in ways that anticipate a male gaze and the need to externalize trauma and render it accountable in the ways that counted for old man Corregidora and, therefore, for the women under his control. The generations of Corregidora women are called upon and call upon each other to redefine themselves as "womb-en."[10] A similar form of accounting occurs in some contemporary discussions about black male–black female relations. Often the text or subtext for intraracial conversations about race, conflicts about "black gender relations" (which usually means relations between heterosexual black men and black women) are frequently staged in the media whether the discussion is about the O. J. Simpson case or *Waiting to Exhale.*[11] The popularity of books like *How to Marry a Black Man: The Real Deal*, which includes commentary by black men who refer to black women as "womb-en" (and with younger generations of black women self-identifying as womb-en), makes the ideological and performative power of the reproductive increasingly visible.[12]

Consider Orlando Patterson's "Blacklash: The Crisis of Gender Relations among African Americans,"[13] an article that appeared in *Transition* twenty years after *Corregidora*'s publication. Patterson and Jones would agree that black people are performing relationships that began in enslavement. However, while *Corregidora* is a text that is about maternal/material reproduction of generations and mimetic reproduction of attitudes, it is also about sex and brutality and their many manifestations and possible alternatives; about translation (what is possible in the space between recollection and reenact-ment), transformation, and performance. In *Corregidora*, Jones addresses the cultural aphasia within black communities around sexuality and attempts a writing of it, its inter- and intraracial manifestations and reproductions. Patterson, too, is concerned with intraracial problems that are a legacy of enslavement—what he terms the "poisoned relationship" between black men and women (Patterson 26). Attempting to work through and work out this poison, or "contagion," as Jones's text does, is Ursa Corregidora. Patterson, however, specifically blames black feminists for obscuring "the problems of gender—which concerns *both* males and females in their relations with each other . . . to privilege the standpoint of women, on the assumption that they are always the victims of the interaction" (Patterson 7). Patterson contends that the "double burden" suffered by black women is, if not a myth, then a burden that has worked to their advantage: "Whereas the burdens of poor African-American men have always been oppressive, dispiriting, demoral-izing, and soul-killing, those of women have always been, at least partly, generative, empowering, and humanizing" (Patterson 11). For Patterson, "lower-class" black men's performances of race are, among other factors, enacted in opposition to black women.

Locating the Anita Hill–Clarence Thomas hearings as a watershed for black Americans, Patterson asserts that the hearings showed that black Americans were "integral" both because they framed "the most intimate problems of white men and women" in terms of "people who happen to be African American" and that they have initiated a "full recognition of this problem [the problematic relationship between black women and men]—and promot[ed] [it] to the top of the agenda of issues for dispassionate study, public discourse, and change" (Patterson 4, 26). After laying out the differ-ential effects of oppression on black women and men and locating the hearings in this fashion, Patterson reinscribes a patriarchal imperative in the need for marriage. Although he would not align himself with the Nation of Islam, he arrives at a point that converges with the rhetoric of the 1995 Million Man March and Day of Atonement: black men need to regain their rightful place. What these cultural articulations share is that they are contemporary per-formances of race, which attempt to control black women's representational and actual bodies and to reinstate patriarchy. These are performances that long for re-productive stasis (reproduction of patriarchy in the form of the dominant culture) in ways similar to the stories of Gram and Great Gram in *Corregidora*.[14]

What's at Stake?

In *Corregidora*, the absence (named in the text as the destruction of written records of slavery: "they burned all the slavery papers so it would be like they never had it" [*C* 9]) of visual evidence to inform Brazilian postemancipation social memory once again leaves only the formerly enslaved to bear witness.

What's at stake is the compulsion to repeat oppressive histories in order to keep them visible. *Corregidora* takes up the unspoken, often unknown, trauma or desire that complicates and structures our lives, that increases and reduplicates with every denial and with every repetition. Both the women and the men in Jones's text struggle under "particular historical and contemporary nightmares," which are legacies of slavery, while it is the Corregidora women who bear the ambiguous twin injunctions to "make generations to bear witness to the horrors of slavery" and to "keep *it* as *visible* as [the] blood" (*C* 22, 72; emphasis mine). We look for the written record to document enslavement and to reckon with the past. The slavery papers would function as a way to hold up irrefutable evidence; they are simultaneously a legal document and one that, for the formerly enslaved, acts as both iconic and textual proof that enslavement actually occurred. Lacking that public record, the mothers reproduce and Ursa sings in an attempt to remember without reproducing.

Particularly relevant to the repetition of spoken and unspoken trauma emphasized in *Corregidora* is the Tawana Brawley case. In 1987, Brawley, a fifteen-year-old African American girl, alleged that six white men—all of whom were public servants—sexually assaulted her, covered her in excrement, wrote obscenities on her, cut her hair, and abandoned her, covered in plastic garbage bags, in a vacant lot.[15] Sequestered and effectively silenced for "her own protection," Brawley's story was disseminated without the benefit of her body and voice. When Brawley's mother spoke about the effects on her daughter's body—the excremental writing, hair pulled out in clumps, and cigarette burns—she was discredited, and the trauma of Brawley's flesh became "alleged" trauma (Williams 171–172). Brawley, unlike Anita Hill four years later, did not break the silence; she did not speak publicly about inter- or intraracial silencing and sexual violence.

Under the "protection" of black men, who disclosed her story for her (and perhaps embellished it), Brawley became further entrenched in her silence.[16] What was at stake in hearing Brawley's story? What if her rearticulation of the events revealed that she was abused both by the white men (whom she accused) and by her black mother and stepfather (whom she did not accuse)?[17] What is at stake in admitting that black women often experience abuse in both interracial and intraracial contexts and that this abuse can and does occur concurrently and with equally devastating effects and repetitions? In *Corregidora*, under Mutt's "protection" in the form of financial support, Ursa would no longer sing the blues even though she sings them "because she has to." She would no longer be allowed the space of audience-performer participation and possible transformation, for which the performance and the performative allow. Analogously, the 1995 Million Man March asked for the silence of black women and their removal to the domestic as black men organized in order to regain their rightful place as patriarchs.[18] In each of these examples, the maintenance of hegemonic patriarchal structures took precedence over the possibility of working out the complications of sexual and racial violence.[19]

In order to get at these complications, Jones's text takes up intraracial violence in ways contrary to the Black Arts Movement's call for "positive images." Committed to the idea that things happen in process, Jones writes of specific situations that may or may not be antithetical to the experiences of "most" black people. For Jones:

> Sometimes politics . . . can also tell you what you cannot do, tell you what you must avoid, tell you that there's a certain territory politics won't allow you to enter, certain questions politics won't allow you to ask—in order to be "politically correct." I think sometimes you just have to be "wrong"; there's a lot of imaginative territory that you have to be "wrong" in order to enter.[20]

In this way, *Corregidora* is explicit about its repetitions, and it is often dismissed because what these repetitions perform is not what is generally expected or accepted in black communities. Jones is interested in complex characters and situations; she is concerned with the necessity of creating an environment within which things happen in process.

Despite her attention to complexity, Jones's nuanced depictions of sexual violence have been read and simplified by critics both as accommodating white audiences with more images of problematically sexual(ized) black women and as statements of how she thinks about black men and black heterosexual relationships.[21] Such readings accord Jones's fiction the status of nonfiction ethnography or autobiography and obscure her importance as a different voice in black women's writing. Asked to discuss positive race images, Jones asserts that such characterizations:

> are fine as long as they're very complex and interesting personalities. Right now I'm not sure how to reconcile the various things that interest me with "positive race images." It's important to me to be able to work with a range of personalities, as well as with a range within one personality.[22]

Jones is committed to foregrounding the obscured and unaccounted for. She most often writes about socially resistant characters who exist peripherally, if at all, in the works of many other African American women writers.[23]

The paucity of critical attention to Jones's work, particularly to *Corregidora*, attests to the fact that we continue to lack access to or have not invented concepts capable of conveying the historical and cultural complexities of sexual violence and the very vexedness of sex(uality) itself within and outside of African American communities. The blues encode pleasure and pain and exist as a marker of the possibility of what Jones calls *tenderness*. For Jones, "What comes out in my work, in those particular novels, is an emphasis on brutality. Something else is also suggested in them . . . namely the alternative to brutality, which is tenderness" (Tate 98). Many readers of *Corregidora* overlook this tenderness, which is so important to Jones. It is largely her complexly layered explorations of intraracial sexual violence and desire that have kept her writing at the margins of African American women's literature. Jones speaks to this when she says that English is inadequate because it uses:

one dimensional words to try to express multi-dimensional things. . . .
There are a lot of things that this language won't account for, that are
outside its perspective, you could say, that it doesn't have either the words
or the forms for. That's what we are all looking for—the words and the
forms to account for certain things we feel need to be accounted for.[24]

In *Corregidora*, although Ursa struggles for the language to speak what is
repressed, speech is ultimately unable to carry the weight that she wants it
to carry. Irene tells Ursa, "She ain't never known no Corregidora to behave
with just telling" (*C* 146–147). Ursa's speech is unable to enact repetitions
with a difference. Ursa discovers that telling alone is not a way through or
outside of the problems; indeed, often speech generates new problems. What
is ultimately at stake in the performance of these particular black female
bodies is the possibility for the exorcism of trauma to prevent further repetitions.

Working It Out

Corregidora begins with a narrative silence around the confrontation between
Ursa and her husband, Mutt. Initially recounting the encounter, Ursa says
simply, "That was when I fell" (*C* 4). Ursa's narrative silence around Mutt's
violent act is also her silence about her own desires, silence around her
participation in her current impasse of biological nonreproduction. What
the narrative does reveal is that an increasingly angry, jealous, and suspicious
Mutt plots to interrupt Ursa's blues performance and remove her from the
stage at Happy's Bar. Not only does Mutt threaten physically to remove Ursa
from the stage while she is singing, but he threatens to enact a part of their
collective past by holding a contemporary slave auction in order to "sell me
a piece a ass" (*C* 159).

A possibility for the exorcism of trauma through another traumatic encounter occurs in *Corregidora* in the interstices of the narrative around Mutt's
violent act (the scuffle between Mutt and Ursa at the top of the stairs).
Contrary to Patterson's reading of the ways in which women=victim in black
women's texts, Jones does not exempt her women characters from participation in oppressive desires. Ursa knows that, without this fall, she will
reproduce Corregidora. Indeed, it is Ursa's never-to-be-born child and the
space of her womb that are the loci of crisis and of possibility. The novel
maintains and relies on ambiguity around the violent incident that renders
Ursa unable to bear children. The result, however, is not ambiguous: Ursa
will produce no new descendants; through the fall, nonreproductive possibility is inscribed on her body. Without this inscription, she will become, as
Bruce Simon points out in an excellent reading of *Corregidora*, her foremothers, like Mama does, as she begins to divulge to Ursa the "terrible" private
memories of her relationship with Martin.[25] The unrealized, unborn child
who Ursa necessarily gives up in *Corregidora* is an absence in reproduction,

which makes possible the changes in the present generation. What is ensured is that the *particular* traumas connected to Corregidora will not be passed on to another generation. Ursa will, however, still be compelled to repeat these structures in her own relationships.

Discussing his plans for a slave auction with Ursa, Mutt and his family history collapse into the story of Corregidora, the slave-owning whoremonger (who fathered Ursa's grandmother and her mother), to create a Corregidora-like Mutt, who threatens to sell Ursa. The narrative space around Mutt's actions, however, allows the reader to complicate both his actions and Ursa's unspoken desires. Might they not be enacting the connections between their marriage and Corregidora's relationships with Ursa's female forebears, connections that Ursa and Mutt have been making consciously and unconsciously since they first began exchanging and re-membering family histories? One can only speculate what might have happened, what demons might have been exorcised and created, had Mutt performed this ritual of ownership. Perhaps he would not have thrown/pushed/otherwise caused Ursa to fall down that flight of stairs after she finished singing. His own staged performance might have offered them an alternative for working out the relations of power between them; nonetheless, Mutt would have had the patriarchal upper hand, which Ursa resists. Instead of relinquishing herself to Mutt's desire for control over her body and her relationship to the gaze of other men, Ursa increases the volume of the song she is singing, drowning out Mutt's shouts as he approaches the stage threateningly. Mutt contends that the men in the audience "mess with [Ursa with] they eyes." Ursa's insistent sexuality—"If it wasn't for your fucking I" (*C* 46)—and the triangulation of desire (Mutt watches the men watch Ursa sing; Ursa watches him and watches him watch the men watching her) become the context of her fall (*C* 4). After his outburst, Mutt is escorted from the bar; he hides, waits for Ursa, grabs her around the waist from behind, she struggles and . . . falls(?) down the stairs. Because of the great cost to the (possible) generations, Ursa insists on the power of the loss of her womb and her singing to work out difference; she attempts to establish an "I" (at least for the duration of the blues performance) to exert control over the productions of her body.

Prior to this, Ursa has begun to see the necessity of marking memory in ways that differ from her foremothers'. The hysterectomy necessitates a renegotiation of her relationship to her own and her female ancestors' pasts, and it is the product of a renegotiation that was already occurring. Prior to the hysterectomy, Ursa has begun to question whether her child would be like "her" or like "them." She transforms the necessity for bodily reproduction into another type of visual and aural production, saying, "Then let me give witness the only way I can. I'll make a fetus out of grounds of coffee to rub inside my eyes. When it's time to give witness I'll make a fetus out of grounds of coffee. I'll stain their hands" (*C* 54). The blues function as testimonials of sexual abuse, abusive relationships, a possible extrabodily site of transformation (of the body, but not on the body): "The blues . . . articulated a new valuation of individual emotional needs and desires" (Davis 5). In Ursa's dream, the grinds from the coffee produced on Corregidora's plantation (and the fertility of Great Gram, the "coffee bean woman") become a means of changing trauma into performance. As Elizabeth Alexander notes, witnessing is both aural and ocular.[26] The future of a black woman is performed: the possibility of a liberatory difference arises out of the repetition of some repressive force.

Keeping It Visible

Ursa maintains that her singing is life-affirming, something that she has to do in order to create a place for her eyes/*Is*. She says, the blues "helps me to explain what I can't explain" (*C* 56), and part of what she cannot explain are the changing roles and relationships between black women and men. Through singing, Ursa begins to move from her Gram's and Great Gram's juridically legislated truth of "no desire"—nonownership of their bodies and the labor (prostitution, childbirth) of their bodies—to her "truth" of an in-process, yet-to-be-articulated subjectivity. Her songs articulate the relatively new ability of black people to choose freely their sexual partners.[27] As other critics have noted, Ursa Corregidora signifies "bearing judgment," and she is called upon alternately to bear daughters to hold up evidence, to be a witness, and to give a verdict.[28] Her value inheres in biological reproduction while Gram and Great Gram were valued for turning their labor (fucking) and their desire (sexual) into gold. Great Gram was old man Corregidora's favorite enslaved woman, his "good little piece. Little gold piece" (*C* 10). Mutt becomes simultaneously the black male partner, absent black son, and a Corregidora stand-in. When Ursa asks her mother, Irene, if her grandmothers had other children, Mama replies, "I think there was some boys, but Corregidora sold the boys off" (*C* 61). Mutt is the strand that connects him and Corregidora, the thread between Ursa and her female ancestors, between Ursa and Corregidora, between Ursa and her father. Echoing all of the relationships, Mutt says to Ursa, "Your pussy's a little gold piece, ain't it Urs? My little gold piece" (*C* 60).

After the hysterectomy, she contends: "I can still feel your [Mutt's? old man Corregidora's? the mothers'?] fucking inside me. If it wasn't for your fucking I" (*C* 46). Through this articulation, Ursa seeks a space that is outside "the cycle of violence that gets passed on . . . as the grammar of love."[29] Jones creates the words and forms with an in-process language, which carries with it an internal conflict to contest objectification. Ursa insists on claiming her subjectivity as she moves within the latter sentence from sexual object to nascent subject.[30] The "fucking I" also plays on the visual: as the fucking I (subject) and the fucking eye (vision), Mutt's gaze appropriates Ursa's body and her sexuality for his pleasure, an appropriation that also occurs when Mutt sees Ursa looking at a photograph of the two of them. He asks, "Don't *we* look good?" (*C* 60; emphasis mine). Ursa remembers looking at the image of Mutt and herself, being seen by Mutt looking at it, and being embarrassed "because it was me I was looking at, not *us*" (*C* 60). While looking at herself, she is once again subjected to the male gaze—Mutt interrupts her contemplation of her own image and shifts the gaze with his query "Don't we look good?" Ursa later says that she would look at the picture when Mutt was not there, "I'd never look when Mutt was home" (*C* 60).

Mutt continually refers to Ursa's eyes saying that she looks tired and wears too much mascara. When Tadpole also talks about Ursa's eyes and expresses a desire to fall to the bottom of them, Ursa thinks, "Fall to the bottom of my eyes. What will you do there?" (*C* 56). Ursa's desires continually conflict with those of the people around her. Mutt says, "*Ain't even took my name. You ain't my woman*" (*C* 61). Mutt attempts to support Ursa, to control her body and, through it, the gazes of the men who comprise her audience, while she maintains that she is able to take care of herself. Mutt's attempts to control Ursa increase to the point that he does not even want the men who come into Happy's to look at her. Ursa says, "Last night you didn't wont nobody to say nothing to me, and tonight they can't even look at me" (*C* 155), an exchange that is echoed by Ursa after her hysterectomy, when Mutt is banned from Happy's. Ursa tells Tadpole half-jokingly, "Tell him that 'can't come in' means 'can't look in' either" (*C* 18). Mutt's desire to control Ursa and Ursa's desire also to exert control converge with Corregidora's beating and selling off black men for looking at "his" women and with her female forebears' exercising of their limited power.

Confronting herself in the mirror, Ursa discovers "for the first time" that she is as much a product of Mutt, Mutt's own history, her ancestors' history, and Corregidora as her mother, grandmother, and great-grandmother are products of Corregidora and their own unexplored (by the text) histories. It is through further examination of the picture on the mirror (which is also her looking at herself in the mirror) that Ursa recognizes herself as one of "them." She collapses herself, Mutt Thomas, Tadpole McCormick (her second husband), and her female ancestors into Corregidora in the ritualistic conversations that she stages with an imaginary old man Corregidora. No longer able to maintain that she knows what evil looks like, Ursa realizes that the "evil," which is in all of the women except Great Gram, is made visible through their "mixed blood"; Corregidora is literally running through their veins. Ursa says, "My veins are centuries meeting" (*C* 46). "Since race is thought to be 'carried' by blood . . . the history of slavery for African American women is also the history of rape" (Phelan 7). Running in Ursa's blood are the traces of interracial violence and the very present threat and enactment of intraracial violence. Tadpole's, Ursa's, and Mutt's immediate families and their larger diasporic (African, North American, and Brazilian) families are all infected with stories of incest and rape.

In *Corregidora*, the effects of that interracial trauma get worked out through the generations as intraracial sex/gender trauma. As the second generation born in North America (Irene was born in Louisiana), the first daughter whose father is not Corregidora, and the second daughter of a black man (presumably

Great Gram is the first), Ursa is marked as different from birth. Ursa, like Irene, is doubly Corregidora (her mother is daughter and granddaughter of Corregidora), and it is he of whom the grandmothers are so possessive. They also have internalized Corregidora's own anxiety about (the visibility of) race. When Ursa was born, she did not look like them. Irene tells her: "You come out bald-headed. . . . I knew they hated me then. Cause you come out all baldheaded. White skin before you got the little pigment you got now, and baldheaded. . . . I used to put a little ribbon on your head so people would know you was a girl" (*C* 117). Bald and white-skinned, Ursa signifies *male* to the mothers—Irene's union with a black man has reproduced the power structure (they think) that they sought to subvert.[31] And, like the photograph they keep of Corregidora to let them know "what evil look like" (*C* 12) and whom to hate, it is important for the women to be able to *see* with whom to align themselves. Ursa may make evident the horror of fulfilling their role of reproducing to bear witness outside of Brazil. Tadpole tells Ursa that she's "mixed up every which way" (nationally, racially, sexually). To which Ursa replies, angrily, that what is in her "she didn't put it there" (*C* 80).

The working out of the traces of enslavement in *Corregidora* takes place partially through the necessity and the vehemence of Ursa's racial explanations to Tadpole and others. They indicate a post-Brazilian enslavement shift in the significance of racial physiognomy and the meanings that attach to skin color and class position once the South American mulatto is transplanted to North America. They also indicate the repressed significance of these meanings in the North American context.[32] Ursa's hybridity contributes to the North American inability to solidly locate her in one race or ethnicity. (Consider the older black man in Detroit who wants to know Ursa's nationality, and Sal, the bartender at Happy's, who tells her that she can pass for Spanish.) In Brazil, there is a continuum of racial identification not an opposition of black-white. *Corregidora* is filled with confusions about the meanings of race in Brazil and in North America and confusions about what counts as strategies of resistance in each context. Infanticide is particularly powerful within the United States, while producing new generations resonates for descendants of Brazilian slavery. This shift, in turn, contributes to the collapsing of the boundaries between Ursa's reflections, her dreams of what she has been told about Corregidora, and what she experiences in her marriages to Mutt and Tadpole. Her two marriages are replete with the traces of her female ancestors' material and emotional relationships with Corregidora and with her husbands' relationships to and with their ancestors. The trace is not always visible (one cannot always see whom to hate), and it is not only Corregidora who is infected. Because of this, Ursa is often unable to differentiate which memories are "hers" and which are "theirs," where "she" begins and where "they" end. She says, "Stained with another's past as well as our own. Their past in my blood. I'm a blood. *Are you mine, Ursa, or theirs?*" (*C* 45). Mutt also recognizes Ursa's desire and ties to Corregidora when he says:

"You one of them," he said. . . .

"If you wasn't one of them you wouldn't like them mens watching after you."

"They don't watch after me, Mutt." (*C* 154)

Ursa's desire and Mutt's escalating violence enable a dialectic that otherwise might not have happened. It is Mutt and Ursa who successfully enact on Ursa's body the kind of violence that Corregidora only threatens to carry out on Gram and Great Gram. Paul Gilroy writes:

> In the context of a discussion of racial authenticity . . . some of the most powerful components of what we experience as racial identity are regularly and frequently drawn from deeply held gender identities, particular ideas about sexuality and a dogged belief that experiencing the conflict between men and women at a special pitch is itself expressive of racial difference. [33]

And while the events that surround her fall exceed representation, Ursa returns again and again to the moment of rupture, the *tone* of the "accident," the way that she *feels* about it; she names the sexual possessiveness, the abuse, and the desire—the desire that persists after and despite the rupture. Ursa thinks:

> I always get back to that. The tobacco fields or coffee ones. Hard because you have to be, but still those tender-eyed women and hands tender behind tobacco calluses with their men. Hurt you into tenderness finally. Is it more his fault than mine? (*C* 41)

The generations of women before Ursa want not only to reproduce a surplus of memory but also a lack. The move to keep visible the horror of enslavement entails an equal move to conceal the libidinal investments of the generations of women: insisting upon the visibility of certain memories also means insisting upon the invisibility of other memories. [34] If they produce generations that include males, memories cannot be transmitted in the same ways. Irene says that, once she was married, her mother and grandmother stopped telling her stories but continued to relate them to each other. "With him there they figured they didn't have to tell me no more, but what they didn't realize was they was telling Martin too" (*C* 128–129). What the women do not really seem to account for is the effect that their stories have on the men who are present and, in turn, on the women with whom they make relationships. Great Gram learned to speak and act like Corregidora, Ursa like Mutt (and her neighbor Cat). They no longer need Corregidora; the codes of the dominant culture are exercised by the family on itself in the absence of the representative of the oppressor. The absent presence of Corregidora and the evidence of the horrors of slavery, which are supposed to be reproduced through making generations, are already internalized and reproduced through the interactions of the women. They dedicate their lives to remembering bodies and power relations preserved from the Corregidora days as much as to remembering particular atrocities (and desires) attached to the experience of being enslaved by Corregidora.

The mothers tell Ursa:

> "They burned all the documents, Ursa, but they didn't burn what they put in their minds. We got to burn out what they put in our minds, like you burn out a wound. Except we got to keep what we need to bear witness. That scar that's left to bear witness. We got to keep it as visible as our blood." (*C* 72)

After her hysterectomy, Ursa is able to discern a difference between herself and her female ancestors. Her productions will not mark memory in the prescribed ways. She will never produce generations that bear witness for men. She has her singing and a visual marker of nonreproductive possibility.

The loss of her womb has produced a void in which Ursa transforms the memories that she was unable to manage before. With the exception of her brief, disastrous marriage to Tadpole, Ursa does initiate movement toward new definitions of making family and witnessing. She says that she feels as if "part of [her] life's already marked out for [her]—the barren part" (*C* 6). "In the analysis of the means of production the unmarked signals the un(re)productive" (Phelan 27). Following the hysterectomy, Ursa comes to consciousness, repeating the words "never her own to me," hungering for the memories that her female ancestors, her mother in particular, have denied her (*C* 102). She begins to conceive of her life in ways that will, among other things, allow her to ask and answer questions that her female ancestors were not allowed.

Ursa thinks, "But I *am* different now. . . . I have everything they had, except the generations. I can't make generations. And even if I still had my womb, even if that first baby had come—what would I have done then? Would I have kept it up? Would I have been like *her*, or *them*?" (*C* 60). In an effort to differentiate herself from "them," Ursa transforms the words forced into her by Gram and Great Gram into song and "sang it as they hummed it"; the possibility of biological reproduction forced out of her is produced in blues songs instead, a music that reflects the experiences of pain, pleasure, and possibility.

After her hysterectomy, Ursa does not sing until she acknowledges to Cat that she is worried about the tone of her voice. "They didn't say anything about my throat. They didn't say it did anything to my throat" (*C* 44). When Ursa sings, Cat tells her:

> "Your voice sounds a little strained, that's all. But if I hadn't heard you before, I wouldn't notice anything. I'd still be moved. Maybe even more, because it sounds like you been through something. Before it was beautiful too, but you sound like you been through more now." (*C* 44)

Ursa's need for witnessing is different after the hysterectomy, and her singing must register that difference. Tellingly, Ursa has not sung for herself, yet even after her sexual encounter with Jeffy, the fourteen-year-old girl who Cat looks after, she sings for Cat. That she does is even more significant for, until this point, performance in *Corregidora* is constructed for a male gaze and functions almost solely within a heterosexual reproductive economy. Ursa sings for Cat after Jeffy has fondled Ursa and after Ursa suspects that Cat (who is sixty) and Jeffy (who is fourteen) are involved in a sexual relationship.[35]

The songs that Ursa sings enact the distance between herself and her ancestors and displace the desires (the desire of Corregidora and the desire to judge) that she recognizes in the photograph of Mutt and her. She sings, "*O Mister who come to my house You do not come to visit You do not come to see me to visit You come to hear me sing with my thighs You come to see me open my door and sing with my thighs*" (*C* 66–67). Mister and master are interchangeable as Ursa experiences the effects of masculine desire in ways similar to her enslaved forebears. Song is both something that is forced into Ursa and something that is forced out of her—she sings because she must. "They squeezed Corregidora into me, and I sung back in return" (*C* 145). In the aftermath of the hysterectomy, Ursa restages her own initial articulate birth, "I came into the world complaining . . . full of teeth and memories" (*C* 102). She is reborn out of the place where her womb used to be. She also reconfigures her conception of *audience* and moves from the performance of singular desire to the possibility of a communal grappling with what is passed on. "It was as if I wanted them to see what he'd done, hear it. All those blues feelings. . . . I felt as if they could see my feelings somewhere in the bottom of my eyes" (*C* 50–51).

Working It Out (Again)

The text maintains a necessary ambiguity around whether Ursa was pushed, and despite this textual ambiguity and the shifting declarations around her "accident," readers often collapse the contradictions and maintain silences around them.[36] In other words, the complexity of agency in the decisive moment in Ursa's life (the "decision" not to reproduce) is signified by an omission. Ursa forgoes (willingly and unwillingly) the making of generations in order to create a rupture. Because she sees Corregidora in herself as well as in Mutt, she is enacting on her body and psyche the experiences that her grandmothers relate to her. She is forcing another possibility on herself outside of the necessity to make generations, which the Corregidora women impose on her life, exercising and exorcising a kind of power on and from herself through Mutt that males, particularly Corregidora (for whom Mutt is a proxy in Ursa's fantasy apprehension), and her grandmothers have wielded. Ursa makes it impossible for herself to fill the female role of reproducer of generations. Now that there is a rupture in the visible transmission of embodied historical memory, Ursa is able to transform her life, the past, and the family memory through performance. She does not want to own those things that have oppressed her.[37] She says, "Let no one pollute my music. I will dig out their temples. I will pluck out their eyes" (*C* 77).

Jones is primarily concerned with what Ursa is unable to ask her ancestors. She wants to ask Cat (and her ancestors): "What are you doing to the girl? [What did you do to me?] Two swollen plums for eyes. . . . What about when it comes to her time? Do you know what *I* mean?" (*C* 65). Ursa wants to question the insistent reproduction of generational desire and memory, which occludes any other subjectivity. Speculation leads Ursa to the memory of a time when:

> "Great Gram sat in the rocker. I was on her lap. She told the same story over and over again . . . and sometimes I'd see the sweat in her palms. . . . Once when she was talking, she started rubbing my thighs with her hands, and I could feel the sweat on my legs. Then she caught herself, and stopped, and held my waist again." (*C* 11)

It seems that Great Gram's desire is, at least in some ways, in her hands. This scene converges with a story that Great Gram relates to a five-year-old Ursa:

> "*{Corregidora's} wife was a skinny stuck-up little woman he got from over in Lisbon and he had her brought over here. He wouldn't sleep with her, so for five years I was sleeping with her and him. That was when I was from about thirteen to about eighteen. . . . But they had me sleeping with both of them.*" (*C* 13)

After hearing this story, Ursa asks her great-grandmother if she is telling the truth. Great Gram "*slapped me. 'When I'm telling you something don't you ever ask if I'm lying. Because they didn't want to leave no evidence of what they done'* " (*C* 14). This fear that aspects of their enslavement will not be believed is part of the reason that the grandmothers insist on leaving visual evidence. Through her repetition of the "fact" of the story, Great Gram continues to repress her own motives and desires, and sex with the master and the mistress becomes only something that was done to her, not something that she participated in (as much as an enslaved person can be said to participate in nonconsensual sexual acts).[38]

What is transmitted to Ursa is more than the text of the story. Great Gram also transmits desire in an instance where she bests Corregidora's wife, a white woman who "couldn't do a damn thing" (*C* 23). "She didn't give him nothing but a little sick rabbit that didn't live but to be a day old. So then he just stopped doing it" (*C* 23). Great Gram takes some pride in the fact that she is, before Corregidora's wife, the primary erotic object:

> "*{The wife} had some hot prongs she come after me with. . . . cause she knew he was getting his from me too. . . . He {Corregidora} grabbed her and knocked the prongs out of her hands and then he started beating her. That woman was black for days to come. After that he just kept her locked up in that bedroom.*" (*C* 172)

Corregidora beating his wife black renders her a sexual object; similarly, Martin, who is denied sexual access to Irene, repeatedly slaps her face until it is blackened: "he just kept slapping me all over my face, twisting me and slapping me all over my face. . . . I know I was going to be black and blue all over, it hurt so bad" (*C* 117). Thus, Corregidora locking his wife "up in that bedroom" means both locking her away (the fetishized) and locking her in for his sexual pleasure (the pornographic). We have read already that Corregidora prefers his women black. As the "coffee bean woman," Great Gram in particular has a libidinal investment in a kind of class-race stasis.

As stated earlier, Gram's and Great Gram's behaviors and the desires that inform them are passed on: Corregidora teaches Great Gram and Gram; they teach Irene and Martin; Great Gram, Gram, and Irene teach Ursa; and Ursa teaches Mutt and Tadpole and vice versa. They all are taught the importance of learning the codes of patriarchy and reproduction, which are, ultimately, important for their survival. (After all, Corregidora's wife dies because she isn't "good for anything.") As Ursa says, "I was made to touch my past at an early age. I found it on my mother's tiddies. In her milk" (*C* 77). Irene also speaks about the stories and their effect on Martin and her:

> "After he come they didn't talk to me about making generations anymore or about anything that happened with Corregidora, but Martin and me could hear them in there talking between theyselves. We'd be in the front room and they'd be back there in the bedroom, Great Gram telling Mama how Corregidora wouldn't let her see some man because he was too black." (*C* 123–124)

Martin is a "kind of satin-black" man (*C* 112), and while Irene's mothers are not primarily concerned with his "complexion" (Corregidora was dark-skinned himself and worried by the fact that he was confused for Creek Indian), they are concerned with "race" and his occupation as a counterman. Great Gram and Gram were taught that looking at black men can be dangerous, for the man and for them. Not only were the enslaved women on Corregidora's plantation punished for making love with and for conversing with enslaved black men, the men (husbands, fathers, lovers) and boys (sons, brothers, lovers) were sold off or killed. Taking on her mothers' voices, Irene relates a story of an enslaved man and woman who defend their right to make a family. The black woman castrates the slave master, and both she and her husband are caught. The enslaved man is castrated, and the woman is hung after being forced to watch her husband bleed to death. For the older Corregidora women, in the move from Brazil to Louisiana to Kentucky, there has been little room and, perhaps, little desire to reconfigure what they have come to know and experience as the always tenuous and dangerous relationships between black men and black women.

While black women's blues are often about sex and the production of desire, they are a performance of desire.[39] Ursa is paid for singing about desire, she is not producing a profit for her owner by another bodily performance of desire. The mothers and Mutt, however, fail to see a difference; Ursa's remuneration for singing the blues collapses the distinction of being "cultivated women," which the Corregidora women fight to maintain.[40] Her work also throws into abeyance Mutt's question: "what's a husband for?" if not to support his wife. It is for these reasons that Mutt and Ursa's female ancestors oppose Ursa's public performances. Tadpole is the exception because it is in his best interests for Ursa to sing—as the proprietor of Happy's, he profits from her performances. Indeed, the marriage between Ursa and Tadpole is her continued performance of the same problems on her body instead of through her songs. She has replaced Corregidora with Mutt and then with Tadpole, other men whose connections to Corregidora she will be compelled to overcome while she engages in a continuing ritualistic dialogue with old man Corregidora.

For Ursa, the process of reconfiguring her relationship to and with Mutt occurs after the hysterectomy. Coming to terms with the persistence of desire, longing, and trauma, she dreams that she births old man Corregidora:

> "*My belly was swollen and restless, and I lay without moving, gave birth without struggle. . . . I never saw what squatted between my knees. . . . Who are you? Who have I born? His hair was like white wings and we were united at birth.*" (*C* 77)

A struggle against the previously oppositional stance of her mothers must take place. The hysterectomy is necessary; successful biological reproduction would have initiated another generation united at birth to Corregidora. By the end of the text, Ursa is able to admit and begin to perform (in a sado-masochistic sense) the complications of her relationship with Mutt: desire is mixed in with hate, and they have similar family histories. Staged through the act of fellatio, "A moment of pleasure and excruciating pain at the same time, a moment of broken skin but not sexlessness, a moment that stops just before sexlessness, a moment that stops before it breaks the skin" (*C* 184), Ursa and Mutt perform the sexual ambiguity that the blues articulate, the crossing and the riding of the lines between pleasure and pain.

Corregidora begins and ends with nonreproductive, (potentially) violent acts encased in nonreproductive performances of a kind of sadomasochistic desire; the circumstances surrounding Ursa's hysterectomy and her performing fellatio.[41] For Michele Wallace:

> The relationship of the problems of visuality (who produces and reproduces vision) to popular culture and material culture and, ultimately, history is vital. We are in danger of getting wasted by ghosts . . . by effusions and visual traces that haunt us because we refuse to study them, to look them in the eye. (Wallace 344)

Corregidora is a text that takes up the profoundly discomfiting task of filling out and complicating the facts of enslavement by looking at the ghosts that haunt our stories and by enacting ritualistic rememberings which reanimate some of the conditions of enslavement.

1. Gayl Jones, *Corregidora* (1975; reprint, London: Camden, 1988), 54. All subsequent references to this text will be made parenthetically.

2. This article appeared on the front page of the *New York Times* with a photo caption that read, "African-Americans paying tribute to their ancestors who died on board the slave ships taking them to the Americas. The fifth annual ceremony of acknowledgment and healing was held last June at Coney Island." Charisse Jones, *New York Times* (2 Apr. 1995): 1, 43.

3. bell hooks, "Performance Practice as a Site of Opposition," in *Let's Get It On: The Politics of Black Performance,* ed. Catherine Ugwu (Seattle, Wash.: Bay Press, 1995), 214.

4. Angela Davis, *Blues Legacies and Black Feminism* (New York: Pantheon, 1998), 5. All subsequent references to this text will be made parenthetically.

5. Peggy Phelan, *Unmarked: The Politics of Performance* (New York: Routledge, 1993), 27. All subsequent references to this article will be made parenthetically.

6. Ursa acknowledges that included among the ancestors are old man Corregidora and her father Martin—the mothers make and leave evidence that they can see.

7. This is the struggle that Toni Morrison articulates in *Beloved* (1987) with the repetition of the phrase "this is not a story to pass on." *Beloved* and *Corregidora* are engaged in an intertextual conversation about the dangers of remembering so well that one is consumed by the past. As Jones's former editor and editor of *Corregidora*, Morrison is intimately acquainted with the text and the problems of memory and possession that it undertakes. That Morrison does not name Jones as her literary predecessor stems in part from the problem of mother-daughter relationships and inheritance, which both *Beloved* and *Corregidora* attempt to work through. For Morrison and Jones, the (literary) daughter makes the work of the (literary) mother possible but, as in *Corregidora*, that is not the trajectory of inheritance.

8. For a discussion of what Spillers calls "hieroglyphics of the flesh," see Hortense Spillers, "Mama's Baby, Papa's Maybe: An American Grammar Book," *Diacritics* (Summer 1987): 64–81.

9. This is a reference to Spillers.

10. See Amy L. Gottfried, "Angry Arts: Silence, Speech, and Song in Gayl Jones's *Corregidora*," *African American Review* 28, no. 4 (Winter 1994): 559–570.

11. Terry McMillan, *Waiting to Exhale* (New York: Washington Square Press, 1994).

12. Mrs. Monique Jellerette de Jongh and Mrs. Cassandra Marshall Cato-Lewis, *How to Marry a Black Man: The Real Deal* (New York: Doubleday, 1996).

13. Orlando Patterson, "Blacklash: The Crisis of Gender Relations among African Americans," *Transition* 62 (1995): 4–26. All subsequent references to this article will be made parenthetically.

14. They also seek to become monumental rather than performative.

15. Patricia Williams notes, "The white men she implicated included the district attorney of Wappinger Falls, a highway patrolman, and a local police officer." She also says that the Reverend Al Sharpton took Brawley into hiding "soon after the police officer she had implicated in her rape committed suicide" (*The Alchemy of Race and Rights* [Cambridge Mass.: Harvard.: University Press, 1991], 171–172).

16. After being silenced by Sharpton and Attorney Alton Maddox, Brawley later joined the Nation of Islam and was further silenced.

17. In fact, Brawley's mother and stepfather were suspects. My point, however, is that these accusations were to the exclusion of the six white men whom Brawley did accuse.

18. "I pledge from this day forward I will never abuse my wife by striking her, disrespecting her, for she is the mother of my children and the producer of my future." Excerpted from the Million Man March Pledge, last revised 7 May 1997. See www.igc.apc.org/africanam/hot; shpledge.html.

19. For further discussion of this, see Michele Wallace, " 'Why Are There No Great Black Artists?' The Problem of Visuality in African American Culture," in *Black Popular Culture*, ed. Gina Dent (Seattle, Wash.: Bay Press, 1992), 333–346. All subsequent references to this text will be made parenthetically.

20. Gayl Jones, "About My Work," in *Black Women Writers,* ed. Mari Evans (London: Pluto, 1985), 233–235. All subsequent references to this text will be made parenthetically.

21. Jerry Ward, Jr. "Escape from Trublem: The Fiction of Gayl Jones," in Evans 249–258, is an example of this sort of criticism. He writes, "Ursa Corregidora begins with the end of her first marriage, and she ends with a description of the vindictive sexual act that makes reconciliation with her first husband possible" (253). And

> Ursa is imbued with this primitive belief in the duty of a Black woman, connected as it is to a circumscribed vision of women's possible development. Ursa never rebels, never seeks alternatives, never breaks free of the constrictive role ordained by others. (253)

The act that reconciles Mutt and Ursa is fellatio—perhaps an unsatisfactory ending but not vindictive. Ursa does seek alternatives through singing and through her participation in the end of her ability to reproduce biologically.

22. Claudia Tate, "Gayl Jones," in *Black Women Writers at Work*, ed. Claudia Tate (New York: Continuum, 1984), 89–99. All subsequent references to this text will be made parenthetically. In relation to the things that she now allows herself to write, Jones says:

> I find myself wanting to back away from some questions. I don't know why. Maybe there's still that feeling that I don't want to analyze things too closely. I should mention that the male characters in those early novels are unfortunate, like the sexual theme—in this society that looks for things to support stereotypes. I'd like to be free of that. I used to think one could be.
>
> Actually, when I wrote those stories I didn't do much thinking about the stories. I just wrote them. Now I do more thinking about the stories and make extensive notes so I can talk about them better. I mean I can talk about them better because they were thought out in a way the others weren't. But it also means that I could write many kinds of stories that I can't write now, and I guess it works the other way too.

Charles Rowell, "An Interview with Gayl Jones," *Callaloo* 16 (Oct. 1982): 32–53.

23. Dorothy West's *The Living Is Easy* (1948), Zora Neale Hurston's *Their Eyes Were Watching God* (1937), Ann Petry's *The Street* (1946), Toni Morrison's *Sula* (1973), and Terry McMillan's *Mama* (1987) are examples of texts concerned with the lives of "marginal" black women.

24. Michael Harper, "Interview with Gayl Jones," in *Chant of Saints: A Gathering of Afro-American Literature, Art and Scholarship*, ed. Michael S. Harper and Robert Stepto (Urbana: University of Illinois Press, 1979), 366.

25. Bruce Simon, "Traumatic Repetition: Gayl Jones's *Corregidora*," in *Race Consciousness: African-American Studies for the New Century*, ed. Judith Jackson Fossett and Jeffrey A. Tucker (New York: New York University Press, 1997), 93–112. See also Gottfried 559–570.

26. Elizabeth Alexander, " 'Can You Be Black and Look at This?': Reading the Rodney King Video," in *Black Male: Representations of Masculinity in Contemporary American Art*, ed. Thelma Golden (New York: Whitney Museum of Art, 1994), 91–111.

27. As Angela Davis writes, "Blues registered sexuality as a tangible expression of freedom" (8).

28. *Ursa* is the constellation of the bear and *corregidor* means "to judge" in Portuguese. *Bear judgment* can mean "to give birth to it, produce it." It can also mean "to be marked by judgment or to carry a judgment." See Melvin Dixon, "Singing a Deep Song: Language as Evidence in the Novels of Gayl Jones," in Evans 236–248.

29. Gina Dent, "Black Pleasure, Black Joy: An Introduction," in her *Black Popular Culture*, 1–19.

30. In the grammar of this sentence, *me* is the object, and *I* also occupies the object position, although it uses the subject pronoun. Ursa is attempting to shift the particular "grammar of love" that she has learned.

31. This is a zeugma. They think that Irene has reproduced the power structure, and they think that they have tried to subvert the power structure.

32. Tadpole tells Ursa about his white grandmother, who was raised by his black grandfather until she was old enough for him to marry her. Tadpole says:

> "My grandmother was white. . . . She was an orphan and they had her working out in the fields along with the blacks and treated her like she was one. She was a little girl about nine, ten, 'leven. My granddaddy took her in and raised her and when she got old enough he married her. She called him Papa. And when they were married she still called him Papa."

Ursa replies, "Maybe I should ask you how you were taught to feel" (13).

33. Paul Gilroy, *The Black Atlantic: Modernity and Double Consciousness* (Cambridge, Mass.: Harvard University Press, 1993), 201–202. All subsequent references to this text will be made parenthetically.

34. Ursa (in relation to both Jeffy and Vivian, the young woman with whom Tadpole takes up) is in the role of experiencing, in regard to her family history, the role that is emptied of power. She occupies the place of Corregidora's white wife over whom her great-grandmother enjoyed some semblance of power. The very sites from which her grandmothers were able to exercise a limited amount of power, because their sex(uality) was productive for Corregidora, are now used against Ursa. This may be part of the reason the mothers are adamant about making generations: it not only empowers them through some sort of future claim to justice, but it empowered them in their relation to Corregidora's wife and her inability to produce children, desire, or a profit for Corregidora. Concentrating on making visible generations involves a move to repress whatever power the women exercised from a place seemingly emptied of power.

35. Another example of what is discomfiting about *Corregidora*: no one escapes the compulsion to repeat. Lesbianism is not an idyllic state (nor is Jones expressly homophobic); the relationship between Cat and Jeffy echoes the relationship between Cat and her white employers and between Corregidora and Gram and Great Gram.

36. See Ann DuCille, "Phallus(ies) of Interpretation: Toward Engendering the Black Critical 'I'," *Callaloo* 16, no. 3 (1993): 559–573. See also Gottfried 559–570; Keith Byerman, "Beyond Realism: The Fictions of Gayl Jones and Toni Morrison," in *Fingering the Jagged Grain*, ed. Keith Byerman (Athens: University of Georgia, 1985): 171–216; and Dixon 236–248. Dixon, however, does note that Mutt breaks the connection with the womb through this act.

37. Similarly, Ursa has no desire to occupy the house that she lived in with her mothers. Nor does she want the china cabinet that she believes must have come from Brazil. The cabinet contained things that she never saw used: "The only time it was opened was to be dusted or polished." Like Great Gram herself, "it was an expensive dark mahogany thing, the best thing we had in the house" (*C* 123).

38. Within an untenable situation, there are still a range of options open to Great Gram, and she chooses to exploit her sexual power in the ways that are available to her.

39. Madhu Dubey writes that the blues was one of the first places that black women could speak of themselves as sexual subjects. Dubey, "Gayl Jones and the Matrilineal Metaphor of Tradition," *Signs* 20 (Winter 1995): 245–267.

40. Of her "class," Great Gram says, Corregidora "called hisself cultivating us, and then didn't send nothing but cultivated mens into us" (*C* 124). However, as Bruce Simon points out, this is actually Irene speaking as if possessed by Gram and Great Gram.

41. Mae G. Henderson has a provocative article, "The Stories of O(Dessa): Stories of Complicity and Resistance," in *Female Subjects in Black and White: Race, Psychoanalysis, Feminism*, ed. Elizabeth Abel, Barbara Christian, and Helene Moglen (Los Angeles: University of California Press, 1997), 285–304. However, Henderson wants to settle the question of chattel slavery and sadomasochistic desire by reading Sherley Anne Williams's *Dessa Rose* (1986) against Pauline Réage's *Story of O* (1954 France, 1965 U.S.) and other accounts of sexual slavery. What Henderson does not allow for is the condition, like in *Corregidora*, where (chattel) sexual slavery constitutes the enslaved's social rank and social/sexual desire. Outside of that system, sadomasochistic desire might be a place from which to exercise power and to exorcise it through the repetition of particular power relations.

Part V

Roundtable Discussion with
Senior Scholars

17

African American Theater

The State of the Profession, Past, Present, and Future

Roundtable discussion edited by
HARRY J. ELAM, JR., & DAVID KRASNER

Panelists:

H. E.	Harry J. Elam
D. K.	David Krasner
J. H.	James V. Hatch
S. R.	Sandra L. Richards
M. W.	Margaret B. Wilkerson

Panel presented at the Association for Theater in Higher Education Conference, 7 August 1997, Chicago.

D. K.: Welcome to African American Theater: The State of the Profession, Past, Present, and Future. Two years ago, Professor Harry Elam and I met in San Francisco at the ATHE conference with the possibility of forming this panel. We had been attending many performance and theater conventions, and there were many state-of-the-profession panels. While these panels were interesting, they were white: they were about white theater and white issues, although they passed themselves off as "universal." We have asked several scholars to be on this panel because they are ground-breaking teachers and researchers; they have made it possible for research and scholarship to flourish.

H. E.: The first question: "In the 1920s, black theater critics, such as Theophilus Lewis and J. A. Jackson, felt it was part of their mission as critics to further and support the development of black theater. In the 1960s, critics such as Larry Neal not only commented on the Black Arts Movement, they were part of the movement themselves. Consider and discuss the role of the critic and scholar of black theater. How has his or her role in relationship to the practice of black theater evolved? Consider the position of the scholar/

critic today: Does the scholar/critic today still have a duty to serve black theater? Why or why not?"

S. R.: It seems to me that unstated in this series of questions is the fact that the location of the black theater critic has shifted to a certain extent. That is, whereas Theophilus Lewis or J. A. Jackson were writing for newspapers in the '20s, today we have a cadre, a small cadre, perhaps, of critic/scholars, like ourselves, who spend a good deal of time attending to the demands of institutions that place relatively little value on black theatrical production.

I'm not quite sure that I know what you mean by "serve black theater," but I suppose on one level I would say that, if I see black theater as my primary research interest, then out of sheer self-interest, I want to see that theater flourish and so need to be active in trying to help that happen. That's perhaps the easy part of the question.

Also related to this question is the issue of audience: to whom should the black theater critic be speaking? The answer to that varies: some of us, perhaps, are better equipped to write, to speak, to a more general public of readers of newspapers and popular magazines like, perhaps, *Emerge, Essence,* or *Black Masks*, and certainly some of us need to be writing in academic venues like *Theatre Journal, TDR,* or *Transition* in order to contribute to, disrupt, or intervene in dominant discourses, particularly now that the academy is devoting some attention to race, some attention to the constitution of whiteness or to issues of postcoloniality.

Whether directed to a general or a specialized public, both critics and types of critical writing are important, first of all, because they document production, so that current and future generations know that we have been here and we've produced. They have some record of what has happened. Also, it seems to me that the critics in both places offer readers and spectators a vocabulary with which to begin to evaluate those productions.

Finally, I would offer at least one other way in which we can "serve black theater" and that's by dramaturgy. After all, we're trained as scholars, so presumably we have research skills that theater companies often do not possess, because they're busy just simply trying to get the production mounted. So we may be able to bring more historical depth and conceptual rigor to a given production.

M. W.: Sandra has spoken well about the scholar as critic, and I just wanted to focus on the role of the newspaper critic, because I've often been troubled by the role that critic plays. I worry that if we do not address the issues of the critic—that is, the newspaper critic and reviewer—then we stand in danger of losing the importance of much of our black theater production that is done, because the failure to cover and to review certain works certainly has a detrimental effect on the production of black theater.

The critic of black theater in particular needs to be very much aware of the contents and the purpose of theater, of what that theater attempts to do, the arguments that it attempts to address. That has to be taken into consideration regardless of the racial background or experience of the critic.

Too often, black theater is reviewed on premises that it does not set for itself, and that's a very unfair way and a very abusive way to look at the work. The critics' role is a role of illuminating the work rather than determining whether it's good, bad, or indifferent. You seek to get inside the work and to understand and to explore it. If you can't get inside of the work and can't illuminate it, then there's no sense in doing it. The critic has the responsibility to reflect and to understand an audience's response.

When I was writing my dissertation, I was reading a review by a critic of a production in Los Angeles—it was about Angela Davis—and the newspaper critic really panned it, and then made a little statement at the end that he seemed to be at odds with the audience, which treated it as if it were a football game. I realized that that critic had missed an opportunity to really try to understand what it was that the audience found so exciting about this work.

We need to examine the role of the critic, particularly the reviewer of live productions, so that we can be in a position to "serve" and to encourage and support the development of black theater.

J. H.: A word about African American critics and their newspaper criticism. The critics for any oppressed group rarely air the group's dirty laundry. If they do, as Stanley Crouch has done in the *Village Voice*, they are roundly abused. All too often, no matter what a critic might not like in a production, he'll praise what he saw, and he does it for the reasons that Margaret spoke about.

In the 1920s, Tony Langston of the *Chicago Defender* and Romeo Dougherty of the *Amsterdam News* gossiped; they knew all the performers on a first-name basis. They knew who was out of town and where they were. Their columns were chatty rather than what we call criticism because theater was a very small world.

Sylvester Russell, James A. Jackson, and Theophilus Lewis are the great exceptions: Lewis had the language, the skills, the vision to set forth what he thought a theater should be, and periodically he would put it down and then say, "Well, this group has made a beginning" and "That group is a start, but we have to do these things." In other words, his chastisement would be general, but his praise, when it came, would be specific. If he criticized Eulalie Spence, he would say something nice about her sister. Lewis tore into white playwrights; he had no problems with it, and he had the wit to do it. Lewis promoted not only art theaters like Krigwa, but he also praised the girlie shows and the low comedians at the Lincoln Theatre because he knew very well the tastes of the "common people"; he knew where the folk roots grew.

To bring criticism into the more modern time, Joe Papp formed his black repertory and Hispanic company in the early '70s; it was roundly criticized by the white critics, partly because of diction and accent: "In *Julius Caesar*, how can we believe that these are citizens of Rome when they're speaking in all these different accents?" Puerto Rican, Dominican, urban black, and southern? The white critics, Walter Kerr and others, were so vicious that, after two shows, *Julius Caesar* and *Coriolanus*, the company closed.

The black critics saw the Shakespeare experiment in different perspective. When Errol Hill placed the company's Shakespearean performances into the context of a movement toward equality, the accent issue became much less of a problem. Loften Mitchell, who wrote regularly for the *Amsterdam News*, found much to praise in the actors, but finally, at the end, he said the diction was horrendous. Now, that is a pioneer remark of a kind.

We don't get helpful criticism from black newspaper critics because the theater is a small world full of vendettas. If you say a bad word publicly about someone, it's never forgotten. The white critics will seize upon it. Therefore, we have to turn to Larry Neal and Theophilus Lewis to find a theoretical and critical view of theater.

D. K.: Next question: "Contemporary African American literary criticism has been much concerned with ideas of essentialism versus constructionism. Essentialists argue that there are certain essential truths of black identity; constructivists suggest that blackness is culturally, politically, and historically constructed with each context of its use. Consider how concerns over essentialism and constructivism affect your work and analysis of black theater history and performance. How does the changing concept of race influence our understanding of the evolution of black theater? Should we dismiss certain periods of black theater practice or certain plays for their essentialism?"

J. H.: I'd like to reinterpret and rephrase the question: "Is there a black aesthetic?" This was a big item in the '60s, particularly among African American artists. Vivian Browne, a black painter, said, "Black art is anything painted by a black painter," and that was a very easy way to deal with it, but it satisfied almost no one. What lies behind the question is more important, and that is racism. If there were no racism, the question wouldn't be discussed to any great extent. There would be questions of form and content, romanticism versus classicism, and a raising of all the questions that you recognize as traditional inquiries into art and theater.

But those questions are often dismissed in favor of the large one, often asked by the culture cops: "Is there a black aesthetic, and does this play conform to it?" And most critical: "How is it different from European?" In the American Negro Theatre's preamble to its constitution, Abram Hill wrote that the Negro had some special contributions to give to America, and he lists one: "rhythm." Now, you know that the word *rhythm* is a word that can trip a white critic; if it's the right day and the right person, yes, "We got rhythm, we've got more than whitey's got," and if it's the wrong person on the wrong day, "You think all black people can do is dance and play basketball?" Or, "You calling me a jungle bunny?" Many of the answers one might bring to the question "Is there a black aesthetic?" are double binds.

The Colored Museum. Remember the scene where the middle-class man is trying to trash the Temptations' recording of "My Girl," and the song climbs back out of the trash to him? That's a wonderful illustration of class discrimination. And this question revolves around class distinction. During the '60s, "street" was the blackest black. Language and attitude to be black had to be street black. It was a revenge of the young artists against their teachers and parents, who they accused of wanting to be white.

Do these attitudes affect me when I write? Yes, they do. When I write, I look over my shoulder all the time to see "who am I likely to offend?" I don't like to do that, and I shouldn't do it, but I do it almost unconsciously.

M. W.: I had more difficulty with this question than any other, because if I examine my own approach to understanding black theater, I've always been aware of the ways in which race is a social construction. You can see it reflected in the ways in which black theater artists have responded down through the years, initially, in response to the stereotyping of African Americans. African American playwrights, in depicting any particular character on stage, brought with them the historical and racial baggage that an audience might bring, regardless of whether the audience was black or white or any other color. When Hansberry puts Lena Younger, for example, on the stage, she's aware that she will be seen, for example, within the context of the black mammy, of being very domineering, and being the head of the household, despite the fact that that family has had a male head of the household until very recently in the family history. Thus, the black writer writes with an understanding, an awareness, of the fact that that audience is going to see the mammy specter in the midst of their play. Therefore, part of the challenge of the writer is somehow to reveal the humanity, the truth, the energy, and the complexity that emerges from a stereotype.

One could argue that almost any writer thinks of that, but the African American writer thinks of it particularly because of the tremendous demonization of African Americans through history. You're dealing with different demonizations now. In the early part of the twentieth century, it was the assumption that African American men were cowardly, and if you look at the early materials on some of the black boxers, the earliest ones coming along even before "The Great White Hope," the newspaper critics wrote and questioned whether or not the black male boxer would have the courage to stay in the ring, whether he would be termed "yellow." Jack London actually wrote an article like that in the early part of the twentieth century. We aren't dealing with that particular stereotyping now, but it's something even more insidious, so that it seems clear to me that race is a social construction. Though it changes as we go through history, it doesn't make it any less dangerous. It could be, in fact, more dangerous, perhaps.

S. R.: Just a little comment: Black Nationalists, like Amiri Baraka, Ron Karenga, and Ed Bullins, can be accused of being essentialists in terms of the '60s, but what's interesting is that "black" was used in two ways. One was an ontological category, the second, a performative category, so that Baraka spends a good deal of time castigating certain black people for not being black—i.e., for not performing or acting in certain ways. "Black" encompasses a presumption of a certain inherent quality, an essentialism, but even more so, a performative quality, that in order to be black, you had to do x, y, and z. We could say that there was certainly an authoritarian dimension to the definition of blackness and black art, but nonetheless some of our critics have given the '60s a bad rap in ways that are undeserved.

H. E.: Your comments have made me think of the movie *Cotton Comes to Harlem*. We saw it way back then, and the guy stands up, and he asks the audience full of black people, "Am I black enough for you?"

D. K.: Along these lines, there was the battle in the 1920s between Charles Gilpin and Eugene O'Neill for the construction of the character of Brutus Jones. Gilpin felt that "O'Neill, he just wrote the role. I understand it, I know it, and I therefore can change the text." Gilpin changed the words to be appropriate to particular audiences, depending upon whether the audience was largely black or largely white. He would adapt and improvise, which eventually led to his firing.

H. E.: Moving to question three, "As evidenced at NCAAT—which is the National Conference of African American Theater—in April of this year, the subject of a black theater canon became a heated topic. So, for the panel, should there be a black theater canon? How would it be determined? Who would choose the works? Would it include works from all over the African diaspora? What purpose would a canon serve?"

M. W.: I am absolutely against [canon formation]. I am against the reasons that were given to me for doing that—that, in developing white institutions, canons are very important, and one of the reasons why black theater is not acceptable is that we have not put forth a canon of our greatest works and so forth, and that in order really to be accepted, we need to do this.

It doesn't really serve the purposes that we should seek to serve, and that is to encourage and develop the best of black theater. The minute you form a canon, you immediately define out of the canon certain works and certain people and certain things. I really feel that a canon does not serve a good purpose for us.

S. R.: Margaret, I would want to ask, what do you teach when you teach a course in African American theater? Do you, in effect, teach a canon? Are there certain plays that just simply have to be there?

M. W.: It depends on what you are trying to get your students to understand about theater, and it's not necessarily that there are certain plays that must be there. There may be plays that you like particularly or that you feel an affinity for, and you should confess that.

S. R.: And what would you include?

M. W.: It's difficult for me to do that, because I'd have to sit down and really think through, "What is it that I'm trying to accomplish in this course, and which plays would allow me to do that?" I did do a course, the most recent course I developed, which was one for an American culture requirement at Berkeley, and you're required to include works by particular cultural groups or underrepresented groups, and I chose four of the following: Euro-Americans, African Americans, Latinos, and Asian Americans. These are freshmen and sophomores.

I titled the course Theater and Cultural Identity. The pieces that I chose were based around those issues. I also chose those that I found to be most accessible in this initial course. I taught it once, and it was a very exciting course for me to teach. From what I gather from the students, it was exciting for them, too.

H. E: Sandra, are you suggesting that a black canon is implicit?

S. R.: Yes. Particularly in choosing to offer an introductory course in African American theater. I guess I would hesitate if I never mentioned, for example, Lorraine Hansberry, because I would be embarrassed and feel that I had done the student a disservice if a student took my course and had no idea who she was. But I certainly do agree with Margaret, I mean, that very often what we don't admit about canons, or haven't up until recently, was that canons are ways supposedly of preserving the past. But we preserve the past in relationship to some sense of where we are in the present and where we want to be in future, so in effect I would be operating within a version of Margaret's comments about context.

I have certain ideas that I would want to offer, certain narratives that I would want to offer, about black cultural production seen through theater; thus, in a certain sense, I construct a canon in teaching a course. But I would hope to transmit ideas in such a way that there's a variety in the course, so that the texts are in dialogue with each other and perhaps at times quarreling with each other.

What I've done in some of my classes is to ask students, "Okay, well, we've got this narrative, how is this narrative produced, and what questions doesn't it allow us to ask? What might be missing?" as a way to try to get them to think, "Well, for every story I've been told, there are certain facts or elements that have been suppressed; I need to look at what's being omitted." I try to challenge them in this way so that they begin to think how ideology operates, that is, by defining parameters and naturalizing them so that certain questions become virtually unthinkable or completely disallowed.

H. E.: Jim, you've created a book that I've used and added to Margaret's class, which could be called, in effect, a black canon. Where do you weigh in on this?

J. H.: The book, *Black Theater USA*, is twenty years old, and in 1974 there was no other comprehensive anthology. So, by circumstance, our book became the standard. As regards the canon, let me speak about our experience at NCAAT in Baltimore this year [1997], where we meet annually to discuss black theater issues. This year, three members were charged with coming up with the black theater canon. But, instead, we circumvented it; we kind of cheated. What we did was declare there would not be a canon but there would be a list of thirty plays (no musicals) that anyone who claimed to be familiar with African American theater should have read. Then we said, "The list should be historical from the beginning to the end. It should represent all kinds of views and styles."

Very quickly, we ended up with thirty; there was some horse trading: "If you'll take this, I'll take that out." But the whole thing happened in an hour, and everyone went away relatively content because we didn't say, *"This is it."* Instead, we said, here are thirty plays that will make you knowledgeable. And the reason that we did it was exactly what Sandra was saying: schoolteachers keep asking, "Which plays should I teach?" Well, here are thirty. Pick some.

D. K.: The next question, the issue of binary structuring, emerged from Samuel Hay's book, *African American Theatre History: An Historical and Critical Analysis* (1994). "While some have argued that the fundamental attributes of African American theater are produced either from the Du Bois tradition of art as propaganda or the Locke tradition of folk art, others say that this binary structuring narrows the frame of African American theater. Is the Locke/Du Bois binary broad enough to accommodate an array of styles, genres, and theatrical functions? Is there room for an alternative position outside this binary?"

J. H.: Art versus propaganda. Humphrey Bogart said, "If you want to send a message, send a telegram." It's an old argument. Ron Karenga said, "All art is propaganda," and, in a very real sense, it is. Take a Camille Billops sculpture, for example. If she manages to get it in the Museum of Modern Art, it is moved up in class and is propaganda for that class; if she gets it in the Met, her sculpture then says, "This is no longer a craft. This is fine art." That is propaganda, too. So I think that's what Karenga must have meant.

S. R.: It seems to me that the historical record does not support this binarism. I think of plays like Georgia Douglas Johnson's *Sunday Morning in the South* or *Blue Eyed Black Boy*. Are they folk plays? Propaganda plays? We know that Locke wrote that he supported Angelina Grimke's *Rachel*, and then later on when it was done before the NAACP, it caused a big controversy, a controversy over art versus propaganda, so that Locke's position evolved over time.

So the question that I would want to ask Sam Hay is, "Why do we want to reify one point in Locke's thinking?" If you also look at, I think, some of the women who were playwrights in the 1920s who were considered to have written "folk plays," they studied with Locke and they were produced by Du Bois, so what does that say about this supposed binarism? We certainly can note that the debate occurred, that these two important figures had different points of view on it, but that those points of view were not all so far apart.

H. E.: The subject of pedagogy: "The issues of race, class, and gender are not mutually exclusive. How are we to understand and teach black theater in such a way that students understand the linkages and interactions among race, class, and gender? What strategies have you found useful?"

J. H.: I would not start with *A Raisin in the Sun* because, if you're going to deal with race, class, and gender, Lorraine Hansberry has dealt with all three of them simultaneously, and you want to start with something that is easier for beginning students to see. Start with some 1920s one-acts by women, where they have the very simple point of view "Lynching is bad" or whatever it is, and it's very clear and it's very direct and it's very short.

Ralph Ellison said, "Change the joke and slip the yoke." That concept applied to a play could be "change the gender and slip the play." Substitute a woman for a male, or a wife for a husband, and so on. Or you can reverse the race, if you like, but gender is the key. Pretty soon, it becomes quite clear what the author intended and how absurd it is if you change the gender of it and then how absurd it is if you leave the gender as it is. It's a way of distancing students from the material so one may have a discussion of gender or race that is truly helpful.

The only way that I've found to teach performance history that has no literary text and where the performance cannot be reenacted is to send the students to the newspapers of the 1920s, the *Amsterdam News, Chicago Defender, Pittsburgh Courier*, and tell them to read three months of ads and cabaret reviews. You give them a report form to turn in [*group laughter*]. They come back with a whole different understanding of what the 1920s theater business was about, and it wasn't the literary plays of Krigwa.

D. K.: "Henry Louis Gates's essay on the Chitlin Circuit [see chap. 7] has increased awareness of black theater that is neither mainstream nor highbrow, but appealing to the masses; it is a theater attentive to issues attached to local concerns and not necessarily to traditional Western aesthetic values of drama. Do you teach in your courses about the Chitlin Circuit, and should black theater courses discuss this theater that is truly—or perhaps—'by, for, and about black people'? Why or why not?"

M. W.: I would applaud it. I've taught a little bit about it, because I'm intrigued with the fact that they are so popular. Whenever something is that popular with a developing black audience, we who are in black theater and are attentive to it need not look down our noses at it but try to understand their standpoint. How is it done? There are particular techniques that they use: they go in and organize the churches, they do networking. They really know how to do it. They do not spend two cents on flyers and posters and amusement grants. It's by grapevine; it's the drum; it's by radio.

It's popular theater. I'm not sure that I agree that it's—and I'm glad you said "perhaps"—truly "by, for, and about black people." I'm not too sure about that. I like to believe that if some of our other theater companies were able to market and had some of the financial backing that they have, then other plays might also be very popular with the new audience.

S. R.: I think *The Beauty Shop* also fits into this *genre* too. Shelly Garrett, the originator of *The Beauty Shop* in 1987, talked about how he wanted to appeal to black women who have a certain amount of disposable income and weren't seeing representations of themselves on stage, and so he went for a particular market. They have produced it rather well.

But, *The Beauty Shop* plays remind me of what I imagine church plays of the 1930s were like, plays like *The Old Ship of Zion* that Winona Fletcher writes about. It seems to me that some of those same dynamics are offered on this Chitlin Circuit. I know, at least in Chicago, whenever such a play comes to town, the producers involve local DJs, so that if you want to see what so-

and-so radio personality looks like, if you want to interact with him or her, you see *The Beauty Shop*. That is, known personalities in a local community are dropped into the show, which means that a certain amount of improvisation occurs during the performance, because these personalities are not learning lines and attending rehearsals.

I think this type of play also raises the question, "Where is the performance? Is the performance on stage, or is it someplace between on stage and in the audience?" because of the kind of dynamic: the laughter, the jokes, and everything that's going on back and forth. Those were some of the things that were also happening in the church plays of the 1930s and on.

Those may be some of the good things that we need to investigate in terms of the Chitlin Circuit. But, at least in terms of *The Beauty Shop* plays, there's a way in which they are very deeply homophobic, and that's troubling. But then, we need to see to what extent we can use some of those marketing skills, because it's not as though people are paying five or ten dollars for a ticket, they're also putting out a good sum of money for a ticket, so the fact that these shows do well financially says that there's more disposable income in black communities than we had previously assumed.

M. W.: I agree. I think we need to help our students develop their own critical framework in dealing with plays and performances that they've seen.

However, I want to go back to that question about race, class, and gender, because I agree with what Jim has said, but I do start with *A Raisin in the Sun*, and I want to just give an example of why I do that. I agree with you that Hansberry deals with these areas quite masterfully.

I'm particularly fond of the scene that is often left out in some of the presentations, and that is Walter's moment alone with his son Travis. It is the only time in that play when we see Walter by himself, without the chorus of women surrounding him and constantly educating him. Here, he dreams about moving up in class, about what he will be as a big corporate executive, and implicit in that dream is a sexist view of female workers.

I like to use that with my students because, at first, they buy it. At first they say, "Yeah, that's great. I have a secretary, I've got a Lincoln in the driveway, I've got a gardener, I've got all of this, but [it's] the secretaries who don't get things right, who're always missing, etc." It's so much a part of the language and the culture that it passes them at first. I like to have them read that and then force them to come back and reexamine Walter's assumptions that are built into his American materialistic dream, and it makes them uncomfortable initially.

H. E.: Turning to the debate—a subject that comes up in other areas of this conference—between Wilson and Brustein.

S. R.: I still can't quite figure out, even though I've read some views and articles on it, what all the excitement was about, what the event actually was. I can't figure out what people thought they were going to see happen there at Town Hall and then why they were so disappointed at what did happen. So, for me, the event is analogous to Genet's play *The Blacks*, where there's this wonderful spectacle happening on stage. People actually referred to the

Town Hall debate as a boxing match. There's a spectacle going on on stage, while something, it seems to me, far more important is happening off stage. Both Wilson and Brustein are compromised in various ways by their rhetoric, their discourse, and their actual practice. But I'll just leave that alone, so that we can get to the more interesting questions of what is happening off stage.

People express shock that Wilson should call for funding for specifically black theater. But the kinds of questions I would love to see and deal with include "What has been the track record of funding multicultural theaters, whatever they are? How many dollars did organizations like the Lila Wallace Fund give to historically white theaters to diversify their repertoires? How many playwrights of color did the theaters produce, and how many designers of color did they employ? How many administrators? How many are there after the one or two ethnic plays are done? And then, at the same time, how many dollars did these same philanthropic organizations give, let's say, to Asian American theater companies, Latino companies, African American theater companies?"

On the topic of color-blind casting: given Brustein's wagging, moralizing finger at Wilson about self-segregation, I would want to ask Brustein: "Well, how many nonwhite actors have you employed?" Is there a "self-segregation" that is also occurring in Brustein's practice as well as a whole lot of other theaters, and why isn't it called "self-segregation"?

If white theaters see color-blind casting as desirable and fruitful, then why don't they simply get on with it and stop making all this noise? Hire minority actors rather than making a lot of noise about "Oh, how horrible, August Wilson doesn't think I should do color-blind casting?" Good nonwhite actors who are employed have already had a history of doing color-blind work. How did they get through B.F.A. programs, M.F.A. programs, if they didn't do color-blind work? [*group laughter*] And they're good. In order to be good, you have to work, right? So black performers have already had a history. I'm sure that those actors would be happy for that decision to be able to work.

The other reality that everybody is dancing around and not admitting is that, for the foreseeable future, even if everybody agreed, "Oh, yes, we're going to do color-blind casting," it's not as though there's going to be a huge influx of Asian American or Latino or African American actors into all these regional companies. That's not going to happen. The sort of notion that "Oh, if they are employed in color-blind casting, they won't get an opportunity to do plays that are consistent with their own ethnic and racial background" simply isn't the case.

I would wonder if these theaters were indeed going to get on with the job of doing color-blind casting, then hopefully they would behave intelligently and begin to ask questions like "Well, what happens to *Death of a Salesman* when I put in people who are not white? If I create a family that is multiracial, how does this text fall apart, or how does it work? How does it help me as a white person, or my audience, see more about whiteness? Or, Am I inviting actors of color in simply to do a kind of whiteface?" These are some of the important questions.

J. H.: I'll add one thing. The word is "access." It is a meaty word for all the issues we're talking about. White people have access to black culture and history, but black people do not have equal access to white culture. There are very few black scholars who write on white subjects. Esther Jackson wrote on Tennessee Williams in approximately 1958 for her dissertation at Wisconsin, and I don't know if there are any other blacks who have written dissertations on white theater subjects.

This inequity is what our conversation is all about. It's a dialogue where Brustein says to Wilson, "Are you going to give up being black?" and Wilson replies, "No, not yet." "Well, why not?" "Because, Mr. Brustein, you keep me black."

M. W.: People often forget when they talk about color-blind casting that the African American men who began that whole effort out of Actors' Equity initiated that national movement around nontraditional casting as their last effort before filing suit for the failure to employ African American actors. It was all about access, as Jim says; it's all about hiring; it's all about the opportunity to do your work. The discussion gets off on another level that may or may not be really appropriate.

S. R.: I would imagine that that debate must have been very funny in terms of a person who hasn't liked a whole lot of American theater since the 1960s— Brustein, you know [*group laughter*]—and a person who's talking about the need for black theaters, and yet a major portion of his work has been done in white theaters. So, that's a compromised position.

J. H.: I'd like to discuss black scholarship in the theater. Our scholarship is the best it's ever been. There are more people writing; there's better writing; there's more intelligence, more background; more people understand world theater history, American theater history, African theater history, and race, class, and gender concepts. There are a dozen young new scholars, both black and white, who are changing the face of this history. I'm old enough to remember when there were very few books, not many plays, and little discussion of any of these issues.

S. R.: I certainly would retain the Du Bois pronouncement that a black play is written by us, understanding "black people" as those people who self-identify as being of African descent and then those people whom the society identifies as such. Under such a definition, a black play can have a Mama on the couch [Hansberry's *A Raisin in the Sun* and George C. Wolfe's *The Colored Museum*] or a purple mountain [Marita Bonner's *The Purple Flower*]; it can have the rind of a watermelon [Suzan-Lori Parks's *The Death of the Last Black Man in the Whole Entire World*]; it can have virtually anything else that the mind can conceive, and it can also have on stage a whole cast of characters, none of whom are black, none of whom are discussing things that are particularly black issues.

We're still at a point where we don't want to weed anybody out, because that's what it becomes: weeding people out of the family. The ghost of the '60s is that "You haven't written a play that's black enough; therefore your own blackness is in question." I don't think that we can afford that.

Also, the question of a white writer. I would want to ask some of the same kinds of questions that I would ask of anybody, namely, "How does your play work? What's its relationship to a material world?" But then, I would also want to conduct a comparison to answer such questions as "Is the white author being received in a way that a black author is not? Is racism operative in this specific instance, and if so, how so?" I would ask these questions because I would fear that we might have a situation analogous to what's happening on our campuses now, where certain black texts are in the syllabus so everybody reads them. The joke's that students, particularly women, read *Their Eyes Are Watching God* at least four times during their careers as undergraduates.

Well, great. So Zora Neale Hurston, Toni Morrison, and a few other people have made it; Lorraine Hansberry made it into the curriculum. But where are those black students sitting in those classrooms? Our society's moving to ensure in whole numbers of different arenas, like education, health, employment, etc., that black and other poor people of color are marginalized and thus unprepared to sit in those college classrooms and read those texts.

I'm reminded of Frantz Fanon's comment, despite the sort of violence of colonialism—the violence that strips the colonized of his or her humanity, that renders him or her black—that despite that black people don't vote in a politician because they want black culture; they vote in the person who they think is going to enhance their life prospects in terms of education, in terms of food, in terms of dignity.

So, while we focus our attention on whether the play is authored by a black or nonblack person, the more important question demanding our attention is this: "Does this play contribute to a larger project of dismantling the present hierarchies, or does it support the status quo?" That may be more important than "Is the author black? Is the author not black?" Rather, "what does this black play do?"

M. W.: I would absolutely agree, in terms of what Sandra said so eloquently, as I struggled with this question, What would I do with a play written by Ward Connelly? There's someone I can drum out of the family. But I think where you ended up, Sandra, really is where I would end up on that same question: that it really has to do with the vision of the work itself and the degree to which it takes into account the life and example in the cauldron of racism and sexism and classism and everything else that black people deal with and that other people deal with as well.

In the final analysis, this has to be the real measure for it, because I'm not sure I could accept a work by Connelly if he were writing on paper what he is acting out in his life in the ways in which he is affecting all of us. But I'd also just like to give a last statement that will affirm the topic of this agenda: I'm very excited, as Jim is, about the virtual explosion of writing about black theater by all kinds of people. It's really very, very exciting and very affirming.

I worry, though, about the response to that writing from some quarters. I worry about the extent to which the whole effort that has been made since the Civil Rights Movement has resulted in what we have now. Many people have said that the Civil Rights Movement didn't accomplish what it intended

Afterword

Change Is Coming

DAVID KRASNER

Commenting on the study of African American theater history, James V. Hatch identified five obstacles to its development: the loss of primary sources, a "severely circumscribed" definition of theater, a "paucity of scholarly publications" in black theater history, a "disgraceful absence of theater scholars who know both black and white theater history," and an "abundance of institutionalized racism." According to Hatch, these problems are exacerbated by the fact that black theater history "has not yet been assimilated into our mainstream bibliographies, directories, biographies, scholarly journals, and history texts."[1] As this is being written, ten years following Hatch's lament, there is evidence that a welcome change is coming. Although lost primary sources can never be replaced, scholars are finding new ways to study available sources; the circumscribed view of theater is opening up to new ideas about performance studies and oral traditions; and scholarly publications are on the increase. During the 1990s the number of essays, books, and Ph.D. dissertations on African American performance and theater history has grown significantly, attesting to the rising interest in the subject. In addition, institutional racism is being chipped away incrementally.

The broad scope of this collection has emphasized the wide impact that African American theater has had on American theater and culture, as well as the wide impact that theater has had on black life and culture. Accessing the various threads of African American theater and its influence on culture is a multilayered task. Wahneema Lubiano contends that the "single greatest difficulty facing Afro-American scholars is the need to figure out, in the space of an article or a book, how to convey the full complexity of periods or genres or intertextual relationships."[2] Instead of one voice defining the subject, our objective has been to include multiple voices; and instead of a single outlook, we have incorporated several, allowing ideas to dialogue and debate in order to comprehend the polyphony of viewpoints in African American performance and theater history.

Notwithstanding several important predecessors, Errol Hill's landmark work, *The Theatre of Black Americans* (1980), initiated a turning point in black theater history. Hill's collection of essays illuminated African American theater history in greater detail than had most earlier works. He claimed that "theatre as an institution can have a significant impact on the relentless struggle of a deprived racial minority for full equality" and that it promoted the "spiritual well-being" for a people "divorced from their ancestral heritage through centuries of degrading slavery."[3] *The Theatre of Black Americans* investigated rituals, playwrights, audiences, actors, and theater companies contributing to black theater history. Hill was among the first African American theater historians who, by rewriting the history of theater from a black perspective, called attention to its multiple formations.

In many ways, our study purports to take up where Hill's book leaves off. Like *The Theatre of Black Americans*, this book has attempted to shed light on African American theater and ways in which black theater counteracted the negative images fostered by minstrel stereotypes. In minstrelsy, white American performers simultaneously emulated and mocked black American culture, style, gesture, and language. White American minstrelsy fashioned what Houston A. Baker, Jr., dubs a "device" that only mattered in its relationship to, and mockery of, "the Afro-American systems of sense from which it is appropriated." By appropriating, imitating, and distorting the behavior of black culture, white minstrel performers enshrined the blackface mask, creating an enduring cultural icon of black effacement and a "device" that, as Baker maintains, "is designed to remind white consciousness that black men and women are *mis-speakers* bereft of humanity."[4] Yet, as Harry J. Elam, Jr., notes in the introduction to this book, race is also a "device" usable in oppositional ways: for promoting social protest and political representation; for shaping cultural traditions and memory; for influencing gender and racial representations; and for informing "performance" in itself, defining the meaning of race at the moment when the performer and the audience interact. Since the advent of blackface minstrelsy nearly two centuries ago, black people have had to come to terms with minstrelsy's insidious representations. There is no denying the fact that black people reacted actively to cultural stereotyping. This work seeks to define the inspiring and ingenious ways black performers have negotiated, subverted, incorporated, resisted, challenged, and ultimately "signified"—the black rhetorical strategy of inversion, parody, and innuendo—on the pervasive minstrel image.

There are, however, other issues besides minstrelsy taken up in this work. Essays here have explored vexing questions that face black artists living in the double worlds of dominant white society and the black community, issues of gender relationships, the oft-neglected history of women in theater, and the way in which distinctions of class in the black community relate to black drama and performance. Judith Williams, for instance, observes how the black female archetype—the Mammy, the tragic mulatto, and the Topsy figure—represent "blackness" that is fraught with controversy and conflict.

Margaret B. Wilkerson takes a fresh look at Lorraine Hansberry, arguing that her work belongs in the pantheon of black revolutionary literature rather than the tepid accommodationism associated with more conventional writers. Wilkerson illuminates the radical elements in Hansberry's work by accentuating the playwright's Marxist and deconstructive view of property rights and neighborhood ownership. Along similar lines, Mike Sell carefully dissects the Black Arts Movement, tracing the subtle nuances of its revolutionary agenda. Implicit in Sell's analysis is the fact that the very success of the Black Arts Movement was the cause of its own erasure. William Sonnega investigates the notion of a "liberal audience"; his unflinching study clarifies the relationship between black performers and white patrons that has complicated this dynamic. By offering personal accounts and observations, Sonnega sheds light on this conflictual relationship from a contemporary perspective.

Three important areas of concern have come to light in the past decade, which have added to this work: the emergence of performance studies as a discipline, the importance of gender and class in the discussion of African American theater history, and the breaking up of hegemony in the analysis of black culture. This work, unlike many others, has sought to move the emphasis of African American theater from playwrights to relations among authors, performers, and audiences. This collection testifies to this new emphasis on performativity; without denying the significance of playwrights, over half the essays focus on performance. Performance can dictate fashion, style, and even identity. Identity is formed in the public sphere, where speech, acts, gestures, fashion, and codes of behavior establish who a person is, what she represents. Performance is also a public art foregrounding expressive powers of cultural memory and traditions; performers often act out cultural codes that are constitutive of the social lexicon. Cultural memory serves as a critical device in Joseph Roach's study of "deep skin." Roach observes that in New Orleans, Congo Square's "mythic status" provides an intersection of trans–Atlantic behaviors, a hybrid connection of gestures and acts inculcated through slave performances and jazz funerals. Telia U. Anderson's discussion of women's performativity in black churches asserts that such performances empower self–assertion. Building on the study of black audience receptivity to August Wilson's plays, Sandra Shannon claims that the Afrocentricity embedded in Wilson's dramaturgy comes to life in performance. In contrast, Henry Louis Gates, Jr., bears witness to black audiences in the working–class theaters of the "Chitlin Circuit." He develops the idea of an alternative Afrocentric theater different from what August Wilson proposes. Yet, implicit in both Shannon and Gates's argument is W. E. B. Du Bois's 1926 notion of a theater that is about, by, for, and near African Americans.[5] The juxtaposition of Shannon and Gates's investigations brings into focus class distinctions and varying perspectives that add to our understanding of the diverse vibrancy and multifaceted intentions of black culture and black theatrical traditions.

Performance is analyzable to the degree to which a performer embodies cultural expression. Sandra L. Richards, commenting on such expressivity, remarks:

> The critical tradition within African American literature locates "authentic" cultural expression on the terrain of the folk, but the folk have articulated their presence most brilliantly in those realms with which literature is uncomfortable, namely in arenas centered in performance.[6]

In the case of the blues, for example, black performativity creates a world perspective that holds together everything that racism would tear apart; the blues acts as a healing process in the face of oppression. Performance also provides definition and, therefore, meaning; it is part of the way black culture has communicated. Edouard Glissant wrote that it is

> nothing new to declare that for us music, gesture, dance are forms of communication, just as important as the gift of speech. This is how we first managed to emerge from the plantation: esthetic form in our cultures must be shaped from these oral traditions.[7]

Similarly, Manthia Diawara contends that performance "records the way in which black people, through communicative action, engender themselves within the American experience. Black agency here involves the redefinition of the tools of Americanness." Diawara adds that "performance presumes an existing tradition and an individual or group of people who interpret that tradition in front of an audience in such a way that the individual or group of people invent themselves for that audience."[8] In this way, social action came to be linked with expressivity. The result was the formation of a communicative infrastructure within the black community, with black performers playing a significant role in structuring black identity.[9]

This study has also investigated how gender is contextualized in African American theater. To this end, Annemarie Bean looks closely at how the concept of black female cross–dressing can destabilize the negative stereotyping of black women. She makes clear that during the nineteenth century the idea of "double inversion"—racial and sexual—cut against the grain of stable representations of identity. Along similar lines, the notion of "primitivism" gained currency by the early twentieth century. Exaggerated perceptions of black sexuality affected the way women were viewed, especially in the realm of dance. In my essay, I call attention to the *Salome* dance craze of the early twentieth century, considering how black female dancers negotiated the minefield of racial and gender representations in their performances. Performance is also a political tool; Kimberly D. Dixon reminds us that contemporary black female playwrights, particularly Suzan–Lori Parks, use the idea of "creative nomadism" to mark a fluid sense of cultural identity. Building on his observations of Pomo Afro Homo's *Dark Fruit*, Jay Plum traces contemporary issues surrounding African American gay and lesbian politics, calling into question conventional notions of black sexuality.

Finally, these essays have born witness to the broad scope of African American culture. They have revealed that the black experience is neither monolithic nor unified. Anthony Appiah, reflecting on the meaning of African American culture, remarks:

> If this means shared beliefs, values, practices, [it] does not exist: what exists are African-American cultures, and though these are created and sustained in large measure by African-Americans, they cannot be understood without reference to the bearers of other American racial identities.[10]

Building diverse cultural and critical perspectives, the essays collected here are a commentary on how varying representations of blackness contribute to the formation of racial identity. Diana R. Paulin, for example, asserts that in the nineteenth century miscegenation was a definitive tool used in the performance of race. According to Paulin, interracial desires upset standards and conventions that were designed to restrict racial differences; the performance of miscegenation and desire challenged racial identity and blurred its distinctions. Analyzing the mechanisms of black–white relations in the construction of theater companies, Tina Redd looks closely at a specific instance, the 1930s Birmingham Alabama's Negro Unit of the Federal Theater Project. Her study ramifies the struggle between white administrators and black creative artists for control of the Negro Unit. Redd's analysis has relevancy for today, given similar repercussions in many current Hollywood projects where white executives and producers dictate control over black directors and actors. Harry J. Elam, Jr., draws a parallel between two seemingly disparate plays. Despite the fact that William Wells Brown's *The Escape, or Leap to Freedom* (1858) and Charles Gordone's *No Place to Be Somebody* (1969) are a century apart, Elam convincingly demonstrates how the performance of race in both dramas acts as a destabilizing force. Both plays, Elam asserts, are rife with conflicting signals and contradictory meanings of race. Christina E. Sharp develops the theme of performance in Gayl Jones's novel, *Corregidora* (1975), calling attention to the unstable notion of reading and performance. Performance functions in the novel as a reenactment of slavery's past, enabling the characters, and by extension the readers, to "reenact" past events.

According to Brenda Dixon Gottschild, American culture "is a panoply of quotations from a wide spectrum of past and present conditioning forces," and, as a result, "we desperately need to cut through the convoluted web of racism that denies acknowledgment of the Africanist part of the whole."[11] This study has examined how the representation of blackness contributes to the American "panoply." The final chapter brings together James V. Hatch, Margaret B. Wilkerson, and Sandra L. Richards, three distinguished scholars of African American performance and theater history, in a roundtable discussion. In her closing remarks, Wilkerson warns us that, despite progress, the goals of the Civil Rights Movement remain unfinished. She laments efforts by many to return to a time when discrimination was tolerated. As a pioneering scholar of African American theater history, Wilkerson has struggled to bring to our attention the works of black playwrights and performers during times when African American scholarship was deemed unfashionable and marginalized. Wilkerson, like many others, fought to make African American theater history part of the curriculum. If change is to come, it will come because of the perseverance and work of scholars who have paved the way. We must now build on their efforts.

NOTES

1. James V. Hatch, "Here Comes Everybody: Scholarship and Black Theatre History," in *Interpreting the Theatrical Past: Essays in the Historiography of Performance*, ed. Thomas Postlewait and Bruce A. McConachie (Iowa City: University of Iowa Press, 1989), 148.

2. Wahneema Lubiano, "Constructing and Reconstructing Afro-American Literary Texts: The Critic as Ambassador and Referee," *American Literary History* 1, no. 2 (Summer 1989): 433.

3. Errol Hill, ed., *The Theatre of Black Americans: A Collection of Critical Essays* (1980, reprint, New York: Applause, 1987), 1.

4. Houston A. Baker, Jr., *Modernism and the Harlem Renaissance* (Chicago: University of Chicago Press, 1987), 21.

5. W. E. B. Du Bois, "Krigwa Players Little Negro Theatre," *Crisis* 32 (July 1926): 134. Du Bois writes that the "plays of a real Negro theatre must be . . . About us, By us, For us, and Near us." Only then, he says, "can a real folk–play movement of American Negroes be built up."

6. Sandra L. Richards, "Writing the Absent Potential: Drama, Performance, and the Canon of African-American Literature," in *Performativity and Performance*, ed. Andrew Parker and Eve Kosofsky Sedgwick (London: Routledge, 1995), 65.

7. Edouard Glissant, *Caribbean Discourse*, trans. J. Michael Dash (Charlottesville: University of Virginia Press, 1989), 248–249.

8. Manthia Diawara, "Cultural Studies/Black Studies," in *Borders, Boundaries, and Frames: Cultural Criticism and Cultural Studies*, ed. Mae Henderson (New York: Routledge, 1995), 209.

9. Language is one form of expression, but performativity explores another "language" of the body, which asserts expressive communication. Hence, performativity becomes another important way in which black people communicate desires, frustrations, and the irony of living in a discriminating world.

10. K. Anthony Appiah, *Color Conscious: The Political Morality of Race* (Princeton, N.J.: Princeton University Press, 1996), 95–96.

11. Brenda Dixon Gottschild, *Digging the Africanist Presence in American Performance: Dance and Other Contexts* (Westport, Conn.: Greenwood, 1996), 3.

Selected Bibliography

Abramson, Doris. *Negro Playwrights in the American Theatre, 1925–1959*. New York: Columbia University Press, 1969.

Anadolu-Okur, Nilgun. *Contemporary African American Theater: Afrocentricity in the Works of Larry Neal, Amiri Baraka, and Charles Fuller*. New York: Garland, 1997.

Anderson, Lisa M. *Mammies No More: The Changing Image of the Black Woman on Stage and Screen*. New York: Rowman & Littlefield, 1997.

Andrews, Bert, and Paul Carter Harrison. *In the Shadow of the Great White Way: Images from the Black Theatre*. New York: Thunder's Mouth, 1989.

Archer, Leonard C. *Black Image in American Theater*. Nashville, Tenn.: Pageant, 1973.

Baker, Houston A. *Afro-American Poetics: Revisions of Harlem and the Black Aesthetic*. Madison: University of Wisconsin Press, 1988.

———, ed. *Black Literature and Literary Theory*. New York: Methuen, 1984.

Bean, Annemarie, ed. *A Sourcebook of African-American Performance: Plays, People, Movements*. New York: Routledge, 1999.

Benston, Kimberly W. *Baraka: The Renegade and the Mask*. New Haven Conno: Yale University Press, 1976.

Bigsby, C. W. E. *Confrontation and Commitment: A Study of Contemporary American Drama, 1959–1966*. Columbia: University of Missouri Press, 1968.

Bogumil, Mary L. *Understanding August Wilson*. Columbia: University of South Carolina Press, 1999.

Bond, Frederick W. *The Negro and the Drama: The Direct and Indirect Contribution which the American Negro Has Made to Drama and the Legitimate Stage*. Washington, D.C.: Associated Publishers, 1940.

Boskin, Joseph. *Sambo: The Rise and Demise of an American Jester*. New York: Oxford University Press, 1986.

Branch, William B. *Black Thunder: An Anthology of Contemporary African-American Drama*. New York: Mentor, 1992.

———, ed. *Crosswinds: An Anthology of Black Dramatists in the Diaspora*. Bloomington: Indiana University Press, 1993.

Brassmer, William, ed. *Black Drama: An Anthology*. Columbus, Ohio: Merrill, 1970.

Brown, Sterling. *Negro Poetry and Drama*. Washington, D.C: Associates in Negro Folk Education, 1937. Reprint. New York: Antheneum, 1969, 1978.

Brown-Guillory, Elizabeth. *Their Place on the Stage: Black Women Playwrights in America*. New York: Greenwood, 1988.

———. *Wines in the Wilderness: Plays by African American Women from the Harlem Renaissance to the Present*. New York: Praeger, 1990.

Bryant-Jackson, Paul K., and Lois More Overbeck. *Intersecting Boundaries: The Theatre of Adrienne Kennedy*. Minneapolis: University of Minnesota Press, 1992.

Bullins, Ed. *New Plays from the Black Theatre*. New York: Bantam, 1969.

Button, Jennifer, ed. *Zora Neale Hurston, Eulalie Spence, Marita Bonner, and Others: The Prize Plays and Other One-Acts Published in Periodicals*. New York: G. K. Hall, 1996.

Carter, Steven R. *Hansberry's Drama: Commitment amid Complexity*. New York: Meridian, 1993.

Cheney, Ann. *Lorraine Hansberry*. New York: Twayne, 1994.

Coleman, Gregory D. *We're Heaven Bound!: Portrait of a Black Sacred Drama*. Athens: University of Georgia Press, 1994.

Couch, William, Jr., ed. *New Black Playwrights*. Baton Rouge: Louisiana State University Press, 1969.

Craig, E. Quita. *Black Drama of the Federal Theatre*. Amherst: University of Massachusetts Press, 1980.

Crow, Brian, and Chris Banfield. *An Introduction to Post-Colonial Theatre*. London: Cambridge University Press, 1996.

Curtis, Susan. *First Black Actors on the Great White Way*. Columbia: University of Missouri Press, 1998.

Davis, Arthur P., and Michael W. Peplow. *The New Negro Renaissance*. New York: Holt, Rinehart and Winston, 1975.

Dent, Gina, ed. *Black Popular Culture*. Seattle, Wash.: Bay Press, 1992.

Dent, Thomas C., Richard Schechner, and Gilbert Moses. *The Free Southern Theater by the Free Southern Theater: A Documentary of the South's Radical Black Theater, with Journals, Letters, Poetry, Essays and a Play Written by Those Who Built It*. Indianapolis, Ind.: Bobbs-Merrill, 1969.

Domina, Lynn. *Understanding "A Raisin in the Sun."* New York: Greenwood, 1998.

Donkin, Ellen, and Susan Clement, eds. *Upstaging Big Daddy: Directing Theater as If Gender and Race Matter*. Ann Arbor: University of Michigan Press, 1993.

Elam, Harry J., Jr. *Taking It to the Streets: The Social Protest Theater of Luis Valdez and Amiri Baraka*. Ann Arbor: University of Michigan Press, 1997.

Elam, Harry J., Jr., and Robert Alexander, eds. *Colored Contradictions: An Anthology of Contemporary African-American Plays*. New York: Plume, 1996.

Elkins, Marilyn, ed. *August Wilson: A Casebook*. New York: Garland, 1994.

Euba, Femi. *Archetypes, Imprecators, and Victims of Fate: Origins and Developments of Satire in Black Drama*. New York: Greenwood, 1989.

Fabre, Genevieve E. *Drumbeats, Masks, and Metaphor: Contemporary Afro-American Theatre*. Translated by Melvin Dixon. Cambridge, Mass.: Harvard University Press, 1983.

Flowers, H. D. *Blacks in American Theatre History*. Edina, Minn.: Burgess International Group Press, 1992.

Fraden, Rena. *Blueprints for a Black Federal Theatre, 1935–1939*. New York: Cambridge University Press, 1996.

Gavin, Christine, and C. James Trotman. *African-American Women Playwrights: A Research Guide*. New York: Garland, 1999.

Gayle, Addison, Jr., ed. *The Black Aesthetic*. Garden City, N.Y.: Doubleday, 1971.

Gill, Glenda. *White Grease Paint on Black Performers: A Study of the Federal Theatre of 1935–1939*. New York: Peter Lang, 1989.

————. *No Surrender! No Retreat! Pioneer African American Performers of the Twentieth-Century American Theater*. New York: St. Martin's Press, 2000.

Gray, Christine Rauchfus. *Willis Richardson, Forgotten Pioneer of African-American Drama*. New York: Greenwood, 1999.

Gray, John, ed. *Black Theatre and Performance: A Pan-African Bibliography*. New York: Greenwood, 1990.

Hamalian, Leo, and James V. Hatch, eds. *The Roots of African American Drama: An Anthology of Early Plays, 1858–1938*. Detroit, Mich.: Wayne State University Press, 1991.

Harris, William, Jr., ed. *The LeRoi Jones/Amiri Baraka Reader*. New York: Thunder's Mouth, 1991.

Harrison, Paul Carter. *The Drama of Nommo*. New York: Grove, 1972.

———. *Kuntu Drama*. New York: Grove, 1974.

———. *Totem Voices: Plays from the Black World Repertory*. New York: Grove, 1989.

Harrison, Paul Carter, and Gus Edwards, eds. *Classic Plays from the Negro Ensemble Company*. Pittsburgh, Pa.: University of Pittsburgh Press, 1995.

Haskins, James. *Black Theater in America*. New York: Thomas Y. Crowell, 1982.

Hatch, James V. *Black Image on the American Stage, 1770–1970*. New York: Drama Book Specialists, 1970.

———. *Sorrow Is the Only Faithful One: The Life of Owen Dodson*. Urbana: University of Illinois Press, 1993.

Hatch, James V., and Leo Hamalian, eds. *Lost Plays of the Harlem Renaissance, 1920–1940*. Detroit, Mich.: Wayne State University Press, 1996.

Hatch, James V., and Ted Shine, eds. *Black Theatre USA: Plays by African Americans, 1847 to Today*. rev. ed. New York: Free Press, 1996.

Hatch, James V., and Brooks McNamara, and Annemarie Bean, eds. *Inside the Minstrel Mask*. Hanover, N.H.: Wesleyan University Press, 1996.

Hay, Samuel. *African American Theatre: An Historical and Critical Analysis*. Cambridge: Oxford University Press, 1994.

———. *Ed Bullins: A Literary Biography*. Detroit, Mich.: Wayne State University Press, 1997.

Heath, Gordon. *Deep Are the Roots: Memoirs of a Black Expatriate*. Amherst: University of Massachusetts Press, 1992.

Herrington, Joan. *I Ain't Sorry for Nothin' I Done: August Wilson's Process of Playwriting*. New York: Limelight, 1998.

Hill, Anthony D. *Pages from the Harlem Renaissance*. New York: Peter Lang, 1996.

Hill, Errol. *Shakespeare in Sable*. Amherst: University of Massachusetts Press, 1984.

———, ed. *The Theatre of Black Americans: A Collection of Critical Essays*. New York: Applause, 1987.

———, ed. *Black Heroes: 7 Plays*. New York: Applause, 1989.

Hudson, Theodore R. *From LeRoi Jones to Amiri Baraka*. Durham, N.C.: Duke University Press, 1973.

Hughes, Langston, and Milton Meltzer. *Black Magic: A Pictorial History of the African-American in the Performing Arts*. New York: Da Capo, 1990.

Isaacs, Edith J. R. *The Negro in the American Theatre*. New York: Theatre Arts, 1947.

Jennis, La Vina Delois. *Alice Childress*. New York: Twayne, 1995.

Kennedy, Adrienne. *People Who Led to My Plays*. New York: Theatre Communications Group, 1989.

Keyssar, Helene. *The Curtain and the Veil: Strategies in Black Drama*. New York: Burt Franklin, 1981.

King, Woodie, Jr. *Black Theatre Present Condition*. New York: Publishing Center for Cultural Resources, 1981.

———, ed. *New Plays for the Black Theatre*. Chicago: Third World Press, 1989.

———, ed. *The National Black Drama Anthology: Eleven Plays from America's Leading African-American Theaters*. New York: Applause, 1995.

King, Woodie, Jr., and Ron Milner, eds. *Black Drama Anthology*. New York: Penguin, 1974.

Krasner, David. *Resistance, Parody, and Double Consciousness in African American Theatre, 1895–1910*. New York: St. Martin's, 1997.

Lacey, Henry C. *To Raise, Destroy and Create: The Poetry, Drama and Fiction of Imamu Amiri Baraka*. Troy, N.Y.: Whitson, 1981.

Leeson, Richard M. *Lorraine Hansberry*. New York: Greenwood, 1997.

Lester, Neal A. *Ntozake Shange: A Critical Study of the Plays*. New York: Garland, 1995.

Lhamon, W. T., Jr., *Raising Cain: Blackface Performance from Jim Crow to Hip Hop*. Cambridge, Mass.: Harvard University Press, 1998.

Littlejohn, David. *Black on White: A Critical Survey of Writings by American Negroes*. New York: Grossman, 1966.

Locke, Alain, and Montgomery Gregory, eds. *Plays of Negro Life: A Source-Book of Native American Drama*. New York: Harper and Brothers, 1927. Reprint. Jackson, Miss.: University Press of Mississippi, 1993.

Lott, Eric. *Love and Theft: Blackface Minstrelsy and the American Working Class*. New York: Oxford University Press, 1993.

Mahone, Sydné, ed. *Moon Marked and Touched by Sun: Plays by African-American Women*. New York: Theatre Communications Group, 1994.

Marshall, Herbert, and Mildred Stock. *Ira Aldridge: The Negro Tragedian*. Carbondale: Southern Illinois University Press, 1968.

Marsh-Lockett, Carol P., ed. *Black Women Playwrights: Visions on the American Stage*. New York: Garland, 1999.

Mitchell, Loften. *Black Drama: The Story of the American Negro in Theatre*. New York: Hawthorn, 1967.

———. *Voices of the Black Theatre*. Clifton, N.J.: James T. White, 1975.

Molette, Carlton W., and Barbara J. Molette. *Black Theatre: Premise and Presentation*. Bristol, Ind.: Wyndham Hall, 1986.

Morrison, Toni. *Playing in the Dark: Whiteness and the Literary Imagination*. Boston, Mass.: Harvard University Press, 1992.

Nadel, Alan, ed. *May All Your Fences Have Gates*. Iowa City: University of Iowa Press, 1994.

Neal, Larry. *Visions of a Liberated Future: Black Arts Movement Writings*. New York: Thunder's Mouth, 1989.

Nemiroff, Robert, ed. *To Be Young, Gifted, and Black: Lorraine Hansberry in Her Own Words*. New York: New American Library, 1970.

———. *"A Raisin in the Sun" (Expanded Twenty-fifth Anniversary Edition) and "The Sign in Sidney Brustein's Window."* New York: New American Library, 1987.

O'Connor, John, and Lorraine Brown, eds. *Free, Adult, Uncensored: The Living History of the Federal Theatre Project*. Washington, D.C.: New Republic, 1978.

Olaniyan, Tejumola. *Scars of Conquest/Masks of Resistance: The Invention of Cultural Identities in African, African-American, and Caribbean Drama*. New York: Oxford University Press, 1995.

Ostrow, Eileen Joyce, ed. *Center Stage: An Anthology of 21 Contemporary Black-American Plays*. Oakland, Calif.: Sea Urchin, 1981.

Patterson, Lindsay. *Black Theater: A Twentieth-Century Collection of the Work of Its Best Playwrights*. New York: New American Library, 1971.

————. ed. *Anthology of the American Negro in the Theatre*. New York: Publishers Co., 1967.

Pereira, Kim. *August Wilson and the African-American Odyssey*. Urbana: University of Illinois Press, 1995.

Perkins, Kathy, ed. *Black Female Playwrights: An Anthology of Plays before 1950*. Bloomington: Indiana University Press, 1989.

Perkins, Kathy, and Judith Stephens, eds. *Strange Fruit: Plays on Lynching by American Women*. Bloomington: Indiana University Press, 1997.

Perkins, Kathy, and Roberta Uno, eds. *Contemporary Plays by Women of Color*. New York: Routledge, 1996.

Peterson, Bernard L. *Early Black American Playwrights and Dramatic Writers: A Biographical Directory and Catalog of Plays, Films, and Broadcast Scripts*. New York: Greenwood, 1990.

————. *The African American Theatre Directory, 1816–1960: A Comprehensive Guide to Early Black Theatre Organizations, Companies, Theatres, and Performing Groups*. Westport, Conn.: Greenwood, 1997.

Reardon, William R., and Thomas D. Pawley. *The Black Teacher and the Dramatic Arts: A Dialogue, Bibliography, and Anthology*. Westport, Conn.: Negro Universities Press, 1970.

Richardson, Willis, ed. *Plays and Pageants from the Life of the Negro*. Washington D.C.: Associated Publishers, 1930. Reprint. Jackson: University Press of Mississippi, 1993.

Richardson, Willis, and May Miller, eds. *Negro History in Thirteen Plays*. Washington, D.C.: Associated Publishers, 1935.

Roach, Joseph R. *Cities of the Dead: Circum-Atlantic Performance*. New York: Columbia University Press, 1996.

Sanders, Leslie Catherine. *The Development of Black Theater in America: From Shadows to Selves*. Baton Rouge: Louisiana State University Press, 1988.

Shafer, Yvonne. *August Wilson*. Westport, Conn.: Greenwood, 1998.

Shannon, Sandra Garrett. *The Dramatic Vision of August Wilson*. Washington, D.C.: Howard University Press, 1995.

Smith, Eric Ledell. *Bert Williams: A Biography of the Pioneer Black Comedian*. Jefferson, N.C.: McFarland, 1992.

Southern, Eileen, ed. *African American Theater*. New York: Garland, 1994.

Southgate, Robert L. *Black Plots and Black Characters: A Handbook for Afro-American Literature*. Syracuse, N.Y.: Gaylord, 1978.

Thomas, Lundeanna, Barbara Ann Teer, and Winona Fletcher. *Barbara Ann Teer and the National Black Theatre: Transformational Forces in Harlem*. New York: Garland, 1997.

Toll, Robert C. *Blacking Up: The Minstrel Show in Nineteenth-Century America*. New York: Oxford University Press, 1974.

Turner, Darwin T., ed. *Black Drama in America: An Anthology*. 2d ed. Washington, D.C.: Howard University Press, 1994.

Ugwu, Catherine, ed. *Let's Get It On: The Politics of Black Performance*. Seattle, Wash.: Bay Press, 1995.

Wilkerson, Margaret, ed. *9 Plays by Black Women*. New York: New American Library, 1986.

Williams, Dana A. *Contemporary African American Female Playwrights*. New York: Greenwood, 1998.

Williams, Mance, ed. *Black Theatre in the 1960s and 1970s: A Historical-Critical Analysis of the Movement*. Westport, Conn.: Greenwood, 1985.

Woll, Allen. *Dictionary of Black Theatre*. Westport, Conn.: Greenwood, 1983.

———. *Black Musical Theatre: From "Coontown" to "Dreamgirls."* Baton Rouge: Louisiana State University Press, 1989.

Index

Ralston, Blanche, 284
Reed, Linda, 85–86
Reid, Mark, 194
religion, African American. *See* church, African American
Rhodes, Colin, 195
Rice, Rebecca, *Everlasting Arms*, 94
Rice, William Henry, 179
Rich, Frank, 142
Richards, Lloyd, 133, 135, 154, 155, 158, 165, 167n.23
Richardson, L. Kenneth, 160
Riggs, Marlon, 235, 239
Riis, Thomas, 177, 178
ring shout, 126, 131nn.45–46
Robbins, Jerome, 185
Roberson, Susan, 29
Robeson, Paul, 45
Robinson, Willie, 182, 184
Rogers, Alex, 186
Román, David, 236
romantic racialism, 20, 291
"Room 222," 244
Rose, Phyllis, 187
Russell, Sylvester, 333

sacred/profane dialectic, 115
Salome, 200
Sampson, Henry T., 178, 185
Sanchez, Sonia
    The Bronx Is Next, 71–72
    Malcolm/Man Don't Live Here No Mo, 71–73
    Sister Son/Ji, 71–72
Sarah Vaughan Concert Hall, 139
Schechner, Richard, 9, 13, 253
Schultz, Alfred P., 253
Schweitzer, Albert, 48–49
Scott-Heron, Gil, 73
Scottsboro Boys, 282
Seale, Bobby, 56
Seidman, Steven, 244–245
Selwyn, Blanche, 187
Shabazz, Betty, 302
Shange, Ntozake, 216–217, 227, 233n.42
    for colored girls . . . , 128
Sharp, Laura, 274–278, 283
Sharpeville Massacre, 50
Shepp, Archie, 70
Shipp, Jesse, 177, 186
Shorenstein, Carol, 165
Showalter, Elain, 200
Shuffle Along, 180
Sidran, Ben, 65
Silverman, Kaja, 239

Simon, Bruce, 313
Singh, Amrijit, 9
Six Degrees of Separation, 236, 238
Skerrett, Joseph, Jr., 9
slavery
    in Great Britain, 25
    in New Orleans, 103, 106–109
    and performance of subservience, 13
    and religious worship, 116–117, 125–126, 129nn.5–6, 129n.10
    in *Sally's Rape*, 93–96
    in *Slave Ship* (Baraka), 70–71
Smart Set, The, 180, 185
Smith, Anna Deavere, 127, 134, 219, 220, 291, 304n.13
    Fires in the Mirror, 233n.42, 292
    On the Road, 233n.42
    Twilight: Los Angeles, 1992, 233n.42, 292
Smith, Bessie, 185
Smith, Gus, 284
Smith, Walter, 182
Snellings, Rolland, 60, 77n.27
social class and nomadism, 217–218
Sollers, Werner, 137
Southern Conference Movement, 85–86
Southern, Eileen, 178
Soyinka, Wole, 133, 150, 165
Spanish Civil War, 51–52
Spear, Robert, 206
Spence, Eulalie, 333
Spillers, Hortense, 308
Spirit Tides from Congo Square, 103–104, 110
Spitz, David, 81–82
Squire (maroon leader), 109
St-Denis, Ruth, 192
Starr, S. Frederick, 108
Steele, Shelby, 84, 96
stereotypes
    of black homosexuals, 236
    in the Chitlin Circuit, 142
    in *Death of a Salesman*, Guthrie production, 91–92
    in *Escape*, 294
    fixity of, 20–21, 177, 335
    in minstrel shows, 173, 177, 181
    in nineteenth-century representation, 20, 23–24, 25
    resistance to, 194, 237
    in *Uncle Tom's Cabin*, 20, 22
Stevedore, 280
Stewart, James, 58, 59, 65, 67
Stewart, Susan, 242
Stowe, Harriet Beecher, 19, 20, 26, 33–34, 293
Strand Theatre, 140